CAL

# The Kander & Ebb Collection

Cover photo © 2003 by Mark Seliger
Courtesy of *Vanity Fair*

ISBN 0-634-07297-8

HAL•LEONARD®
CORPORATION

7777 W. Bluemound Rd. P.O. Box 13819 Milwaukee, WI 53213



Visit Hal Leonard Online at
**www.halleonard.com**

# John Kander & Fred Ebb
## A profile

John Kander and Fred Ebb are sometimes credited as the Rodgers and Hart and Hammerstein of the second half of the twentieth century. They've given the world some of the great creations of the American musical stage, including *Cabaret; Chicago; Kiss of the Spider Woman*, and nearly a dozen more, ranging from *The Act* to *Zorba*. Their scores have a breathtaking ability to capture the flavor of the specific time and place, with gutsy music brimming with vitality and brilliantly droll, penetrating lyrics.

Kander and Ebb have written for many well-known musical performers, including Lauren Bacall, Joel Grey, Gwen Verdon, Frank Sinatra, Robert Goulet, Chita Rivera, Liza Minnelli and Barbra Streisand. They are the winners of numerous awards, including Broadway's most-coveted award, the Tony.

The team's other musicals include *Flora, The Red Menace; The Happy Time; 70, Girls, 70; Woman of the Year; The Rink; And the World Goes 'Round* and *The Visit*, which premiered in October 2001 in Chicago, Illinois and starred Chita Rivera.

Kander and Ebb's writing for films has been no less notable. In 1975, they wrote five new songs for Barbra Streisand's *Funny Lady*, including "How Lucky Can You Get" and "Let's Hear It for Me." One year later, the title song for the film musical *New York, New York*, directed by Martin Scorsese and starring Liza Minnelli and Robert De Niro, became their biggest hit since *Cabaret*. Introduced by Minnelli and popularized by both her and Sinatra, the song became an instant standard and the unofficial theme song for New York City.

Throughout their long, fruitful careers, Kander and Ebb have let their differences serve to complement each other. "When we're at our best, we sound like one person," says Kander. They exult in writing songs that stand out on their own, even while adhering to the storyline for which they were created. "And their collaboration isn't just with each other," says David Thompson, book author for *Steel Pier*. "It's with the book writer, choreographer, director, actors—ultimately, with the audience."

Harold Prince sums up the talent of Kander and Ebb nicely: "They write Broadway—in the best sense."

— Beth Tuszynski
for the William Inge Center for the Arts

### Production Credits

**Theatre:** *Flora, The Red Menace; Cabaret; The Happy Time; Zorba; 70, Girls, 70; The Act; Woman of the Year; The Rink; And the World Goes 'Round – The Kander & Ebb Musical; Kiss of the Spider Woman; Steel Pier; The Visit; The Skin of Our Teeth (Over and Over); Curtains (upcoming).*

**Films:** *Cabaret; Lucky Lady; New York, New York; Funny Lady; Kramer vs. Kramer; A Matter of Time; Still of the Night; Places in the Heart; French Postcards; Stepping Out; Chicago.*

**Television:** *"Liza with a Z" (Liza Minnelli); "Goldie and Liza Together" (with Goldie Hawn); "Ol' Blue Eyes Is Back" (Frank Sinatra); "Baryshnikov on Broadway" (Mikhail Baryshnikov); "An Early Frost" (TV film score); "Liza in London" (special); "Breathing Lessons" (TV film score); "The Boys Next Door" (TV film score).*

# Which Came First?

I am waiting to be interviewed for some music magazine. I'm to be on my own today although generally the interviews are with my partner, John Kander. Today, though, I am "flying solo." I am an old hand at this, as I have been interviewed many times in the past. So many times, in fact, that I feel I can reasonably anticipate how at least a portion of the interview is likely to go.

Where were you born, Mr. Ebb, they are likely to ask, and I will probably answer, New York City.

And how long have you been working with Mr. Kander, they will probably ask, and I will probably answer, I'm not exactly sure, because the truth is I am *not* exactly sure. John knows and I hate hearing about it.

And who are your favorite songwriters, they are likely to ask, and I will probably answer, Rodgers & Hart or Frank Loesser or Alan Jay Lerner or Johnny Mercer or Irving Berlin, depending on which name pops into my head at that particular moment.

And what was the first musical you ever saw, they are likely to ask, and I will probably answer, I don't remember, because I don't.

And how old are you, they are likely to ask, and I am likely to change the subject.

So these are some of the probabilities of the interview, and in fact, depending on how clever, well-informed or intrepid the interviewer might be, the questions might surprise you, intrigue you and challenge you. Actually, when that happens the interview can be a really stimulating experience. What amazes me, however, is no matter what the caliber of the interview might be, and how different from each other, they all have one thing in common. There has never been one interviewer able to resist one question: Tell me, Mr. Ebb, which comes first, the music or the lyrics?

Since it is a well-known fact that Mr. Kander writes the music and I write the lyrics, the question seems irresistible to the people interviewing us. Since Jerry Herman, Frank Loesser, Cole Porter and my revered Irving Berlin all wrote both music and lyrics, I feel confident they never had to deal with this question. Here are two of the replies John and I have given over the years in response.

1. We work in the same room at the same time. I can improvise in words and John can improvise in music. Out of that improvisation comes our product. We work in the same room at the same time.

2. When we walk into our music room, I am Fred Ebb and he is John Kander. When we come out, we are Kander & Ebb.

With some variations, that is how we respond to the question.

In summation, let me quote James Barrie: Though it's a little bit perplexing at times and maybe annoying too, the point is you *are* being interviewed which means somebody values what you are about to say. And Gee Whiz, folks, "It's good to be asked." (*What Every Woman Knows*, Act III)

**Fred Ebb**
February 11, 2004
New York City

# Contents by Show



*At this time (2004) these are new shows in development.

# Contents by Song



*At this time (2004) these are new shows in development.

# And All That Jazz

*from the Musical* **CHICAGO**

Words by
**FRED EBB**

Music by
**JOHN KANDER**

**Bluesy vamp, not too fast**

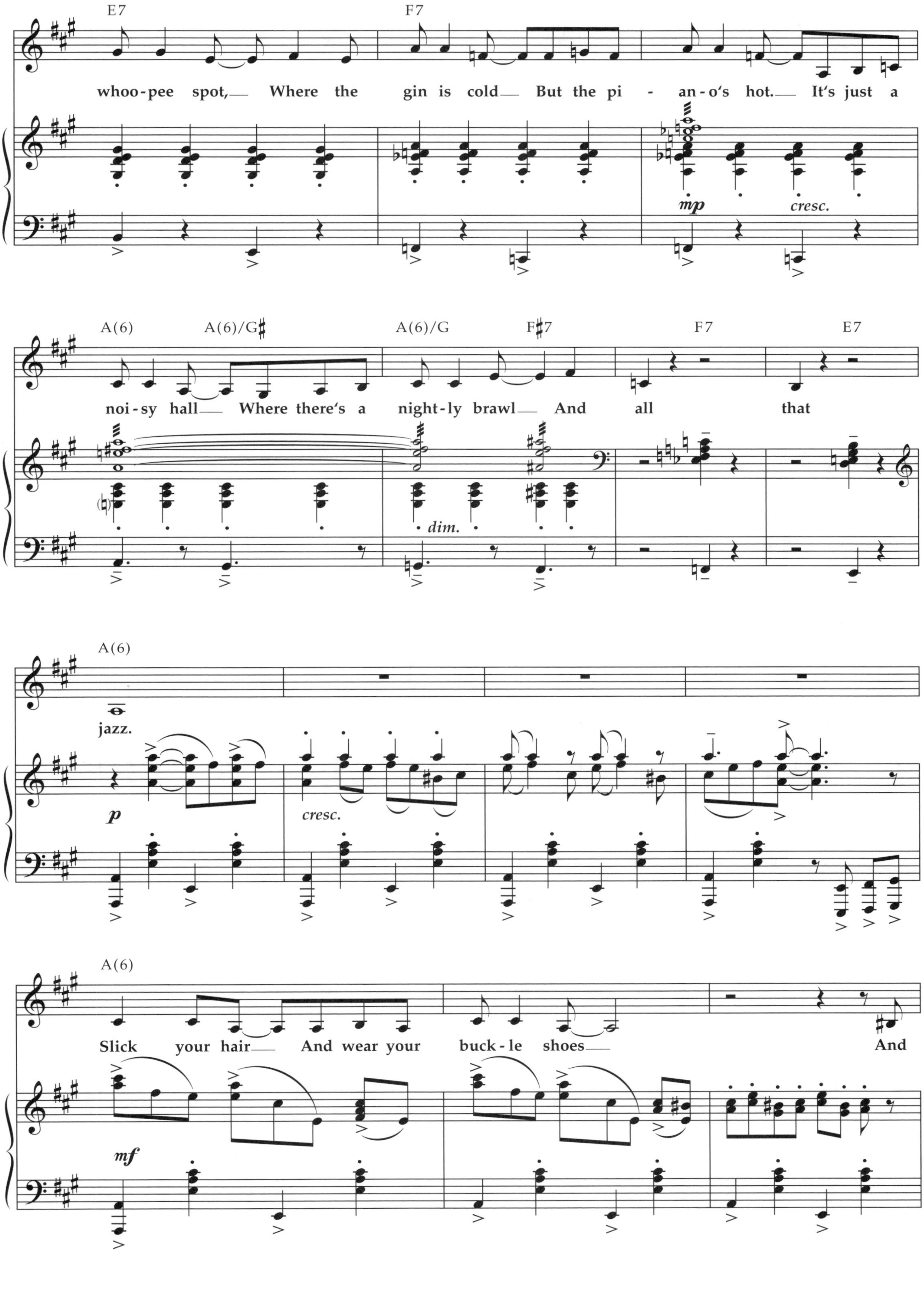
E7 F7
whoo-pee spot, Where the gin is cold But the pi - an-o's hot. It's just a
mp cresc.
A(6) A(6)/G♯ A(6)/G F♯7 F7 E7
noi-sy hall Where there's a night-ly brawl And all that
dim.
A(6)
jazz.
p cresc.
A(6)
Slick your hair And wear your buck-le shoes And
mf

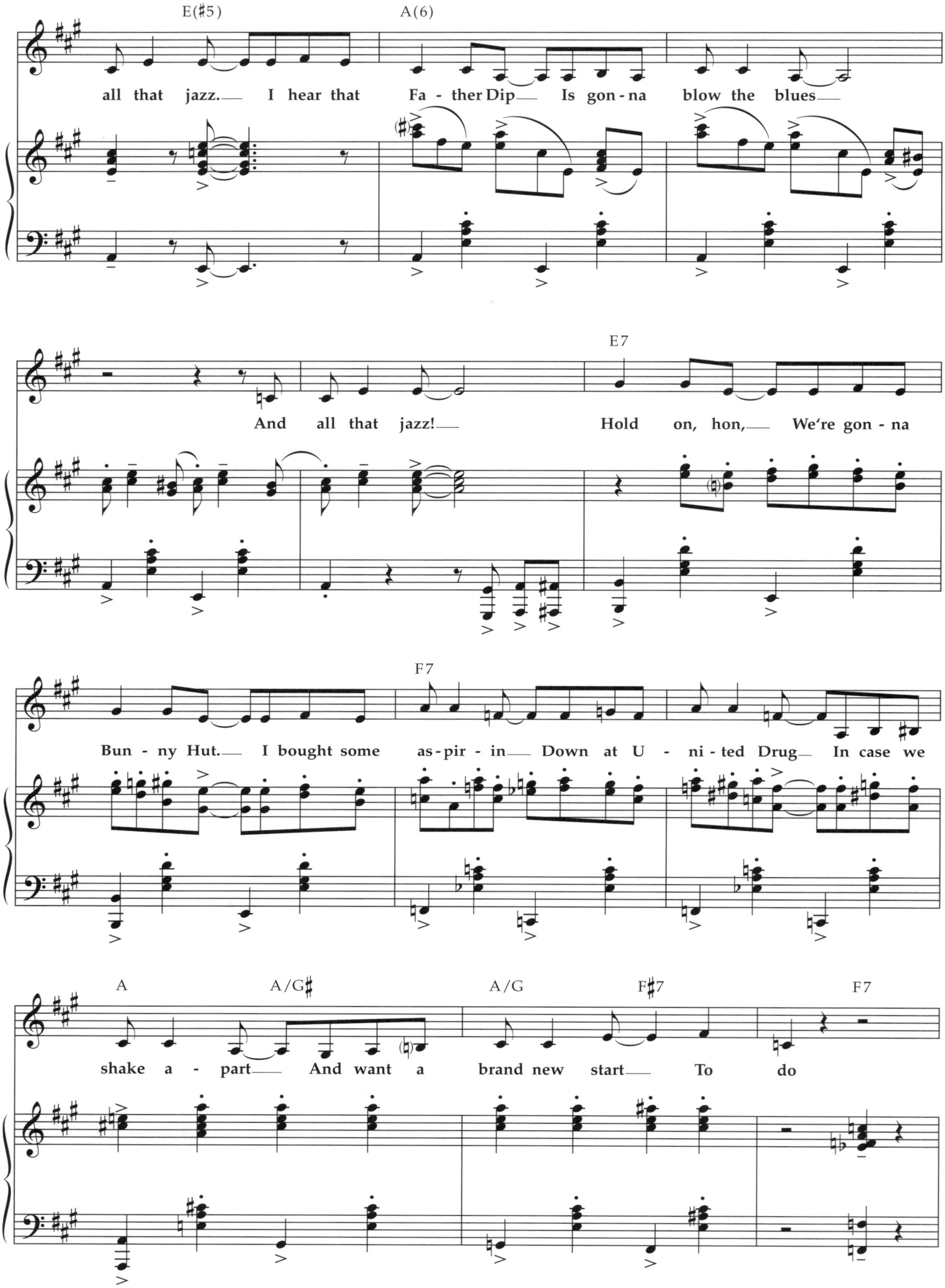
E(♯5)
A(6)
all that jazz. I hear that Fa - ther Dip Is gon - na blow the blues
And all that jazz!
E7
Hold on, hon, We're gon - na
Bun - ny Hut. I bought some
F7
as - pir - in Down at U - ni - ted Drug In case we
A
A/G♯
shake a - part And want a
A/G
F♯7
brand new start
F7
To do

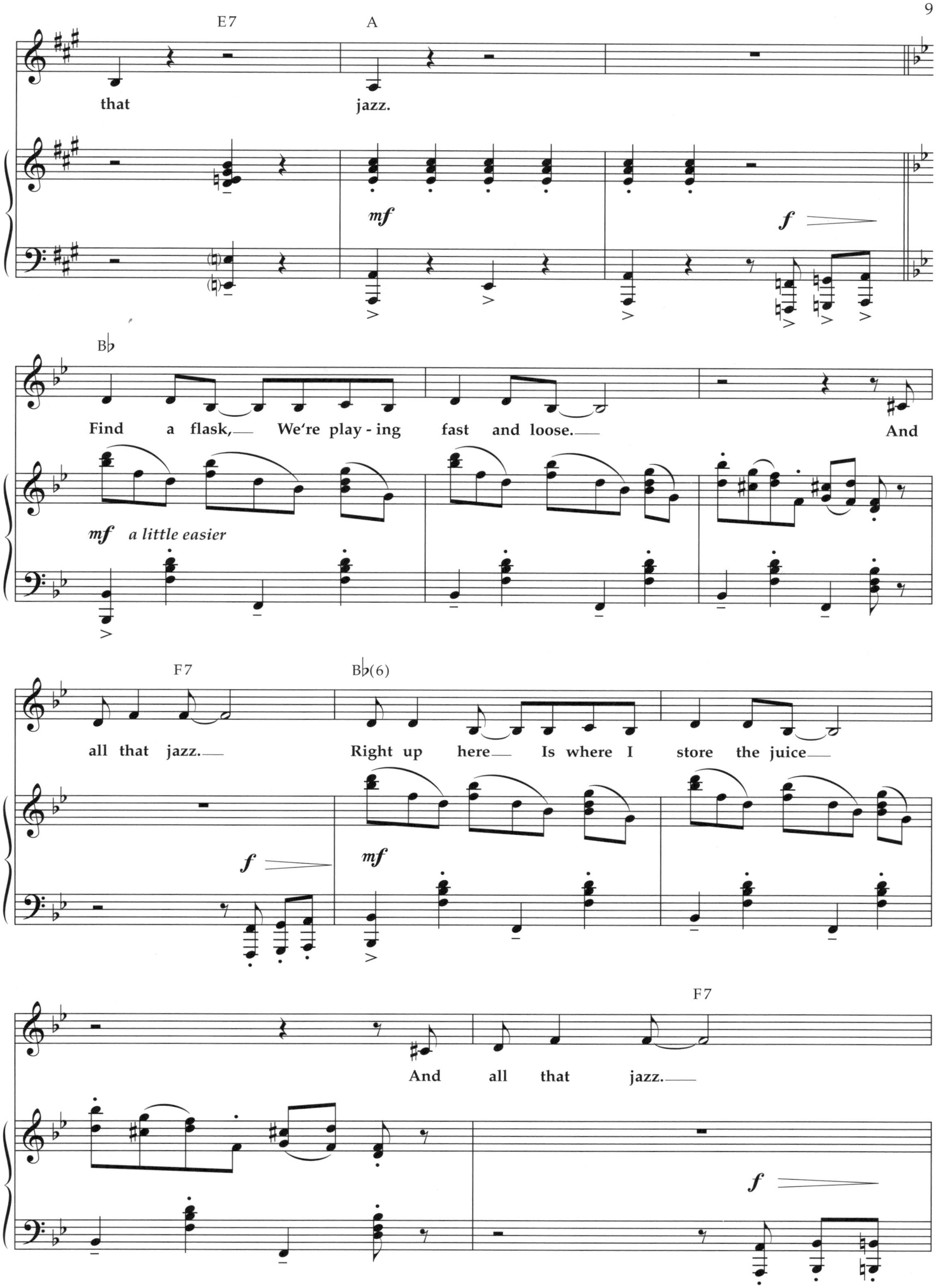
E7
A
that
jazz.
mf
f
B♭
Find a flask, We're play - ing fast and loose. And
mf a little easier
F7
B♭(6)
all that jazz.
Right up here Is where I store the juice
f
mf
F7
And all that jazz.
f

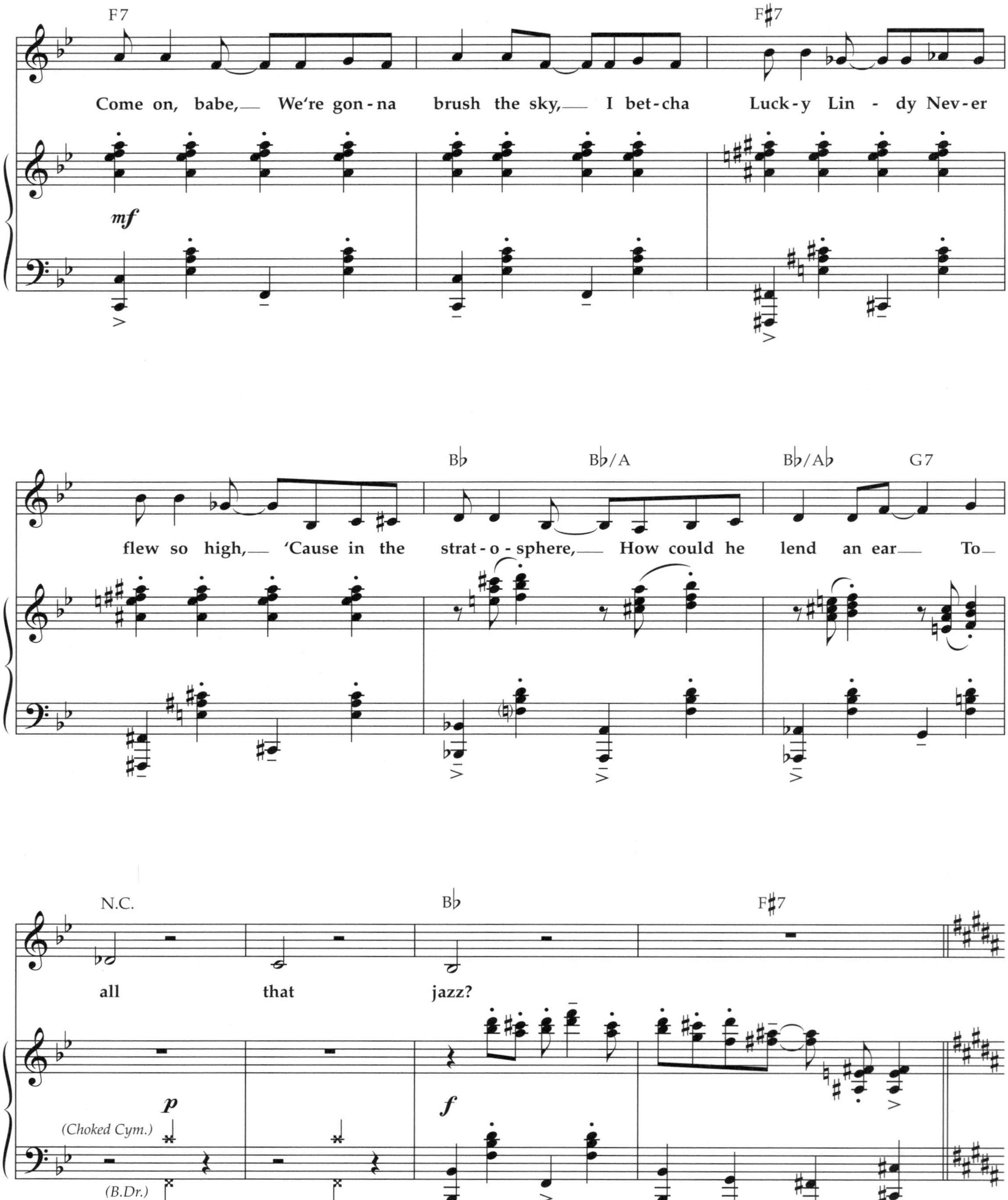
F7
F♯7
Come on, babe, We're gon-na brush the sky, I bet-cha Luck-y Lin - dy Nev-er
mf
B♭
B♭/A
B♭/A♭
G7
flew so high, 'Cause in the strat-o-sphere, How could he lend an ear To
N.C.
B♭
F♯7
all that jazz?
p
f
(Choked Cym.)
(B.Dr.)

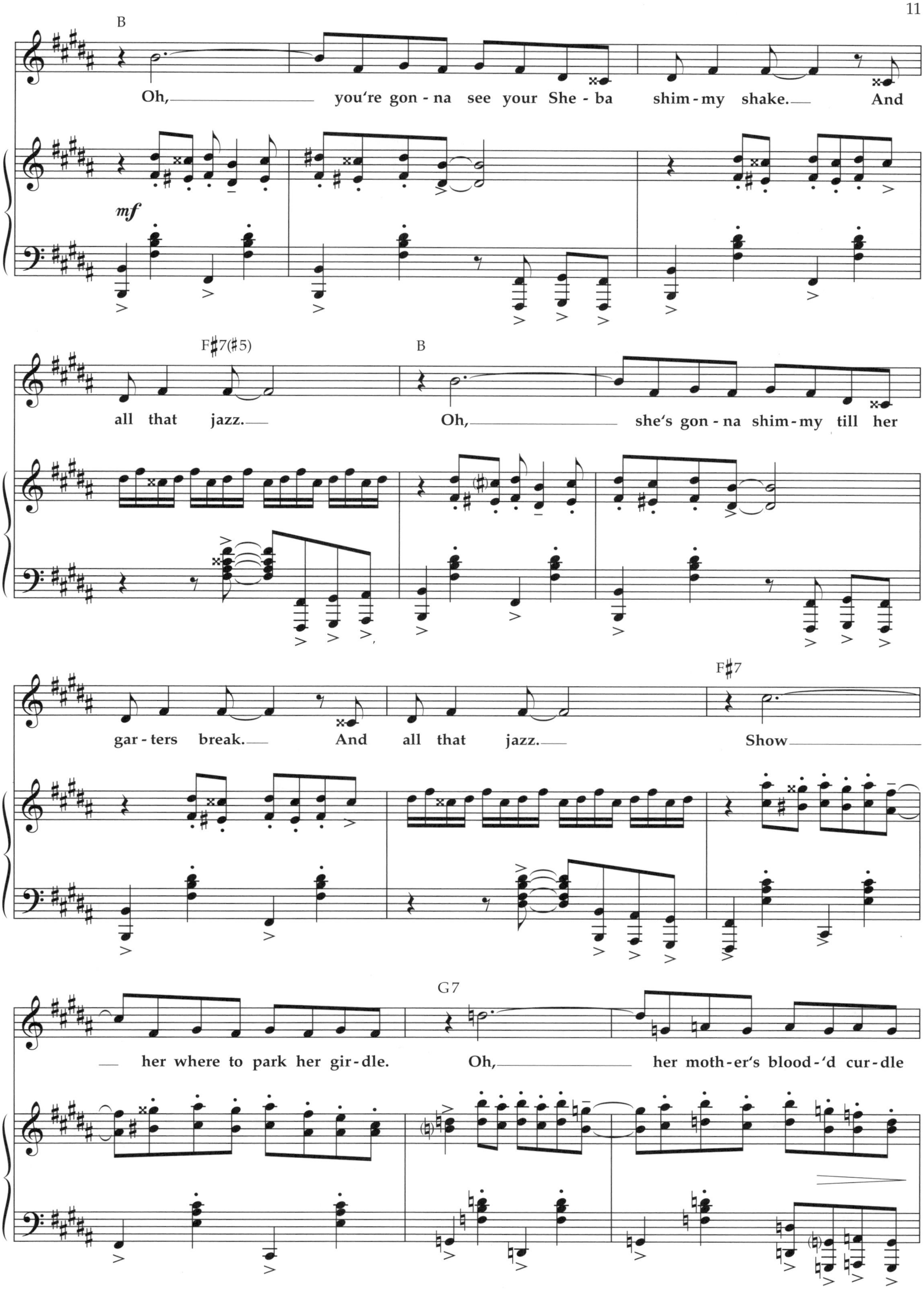
B
Oh, you're gon-na see your She-ba shim-my shake. And
mf
F♯7(♯5)
B
all that jazz. Oh, she's gon-na shim-my till her
F♯7
gar-ters break. And all that jazz. Show
G7
her where to park her gir-dle. Oh, her moth-er's blood-'d cur-dle

B B/A♯ B/A G♯7 G7
(Whispered) If she'd hear her ba - by's queer for all
p
pp
F♯7 B G7 C
that jazz. (Sung) Come on, babe, Why don't we
Oh,
f
paint the town, And all that jazz? I'm gon-na
G7
you're gon - na see your She - ba shim-my shake. And all that jazz.

C
rouge my knees And roll my stock-ings down, And all that jazz.
Oh, she's gon-na shim-my till her gar-ters break. And
G7
Start the car, I know a whoo-pee spot, Where the
all that jazz. Show her where to park her gir-dle.
A♭7
gin is cold But the pi-an-o's hot. It's just a
Oh, her moth-er's blood-'d cur-dle

C C/B C/B♭ A7 A♭7
noi - sy hall Where there's a night - ly brawl And all
If she'd hear her ba - by's queer for all
f
G7 N.C.
that jazz.
that jazz.
p
(Hi hats)
pp
Piu mosso
F7 Gdim7 F7/A
8va
ff
B♭ B♭/A B♭/A♭
No, I'm no one's wife, but Oh, I
loco
f
marc.

G7
C7
love my life
And
all
F9sus
that
Bb
Bb/A
Bb/Ab
Gmin7
F#(#5)
F7
Bb/F
Bb
jazz!
That jazz!
sfz

# But the World Goes 'Round

*from the Motion Picture* **NEW YORK, NEW YORK**

Lyrics by
**FRED EBB**

Music by
**JOHN KANDER**

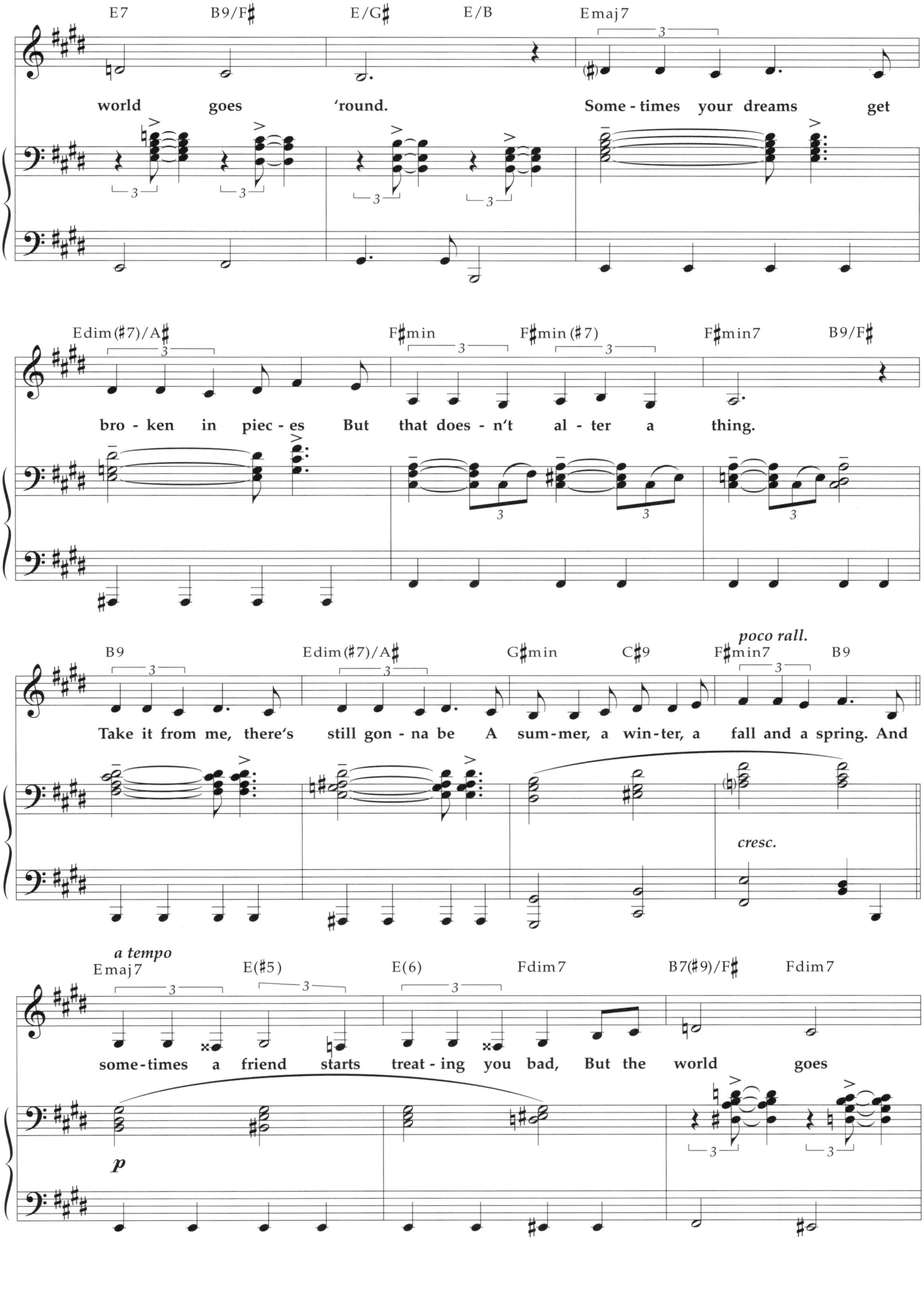
E7 B9/F♯ E/G♯ E/B Emaj7
world goes 'round. Some - times your dreams get
Edim(♯7)/A♯ F♯min F♯min(♯7) F♯min7 B9/F♯
bro - ken in piec - es But that does - n't al - ter a thing.
B9 Edim(♯7)/A♯ G♯min C♯9 F♯min7 B9
poco rall.
Take it from me, there's still gon - na be A sum - mer, a win - ter, a fall and a spring. And
cresc.
a tempo
Emaj7 E(♯5) E(6) Fdim7 B7(♯9)/F♯ Fdim7
some - times a friend starts treat - ing you bad, But the world goes
p

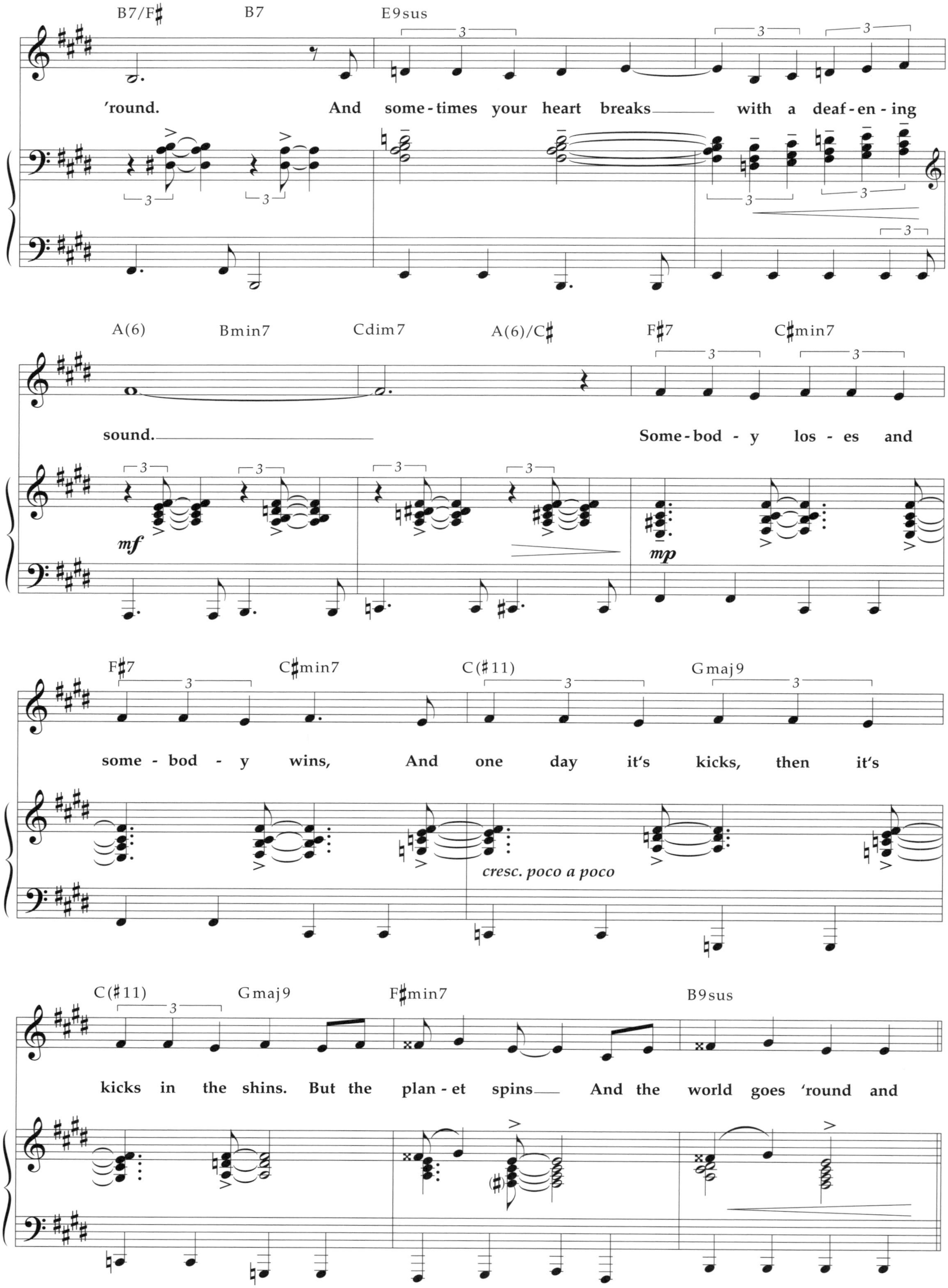
B7/F♯ B7 E9sus
'round. And some-times your heart breaks with a deaf-en-ing
A(6) Bmin7 Cdim7 A(6)/C♯ F♯7 C♯min7
sound. Some-bod-y los-es and
mf
mp
F♯7 C♯min7 C(♯11) Gmaj9
some-bod-y wins, And one day it's kicks, then it's
cresc. poco a poco
C(♯11) Gmaj9 F♯min7 B9sus
kicks in the shins. But the plan-et spins And the world goes 'round and

E E(♯5) E(6) Fdim7 B7(♯9)/F♯ Fdim7 B7/F♯ B7
'round. The world goes 'round.
f marc.
mp
F♯min F♯min(♯7) F♯min7 B9 E7 B9/F♯ E/G♯
The world goes 'round.
f
mp
Emaj7 Edim(♯7)/A♯ F♯min F♯min(♯7)
Some-times your dreams get bro-ken in piec-es But that does-n't mat-ter at
F♯min7 B7/F♯ B9 Edim(♯7)/A♯
all. Take it from me, there's still gon-na be A
cresc. poco a poco

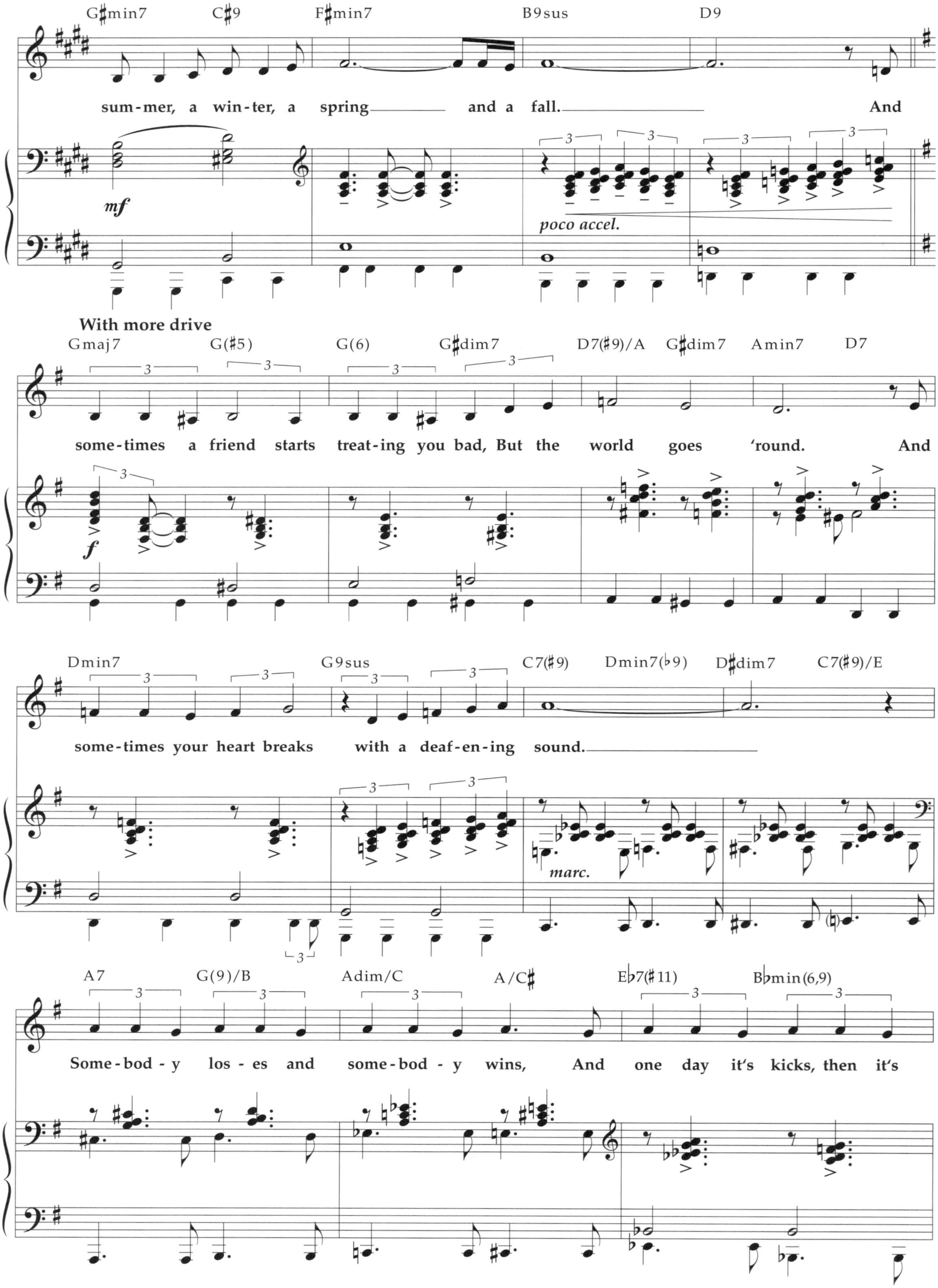
G♯min7 C♯9 F♯min7 B9sus D9
sum-mer, a win-ter, a spring and a fall. And
mf
poco accel.
With more drive
Gmaj7 G(♯5) G(6) G♯dim7 D7(♯9)/A G♯dim7 Amin7 D7
some-times a friend starts treat-ing you bad, But the world goes 'round. And
f
Dmin7 G9sus C7(♯9) Dmin7(♭9) D♯dim7 C7(♯9)/E
some-times your heart breaks with a deaf-en-ing sound.
marc.
A7 G(9)/B Adim/C A/C♯ E♭7(♯11) B♭min(6,9)
Some-bod-y los-es and some-bod-y wins, And one day it's kicks, then it's

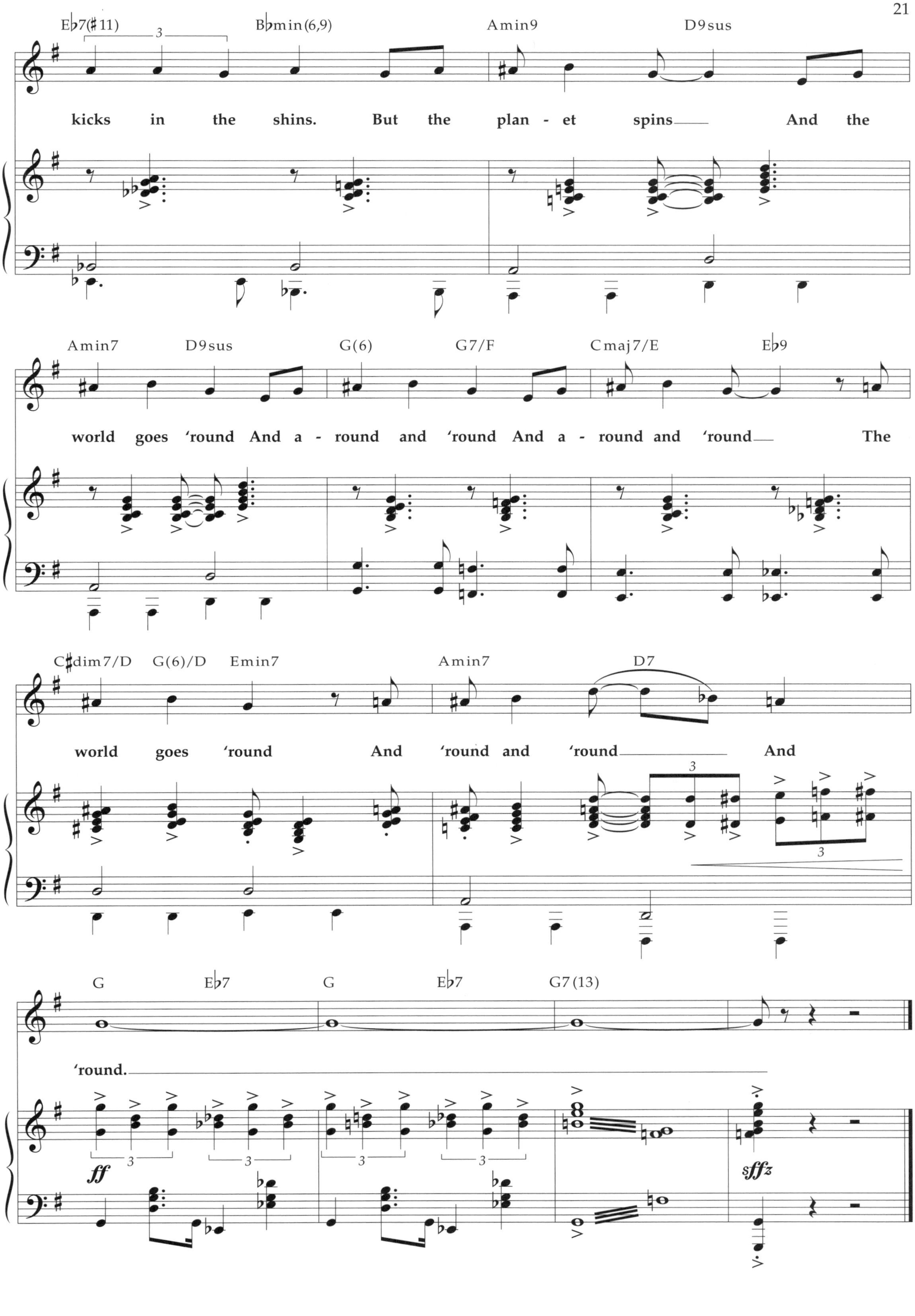
E♭7(♯11) B♭min(6,9) Amin9 D9sus
kicks in the shins. But the plan - et spins And the
Amin7 D9sus G(6) G7/F Cmaj7/E E♭9
world goes 'round And a - round and 'round And a - round and 'round The
C♯dim7/D G(6)/D Emin7 Amin7 D7
world goes 'round And 'round and 'round And
G E♭7 G E♭7 G7(13)
'round.
ff
sffz

# Cabaret

*from the Musical* ***CABARET***

Words by
**FRED EBB**

Music by
**JOHN KANDER**

D(6)
E♭dim
A(6)/C♯
F♯7
Life is a cab - a - ret, old chum,
Bmin9
E7
A(6)
E7(13)
Come to the cab - a - ret.
mf
dim.
A(6)
E(♯5)
A(6)
E7(♯5)
Put down the knit-ting, the book and the broom.
mp
A(6)
Amaj7
A9
Time for a hol - i - day.

D(6)
E♭dim
A(6)/C♯
F♯7
Life is a cab - a - ret, old chum,
Bmin9
E7
A(6)
Come to the cab - a - ret.
Come taste the
mf
Dmin(6)
A(6)
wine,
Come hear the band.
Come blow a
mp stacc.
poco rit.
F♯min
F♯min(♯7)
F♯min7
B7
E7
horn, start cel - e - brat - ing: Right this way, your ta - ble's wait - ing.

a tempo
A(6) E7(♯5) A(6) E7(♯5)
No use per - mit - ting some proph - et of doom To
mp marc.
A(6) E♭dim Emin7 A7
wipe ev - 'ry smile a - way.
cresc.
D(6) E♭dim C♯min7 F♯7 Bmin7 E7(♭9) A(6)
Life is a cab - a - ret, old chum, Come to the cab - a -
mf
cresc.
Slightly faster
A(6) A(♯5) A7 A(♯5) A A(♯5) A7 A(♯5)
ret! I
f
dim.

A(6)
E9(♯5)
A(6)
E7(♯5)
A(6)
used to have a girl - friend known as El - sie. With
f
p
A(6)
E9(♯5)
A(6)
E7(♯5)
A7
whom I shared four sor - did rooms in Chel - sea. She
p
f
D(6)
G♯min7
C♯7
F♯min7
was - n't what you'd call a blush - ing flow - er. As a
mp
B9
Bmin7 E7 Bmin7 E7
mat - ter of fact, she rent - ed by the ho - ur. The
f
sfz

A(6) E7(♯5) A(6) E7(♯5) A(6)
day she died the neigh - bors came to snick - er: "Well,
mf mp
E7(♯5) A(6) A7
that's what comes of too much pills and li - quor." But
mf mp
D(6) G♯min7 C♯7 F♯min
Held back
when I saw her laid out like a queen, She was the
3
f sfz
Rubato
Bmin7 E9sus E7(♭9) A(6)
hap - pi - est corpse I'd ev - er seen. I
p mp

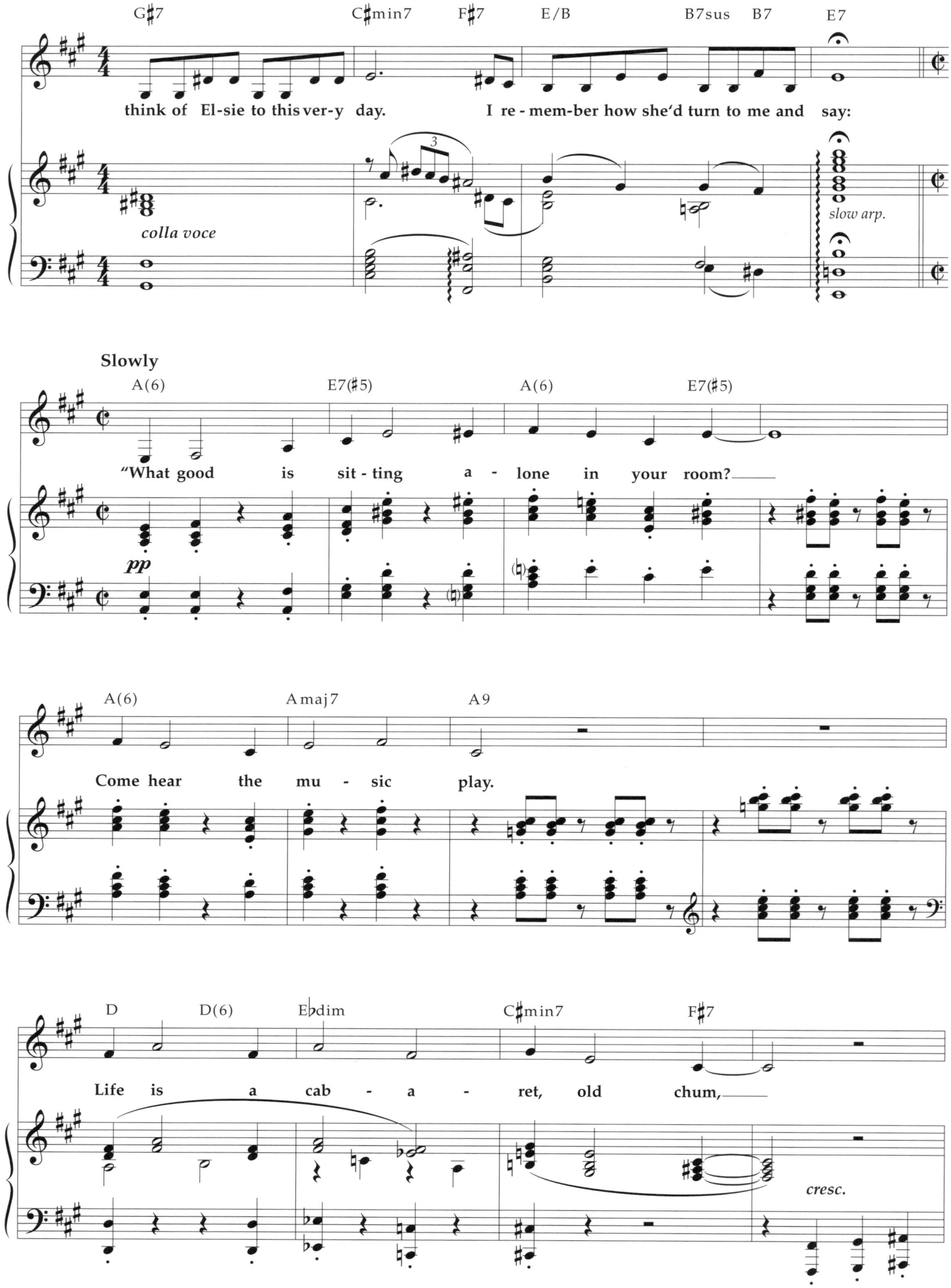
G♯7 C♯min7 F♯7 E/B B7sus B7 E7
think of El-sie to this ver-y day. I re-mem-ber how she'd turn to me and say:
colla voce
slow arp.
Slowly
A(6) E7(♯5) A(6) E7(♯5)
"What good is sit-ting a-lone in your room?
pp
A(6) Amaj7 A9
Come hear the mu-sic play.
D D(6) E♭dim C♯min7 F♯7
Life is a cab-a-ret, old chum,
cresc.

Bmin9
E7
E9(♯5)
A(6)
E7
Come to the cab - a - ret.
accel.
f
A(6)
E7(♯5)
A(6)
E7(♯5)
Put down the knit-ting, the book and the broom,
mf marc.
A(6)
Amaj7
A9
Time for a hol - i - day.
D(6)
E♭dim
C♯min7
F♯7
Life is a cab - a - ret, old chum,

Bmin9
E7(13)
A
Come to the cab - a - ret." And as for
Dmin(6)
A(6)
me, as for me, I made my
mp
rall.
Rubato
F♯min
F♯min(♯7)
F♯min7
B7
E7
F7
mind up, back in Chel-sea, When I go I'm go-ing like El - sie.
cresc. poco a poco

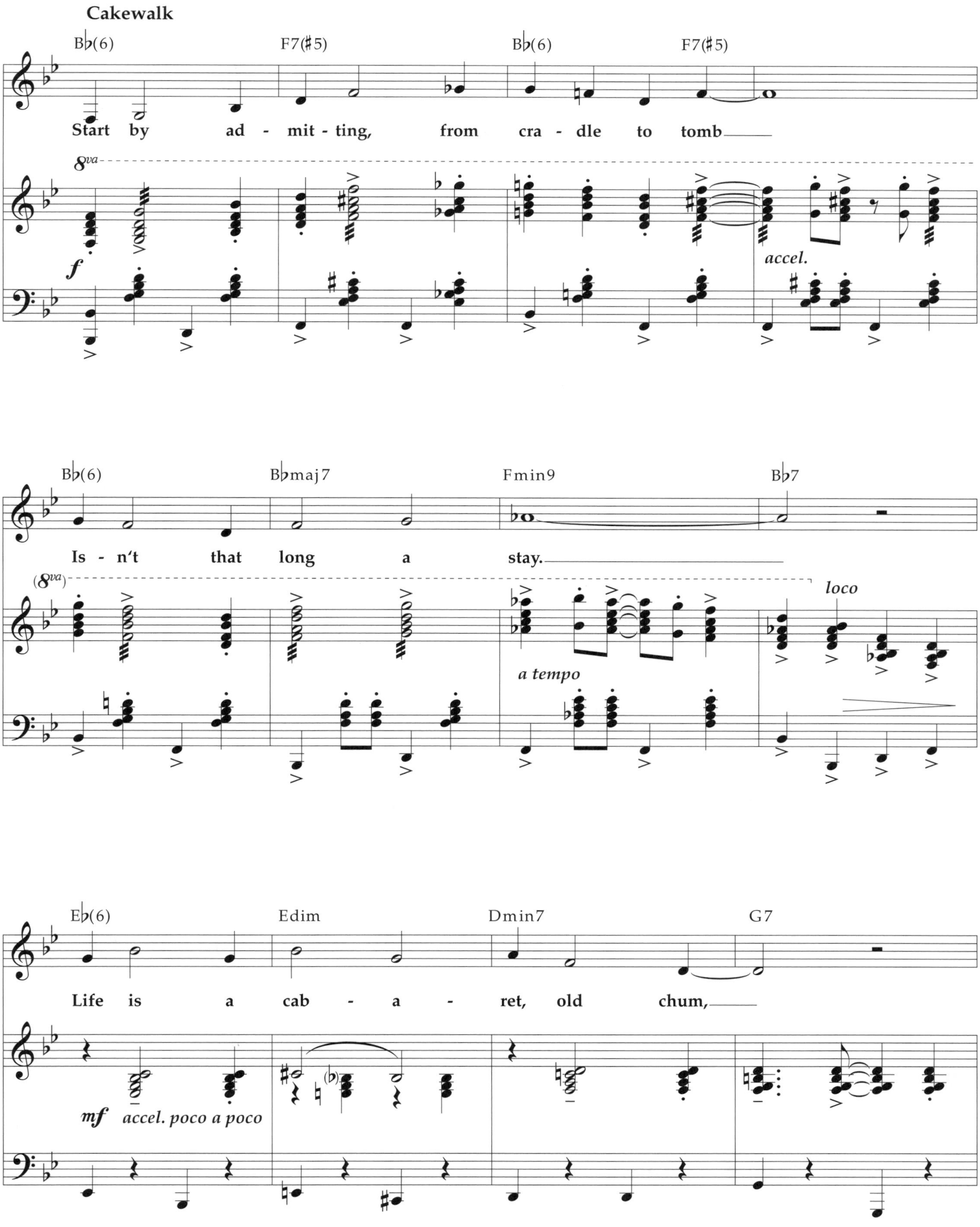
Cakewalk
B♭(6)
F7(♯5)
B♭(6)
F7(♯5)
Start by ad - mit - ting, from cra - dle to tomb
8va
f
accel.
B♭(6)
B♭maj7
Fmin9
B♭7
Is - n't that long a stay.
(8va)
loco
a tempo
E♭(6)
Edim
Dmin7
G7
Life is a cab - a - ret, old chum,
mf
accel. poco a poco

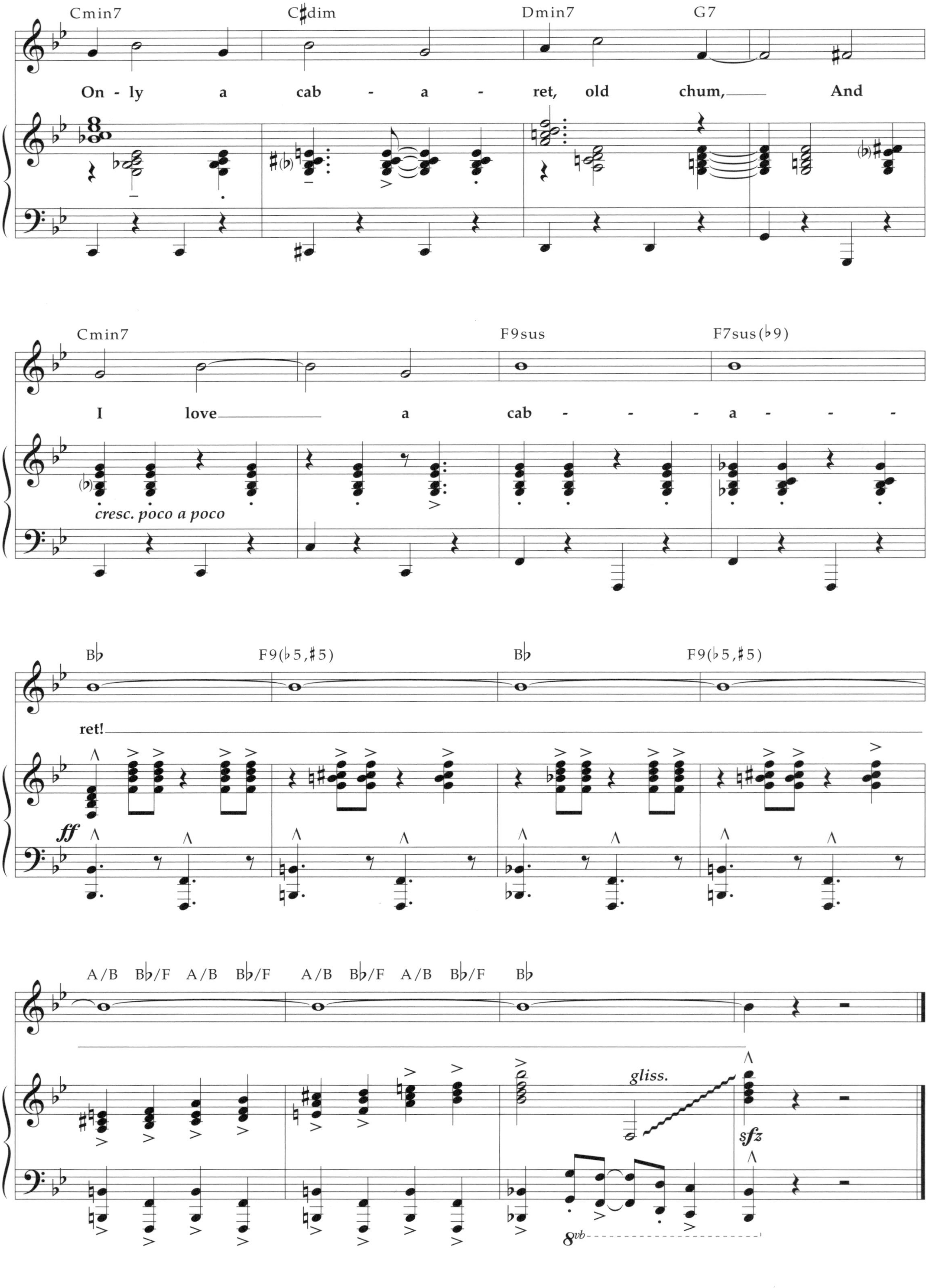
Cmin7
C♯dim
Dmin7
G7
On - ly a cab - a - ret, old chum, And
Cmin7
F9sus
F7sus(♭9)
I love a cab - - - a - - -
cresc. poco a poco
B♭
F9(♭5,♯5)
B♭
F9(♭5,♯5)
ret!
ff
A/B
B♭/F
A/B
B♭/F
A/B
B♭/F
A/B
B♭/F
B♭
gliss.
sfz
8vb

# Class

*from the Musical* **CHICAGO**

Words by
**FRED EBB**

Music by
**JOHN KANDER**

Emin7(♭5)
MATRON:
A7
What-ev-er hap-pened to class?
Class!
D
(MATRON):
Dmin(9)
What-ev-er hap-pened to "Please, may I?" And "Yes, thank you." And "How charm-ing!"
p
A
D
D(♯5)
Now, ev-'ry son of a bitch is a snake in the
Gmin
Emin7(♭5)
BOTH:
A7/C♯
grass. What-ev-er hap-pened to class? Class!
cresc.

B
Ah, there ain't no gen - tle - men to o - pen up the
mf
A♯min
doors. There ain't no la - dies now, There's on - ly pigs and
G♯min
C♯9sus
whores. And e - ven kids - 'll knock ya down so's they can
A♯min
D♯7
G♯min
C♯9sus
C♯7
pass, No - bod - y's got no

D
VELMA:
MATRON:
class.
What - ev - er hap - pened to old val - ues And
dim.
mp
Dmin
VELMA:
A
fine mor - als And good breed - ing?
D
MATRON:
D(♯5)
Gmin
Now no one e - ven says "Oops" When they're pass - ing their gas.
Emin7(♭5)
BOTH:
C♯7
What - ev - er hap - pened to class? Class!
cresc.

B
A♯min
VELMA:
Ah, there ain't no gen-tle-man that's fit for an-y use, And an-y
MATRON:
Ah, there ain't no gen-tle-man that's fit for an-y use, And an-y
mf
G♯min
C♯9sus
C♯7
girl-'d touch your pri-vates for a deuce. And e-ven
girl-'d touch your pri-vates for a deuce. And e-ven kids-'ll kick your shins and give ya
A♯min
G♯min
C♯7
kids-'ll kick your shins and give ya sass, No-bod-y's got no
sass, No-bod-y's got no

B
VELMA:
class.
All you read a - bout to - day is
A♯min
rape and theft.
MATRON:
Je - sus
G♯min
Christ!
C♯9sus
C♯7
Ain't there no de - cen - cy

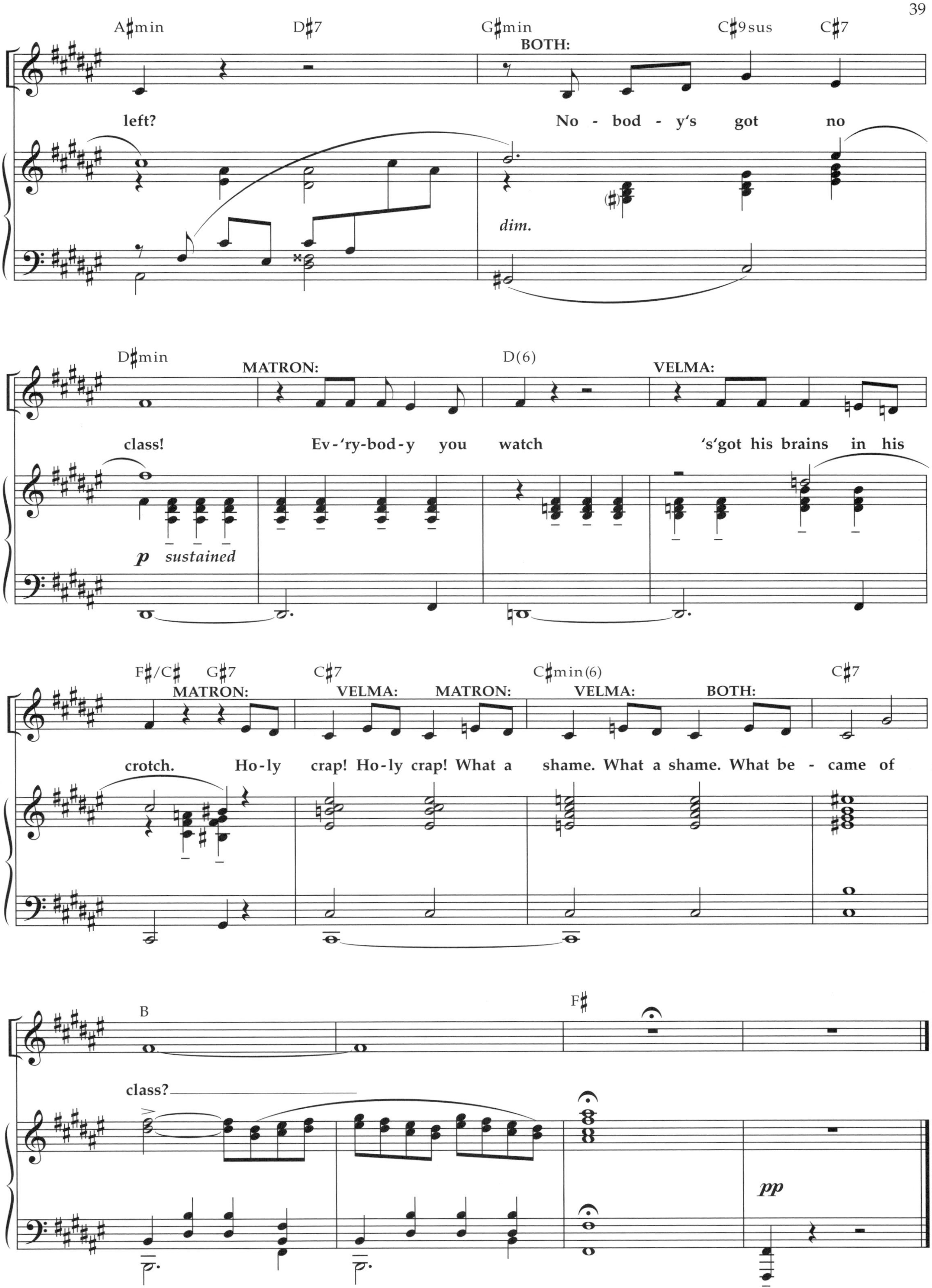
A♯min D♯7 G♯min C♯9sus C♯7
BOTH:
left? No - bod - y's got no
dim.
D♯min D(6)
MATRON:
VELMA:
class! Ev - 'ry - bod - y you watch 's'got his brains in his
p sustained
F♯/C♯ G♯7 C♯7 C♯min(6) C♯7
MATRON:
VELMA:
MATRON:
VELMA:
BOTH:
crotch. Ho - ly crap! Ho - ly crap! What a shame. What a shame. What be - came of
B F♯
class?
pp

# City Lights

*from the Musical* ***THE ACT***

Words by
**FRED EBB**

Music by
**JOHN KANDER**

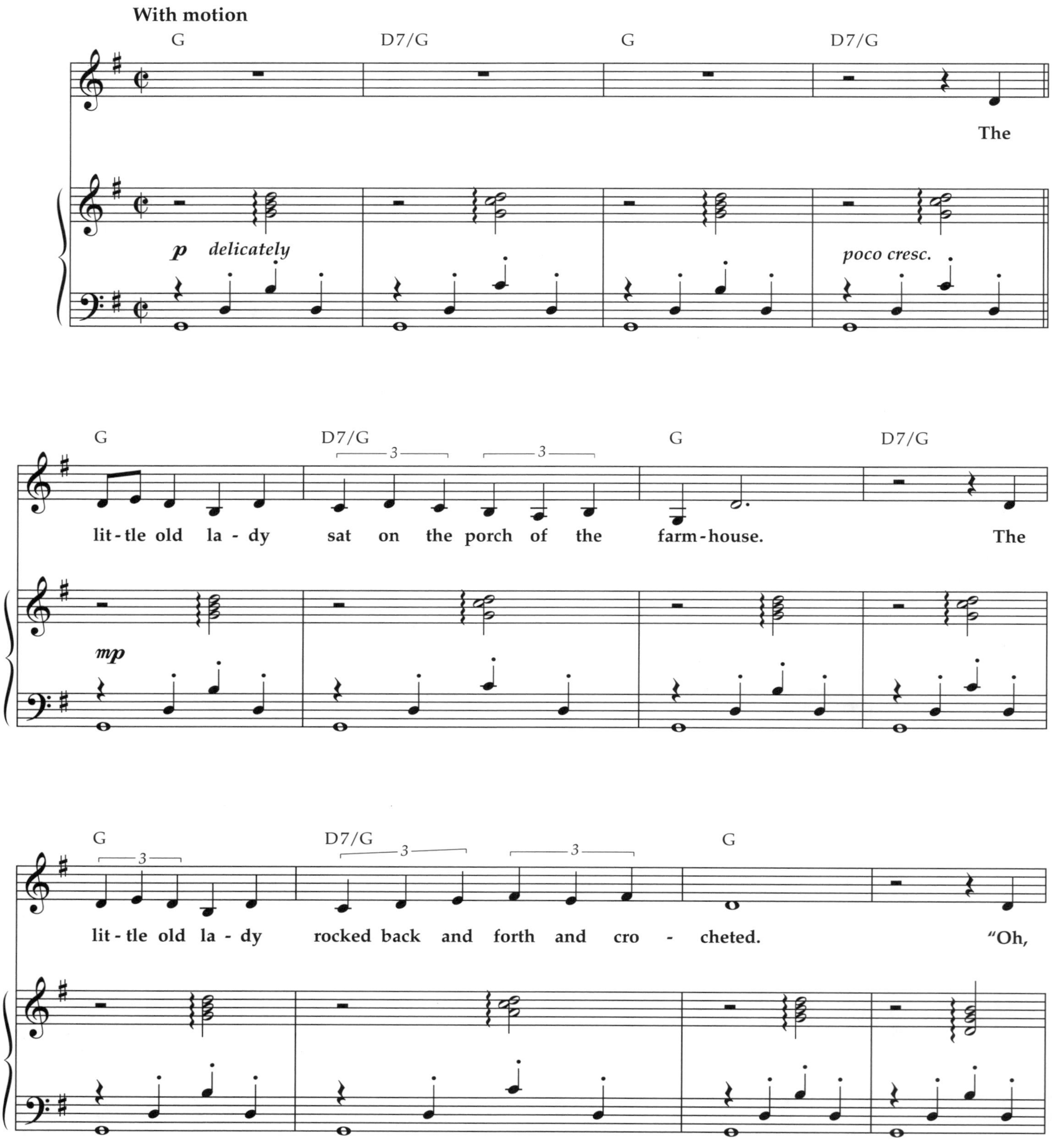

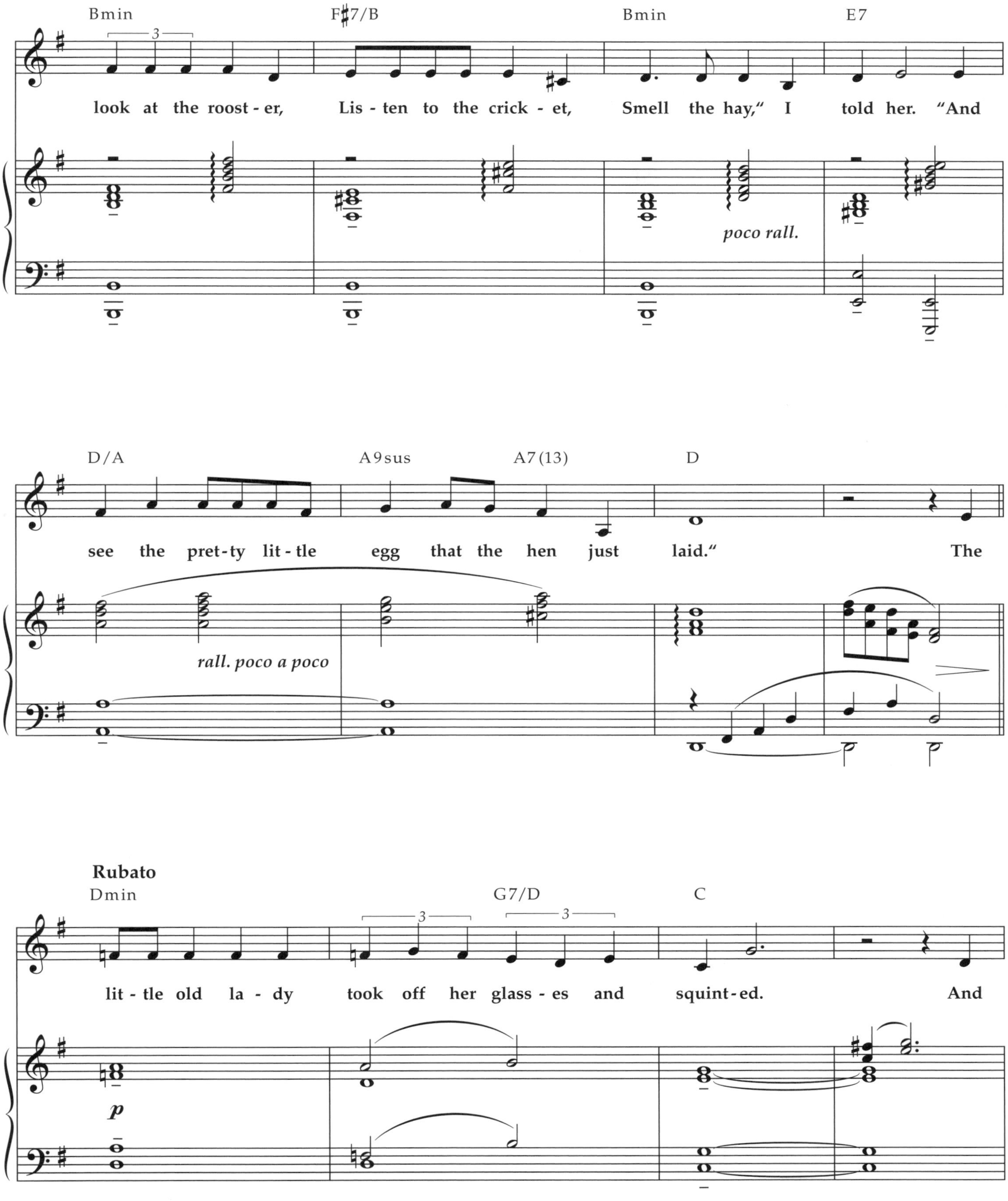
Bmin
F♯7/B
Bmin
E7
look at the roost - er, Lis - ten to the crick - et, Smell the hay," I told her. "And
poco rall.
D/A
A9sus
A7(13)
D
see the pret - ty lit - tle egg that the hen just laid." The
rall. poco a poco
Rubato
Dmin
G7/D
C
lit - tle old la - dy took off her glass - es and squint - ed. And
p

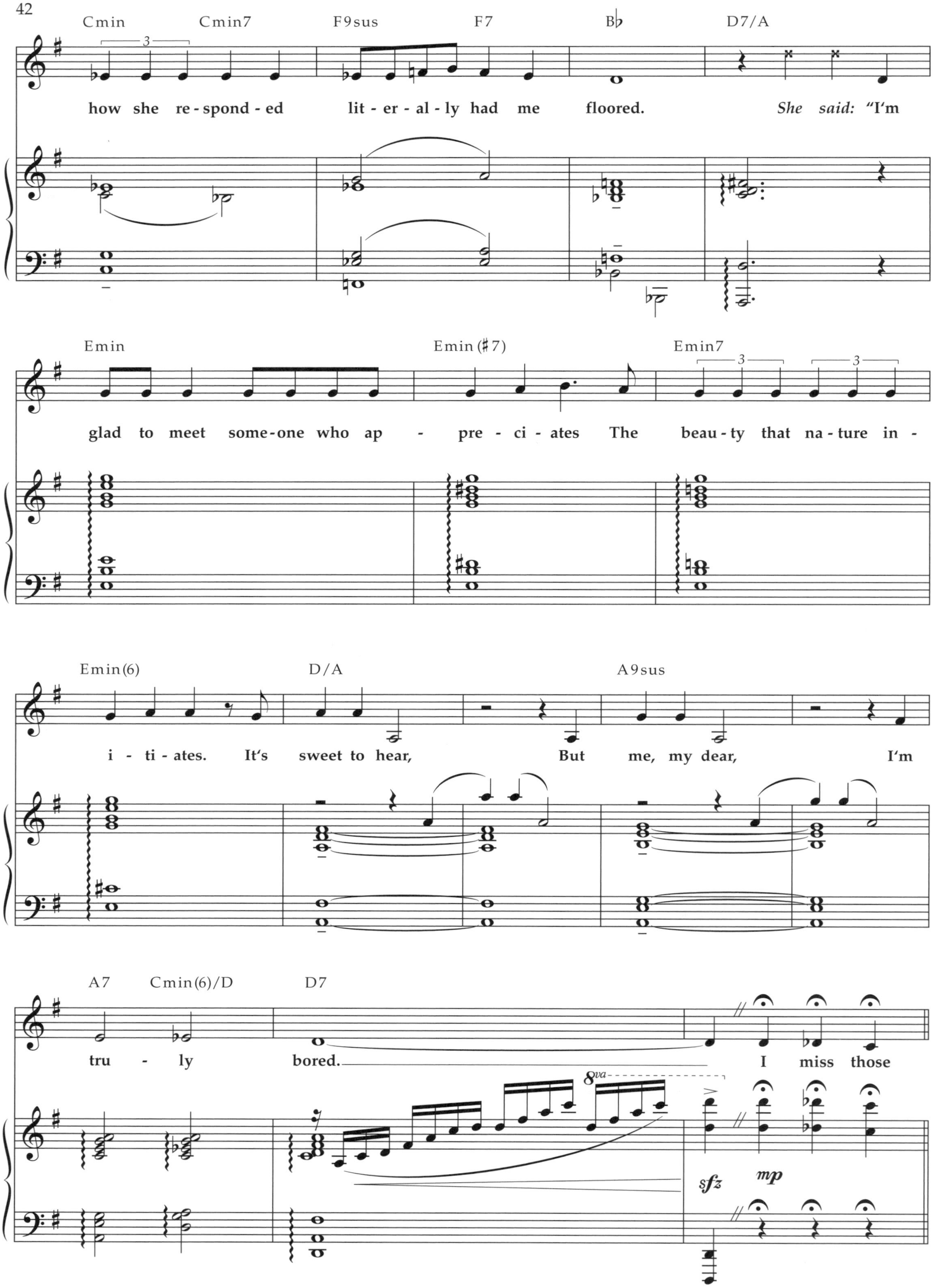
Cmin Cmin7 F9sus F7 B♭ D7/A
how she re-spond-ed lit-er-al-ly had me floored. She said: "I'm
Emin Emin(♯7) Emin7
glad to meet some-one who ap - pre - ci - ates The beau-ty that na-ture in -
Emin(6) D/A A9sus
i - ti - ates. It's sweet to hear, But me, my dear, I'm
A7 Cmin(6)/D D7
tru - ly bored. I miss those
8va
sfz
mp

Medium slow Rag
G
G(6)
Gmaj7
cit - y lights
Those spark - a - ling
cit - y lights,
marc.
sim.
G7
Cmaj7
C♯dim7
3
Those twink - a - ling
cit - y lights
blur - ring my
Bmin
F♯/A♯
Amin
D7
G
eyes.
I love those
cit - y lights,
marc.
G(6)
Gmaj7
G7
The col - or of
cit - y sights
That shine under

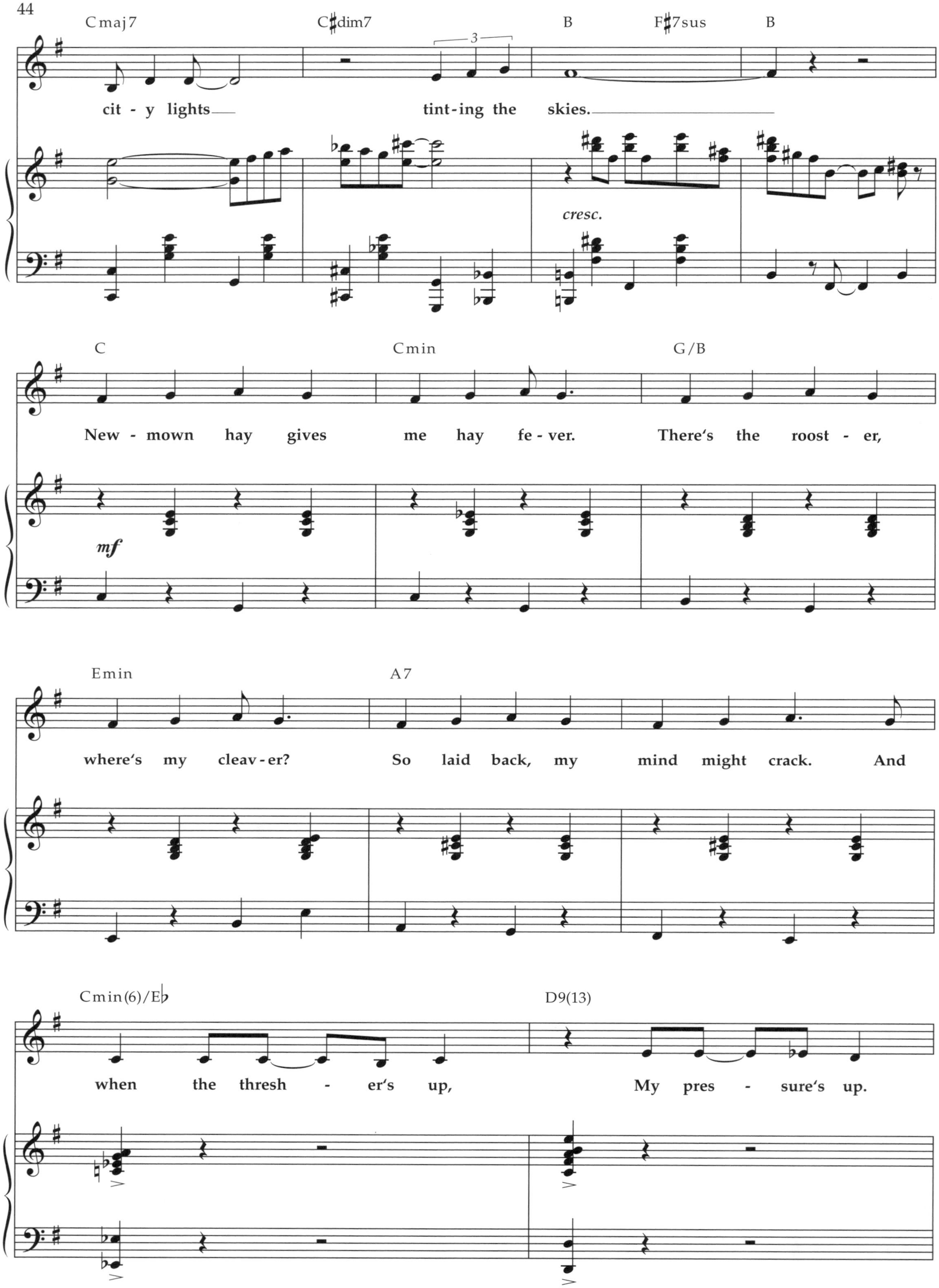
Cmaj7
C♯dim7
B
F♯7sus
B
3
cit - y lights
tint-ing the
skies.
cresc.
C
Cmin
G/B
New - mown hay gives me hay fe - ver. There's the roost - er,
mf
Emin
A7
where's my cleav - er? So laid back, my mind might crack. And
Cmin(6)/E♭
D9(13)
when the thresh - er's up, My pres - sure's up.

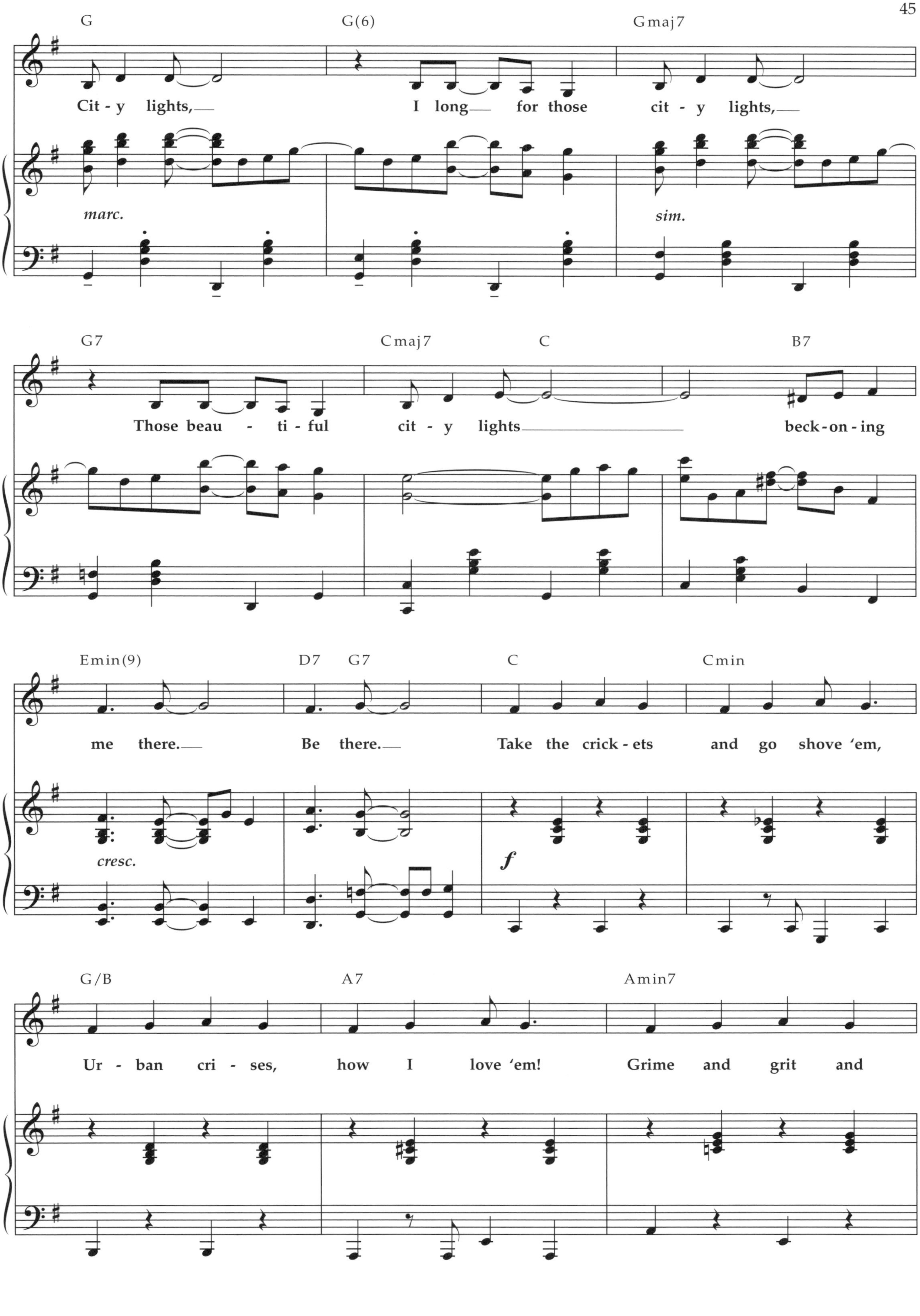
G
G(6)
Gmaj7
Cit - y lights,
I long for those
cit - y lights,
marc.
sim.
G7
Cmaj7
C
B7
Those beau - ti - ful
cit - y lights
beck - on - ing
Emin(9)
D7
G7
C
Cmin
me there.
Be there.
Take the crick - ets
and go shove 'em,
cresc.
f
G/B
A7
Amin7
Ur - ban cri - ses,
how I love 'em!
Grime and grit and

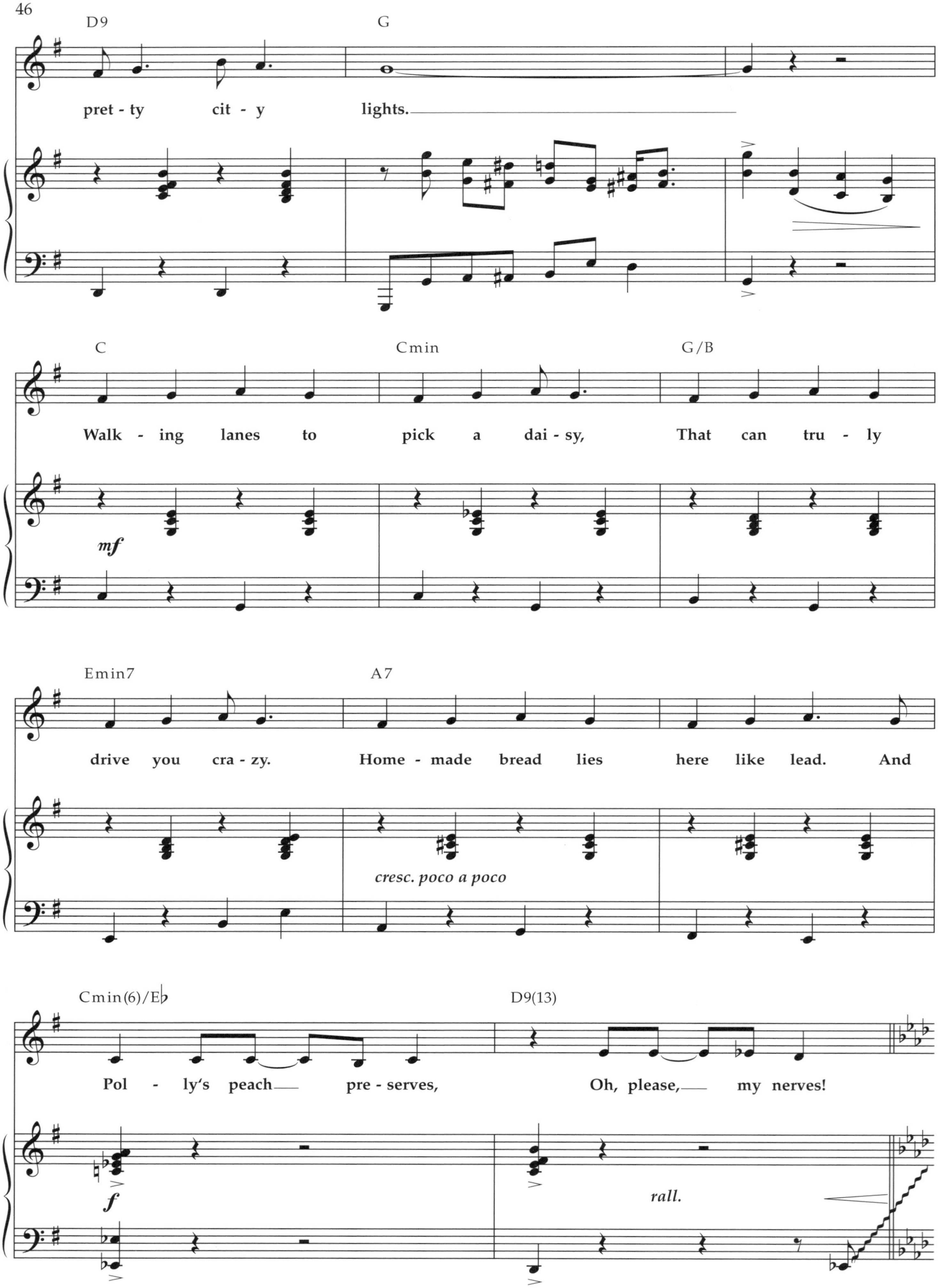
D9
G
pret - ty cit - y lights.
C
Cmin
G/B
Walk - ing lanes to pick a dai - sy, That can tru - ly
mf
Emin7
A7
drive you cra - zy. Home - made bread lies here like lead. And
cresc. poco a poco
Cmin(6)/E♭
D9(13)
Pol - ly's peach pre - serves, Oh, please, my nerves!
f
rall.

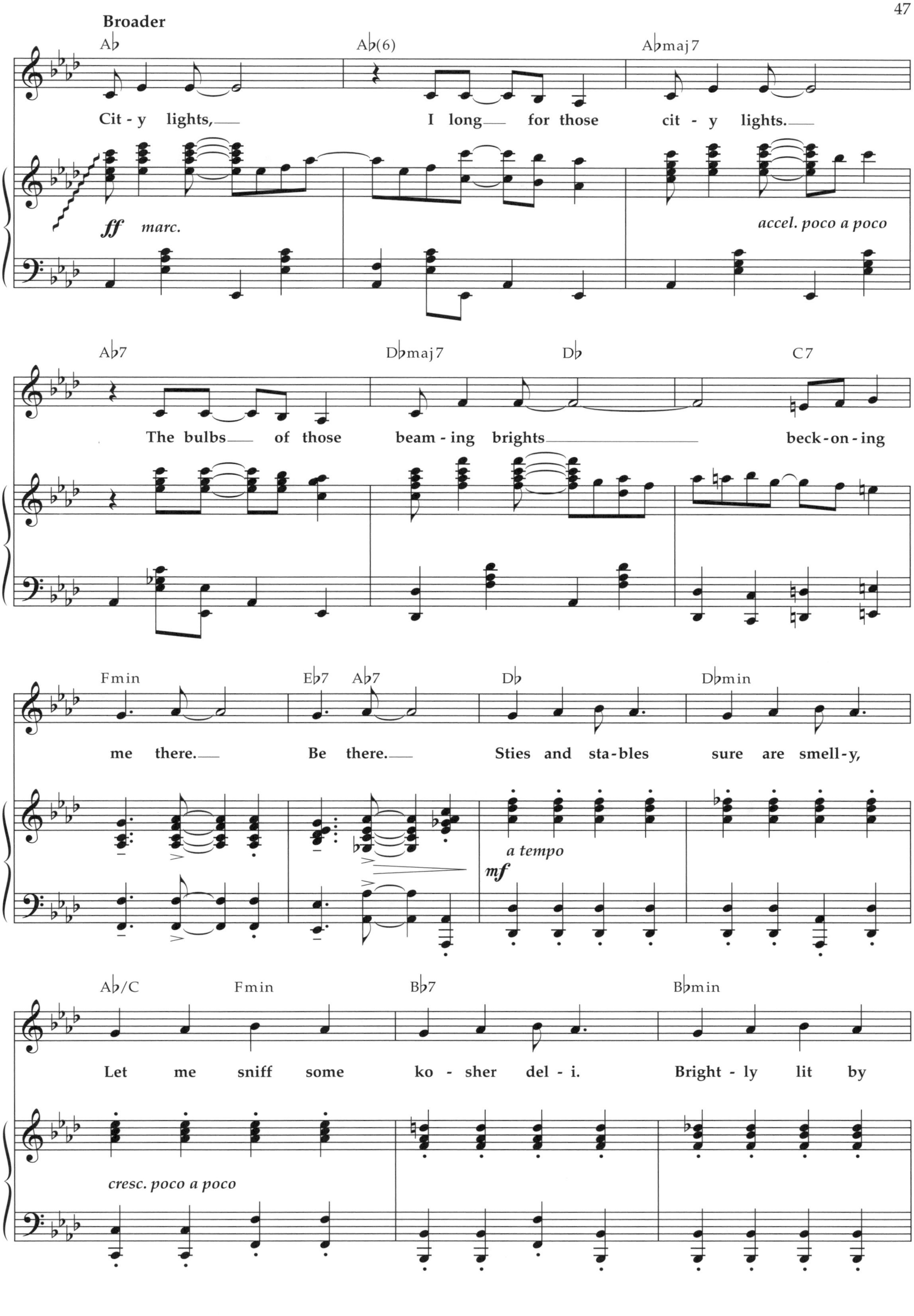
Broader
A♭
A♭(6)
A♭maj7
City lights, I long for those city lights.
ff marc.
accel. poco a poco
A♭7
D♭maj7
D♭
C7
The bulbs of those beaming brights beckoning
Fmin
E♭7
A♭7
D♭
D♭min
me there. Be there. Sties and stables sure are smelly,
a tempo
mf
A♭/C
Fmin
B♭7
B♭min
Let me sniff some kosher deli. Brightly lit by
cresc. poco a poco

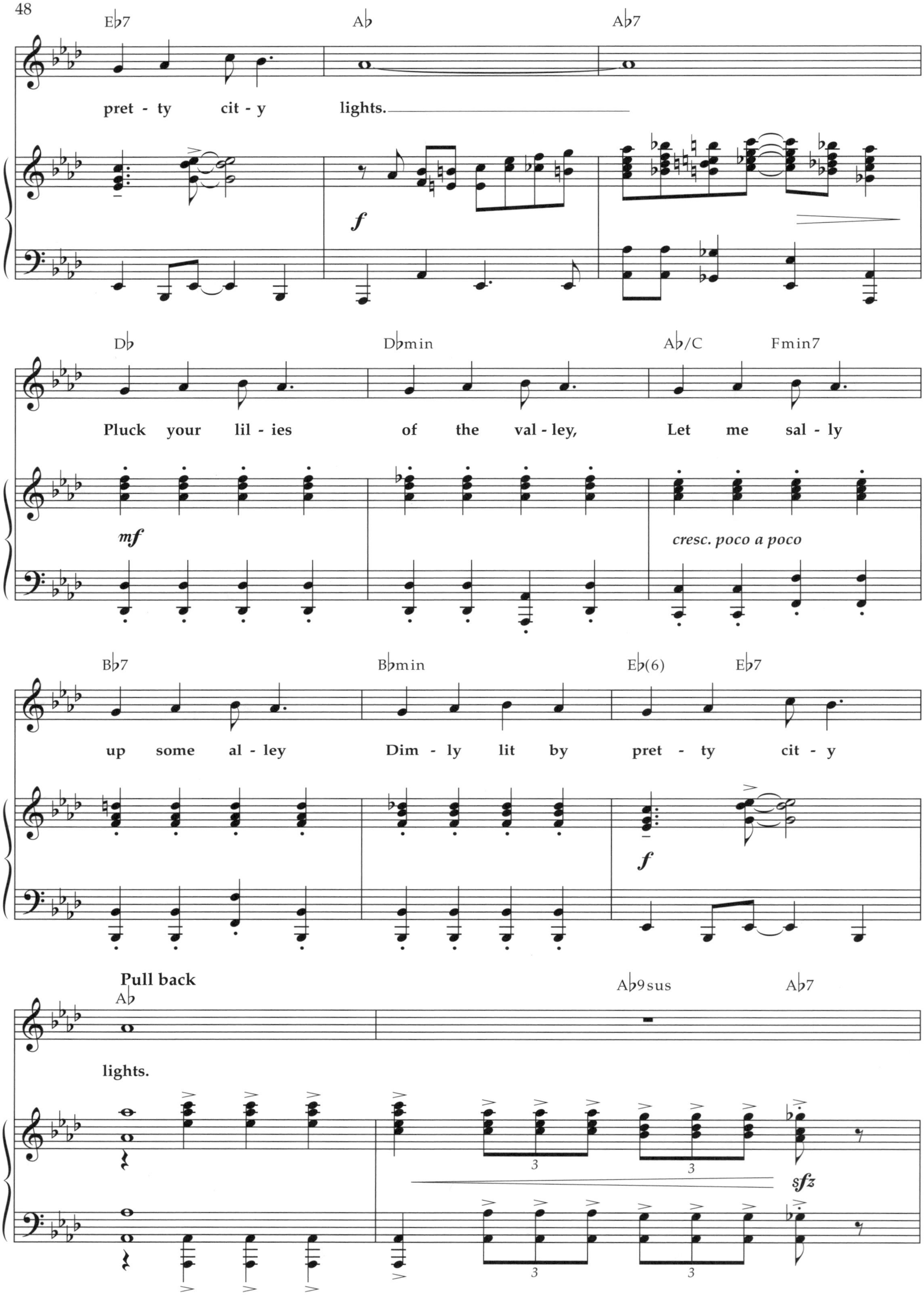

E♭7
A♭
A♭7
pret - ty cit - y lights.
f
D♭
D♭min
A♭/C
Fmin7
Pluck your lil - ies of the val - ley, Let me sal - ly
mf
cresc. poco a poco
B♭7
B♭min
E♭(6)
E♭7
up some al - ley Dim - ly lit by pret - ty cit - y
f
Pull back
A♭
A♭9sus
A♭7
lights.
sfz

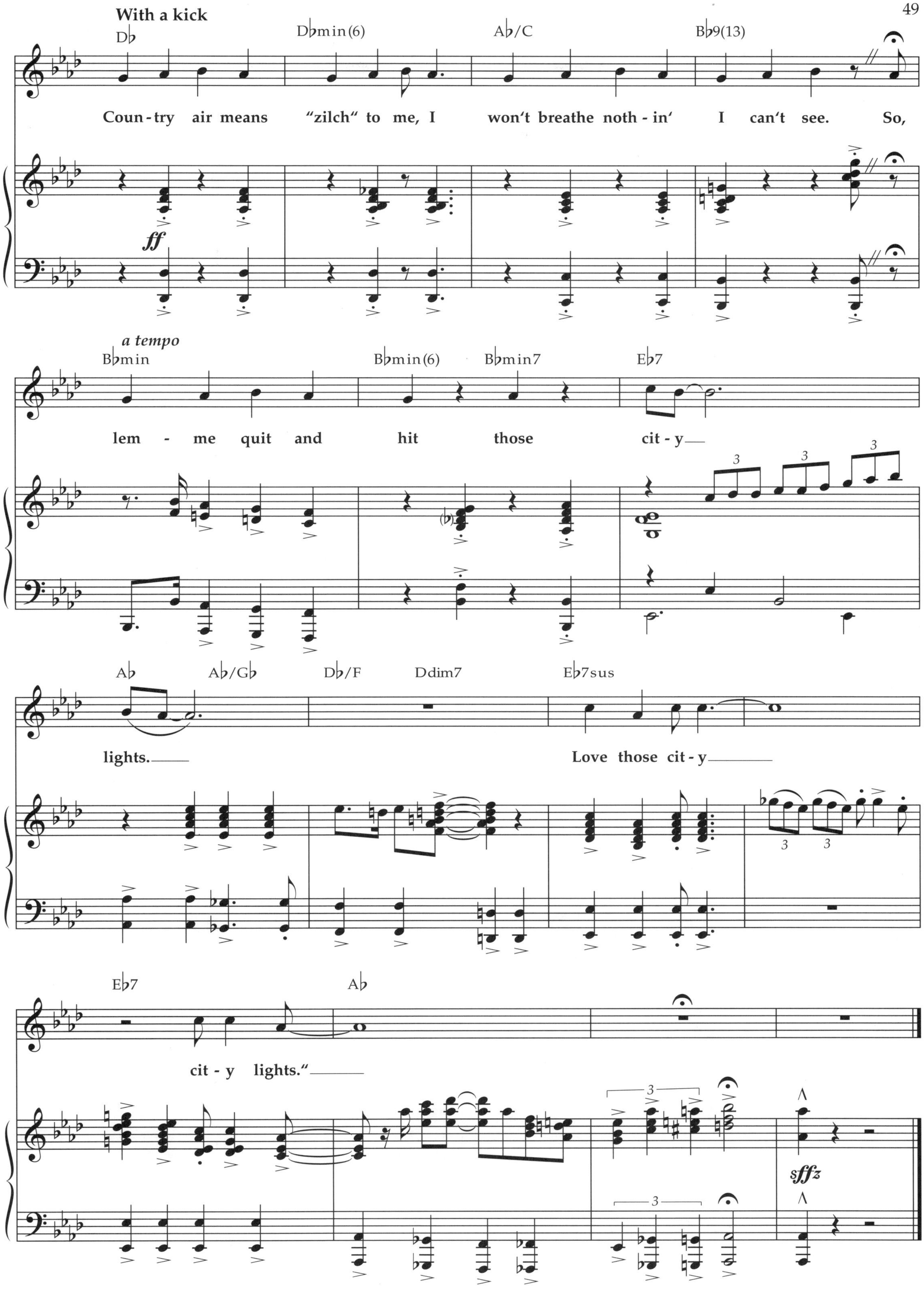
With a kick
D♭
D♭min(6)
A♭/C
B♭9(13)
Coun - try air means "zilch" to me, I won't breathe noth - in' I can't see. So,
ff
a tempo
B♭min
B♭min(6)
B♭min7
E♭7
lem - me quit and hit those cit - y
A♭
A♭/G♭
D♭/F
Ddim7
E♭7sus
lights.
Love those cit - y
E♭7
A♭
cit - y lights."
sffz

# Coffee (In a Cardboard Cup)

*from the Musical* ***70, GIRLS, 70***

Words by
**FRED EBB**

Music by
**JOHN KANDER**

E♭ D D♭ C B♭ E♭(6)
WOMAN 3:
cup. The trou - ble with the af - flu - ent so -
F7 Fmin9 B♭9 E♭
ci - e - ty Is cof - fee in a card - board cup.
A♭(6) Adim7 E♭/B♭ A♭(6) Adim7
MAN 1:
No one's ev - er ca - su - al or non - cha - lant.
MAN 2:
No one wastes a min - ute in a
E♭/B♭ Cmin(6) D7(♭9) Gmin C7sus C7
WOMAN 1:
res - tau - rant. No one wants a wait - ress pass - ing pleas - an - tries, Like

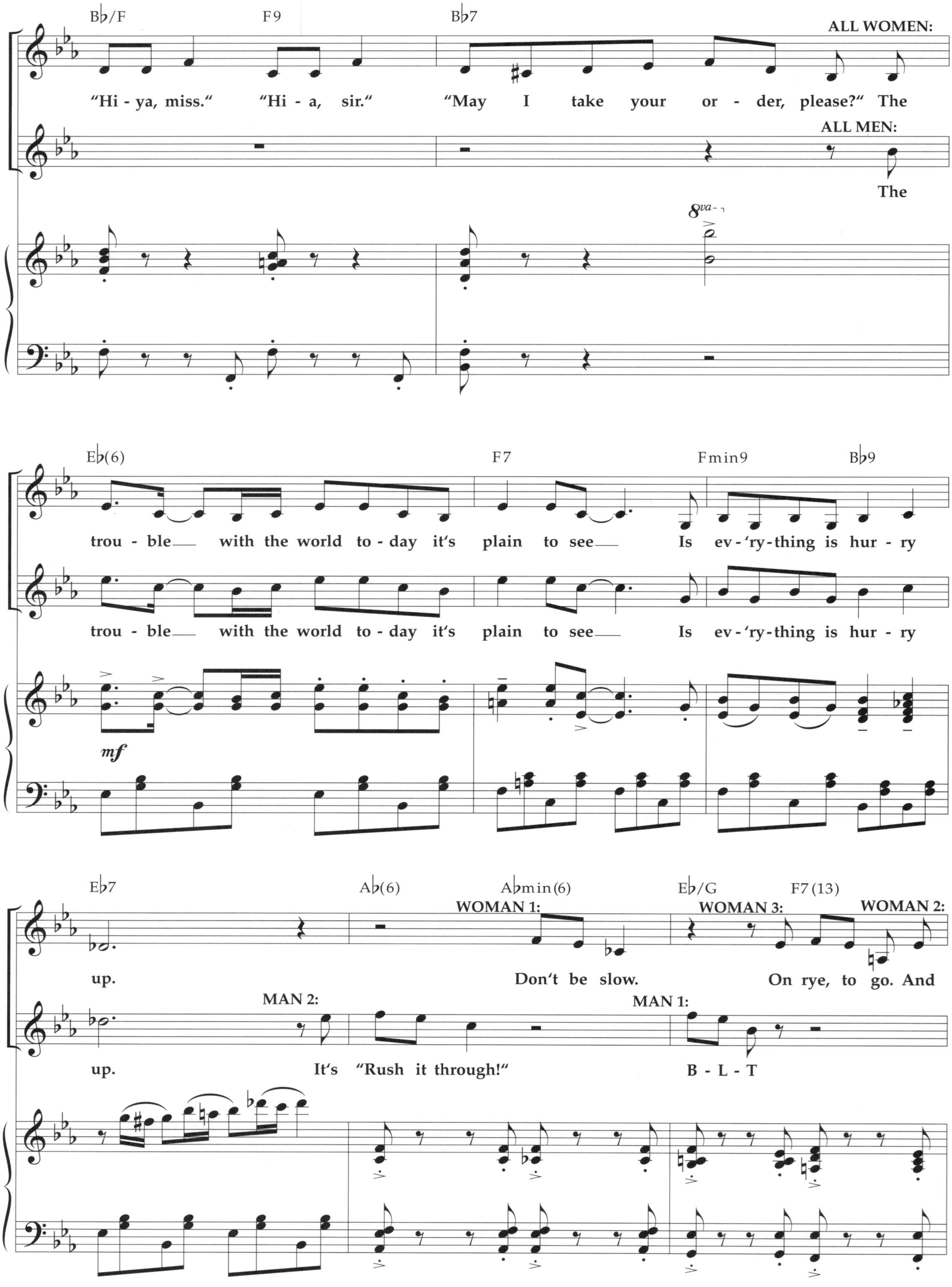
B♭/F
F9
B♭7
ALL WOMEN:
"Hi - ya, miss." "Hi - a, sir." "May I take your or - der, please?" The
ALL MEN:
The
8va
E♭(6)
F7
Fmin9
B♭9
trou - ble with the world to - day it's plain to see Is ev - 'ry-thing is hur - ry
trou - ble with the world to - day it's plain to see Is ev - 'ry-thing is hur - ry
mf
E♭7
A♭(6)
A♭min(6)
E♭/G
F7 (13)
WOMAN 1:
WOMAN 3:
WOMAN 2:
up. Don't be slow. On rye, to go. And
MAN 2:
MAN 1:
up. It's "Rush it through!" B - L - T

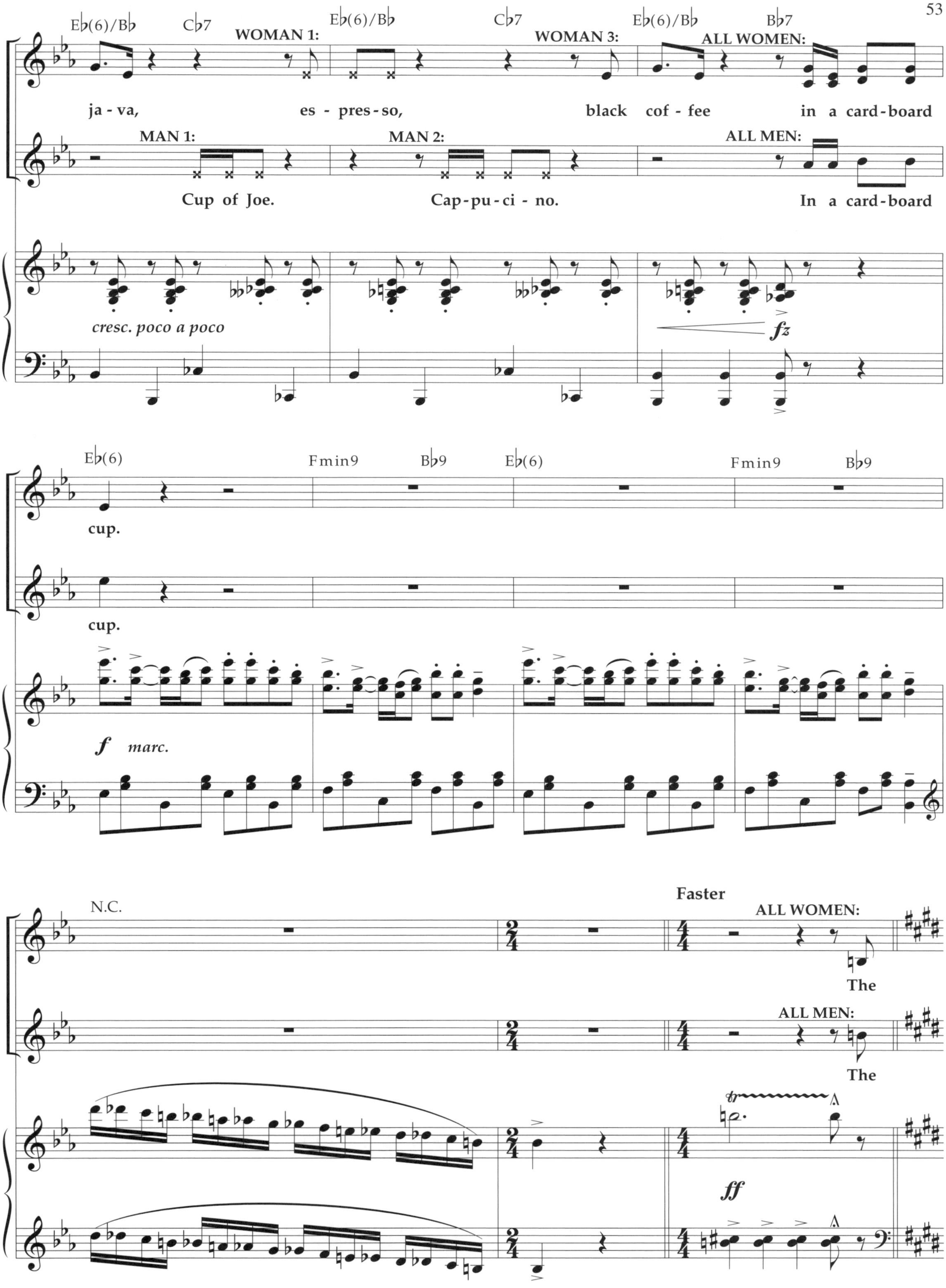

Eb(6)/Bb Cb7 Eb(6)/Bb Cb7 Eb(6)/Bb Bb7
WOMAN 1:
WOMAN 3:
ALL WOMEN:
ja - va, es - pres - so, black cof - fee in a card - board
MAN 1:
MAN 2:
ALL MEN:
Cup of Joe. Cap - pu - ci - no. In a card - board
cresc. poco a poco
fz
Eb(6) Fmin9 Bb9 Eb(6) Fmin9 Bb9
cup.
cup.
f marc.
N.C.
Faster
ALL WOMEN:
The
ALL MEN:
The
tr
ff

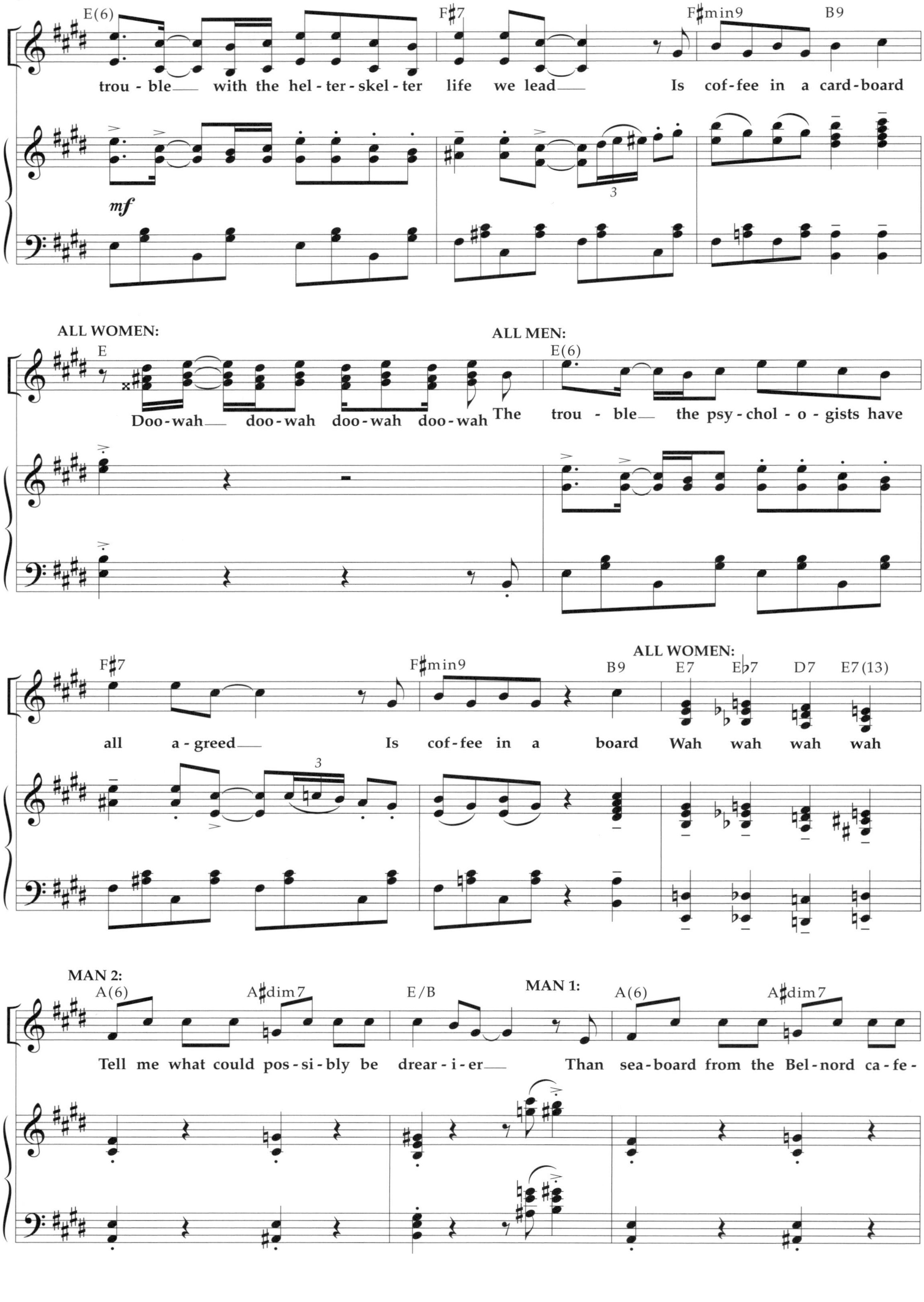
E(6) F♯7 F♯min9 B9
trou - ble with the hel - ter - skel - ter life we lead Is cof - fee in a card - board
mf
ALL WOMEN:
E
Doo - wah doo - wah doo - wah doo - wah
ALL MEN:
E(6)
The trou - ble the psy - chol - o - gists have
F♯7 F♯min9 B9
all a - greed Is cof - fee in a board
ALL WOMEN:
E7 E♭7 D7 E7(13)
Wah wah wah wah
MAN 2:
A(6) A♯dim7 E/B
Tell me what could pos - si - bly be drear - i - er
MAN 1:
A(6) A♯dim7
Than sea - board from the Bel - nord ca - fe -

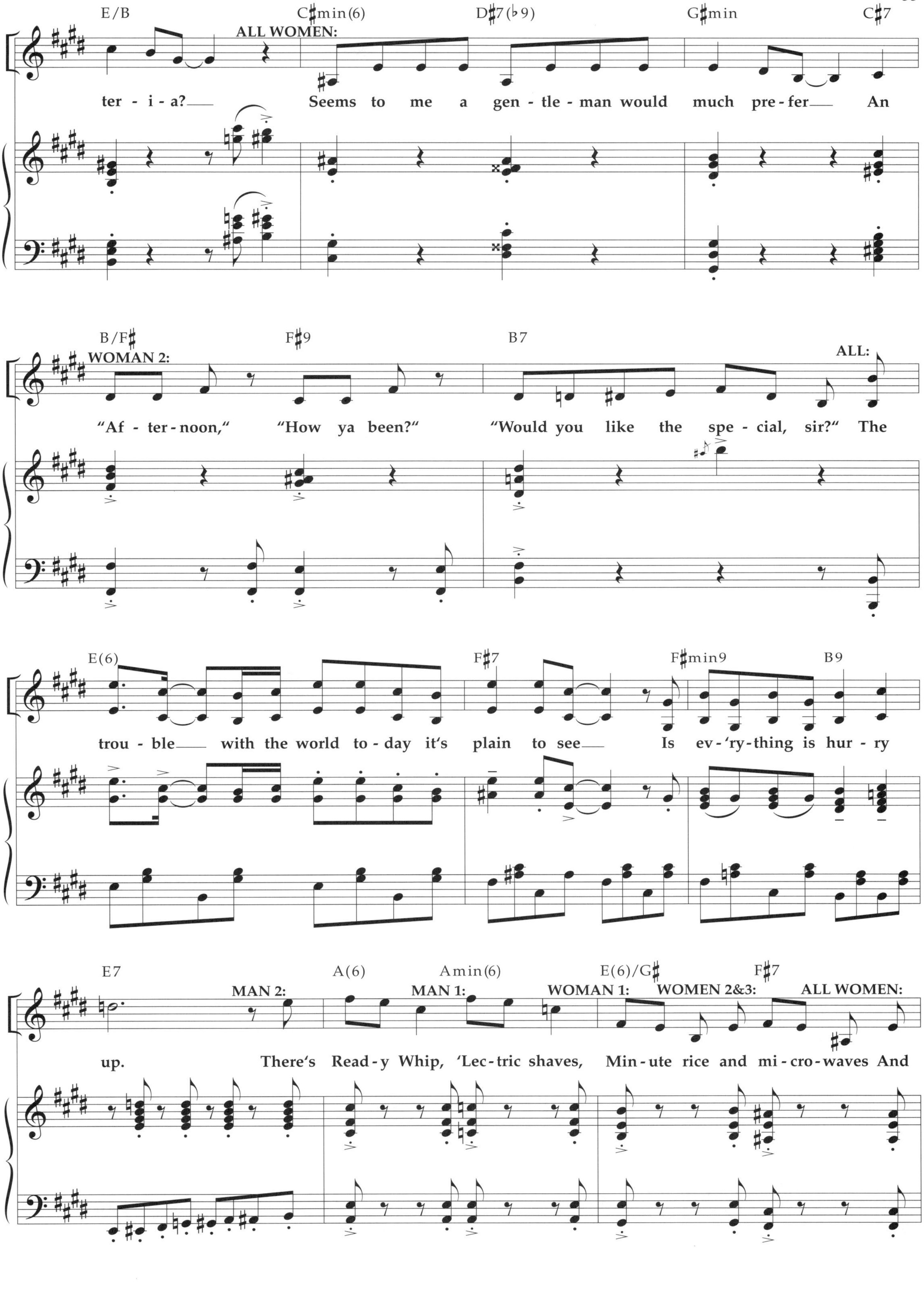
E/B
C♯min(6)
D♯7(♭9)
G♯min
C♯7
ALL WOMEN:
ter - i - a? Seems to me a gen - tle - man would much pre - fer An
B/F♯
F♯9
B7
WOMAN 2:
ALL:
"Af - ter - noon," "How ya been?" "Would you like the spe - cial, sir?" The
E(6)
F♯7
F♯min9
B9
trou - ble with the world to - day it's plain to see Is ev - 'ry - thing is hur - ry
E7
A(6)
Amin(6)
E(6)/G♯
F♯7
MAN 2:
MAN 1:
WOMAN 1:
WOMEN 2&3:
ALL WOMEN:
up. There's Read - y Whip, 'Lec - tric shaves, Min - ute rice and mi - cro - waves And

E/B C7 E/B C7
ALL WOMEN:
cof - fee, cof - fee,
ALL MEN:
I think she said I know she said
cresc. poco a poco
E/B C7 E/B F#7 E(6)
cof - fee, Cof - fee in a card - board cup.
I'm sure she said In a card - board cup.
f
N.C.
Faster
ALL:
The
cresc.
ff

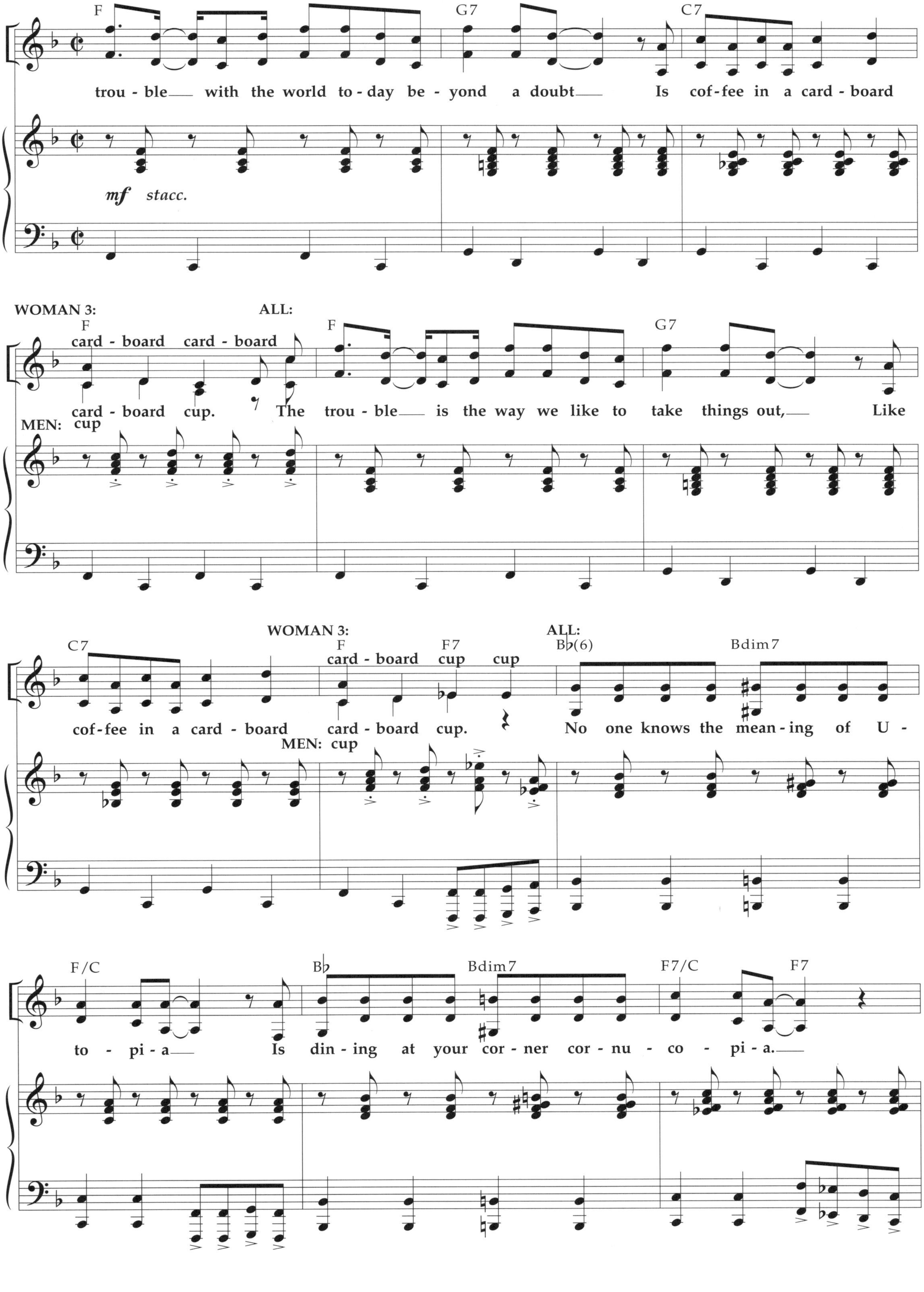
F G7 C7
trou - ble with the world to - day be - yond a doubt Is cof - fee in a card - board
mf stacc.
WOMAN 3: ALL:
F F G7
card - board card - board
card - board cup. The trou - ble is the way we like to take things out, Like
MEN: cup
C7 WOMAN 3: ALL:
F F7 B♭(6) Bdim7
card - board cup cup
cof - fee in a card - board card - board cup. No one knows the mean - ing of U -
MEN: cup
F/C B♭ Bdim7 F7/C F7
to - pi - a Is din - ing at your cor - ner cor - nu - co - pi - a.

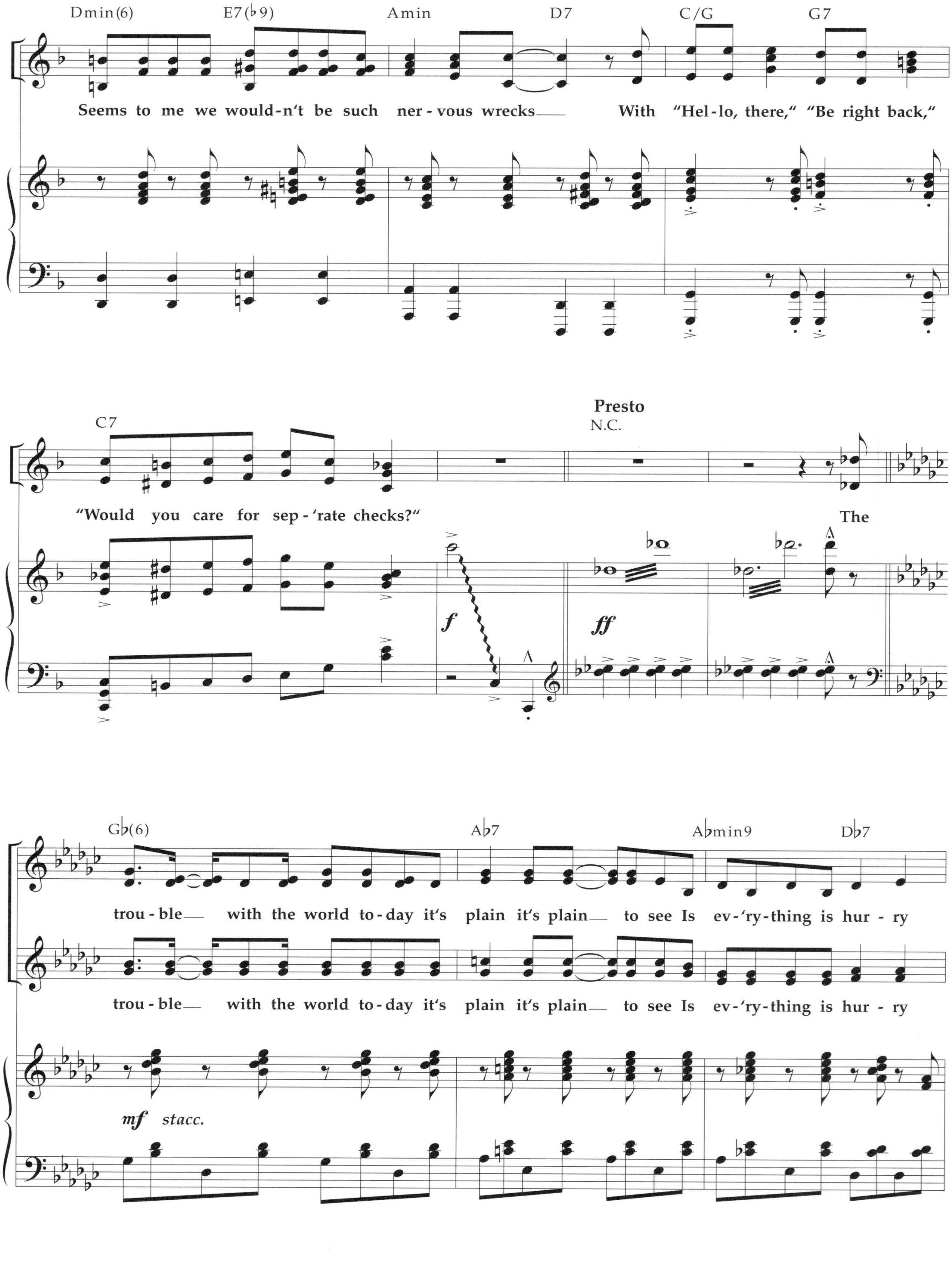
Dmin(6) E7(♭9) Amin D7 C/G G7
Seems to me we would-n't be such ner-vous wrecks With "Hel-lo, there," "Be right back,"
C7
"Would you care for sep-'rate checks?"
Presto
N.C.
The
f
ff
G♭(6) A♭7 A♭min9 D♭7
trou-ble with the world to-day it's plain it's plain to see Is ev-'ry-thing is hur-ry
trou-ble with the world to-day it's plain it's plain to see Is ev-'ry-thing is hur-ry
mf stacc.

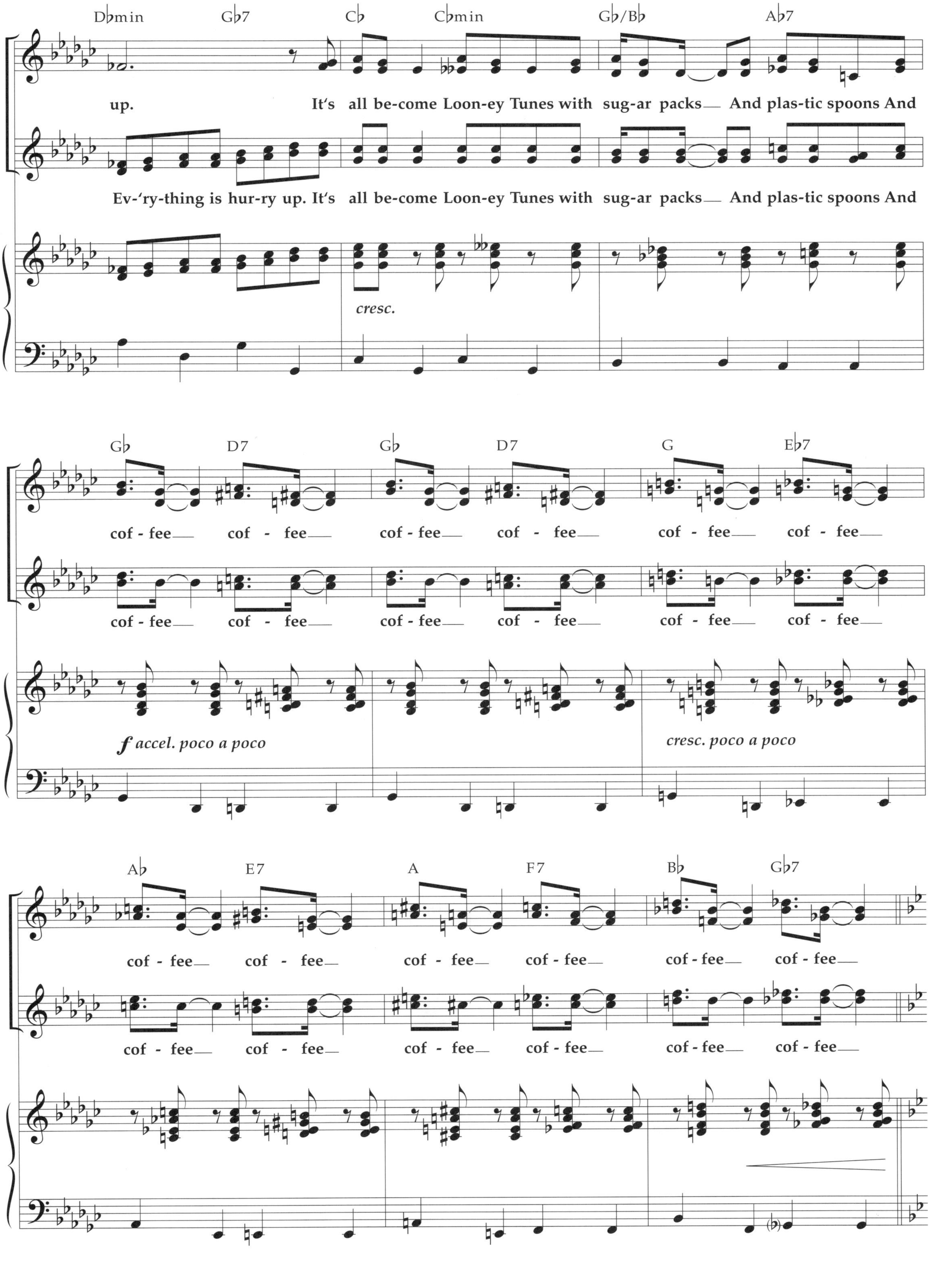

D♭min G♭7 C♭ C♭min G♭/B♭ A♭7
up. It's all be-come Loon-ey Tunes with sug-ar packs And plas-tic spoons And
Ev-'ry-thing is hur-ry up. It's all be-come Loon-ey Tunes with sug-ar packs And plas-tic spoons And
cresc.
G♭ D7 G♭ D7 G E♭7
cof - fee cof - fee cof - fee cof - fee cof - fee cof - fee
cof - fee cof - fee cof - fee cof - fee cof - fee cof - fee
f accel. poco a poco
cresc. poco a poco
A♭ E7 A F7 B♭ G♭7
cof - fee cof - fee cof - fee cof - fee cof - fee cof - fee
cof - fee cof - fee cof - fee cof - fee cof - fee cof - fee

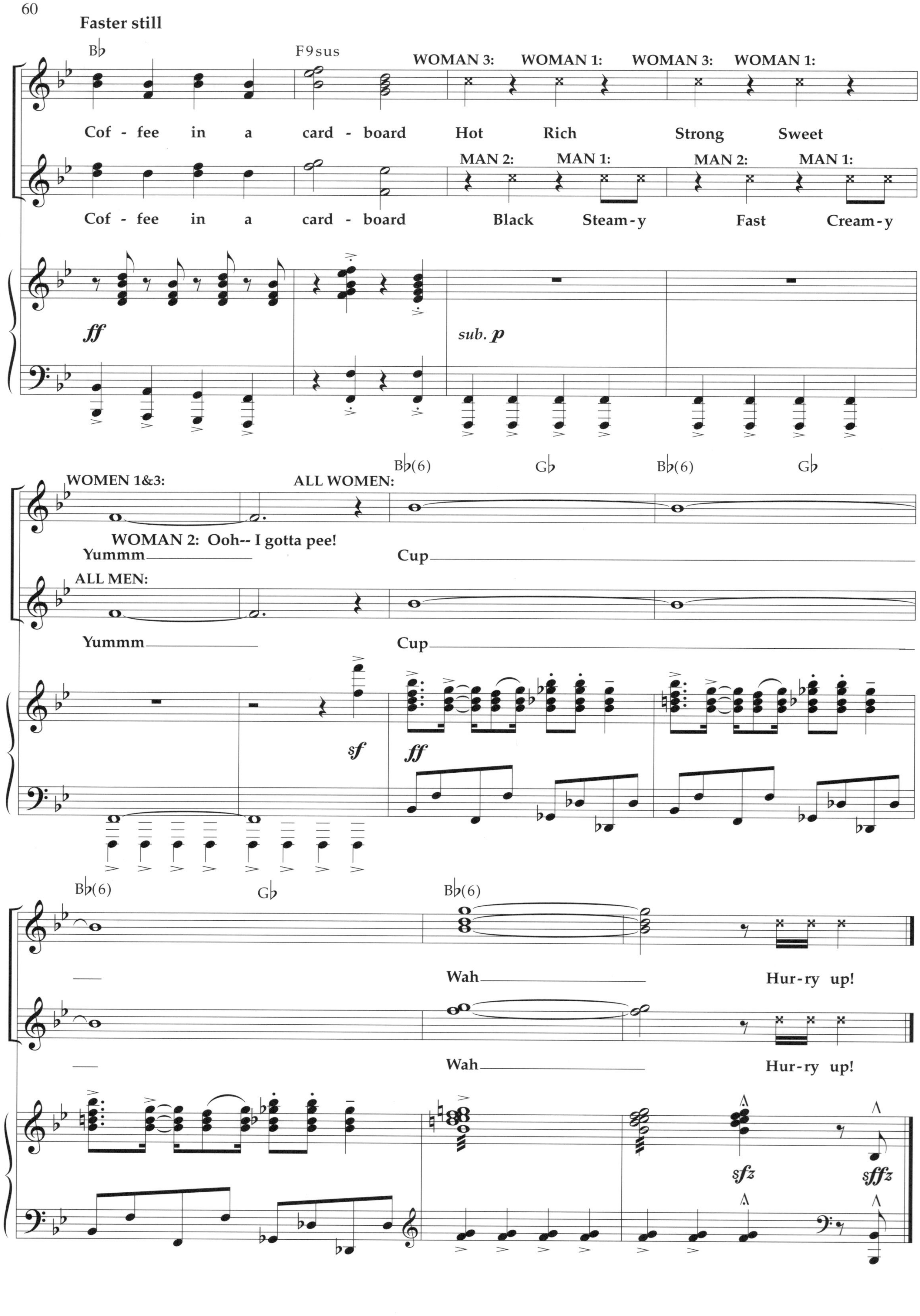
Faster still
B♭
F9sus
WOMAN 3: WOMAN 1: WOMAN 3: WOMAN 1:
Cof - fee in a card - board Hot Rich Strong Sweet
MAN 2: MAN 1: MAN 2: MAN 1:
Cof - fee in a card - board Black Steam-y Fast Cream-y
ff
sub. p
WOMEN 1&3: ALL WOMEN:
B♭(6) G♭ B♭(6) G♭
WOMAN 2: Ooh-- I gotta pee!
Yummm Cup
ALL MEN:
Yummm Cup
sf
ff
B♭(6) G♭ B♭(6)
Wah Hur-ry up!
Wah Hur-ry up!
sfz
sffz

# Colored Lights

*from the Musical* **THE RINK**

Words by
**FRED EBB**

Music by
**JOHN KANDER**

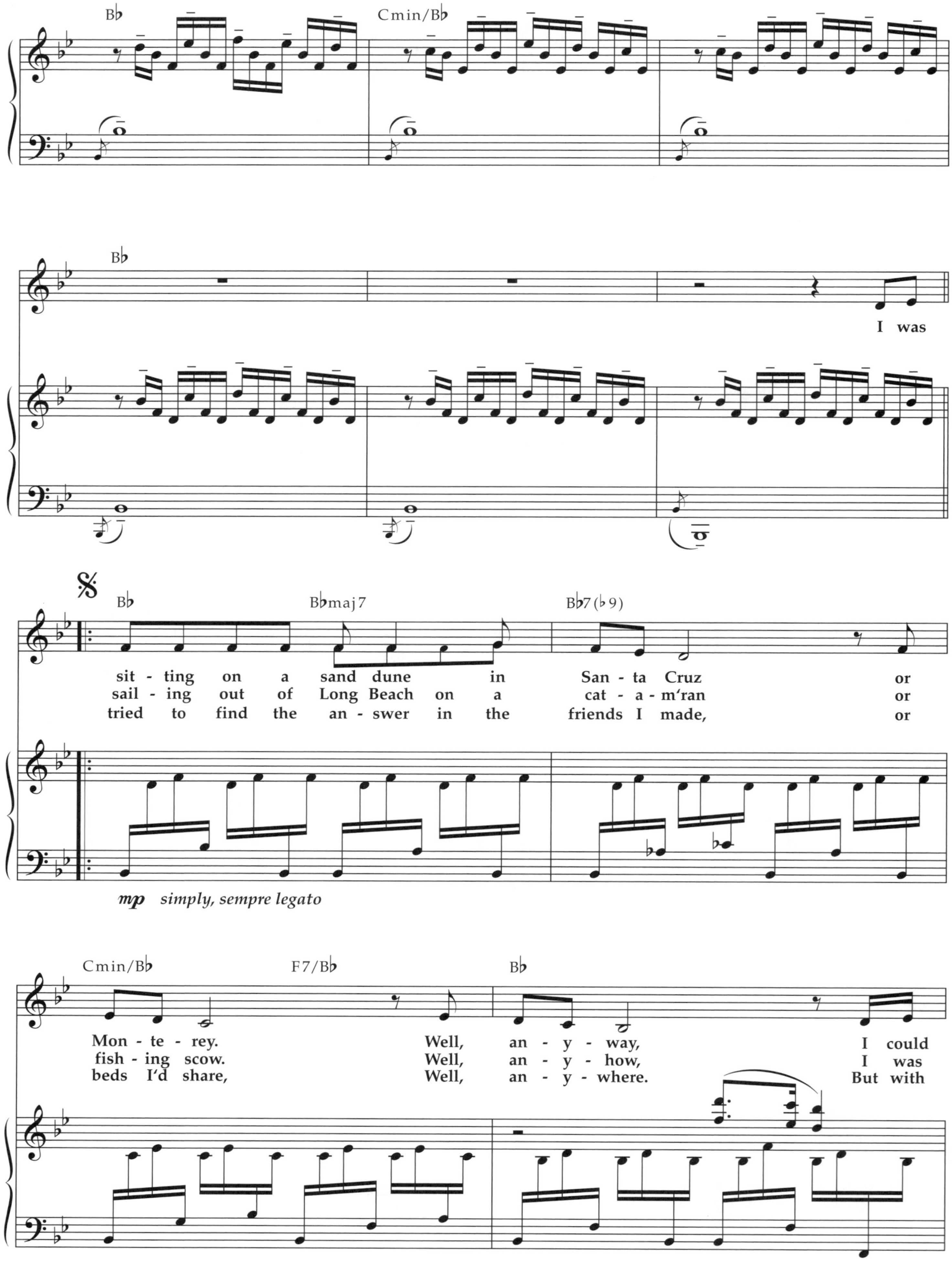
B♭
Cmin/B♭
B♭
I was
B♭
B♭maj7
B♭7(♭9)
sit - ting on a sand dune in San - ta Cruz or
sail - ing out of Long Beach on a cat - a - m'ran or
tried to find the an - swer in the friends I made, or
mp simply, sempre legato
Cmin/B♭
F7/B♭
B♭
Mon - te - rey. Well, an - y - way, I could
fish - ing scow. Well, an - y - how, I was
beds I'd share, Well, an - y - where. But with

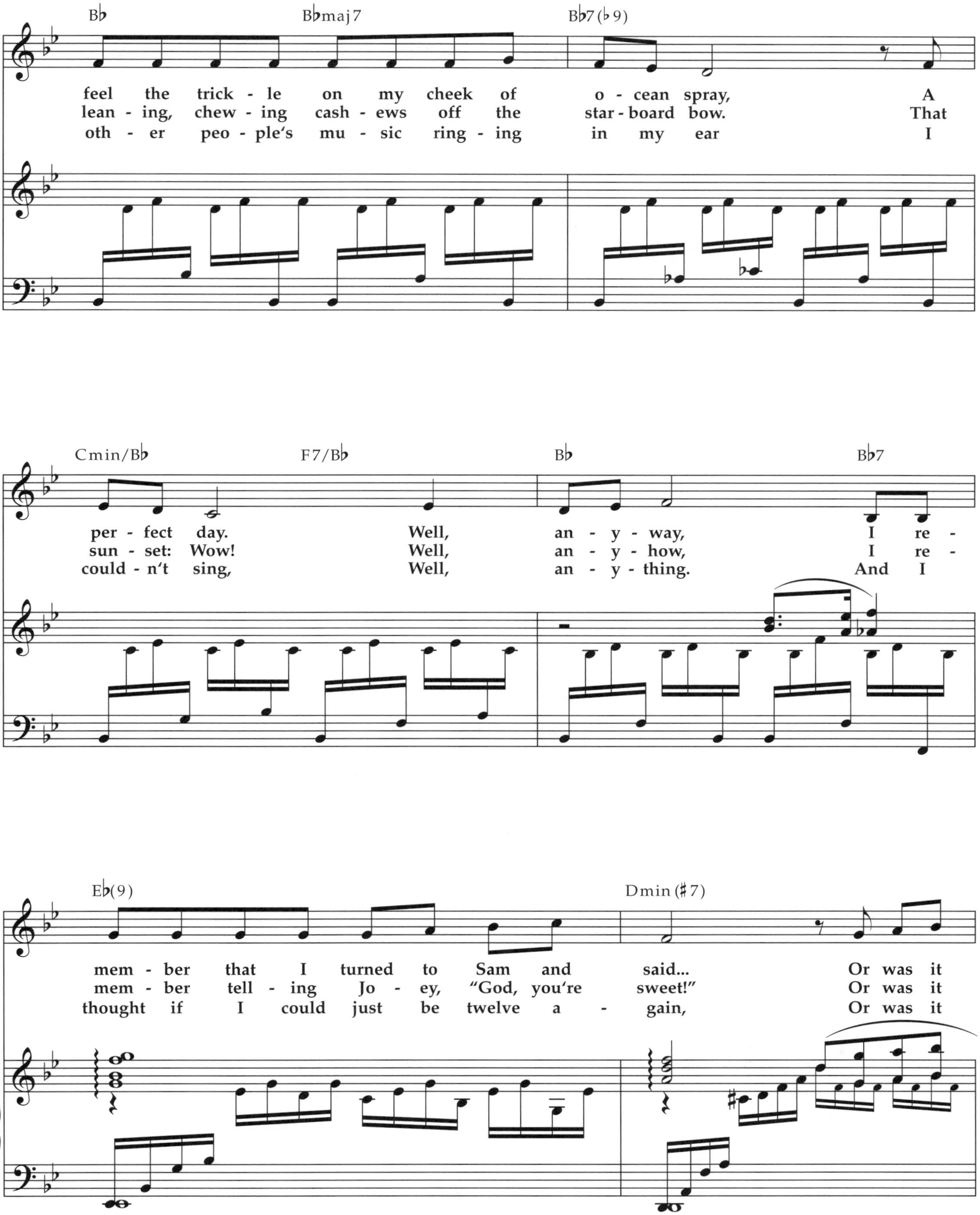
B♭ B♭maj7 B♭7(♭9)
feel the trick - le on my cheek of o - cean spray, A
lean - ing, chew - ing cash - ews off the star - board bow. That
oth - er peo - ple's mu - sic ring - ing in my ear I
Cmin/B♭ F7/B♭ B♭ B♭7
per - fect day. Well, an - y - way, I re -
sun - set: Wow! Well, an - y - how, I re -
could - n't sing, Well, an - y - thing. And I
E♭(9) Dmin(♯7)
mem - ber that I turned to Sam and said... Or was it
mem - ber tell - ing Jo - ey, "God, you're sweet!" Or was it
thought if I could just be twelve a - gain, Or was it

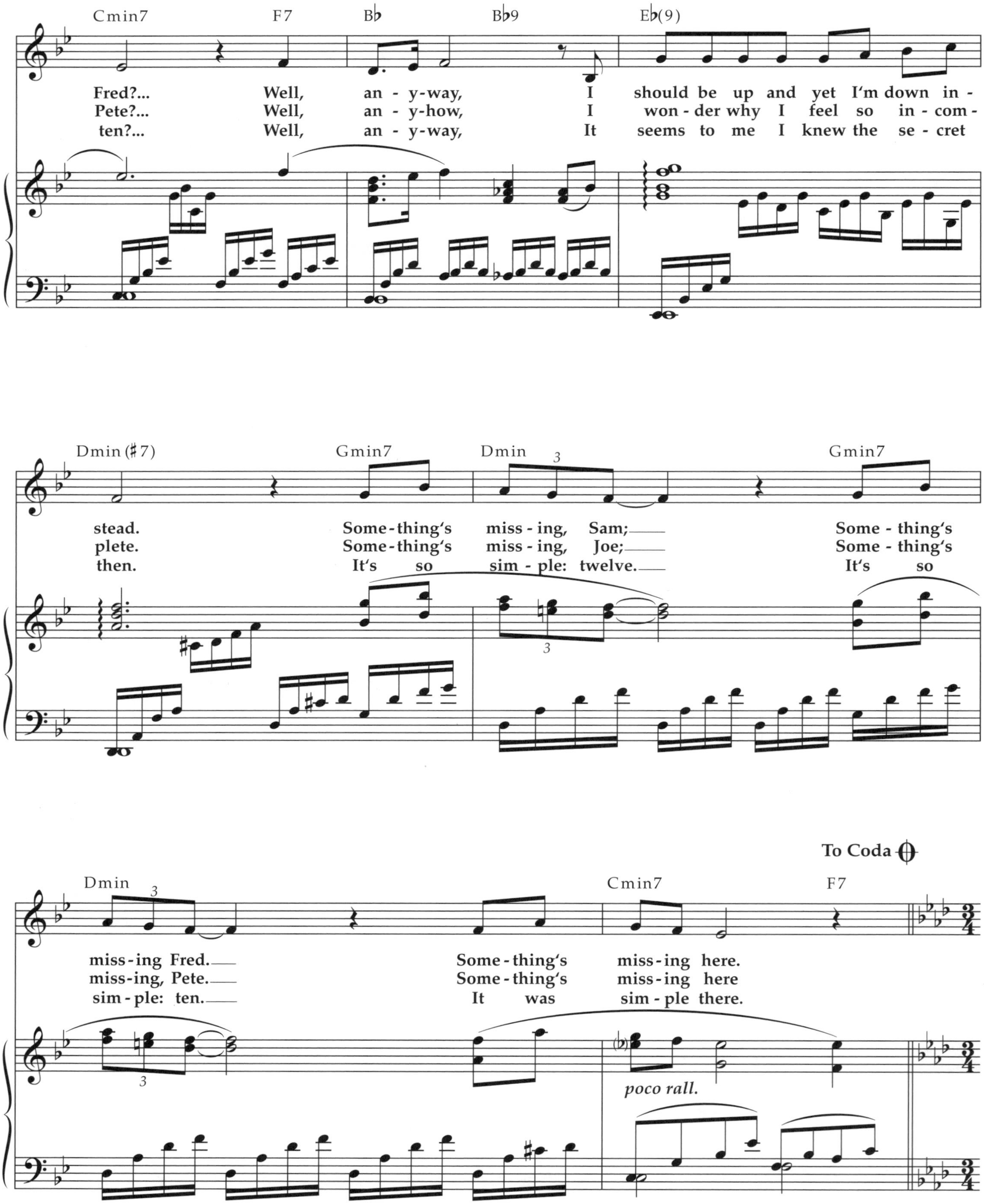
Cmin7 F7 B♭ B♭9 E♭(9)
Fred?... Well, an - y-way, I should be up and yet I'm down in -
Pete?... Well, an - y-how, I won - der why I feel so in - com -
ten?... Well, an - y-way, It seems to me I knew the se - cret
Dmin(♯7) Gmin7 Dmin Gmin7
stead. Some-thing's miss - ing, Sam; Some - thing's
plete. Some-thing's miss - ing, Joe; Some - thing's
then. It's so sim - ple: twelve. It's so
To Coda
Dmin Cmin7 F7
miss-ing Fred. Some-thing's miss-ing here.
miss-ing, Pete. Some-thing's miss-ing here
sim - ple: ten. It was sim - ple there.
poco rall.

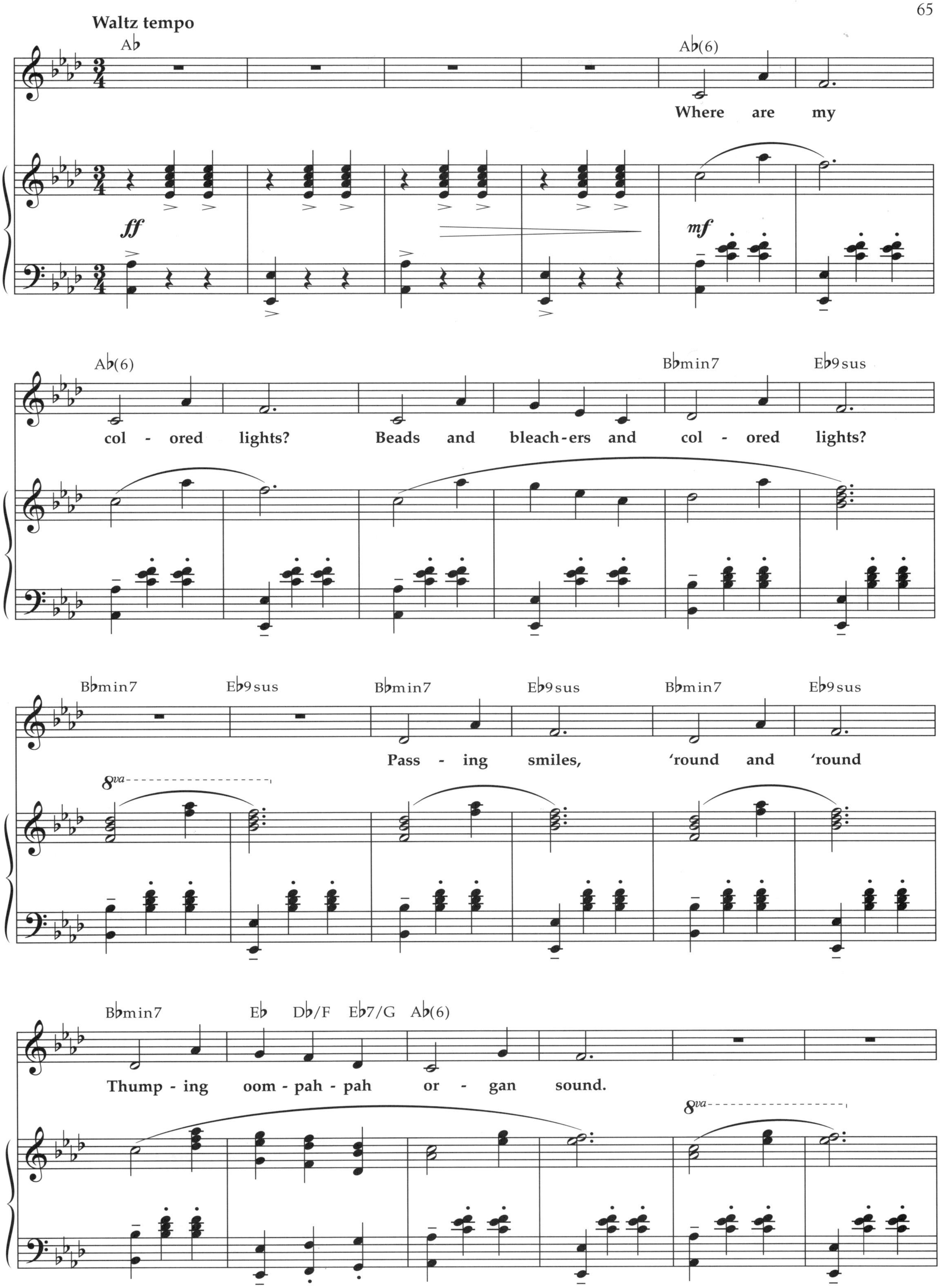
Waltz tempo
A♭
A♭(6)
Where are my
ff
mf
A♭(6)
B♭min7
E♭9sus
col - ored lights? Beads and bleach-ers and col - ored lights?
B♭min7
E♭9sus
B♭min7
E♭9sus
B♭min7
E♭9sus
Pass - ing smiles, 'round and 'round
8va
B♭min7
E♭
D♭/F
E♭7/G
A♭(6)
Thump - ing oom - pah - pah or - gan sound.
8va

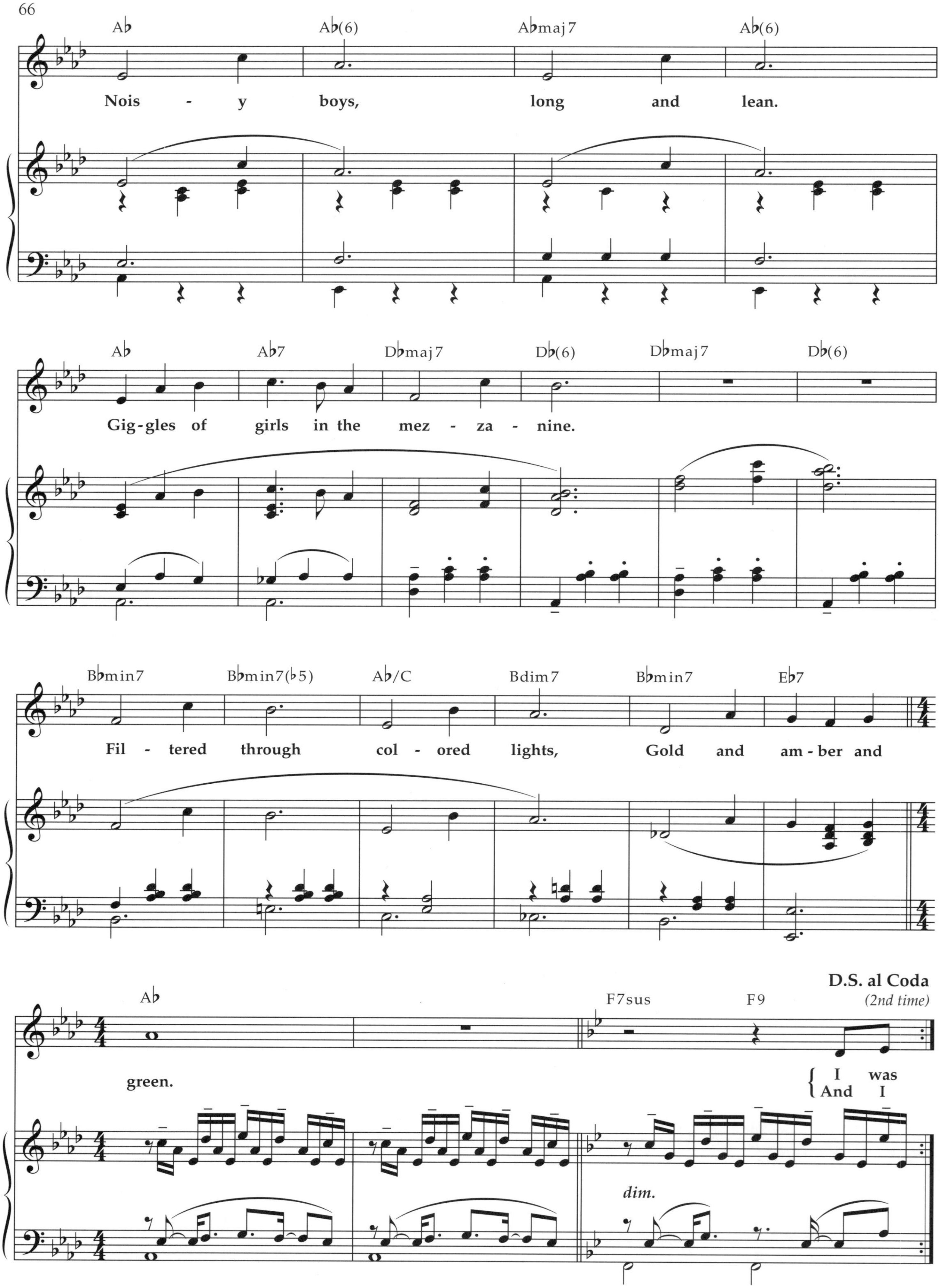
A♭
A♭(6)
A♭maj7
A♭(6)
Nois - y boys, long and lean.
A♭
A♭7
D♭maj7
D♭(6)
D♭maj7
D♭(6)
Gig-gles of girls in the mez - za - nine.
B♭min7
B♭min7(♭5)
A♭/C
Bdim7
B♭min7
E♭7
Fil - tered through col - ored lights, Gold and am-ber and
A♭
F7sus
F9
D.S. al Coda
(2nd time)
green.
I was
And I
dim.

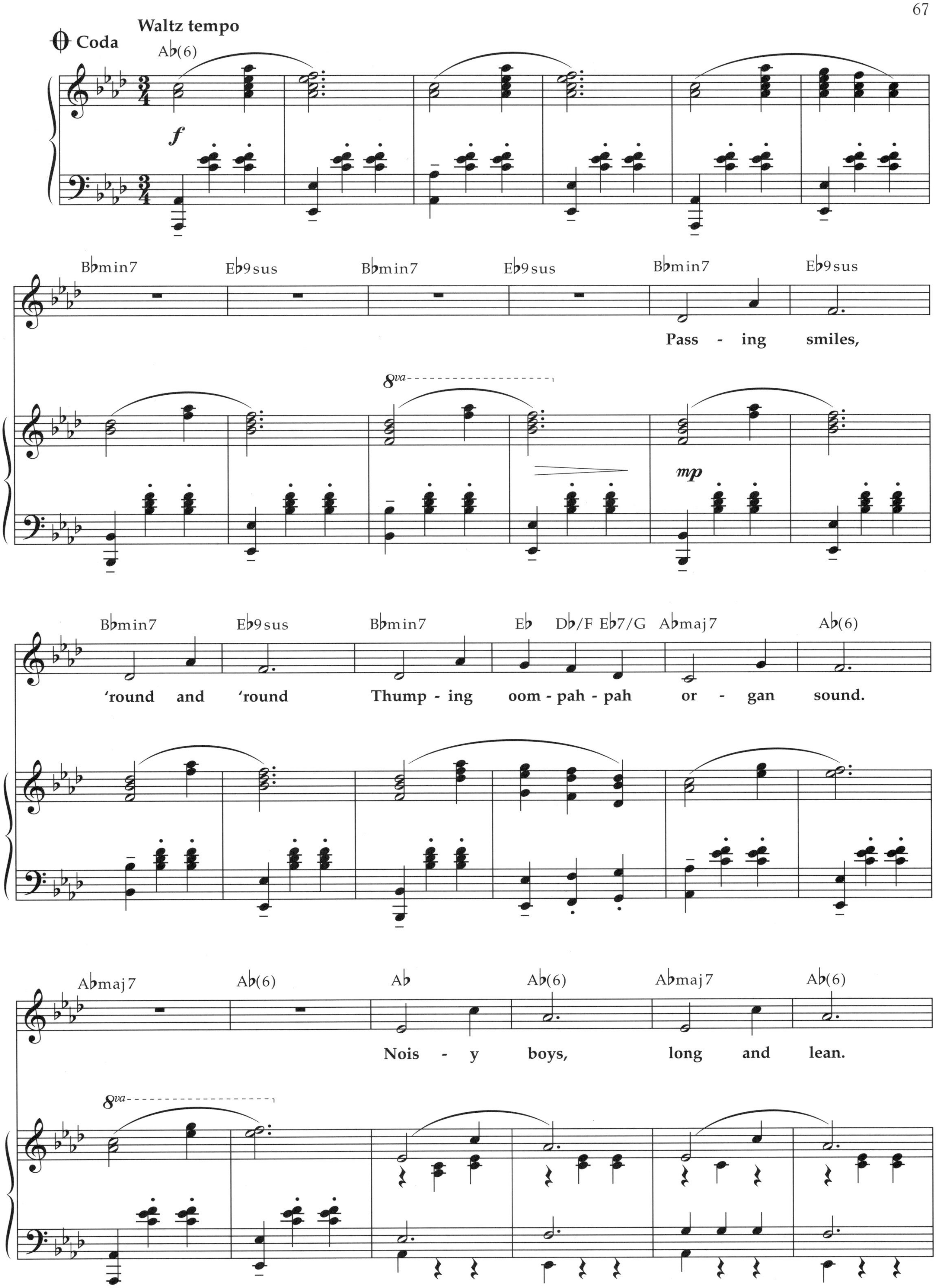
Coda
Waltz tempo
Ab(6)
f
Bbmin7 Eb9sus Bbmin7 Eb9sus Bbmin7 Eb9sus
Pass - ing smiles,
8va
mp
Bbmin7 Eb9sus Bbmin7 Eb Db/F Eb7/G Abmaj7 Ab(6)
'round and 'round Thump - ing oom - pah - pah or - gan sound.
Abmaj7 Ab(6) Ab Ab(6) Abmaj7 Ab(6)
Nois - y boys, long and lean.
8va

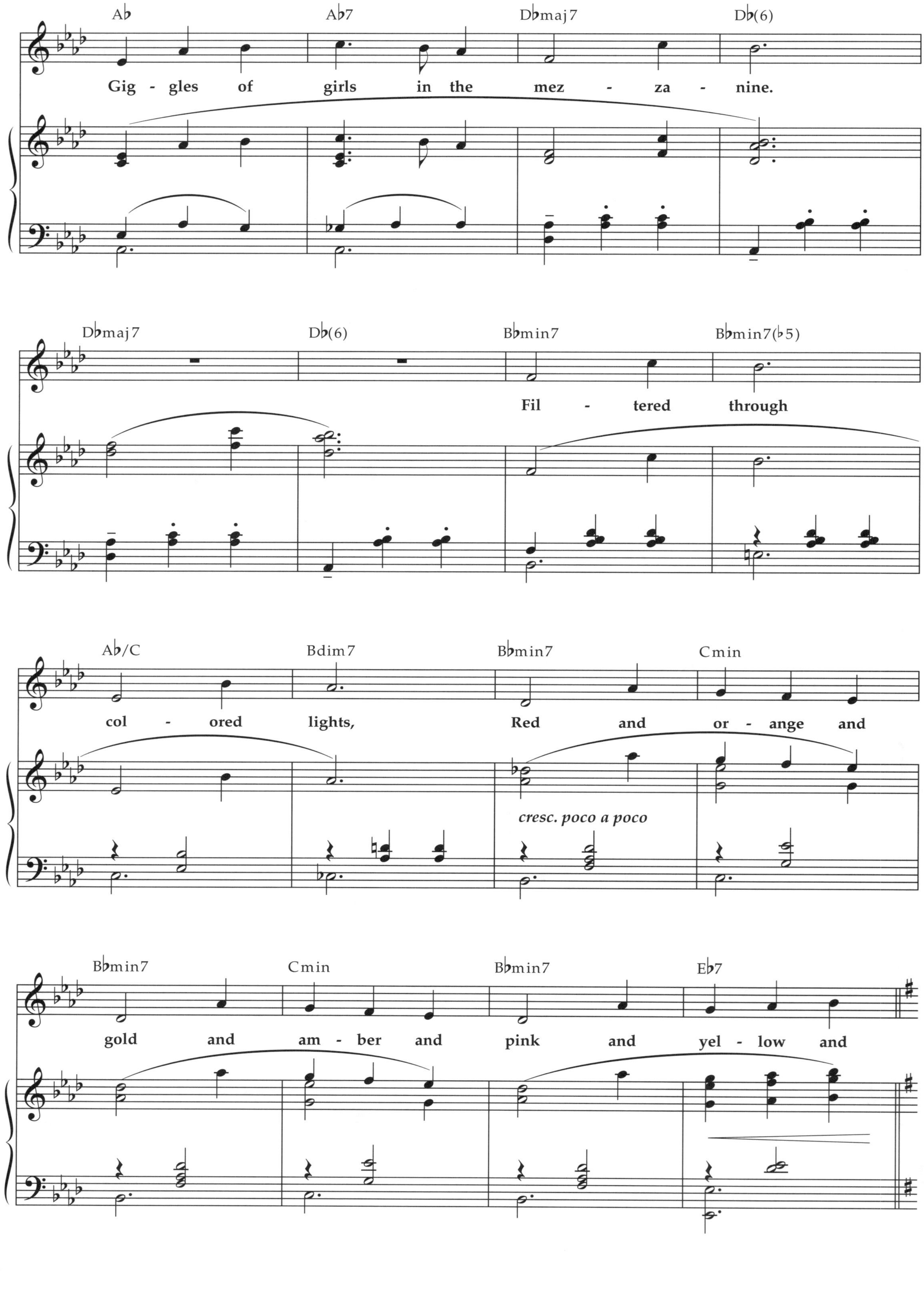
A♭
A♭7
D♭maj7
D♭(6)
Gig - gles of girls in the mez - za - nine.
D♭maj7
D♭(6)
B♭min7
B♭min7(♭5)
Fil - tered through
A♭/C
Bdim7
B♭min7
Cmin
col - ored lights, Red and or - ange and
cresc. poco a poco
B♭min7
Cmin
B♭min7
E♭7
gold and am - ber and pink and yel - low and

G/D
green.
8va
ff
8va
(8va)
D9sus
8va
D9sus
D7 Amin/E D7/F♯
G
G(6)
dim. e rall.
Rubato
A♭/E♭
A♭maj7/E♭
A♭maj9
A♭maj7
Leav - ing home years a - go, What was I look-ing for?
poco legato
mf

D♭
D♭(6)
D♭maj7
D♭(6)
I don't know. I
mp
D♭maj7
D♭min(6)
A♭/C
Bdim7
can't re - call well, an - y - way.
p
B♭min7
Cmin
B♭min7
Cmin
Soon I'll have my days and nights of
cresc. e accel. poco a poco
B♭min7
Cmin7
B♭min7
Won - der - ful, glim - mer - ing, beau - ti - ful, shim - mer - ing
a tempo

E♭9sus
E♭7(13)
Col - ored
f
A♭(6)
lights!
8va
ff
A♭ A/G B♭/G♭ B/F C/E D♭/E♭ D♭ D E♭ A♭
(8va)
sfz

# Don't Tell Mama

*from the Musical* ***CABARET***

Words by
**FRED EBB**

Music by
**JOHN KANDER**

A♭7 D7 G7 Cmin(9) G7(♭5)
night club in a pair of la - cy pants.
Ant - werp and I'm tour-ing on my own.
So
Fmin7 B♭7 E♭maj7 Cmin7
please, sir, if you run in - to my ma - ma, Don't re - veal my in - dis -
Fmin7 Dmin7(♭5) G7
cre - tion,
Give a work - ing girl a chance.
Just leave well e - nough a - lone.
poco rit.
Charleston tempo
C(6) A♭7 G7 C(6) A♭7 G7
Hush up, don't tell ma - ma, Shush up, don't tell ma - ma,
mf rhythmically

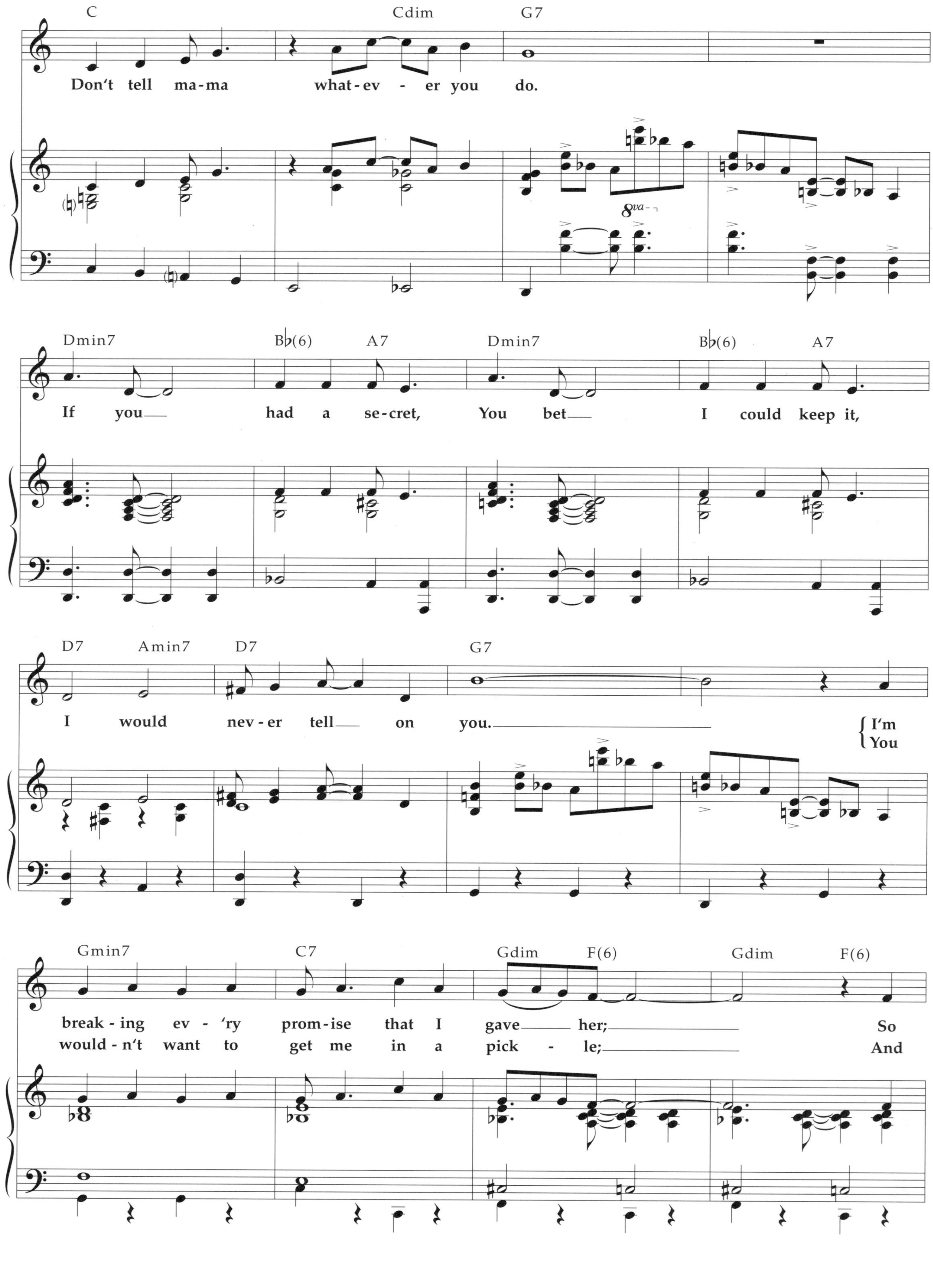
C Cdim G7
Don't tell ma-ma what-ev - er you do.
8va
Dmin7 B♭(6) A7 Dmin7 B♭(6) A7
If you had a se-cret, You bet I could keep it,
D7 Amin7 D7 G7
I would nev-er tell on you.
I'm
You
Gmin7 C7 Gdim F(6) Gdim F(6)
break-ing ev - 'ry prom-ise that I gave her;
So
would-n't want to get me in a pick - le;
And

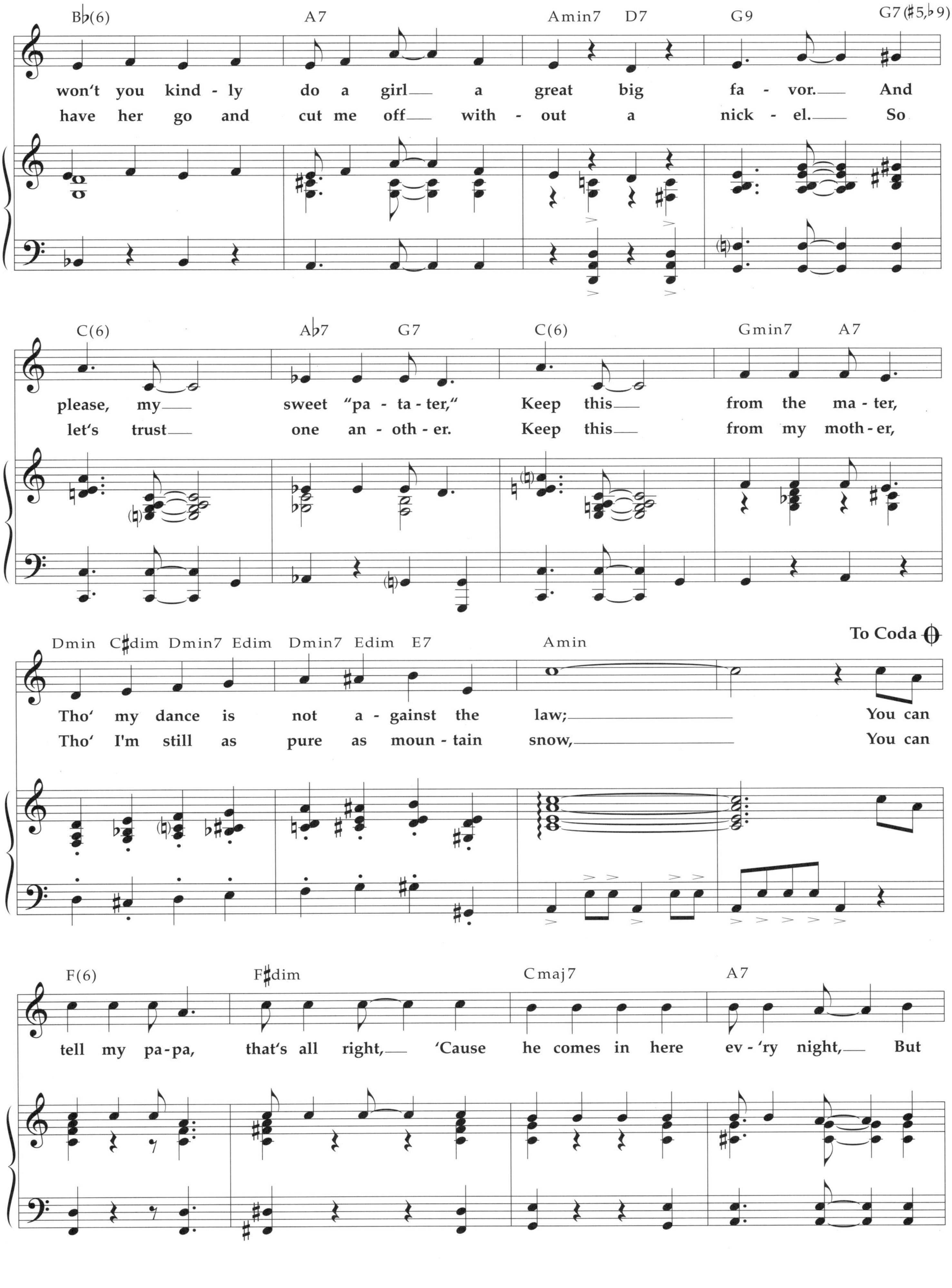
B♭(6) A7 Amin7 D7 G9 G7(♯5,♭9)
won't you kind - ly do a girl a great big fa - vor. And
have her go and cut me off with - out a nick - el. So
C(6) A♭7 G7 C(6) Gmin7 A7
please, my sweet "pa - ter," Keep this from the ma - ter,
let's trust one an - oth - er. Keep this from my moth - er,
Dmin C♯dim Dmin7 Edim Dmin7 Edim E7 Amin
To Coda
Tho' my dance is not a - gainst the law; You can
Tho' I'm still as pure as moun - tain snow, You can
F(6) F♯dim Cmaj7 A7
tell my pa - pa, that's all right, 'Cause he comes in here ev - 'ry night, But

D.S. al Coda
Dmin7 G7(13) Cmin(9) G7(♭5)
don't tell ma-ma what you saw.
Coda
F(6) F♯dim Cmaj7/G A9
tell my un - cle, here and now, 'Cause he's my a - gent an - y - how;
tell my grand - maw, suits me fine, just yes - ter - day she joined the line;
But
Dmin7 G7 Amin
don't tell ma-ma what you know. You can

F(6)
F♯dim
Cmaj7/G
A9
tell my broth-er, that's not grim, 'Cause if he squeals on me, I'll squeal on him; But
Dmin7
G9(13)
Dmin7
G9(13)
Dmin7
don't tell ma-ma, bit - te, Don't tell ma-ma, please, sir, Don't tell
G9sus
G7
Cmin(9)
G7(♭5)
Cmin
ma-ma what you know. Sssh!
G7(♭5)
C
Sssh! So if you see my mum-my, mum's the word!

# First You Dream

*from the Musical* **STEEL PIER**

Words by
**FRED EBB**

Music by
**JOHN KANDER**

**Con moto, poco rubato**

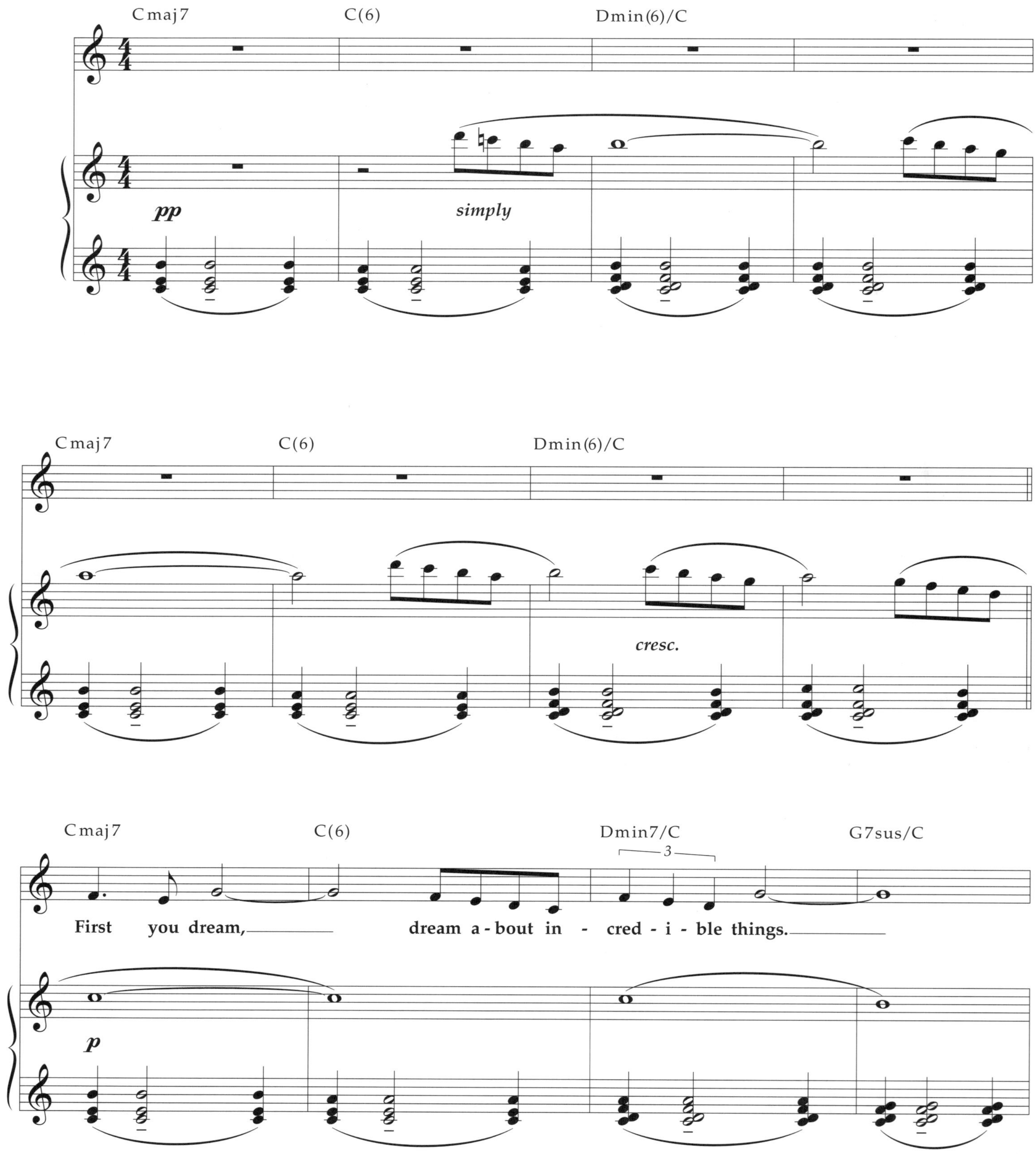

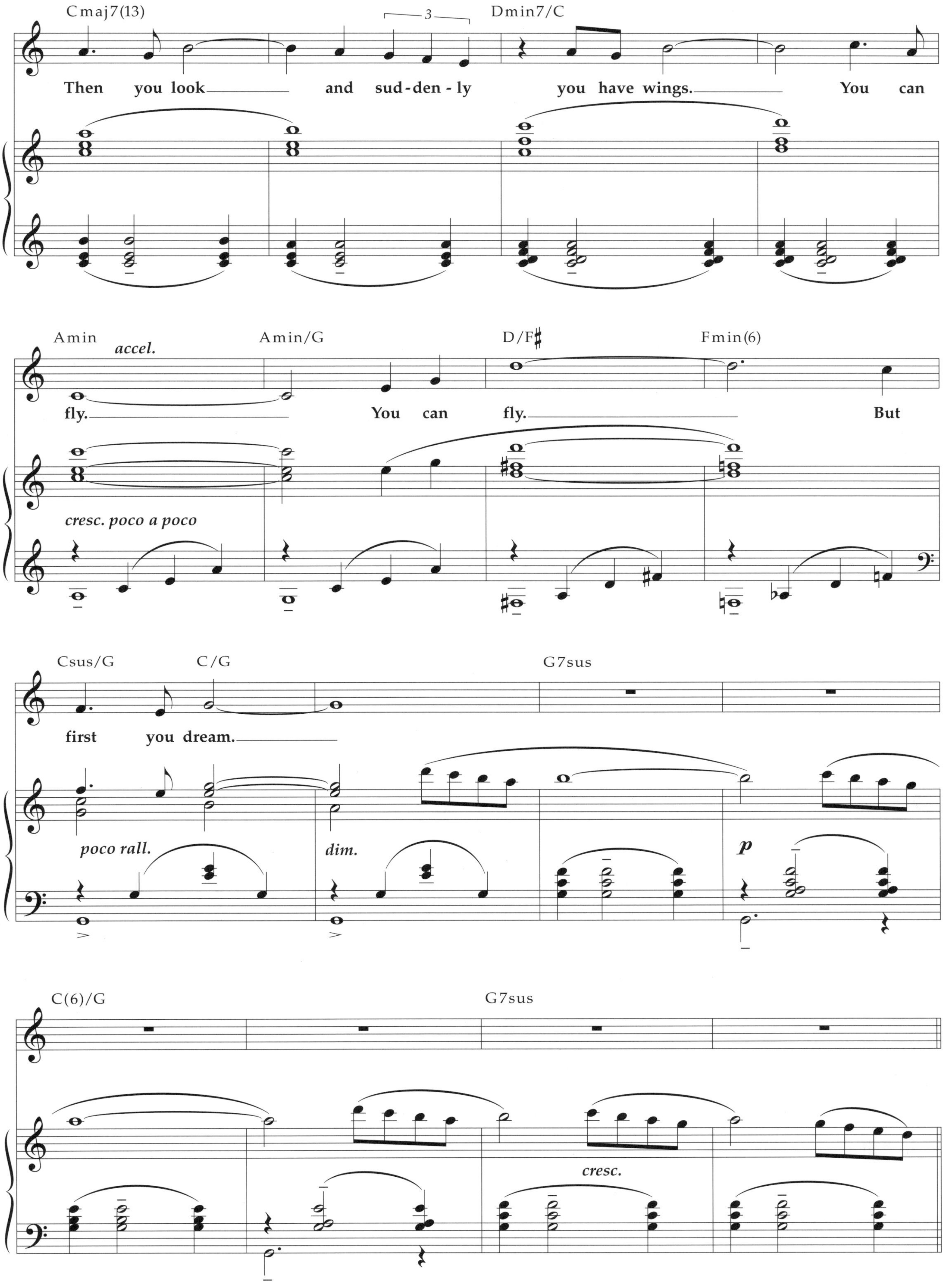
Cmaj7(13)
Dmin7/C
Then you look and sud-den-ly you have wings. You can
Amin
accel.
Amin/G
D/F♯
Fmin(6)
fly. You can fly. But
cresc. poco a poco
Csus/G
C/G
G7sus
first you dream.
poco rall.
dim.
p
C(6)/G
G7sus
cresc.

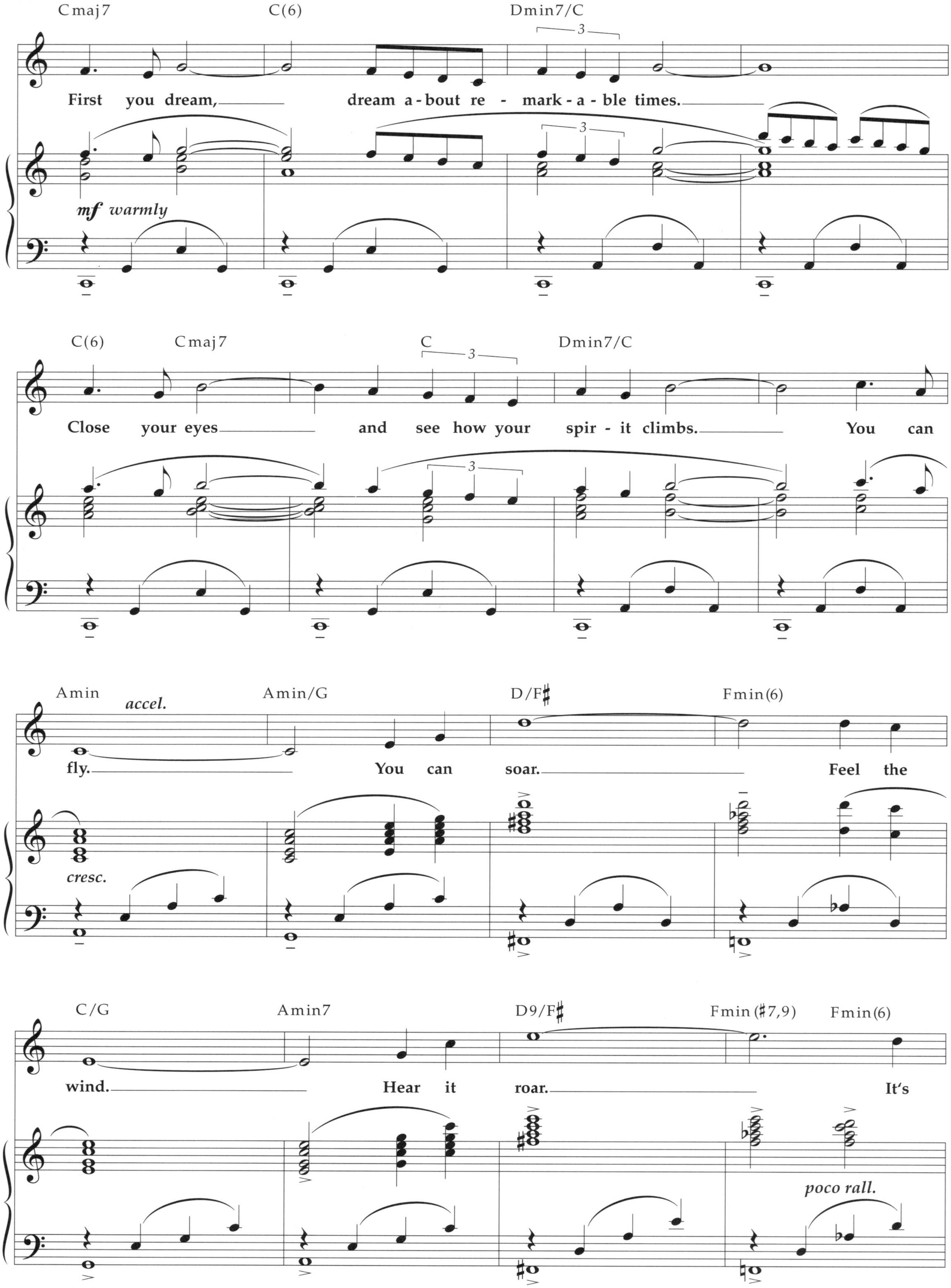
Cmaj7 C(6) Dmin7/C
First you dream, dream a-bout re-mark-a-ble times.
mf warmly
C(6) Cmaj7 C Dmin7/C
Close your eyes and see how your spir-it climbs. You can
Amin Amin/G D/F♯ Fmin(6)
accel.
fly. You can soar. Feel the
cresc.
C/G Amin7 D9/F♯ Fmin(♯7,9) Fmin(6)
wind. Hear it roar. It's
poco rall.

G7sus C/G G7sus C/G G7sus rit. G7
eas - y now. I - mag - ine that. But
dim. poco a poco
Slower
Amin
first you dream.
Ab(#11) Ab
mp
C/G
G7sus
(Instrumental)
Con moto
Ab(6)
pp legato

A♭(6)
E♭9sus
A♭(6)
cresc.
A♭maj7
A♭(6)
A♭maj7
A♭(6)
B♭min7
Here we are high a-bove the roof - tops.
mp warmly
B♭min7
E♭7
A♭maj7
A♭(6)
A♭maj7
A♭(6)
There's a barn, there's a field of

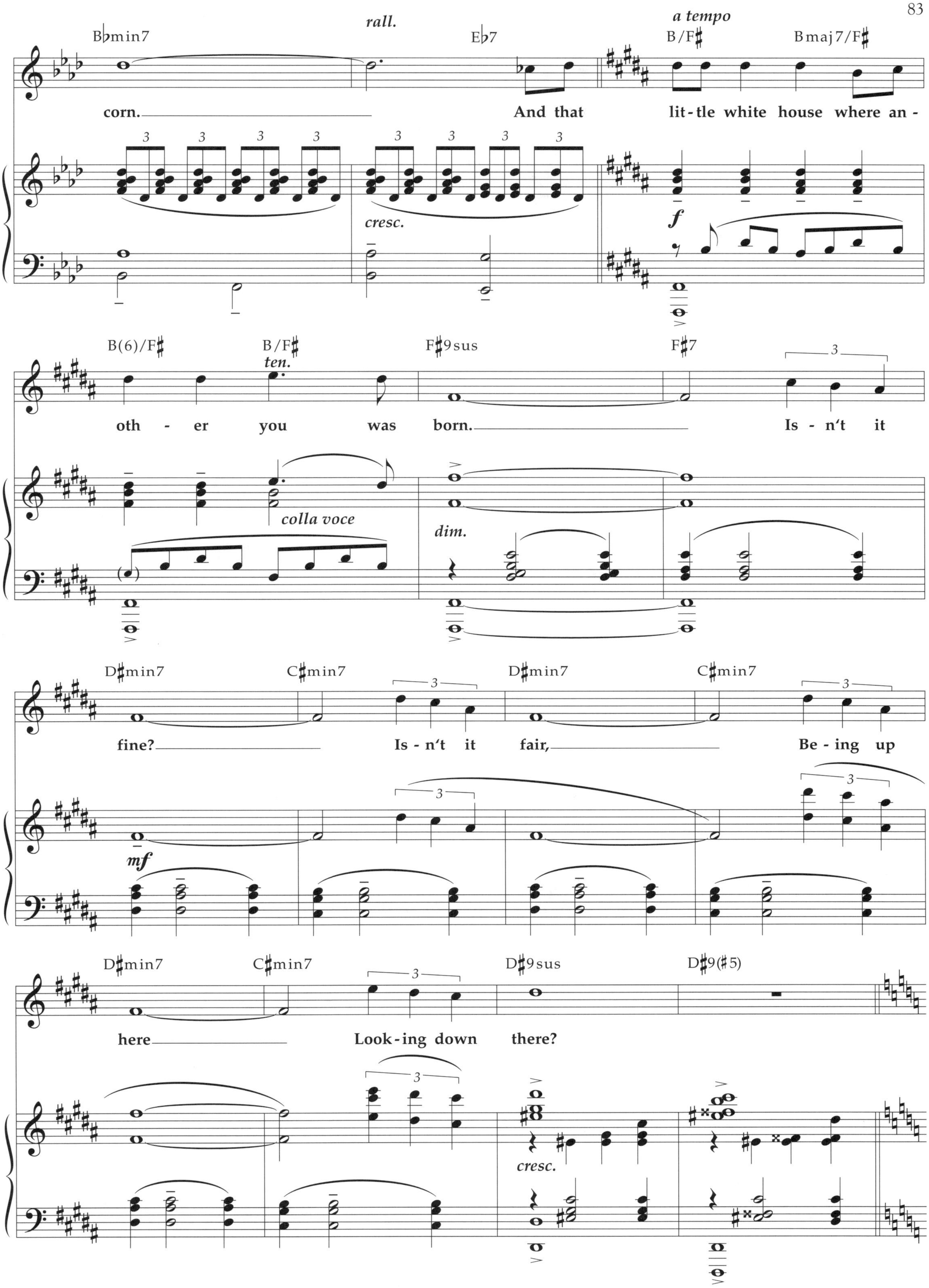
rall.
a tempo
B♭min7
E♭7
B/F♯
Bmaj7/F♯
corn. And that lit-tle white house where an -
cresc.
f
B(6)/F♯
B/F♯
ten.
F♯9sus
F♯7
oth - er you was born. Is - n't it
colla voce
dim.
D♯min7
C♯min7
D♯min7
C♯min7
fine? Is - n't it fair, Be - ing up
mf
D♯min7
C♯min7
D♯9sus
D♯9(♯5)
here Look-ing down there?
cresc.

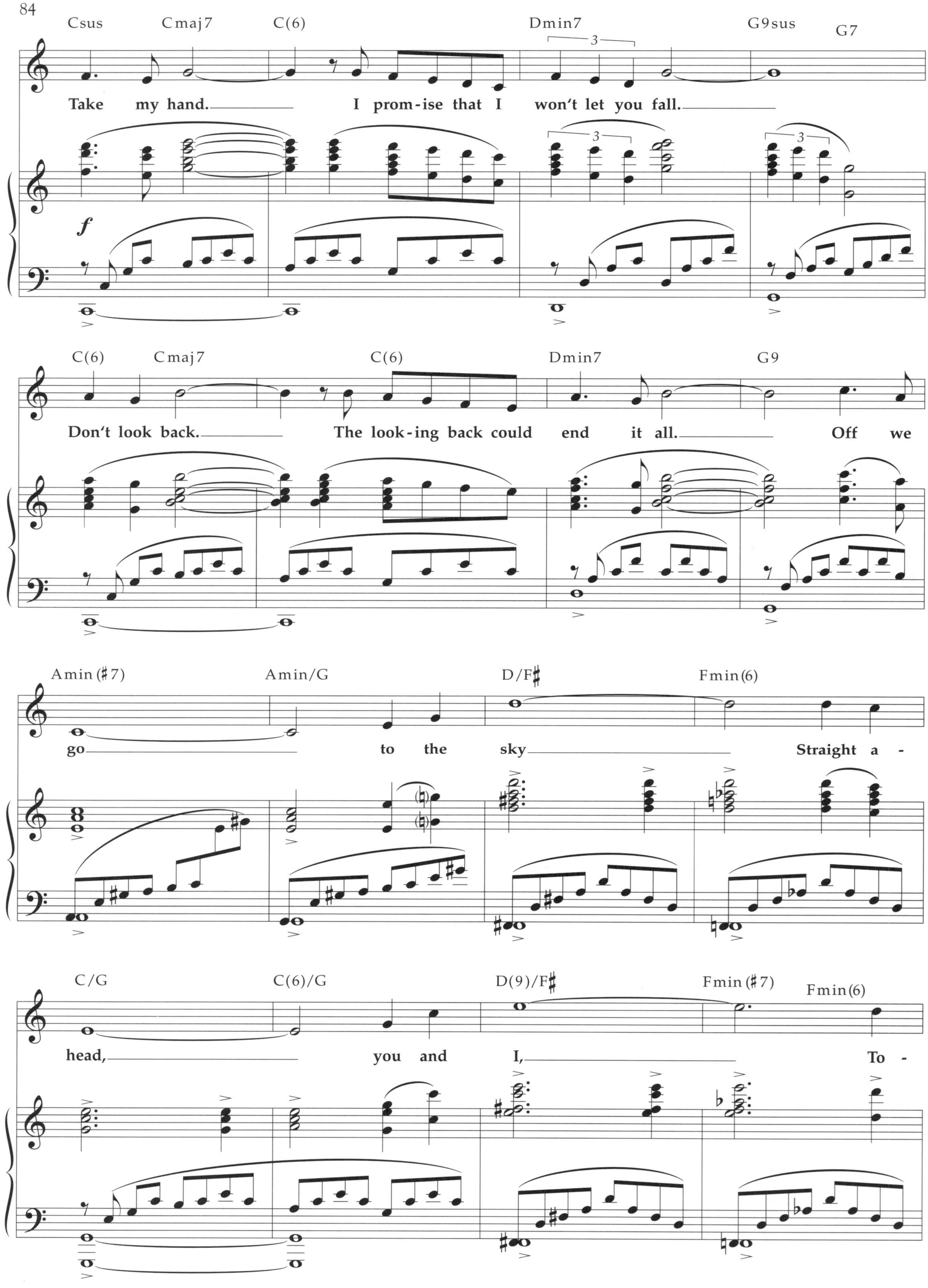
Csus Cmaj7 C(6) Dmin7 G9sus G7
Take my hand. I prom-ise that I won't let you fall.
f
C(6) Cmaj7 C(6) Dmin7 G9
Don't look back. The look-ing back could end it all. Off we
Amin(♯7) Amin/G D/F♯ Fmin(6)
go to the sky Straight a-
C/G C(6)/G D(9)/F♯ Fmin(♯7) Fmin(6)
head, you and I, To-

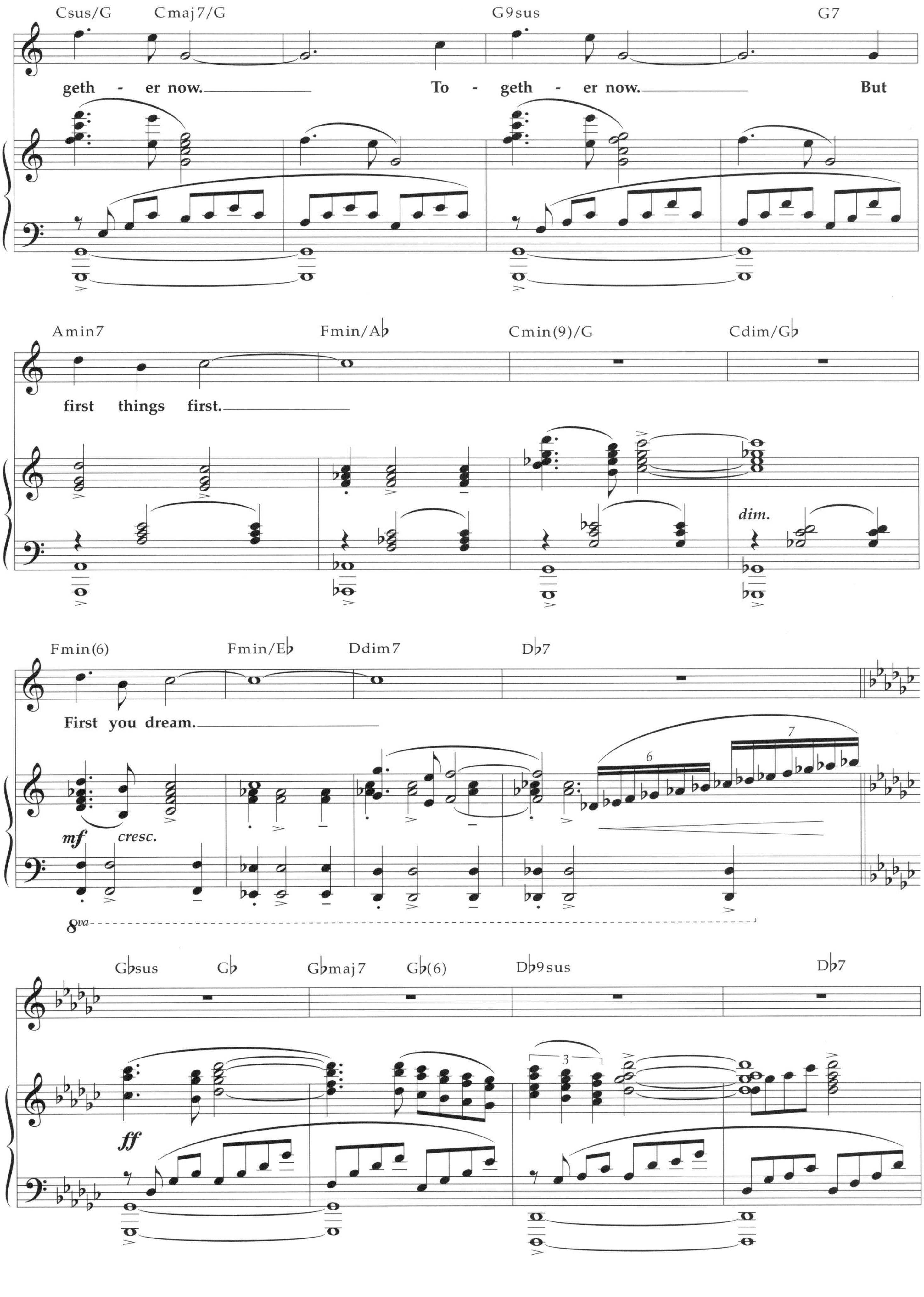
Csus/G
Cmaj7/G
G9sus
G7
geth - er now.
To - geth - er now.
But
Amin7
Fmin/A♭
Cmin(9)/G
Cdim/G♭
first things first.
dim.
Fmin(6)
Fmin/E♭
Ddim7
D♭7
First you dream.
mf
cresc.
6
7
8va
G♭sus
G♭
G♭maj7
G♭(6)
D♭9sus
D♭7
ff
3

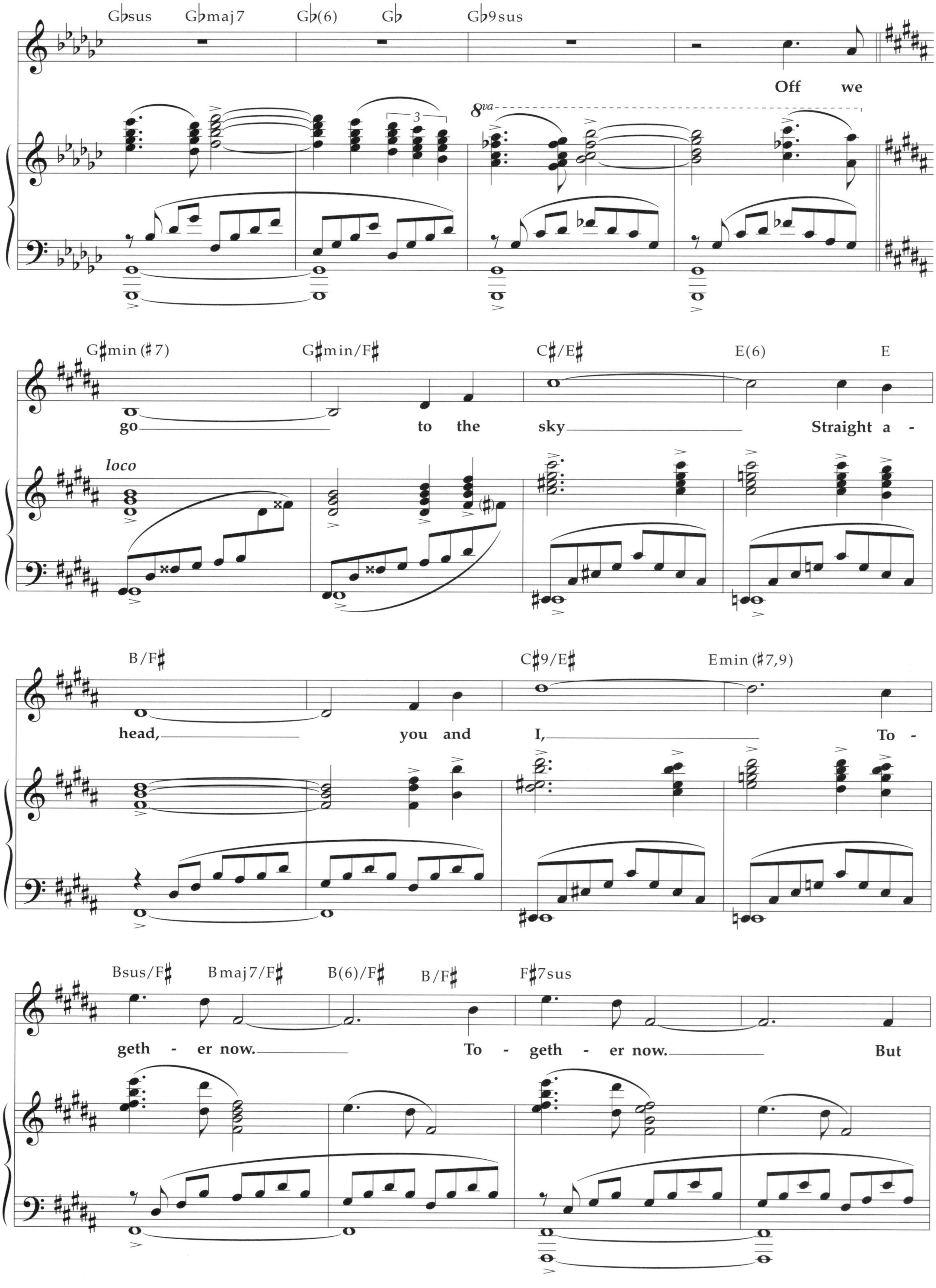

G♭sus G♭maj7 G♭(6) G♭ G♭9sus
Off we
8va
3
G♯min(♯7) G♯min/F♯ C♯/E♯ E(6) E
go to the sky Straight a -
loco
B/F♯ C♯9/E♯ Emin(♯7,9)
head, you and I, To -
Bsus/F♯ Bmaj7/F♯ B(6)/F♯ B/F♯ F♯7sus
geth - er now. To - geth - er now. But

G♯min(11) G♯min Emin/G Bmin/F♯ C♯7/E♯
first things first. First you dream.
dim. poco a poco
Emin(6) B
First you dream.
p
B/F♯ Bsus
rall. poco a poco
B
dim.
pp

# The Grass Is Always Greener

*from the Musical* **WOMAN OF THE YEAR**

Words by
**FRED EBB**

Music by
**JOHN KANDER**

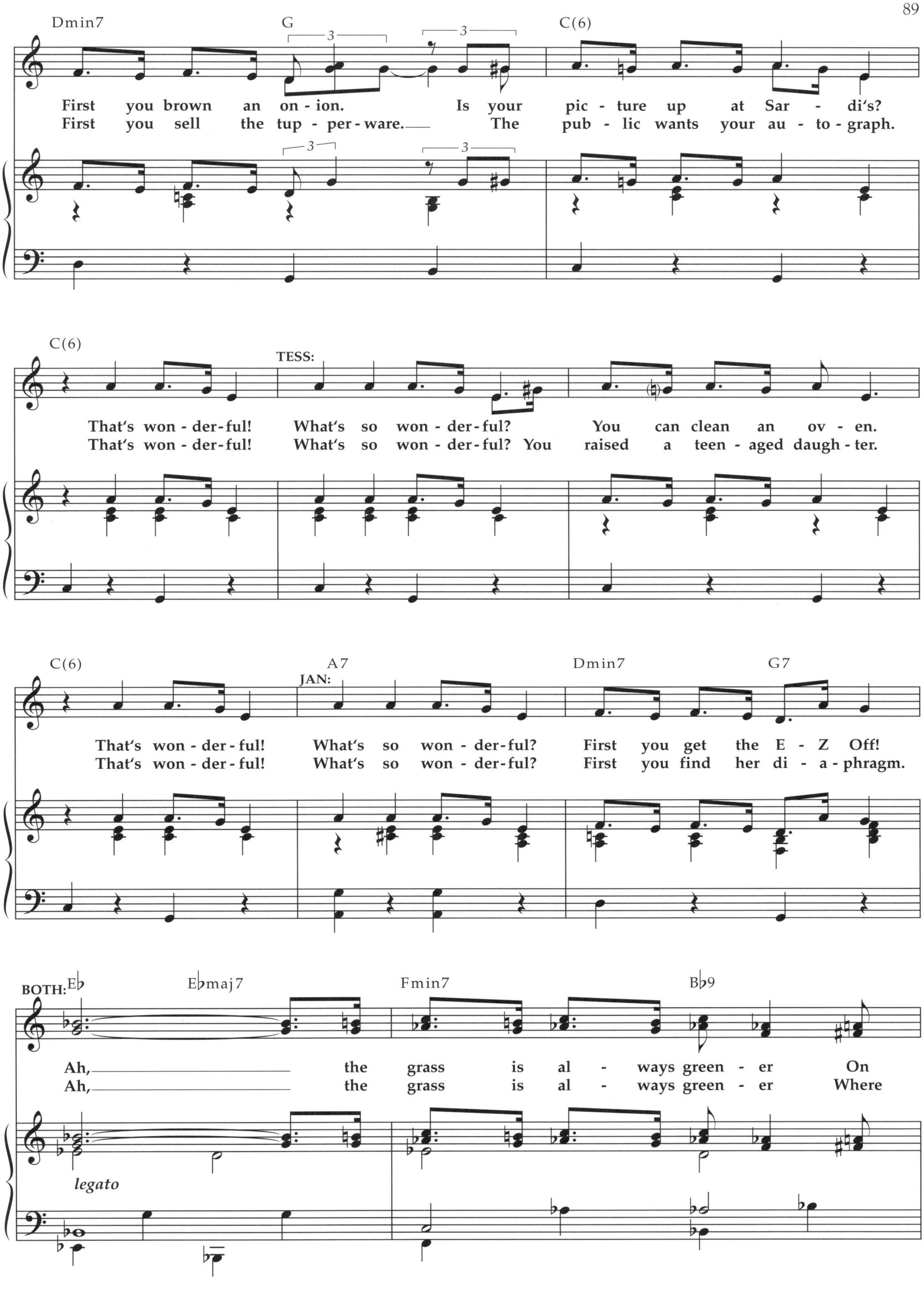
Dmin7
G
3
3
C(6)
First you brown an on - ion. Is your pic - ture up at Sar - di's?
First you sell the tup - per - ware. The pub - lic wants your au - to - graph.
C(6)
TESS:
That's won - der - ful! What's so won - der - ful? You can clean an ov - en.
That's won - der - ful! What's so won - der - ful? You raised a teen - aged daugh - ter.
C(6)
A7
JAN:
Dmin7
G7
That's won - der - ful! What's so won - der - ful? First you get the E - Z Off!
That's won - der - ful! What's so won - der - ful? First you find her di - a - phragm.
BOTH:
E♭
E♭maj7
Fmin7
B♭9
Ah, the grass is al - ways green - er On
Ah, the grass is al - ways green - er Where
legato

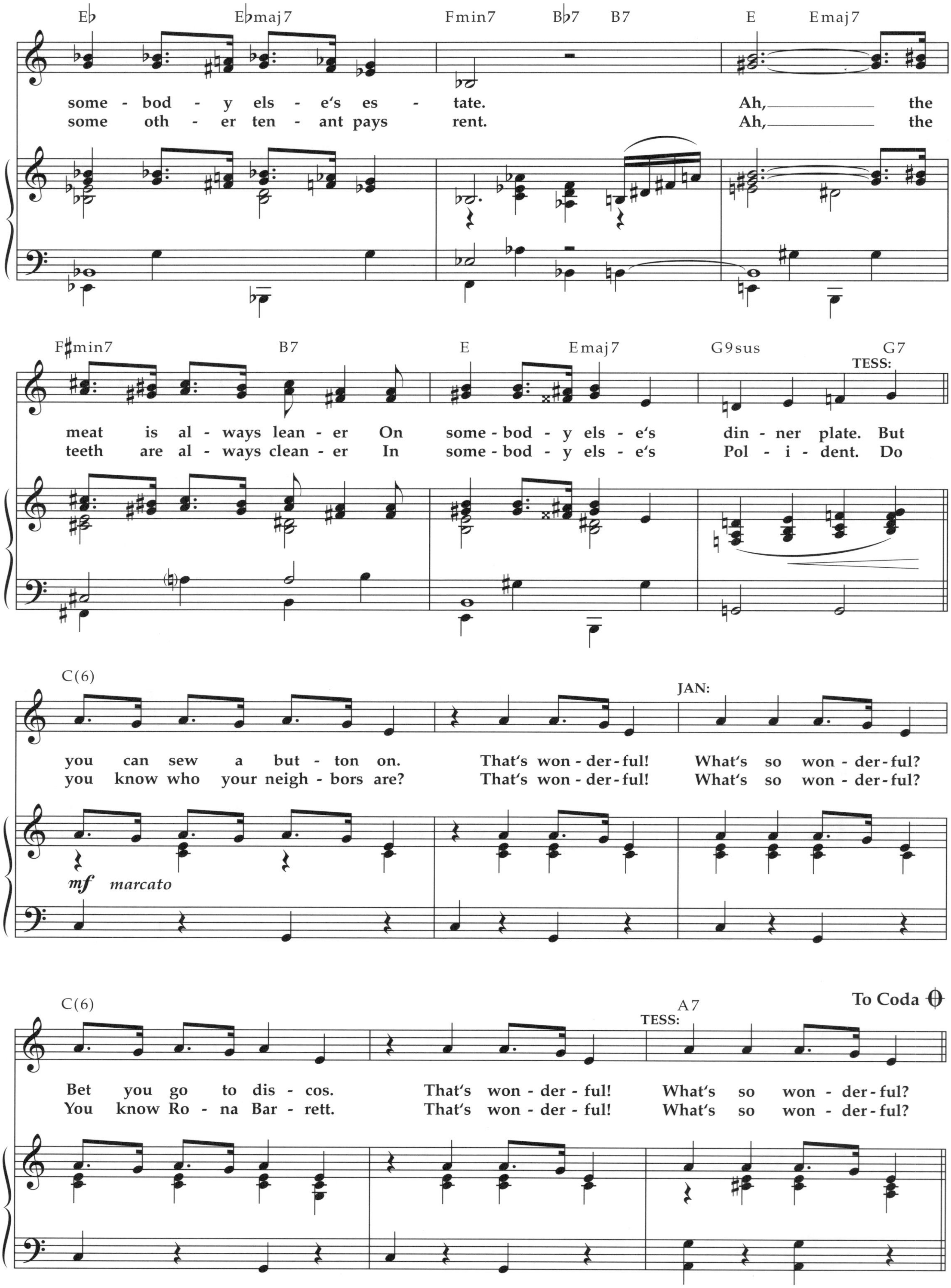
E♭ E♭maj7 Fmin7 B♭7 B7 E Emaj7
some - bod - y els - e's es - tate. Ah, the
some oth - er ten - ant pays rent. Ah, the
F♯min7 B7 E Emaj7 G9sus G7
TESS:
meat is al - ways lean - er On some - bod - y els - e's din - ner plate. But
teeth are al - ways clean - er In some - bod - y els - e's Pol - i - dent. Do
C(6)
JAN:
you can sew a but - ton on. That's won - der - ful! What's so won - der - ful?
you know who your neigh - bors are? That's won - der - ful! What's so won - der - ful?
mf marcato
C(6) A7
To Coda
TESS:
Bet you go to dis - cos. That's won - der - ful! What's so won - der - ful?
You know Ro - na Bar - rett. That's won - der - ful! What's so won - der - ful?

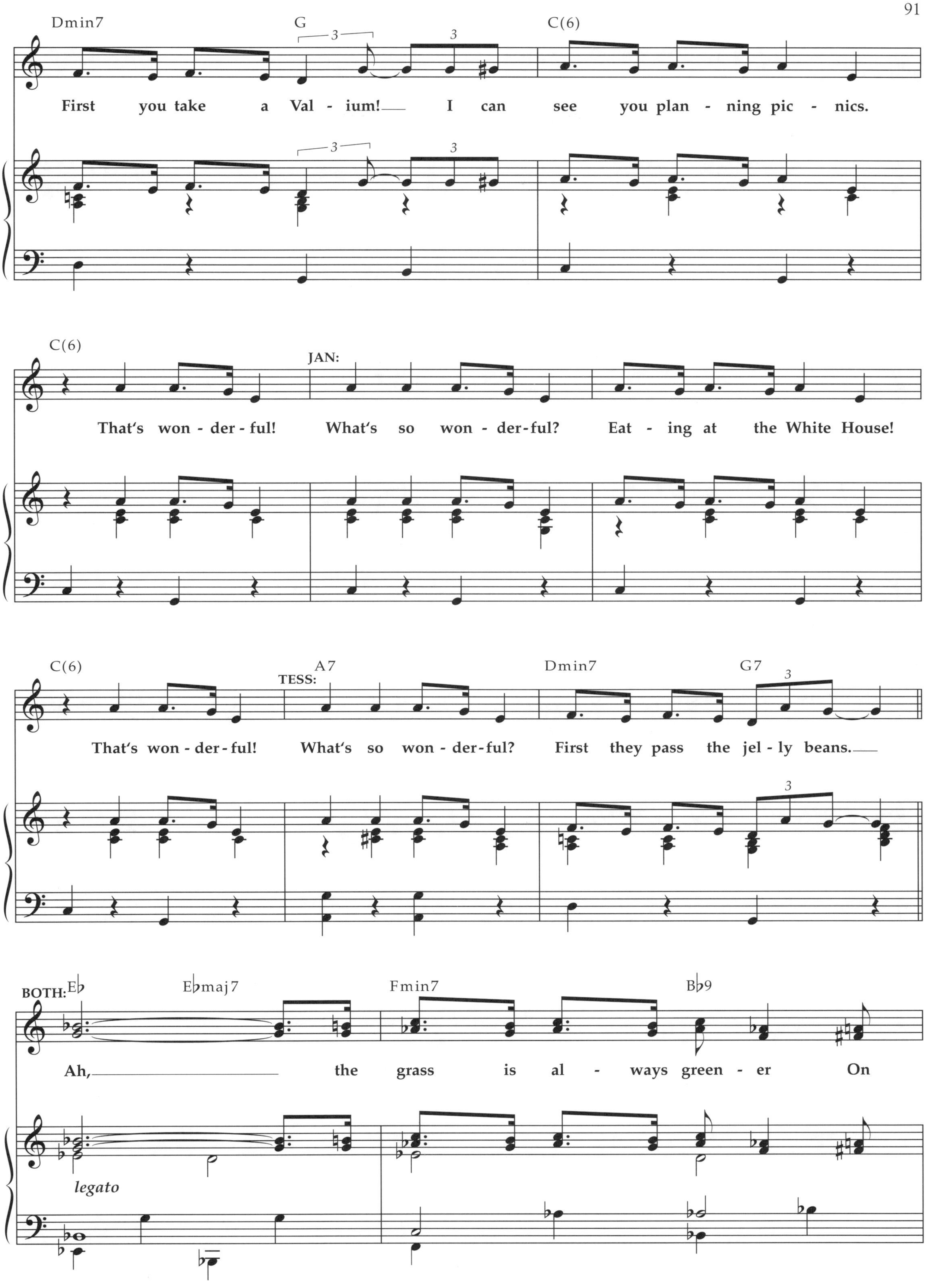
Dmin7
G
C(6)
First you take a Val - ium! I can see you plan - ning pic - nics.
C(6)
JAN:
That's won - der - ful! What's so won - der - ful? Eat - ing at the White House!
C(6)
A7
TESS:
Dmin7
G7
That's won - der - ful! What's so won - der - ful? First they pass the jel - ly beans.
BOTH:
E♭
E♭maj7
Fmin7
B♭9
Ah, the grass is al - ways green - er On
legato

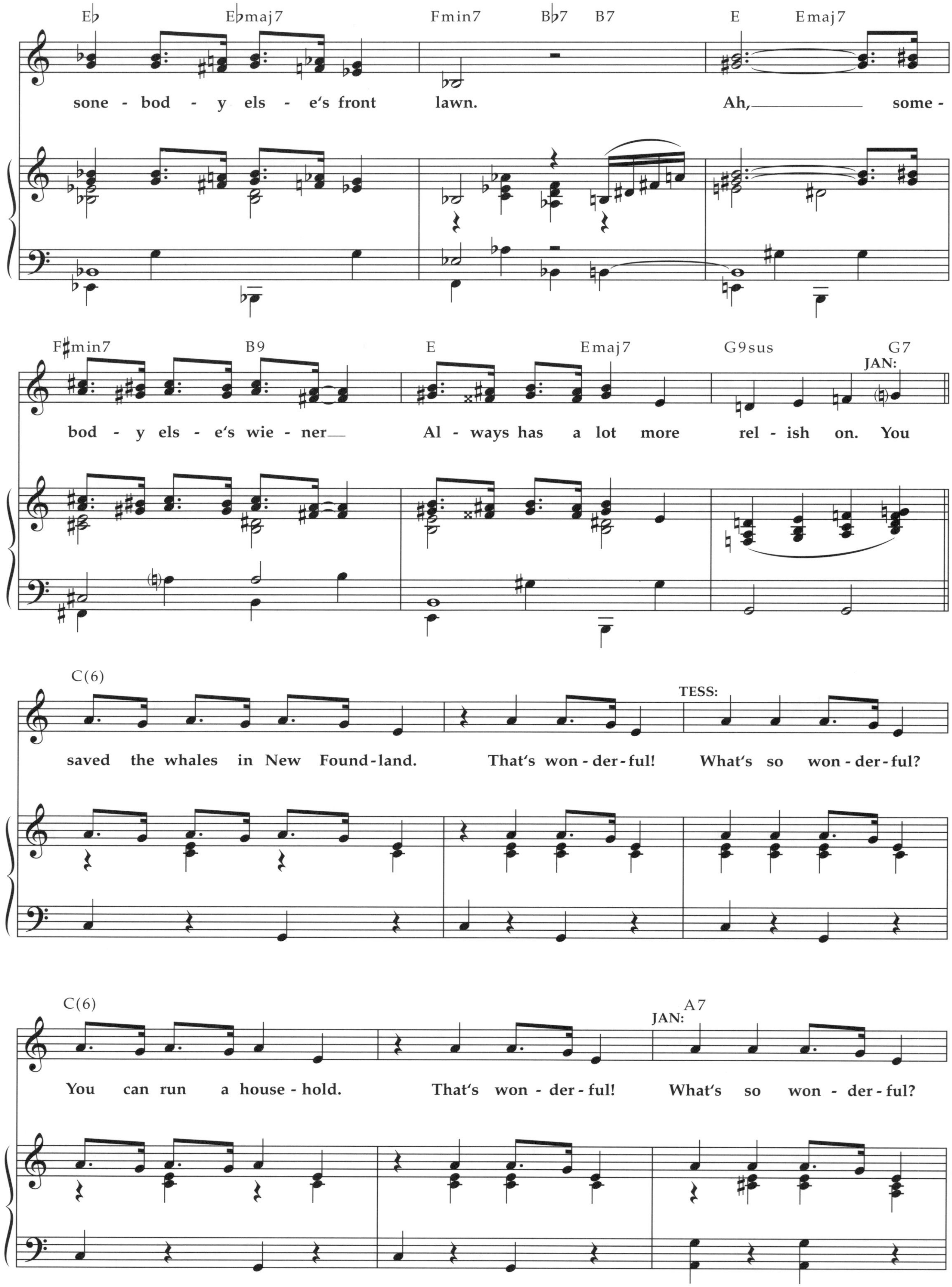
E♭ E♭maj7 Fmin7 B♭7 B7 E Emaj7
sone - bod - y els - e's front lawn. Ah, some -
F♯min7 B9 E Emaj7 G9sus G7
JAN:
bod - y els - e's wie - ner Al - ways has a lot more rel - ish on. You
C(6)
TESS:
saved the whales in New Found - land. That's won - der - ful! What's so won - der - ful?
C(6) A7
JAN:
You can run a house - hold. That's won - der - ful! What's so won - der - ful?

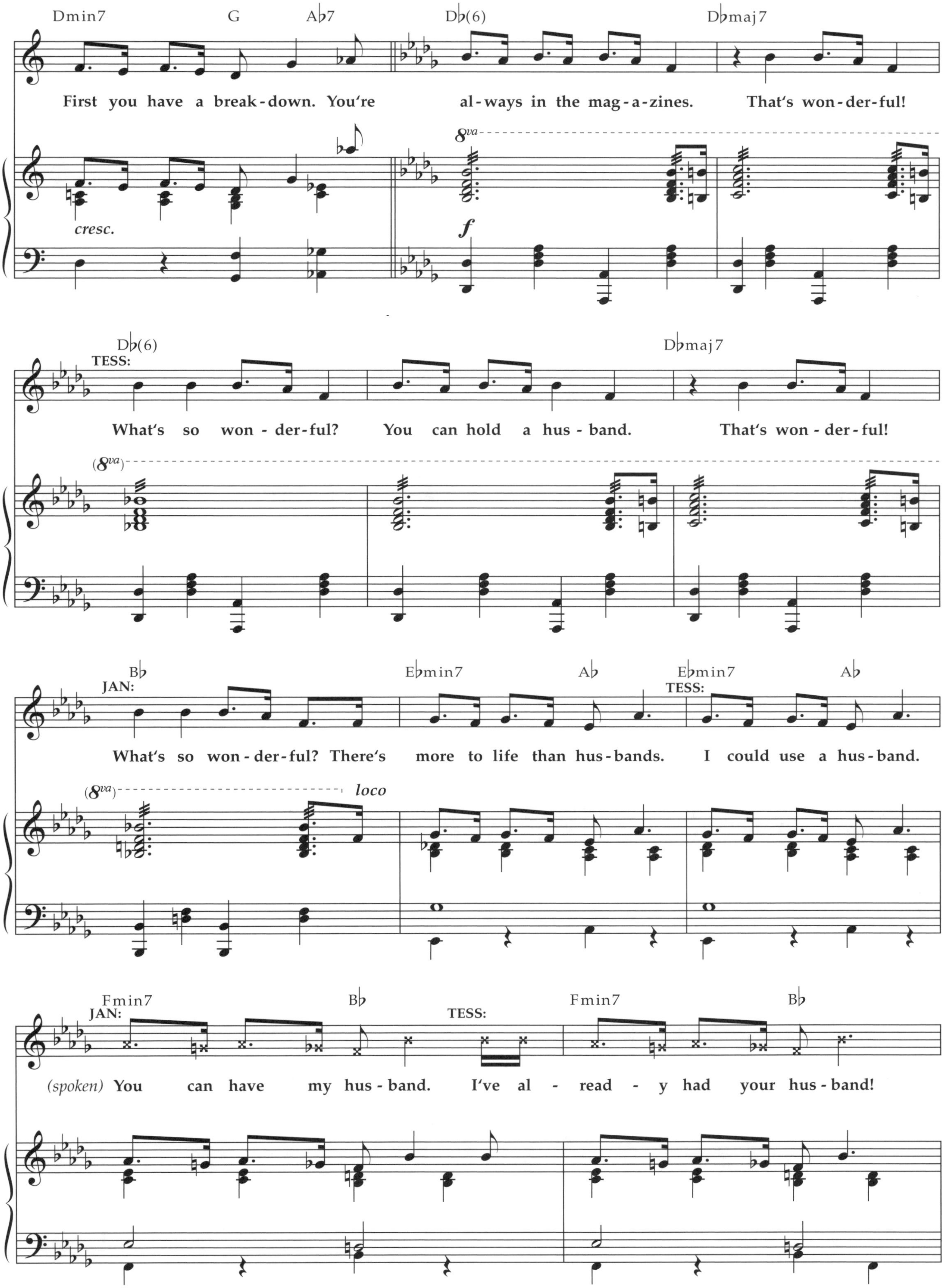
Dmin7 G A♭7 D♭(6) D♭maj7
First you have a break-down. You're al-ways in the mag-a-zines. That's won-der-ful!
8va
cresc.
f
D♭(6) D♭maj7
TESS:
What's so won-der-ful? You can hold a hus-band. That's won-der-ful!
(8va)
B♭ E♭min7 A♭ E♭min7 A♭
JAN:
TESS:
What's so won-der-ful? There's more to life than hus-bands. I could use a hus-band.
(8va)
loco
Fmin7 B♭ Fmin7 B♭
JAN:
TESS:
(spoken) You can have my hus-band. I've al-read-y had your hus-band!

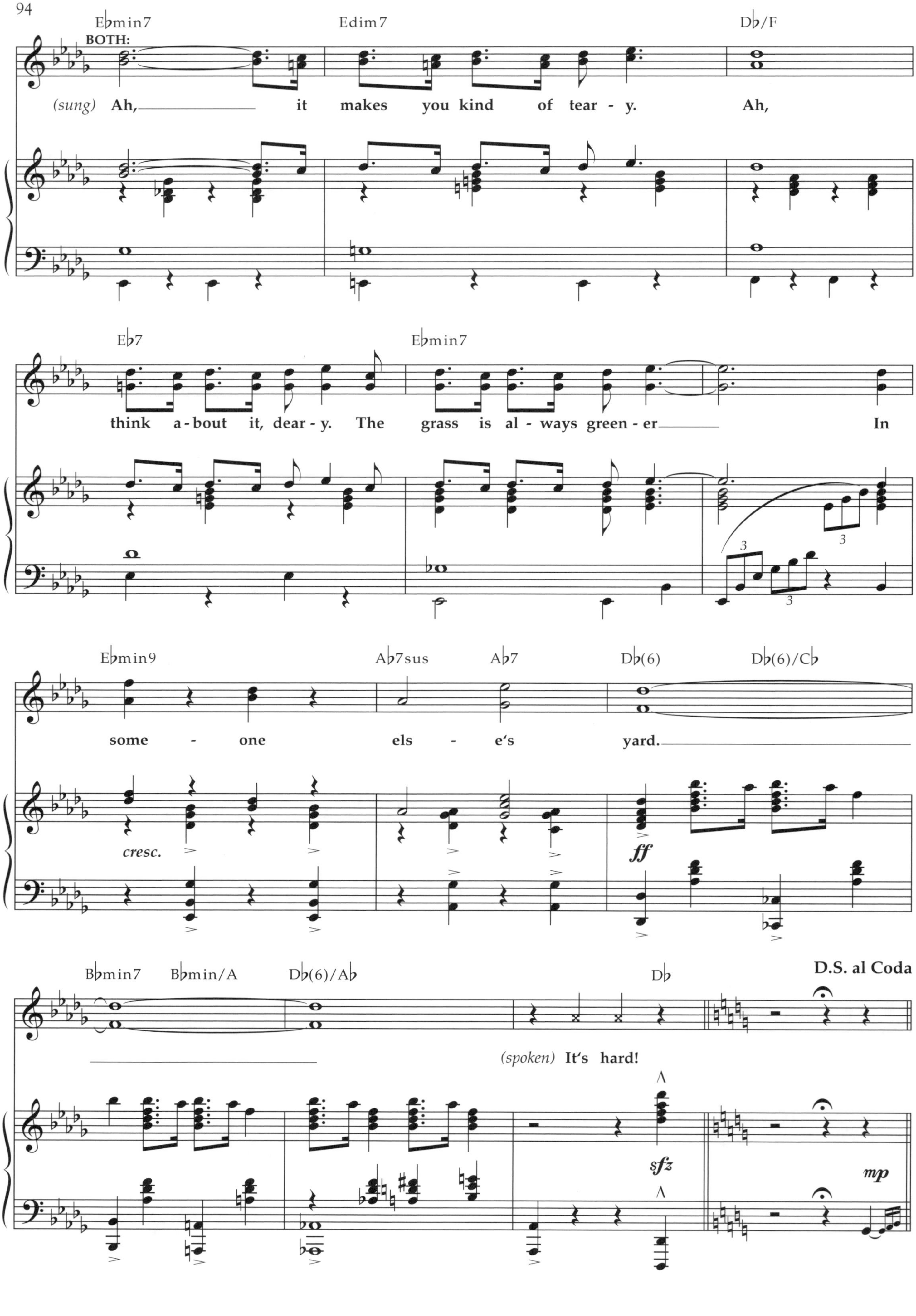

E♭min7
Edim7
D♭/F
BOTH:
(sung) Ah, it makes you kind of tear - y. Ah,
E♭7
E♭min7
think a - bout it, dear - y. The grass is al - ways green - er In
3
3
3
E♭min9
A♭7sus
A♭7
D♭(6)
D♭(6)/C♭
some - one els - e's yard.
cresc.
ff
B♭min7
B♭min/A
D♭(6)/A♭
D♭
D.S. al Coda
(spoken) It's hard!
sfz
mp

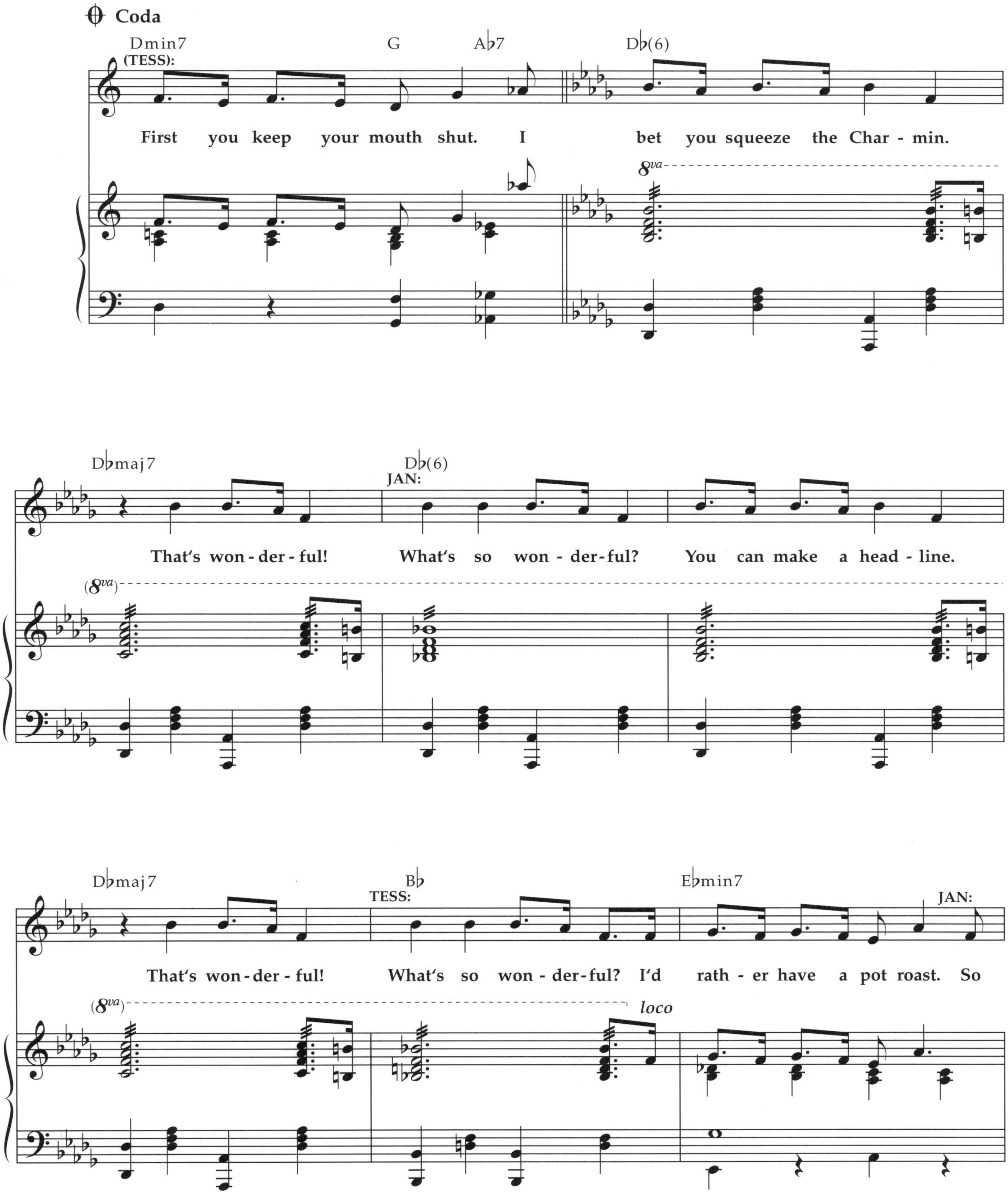
Coda
Dmin7 G A♭7 D♭(6)
(TESS):
First you keep your mouth shut. I bet you squeeze the Char - min.
8va
D♭maj7 D♭(6)
JAN:
That's won-der-ful! What's so won - der-ful? You can make a head - line.
(8va)
D♭maj7 B♭ E♭min7
TESS:
JAN:
That's won-der - ful! What's so won - der-ful? I'd rath - er have a pot roast. So
(8va)
loco

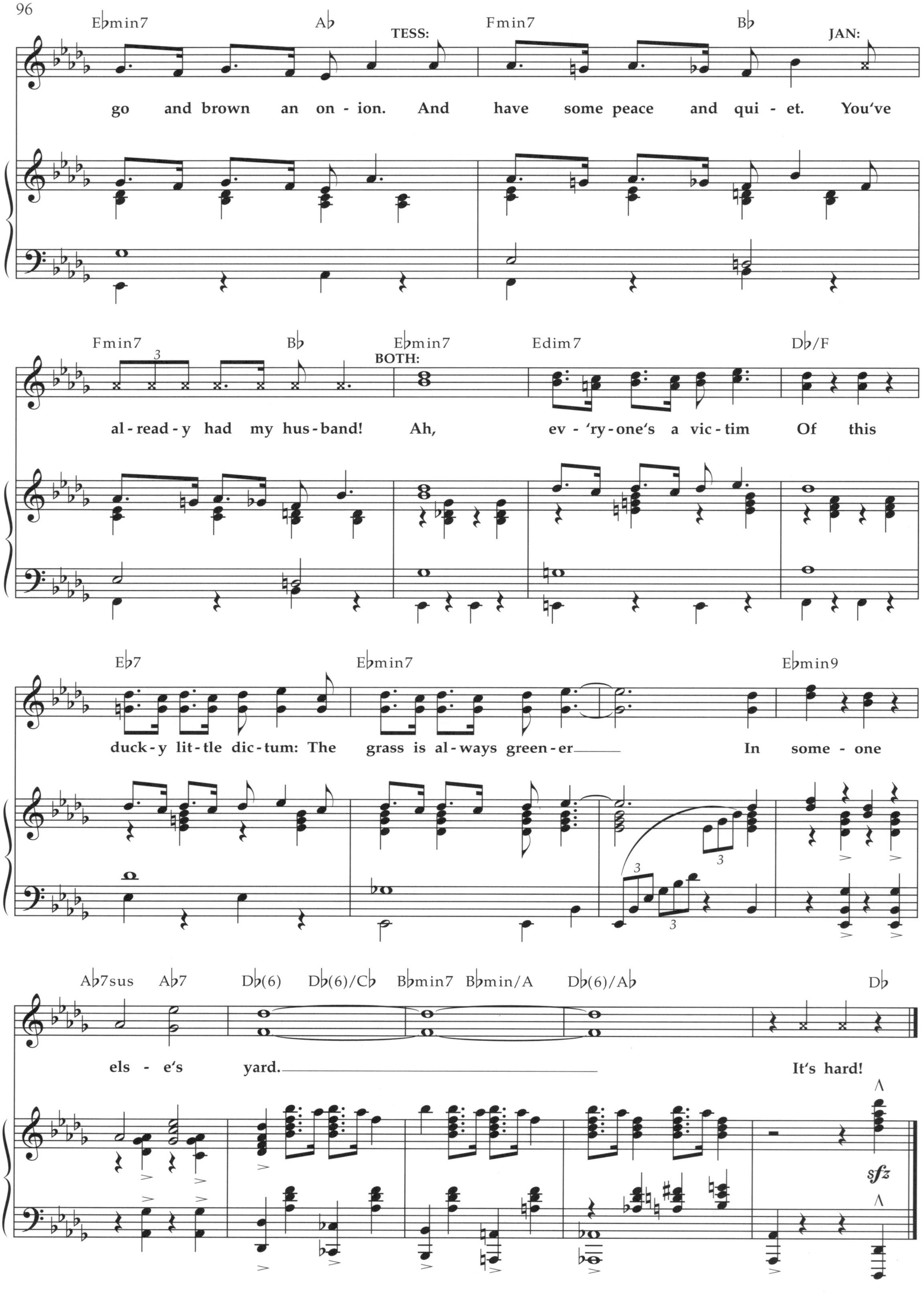
E♭min7 A♭ Fmin7 B♭
TESS:
JAN:
go and brown an on - ion. And have some peace and qui - et. You've
Fmin7 B♭ E♭min7 Edim7 D♭/F
BOTH:
al - read - y had my hus - band! Ah, ev - 'ry - one's a vic - tim Of this
E♭7 E♭min7 E♭min9
duck - y lit - tle dic - tum: The grass is al - ways green - er In some - one
A♭7sus A♭7 D♭(6) D♭(6)/C♭ B♭min7 B♭min/A D♭(6)/A♭ D♭
els - e's yard. It's hard!
sfz

# The Happy Time

*from the Musical* ***THE HAPPY TIME***

Words by
**FRED EBB**

Music by
**JOHN KANDER**

C♭/G♭ D♭7 G♭
Re - mem-ber the paint - ed horse, the car - ou - sel, The
G♭ D♭7 C♭/G♭ G♭
choc - 'late kiss, the car - a - mel, The hap - py time.
cresc.
mp
Fmin7 B♭7 E♭min E♭min7 A♭7
Re - mem-ber a pale pink sky, your first Eas - ter
D♭(♯5) D♭ D♭(♯5) D♭ D♭(♯5) D♭ A♭7sus A♭7
hat. And if you should

D♭min
D♭min7
G♭7
C♭
C♭/B♭♭
ask me why, The rea - son I ask you this is
A♭7
D♭7
G♭
G♭/F♭
E♭7(♯5)
that I want to re - mem - ber you re - mem - ber - ing the
cresc.
A♭min9
D♭7
G♭
G♭maj7
hap - py time.
mf
G♭
G♭maj7
G♭
G♭maj7

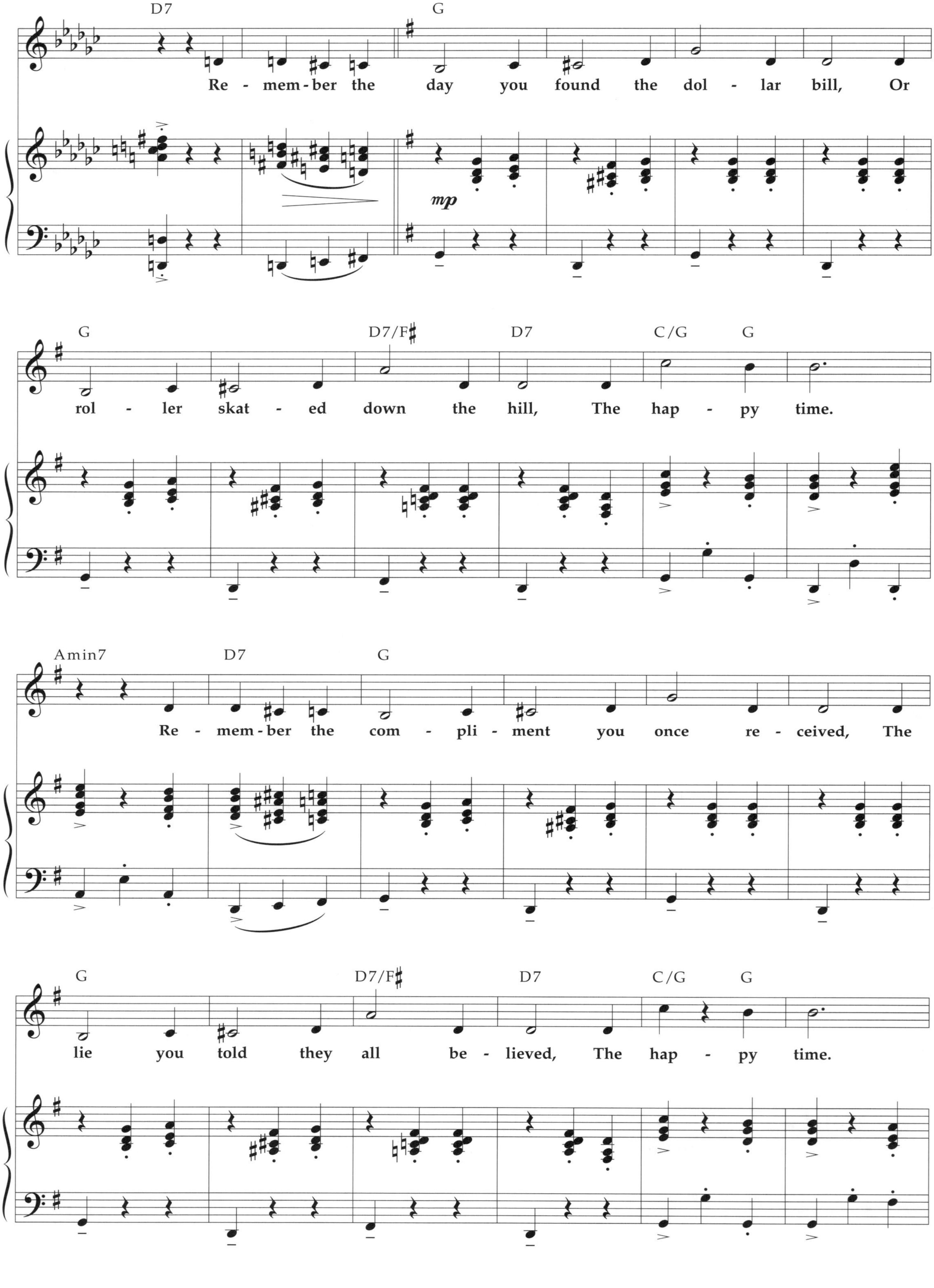
D7
G
Re - mem - ber the day you found the dol - lar bill, Or
mp
G
D7/F♯
D7
C/G
G
rol - ler skat - ed down the hill, The hap - py time.
Amin7
D7
G
Re - mem - ber the com - pli - ment you once re - ceived, The
G
D7/F♯
D7
C/G
G
lie you told they all be - lieved, The hap - py time.

F♯min7(♭5) B7 Emin Emin7 A7
Re - mem - ber your first school play, the sound of ap -
G A7 Dmin Dmin7
plause. Why do I go on this
G7 C C/B♭ A7 D7
way? I'm on - ly re - mind - ing you be - cause I want to re -
G G/F E7(♯5) B♭dim7
mem - ber you re - mem - ber - ing the

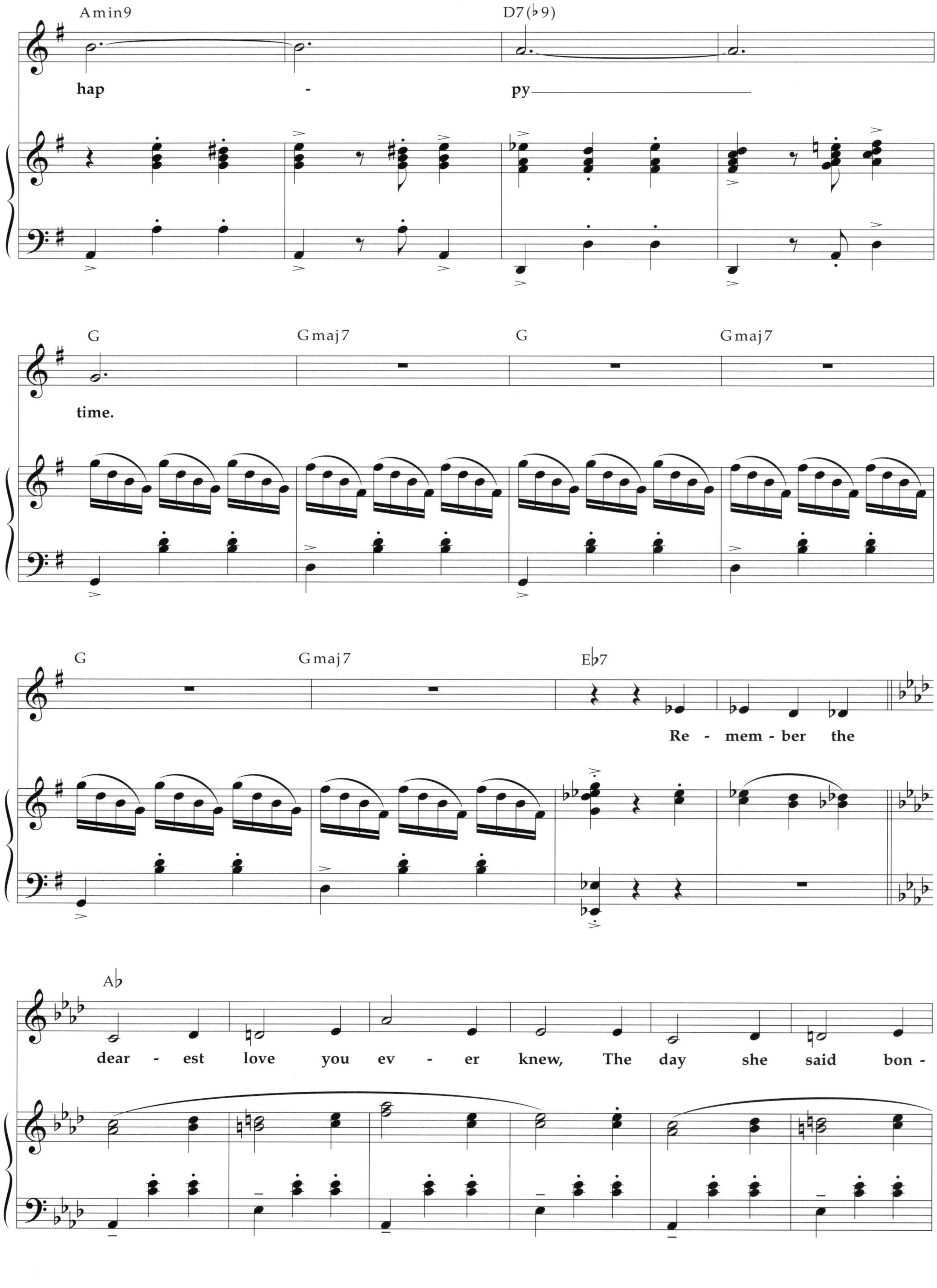
Amin9
D7(♭9)
hap - py
G
Gmaj7
G
Gmaj7
time.
G
Gmaj7
E♭7
Re - mem - ber the
A♭
dear - est love you ev - er knew, The day she said bon -

E♭9/G E♭7 D♭/A♭ A♭ B♭min7 E♭7
jour to you, The hap - py time. Re - mem - ber the
A♭
tu - lip trees you walked a - mong, The game was old, the
E♭9/G E♭7 D♭/A♭ A♭ C7
play - er young, The hap - py time. Re - mem - ber a
Fmin Fmin7 B♭7 E♭
long deep sigh, a ten - ta - tive kiss.

B♭7/F
E♭min
E♭min7
A♭7
And if you should ask me why, The rea - son I
D♭
D♭/C♭
B♭7
E♭7
ask you this is that I'm long - ing to
A♭
see you smile and hear you laugh So
A♭
E♭9/G
E♭7
I can have the pho - to - graph to re -

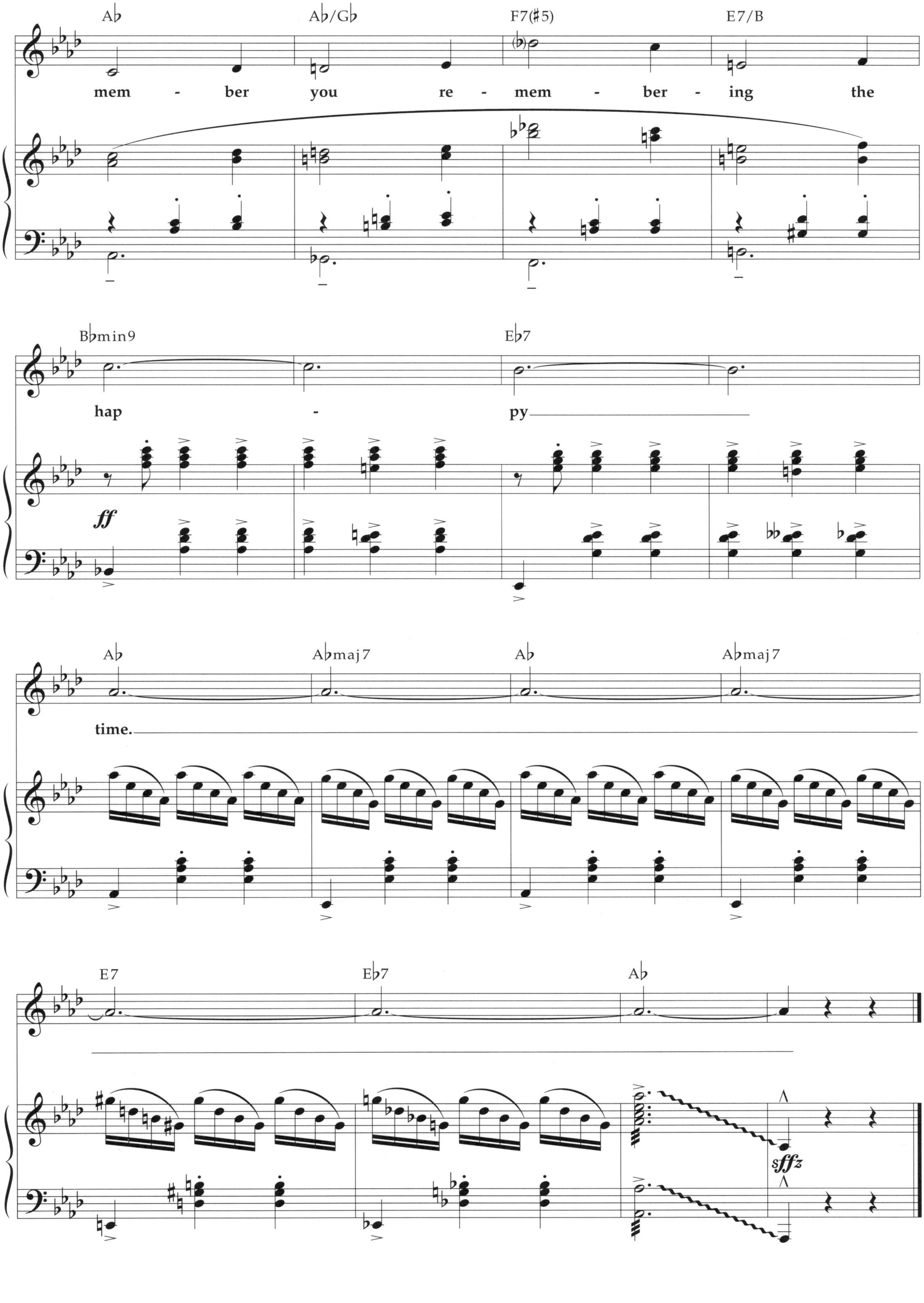
A♭
A♭/G♭
F7(♯5)
E7/B
mem - ber you re - mem - ber - ing the
B♭min9
E♭7
hap - py
ff
A♭
A♭maj7
A♭
A♭maj7
time.
E7
E♭7
A♭
sffz

# How Lucky Can You Get

*from the Motion Picture* ***FUNNY LADY***

Words by
**FRED EBB**

Music by
**JOHN KANDER**

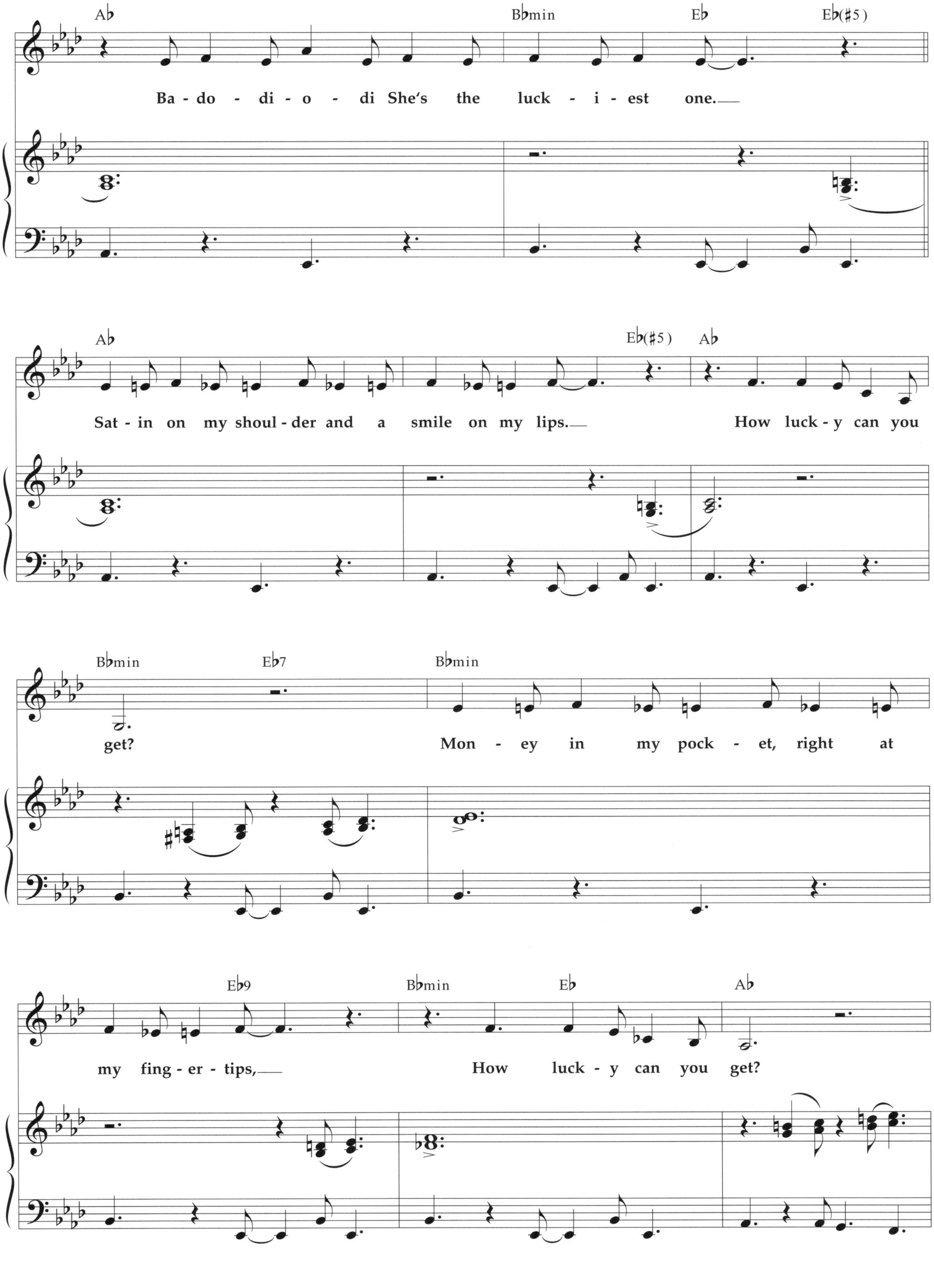
A♭
B♭min
E♭
E♭(♯5)
Ba - do - di - o - di She's the luck - i - est one.
A♭
E♭(♯5)
A♭
Sat - in on my shoul - der and a smile on my lips.
How luck - y can you
B♭min
E♭7
B♭min
get?
Mon - ey in my pock - et, right at
E♭9
B♭min
E♭
A♭
my fing - er - tips,
How luck - y can you get?

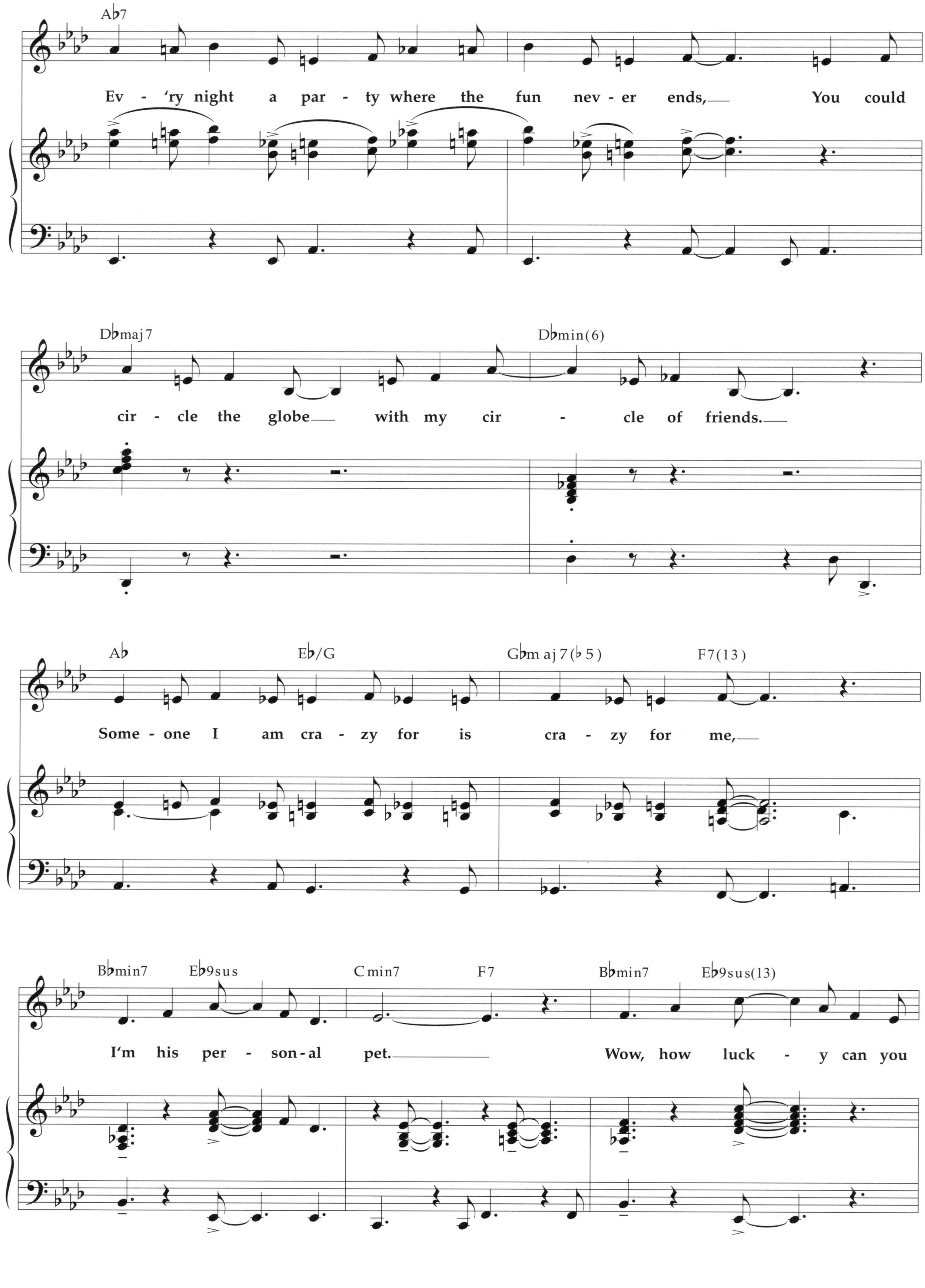
A♭7
Ev - 'ry night a par - ty where the fun nev - er ends, You could
D♭maj7
D♭min(6)
cir - cle the globe with my cir - cle of friends.
A♭
E♭/G
G♭maj7(♭5)
F7(13)
Some - one I am cra - zy for is cra - zy for me,
B♭min7
E♭9sus
Cmin7
F7
B♭min7
E♭9sus(13)
I'm his per - son-al pet. Wow, how luck - y can you

A♭
B♭min
E♭7
E♭(♯5)
A♭
get? Ba-do-di-o-di See her dia-monds a-gleam.
Ba-do-di-o-di-o Her
p
B♭min
E♭7
E♭(♯5)
A♭
E♭(♯5)
life is a dream.
Wrap it up and charge it that's my fa-vor-ite phrase,
cresc.
mp
A♭
B♭min
E♭
B♭min
E♭7
How luck-y can you get?
When I see the chauf-feur, think I'll

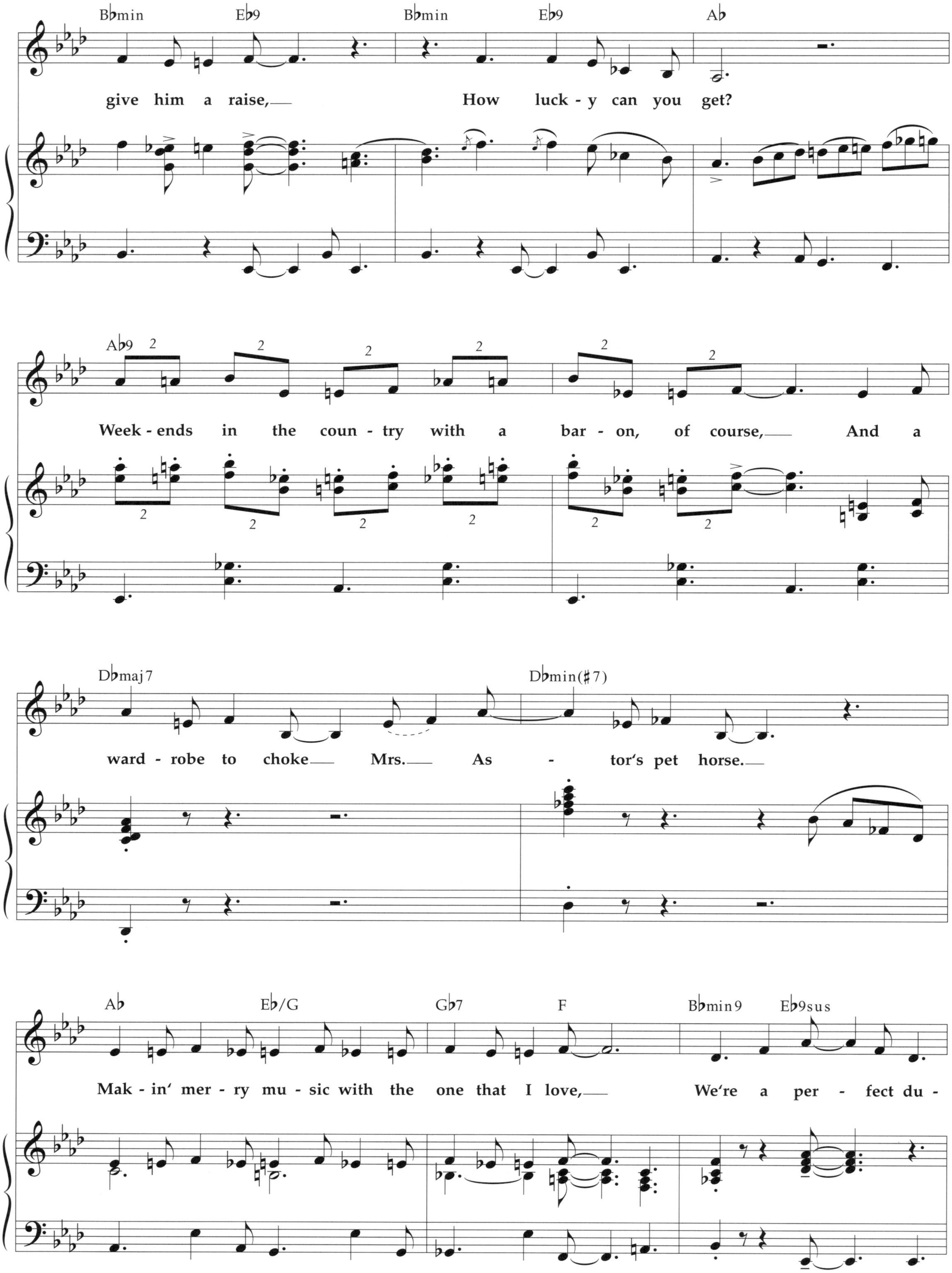
B♭min E♭9 B♭min E♭9 A♭
give him a raise, How luck - y can you get?
A♭9
Week - ends in the coun - try with a bar - on, of course, And a
D♭maj7 D♭min(♯7)
ward - robe to choke Mrs. As - tor's pet horse.
A♭ E♭/G G♭7 F B♭min9 E♭9sus
Mak - in' mer - ry mu - sic with the one that I love, We're a per - fect du -

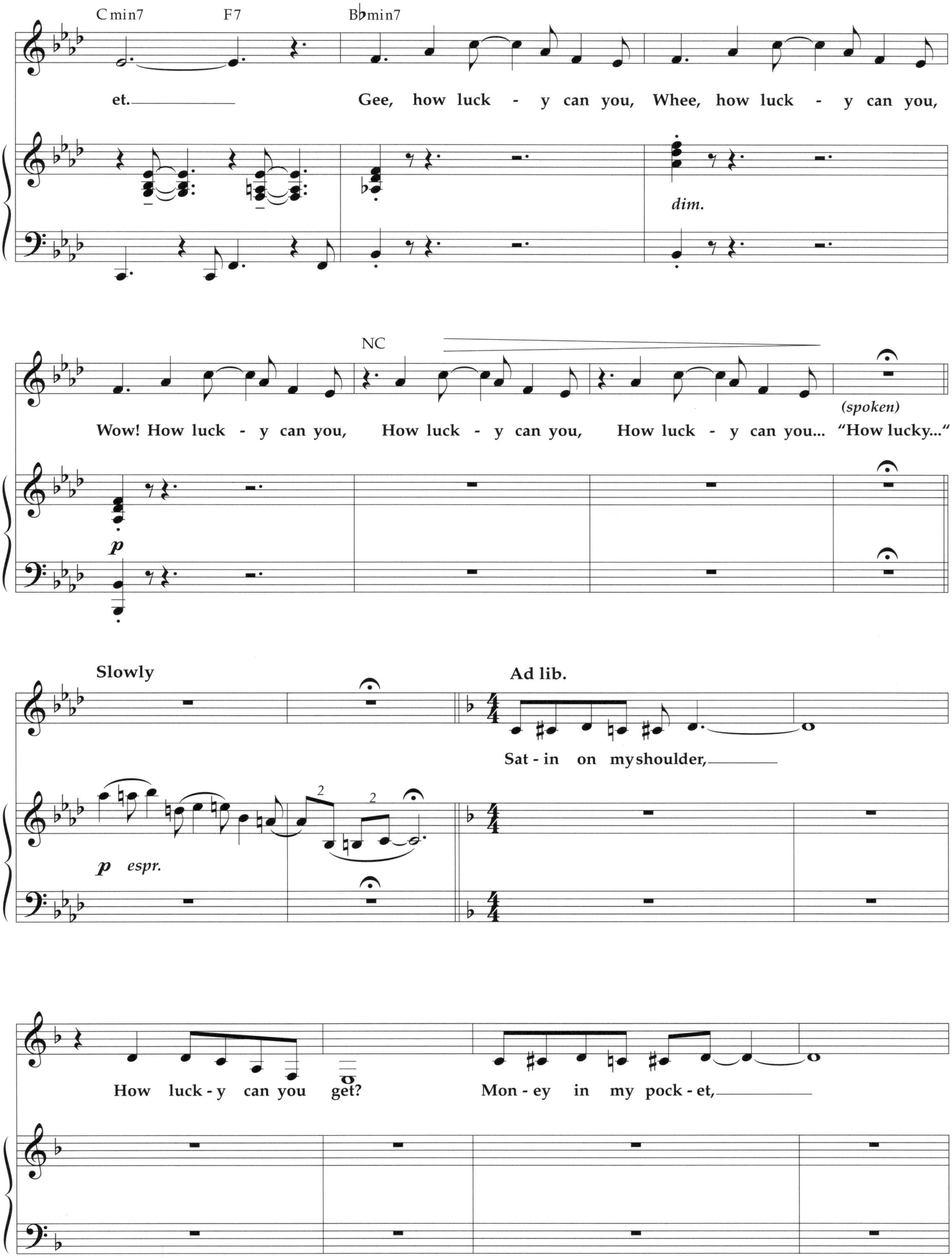
Cmin7 F7 B♭min7
et. Gee, how luck - y can you, Whee, how luck - y can you,
dim.
NC
Wow! How luck - y can you, How luck - y can you, How luck - y can you... "How lucky..."
(spoken)
p
Slowly
Ad lib.
Sat - in on my shoulder,
p espr.
How luck - y can you get? Mon - ey in my pock - et,

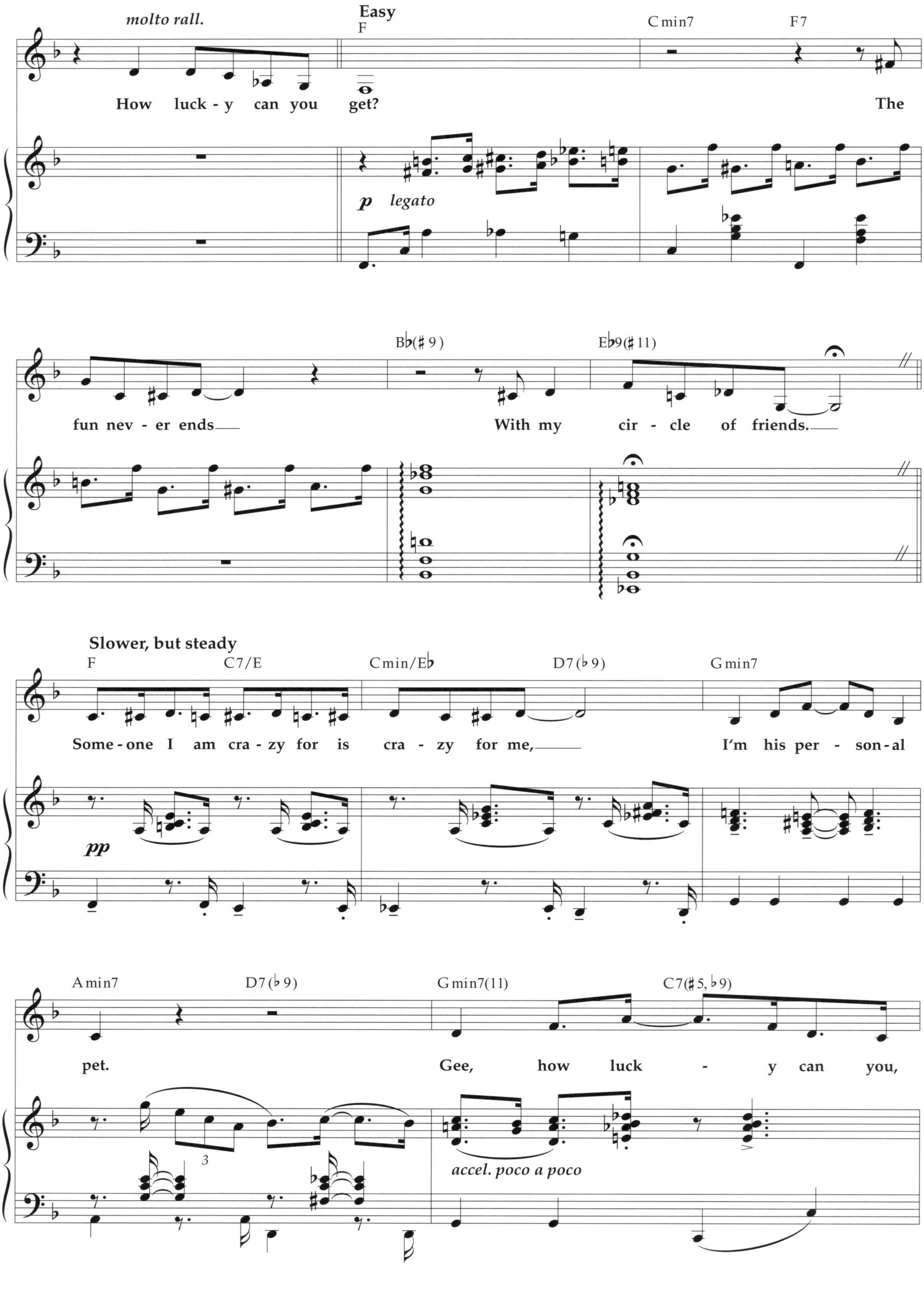
molto rall.
Easy
F
Cmin7
F7
How luck - y can you get?
The
p legato
Bb(#9)
Eb9(#11)
fun nev - er ends
With my cir - cle of friends.
Slower, but steady
F
C7/E
Cmin/Eb
D7(b9)
Gmin7
Some - one I am cra - zy for is cra - zy for me,
I'm his per - son - al
pp
Amin7
D7(b9)
Gmin7(11)
C7(#5, b9)
pet.
Gee, how luck - y can you,
accel. poco a poco

Gmin7
C7(♯5, ♭9)
Gmin7
C7(♯5, ♭9)
Whee, how luck - y can you, Wow, how luck - y can you
accel.
F
D♭9sus
get?
cresc.
Pesante
G♭
Hey there, gor - geous, Big suc -
8va
f

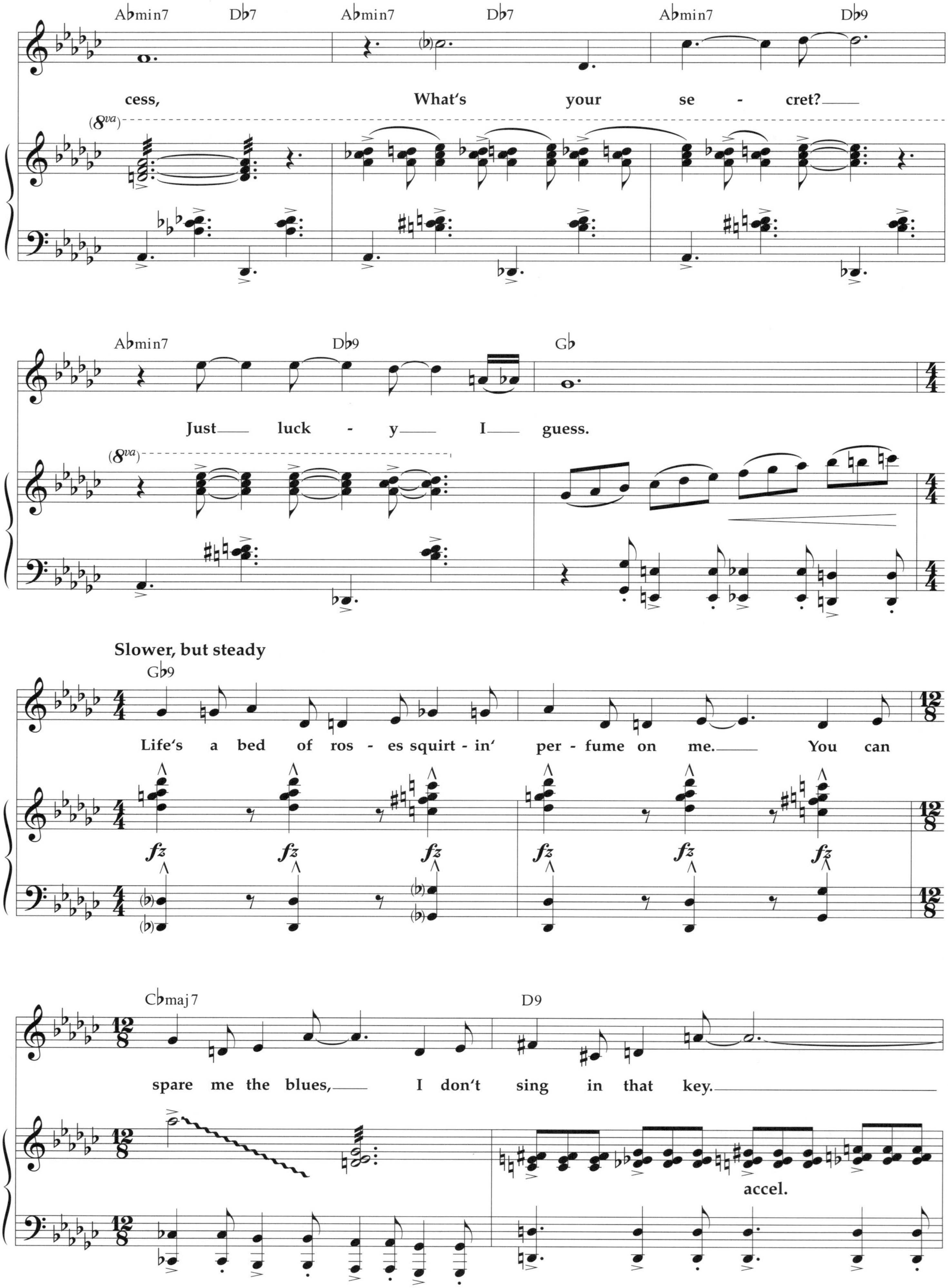
A♭min7 D♭7 A♭min7 D♭7 A♭min7 D♭9
cess, What's your se - cret?
(8va)
A♭min7 D♭9 G♭
Just luck - y I guess.
(8va)
Slower, but steady
G♭9
Life's a bed of ros - es squirt - in' per - fume on me. You can
fz fz fz fz fz fz
C♭maj7 D9
spare me the blues, I don't sing in that key.
accel.

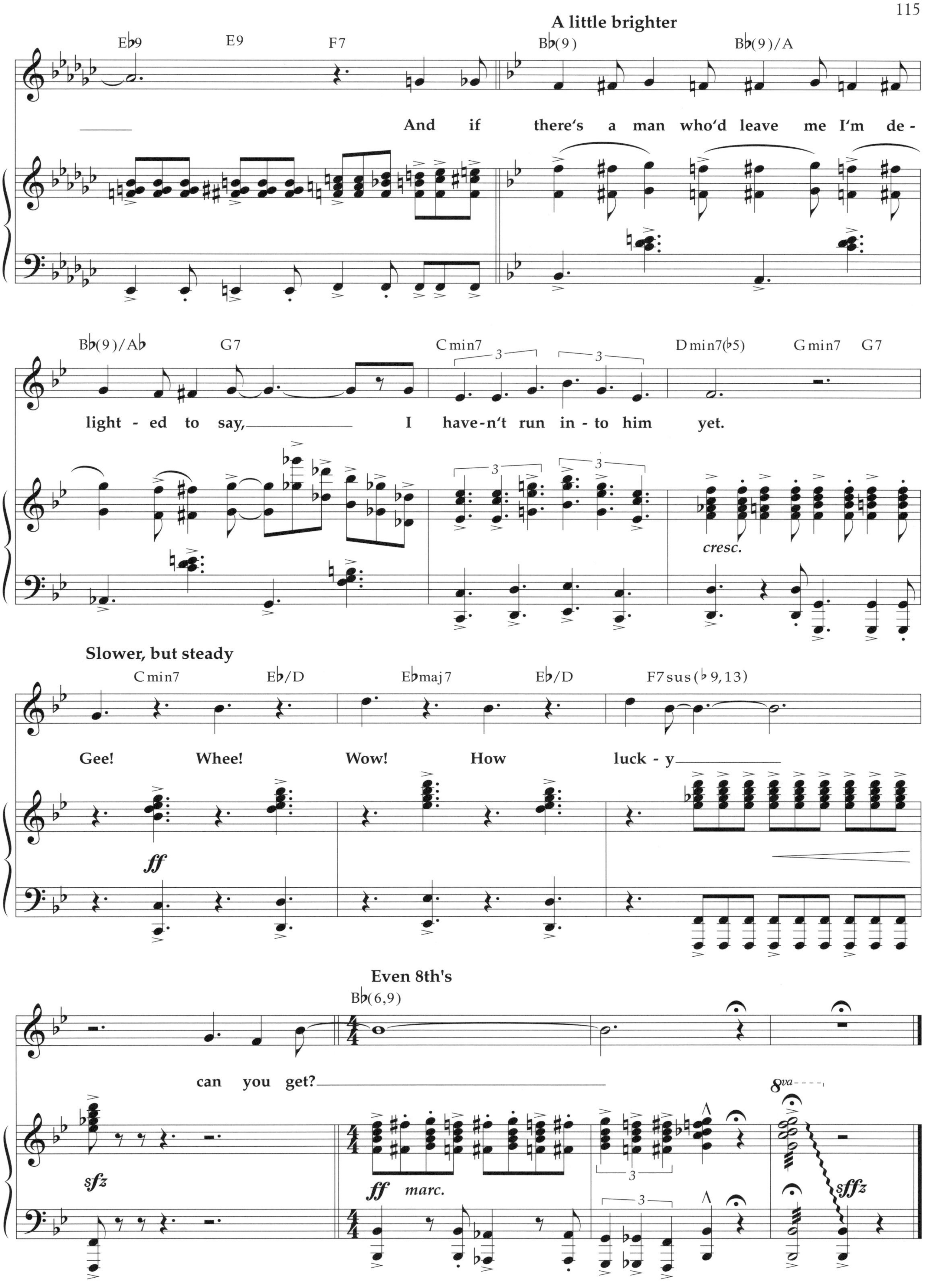
A little brighter
E♭9 E9 F7 B♭(9) B♭(9)/A
And if there's a man who'd leave me I'm de-
B♭(9)/A♭ G7 C min7 D min7(♭5) G min7 G7
light-ed to say, I have-n't run in-to him yet.
cresc.
Slower, but steady
C min7 E♭/D E♭maj7 E♭/D F7sus(♭9,13)
Gee! Whee! Wow! How luck-y
ff
Even 8th's
B♭(6,9)
can you get?
sfz
ff marc.
8va
sffz

# I Don't Care Much

*from the Musical* ***CABARET***

Words by
**FRED EBB**

Music by
**JOHN KANDER**

Cmin7
Cmin9
F9sus(13)
F7
I don't care ___ ver - y
B♭(9)
Amin7(♭5)
D7
much ei - ther way. ___
Gmin(9)
Cmin(6)
Hearts grow hard On a
Gmin(9)
G9
wind - y street. ___

Cmin7
Cmin9
F9sus(13)
F7
Lips grow cold With the
B♭(9)
B♭7
rent to meet. So
cresc.
E♭(9)
E♭min
B♭/F
Dmin
if you kiss me,
mp
Cmin7
F9sus
F7
Dmin7(♭5)
G7
If we touch, Warn - ing's
dim.

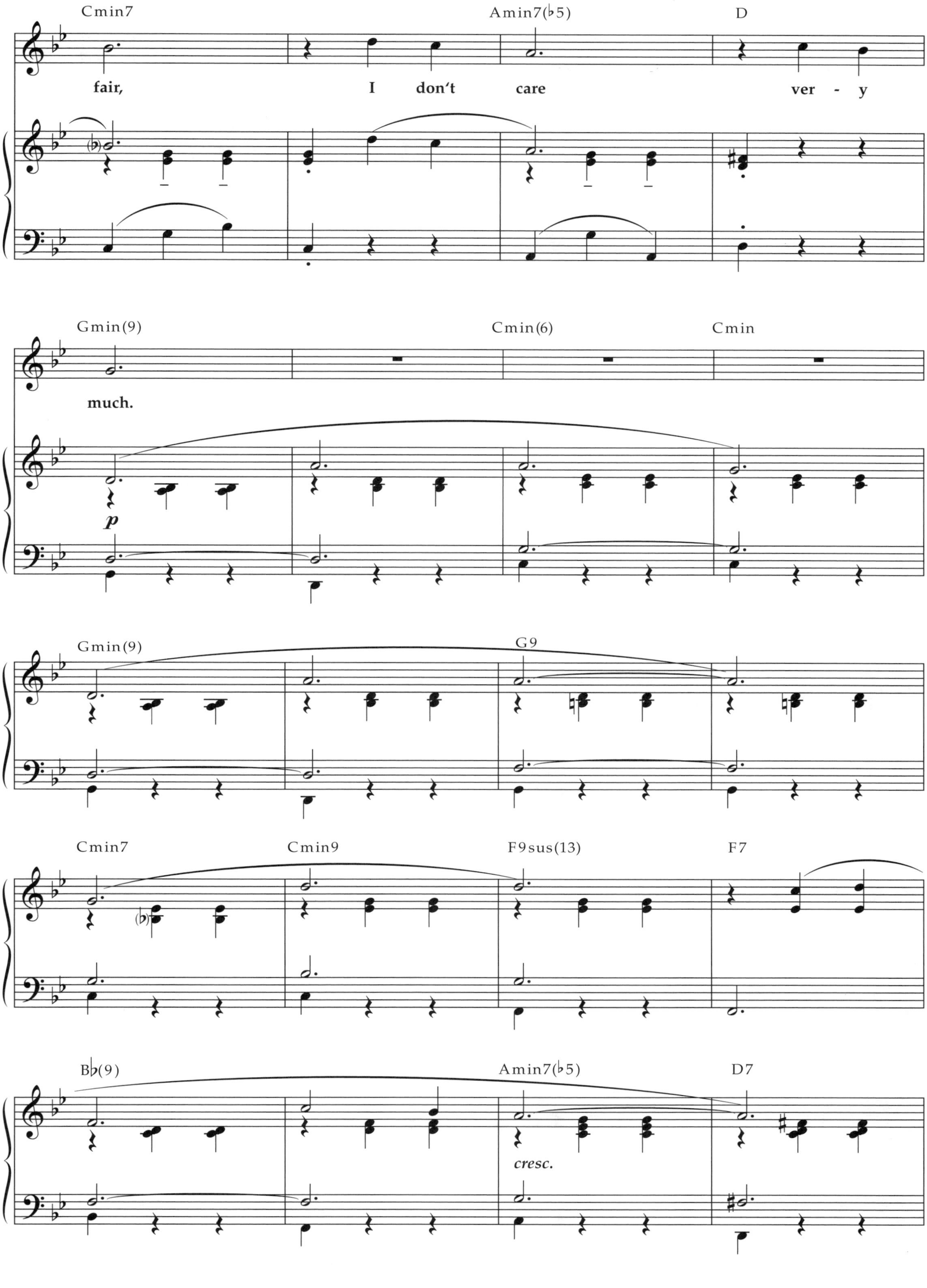
Cmin7
Amin7(♭5)
D
fair, I don't care ver - y
Gmin(9)
Cmin(6)
Cmin
much.
p
Gmin(9)
G9
Cmin7
Cmin9
F9sus(13)
F7
B♭(9)
Amin7(♭5)
D7
cresc.

Gmin(9)
Cmin(6)
Words sound false When your
mf
Gmin(9)
G9
coat's too thin.
Cmin7
Cmin9
F9sus(13)
F7
Feet don't waltz When the
B♭(9)
B♭7
roof caves in So
cresc.

E♭(9) E♭min B♭/F Dmin
if you kiss me,
f
Cmin7 F9sus F7 Dmin7(♭5) G7
If we touch, Warn - ing's
Cmin7 Amin7(♭5) D Gmin Gmin(9)
fair, I don't care ver - y much.
mp
rit.
a tempo
Cmin Cmin(6) Gmin(9)

# I Don't Remember You

*from the Musical* **THE HAPPY TIME**

Words by
**FRED EBB**

Music by
**JOHN KANDER**

A♭(9) D♭/A♭ A♭(9) D♭/A♭
in the park? What laugh - ter in the dark? What smol - d'ring
cross the hill? What laugh - ter by the mill? What whis - per
A♭(9) D♭/A♭ A♭sus A♭(9)
fi - re - place That lit your face With ev - 'ry spark? And if I
in the snow I heard be - low my win - dow - sill? And if you
cresc.
E♭(9)/G E♭min/G♭ Fmin7 B♭7
left you once be - fore, Some - how I
left me once be - fore, Some - how I
mf
poco dim.
A♭(9) Gmin Fmin7 B♭
can't re - call it an - y - more. That was an -
can't re - call it an - y - more. That was an -
poco cresc.

A tempo
E♭(9) A♭/E♭ E♭(9) A♭/E♭
oth - er girl. You're not at all like her Though for an
oth - er time. An - oth - er time and place. Al - though you
mf
E♭(9) A♭/E♭ E♭9sus E♭9
in - stant when you touched me, I be - lieved you were. But I was
bear a faint re - sem - blance You're an - oth - er face. Yes, I was
cresc.
A♭ A♭(♯5) Fmin7 B♭7 Gmin Cmin
wrong This mo - ment is new Be - cause I
wrong This mo - ment is new
f
dim.
3

Freely
Fmin7 Gmin A♭ Fmin7 Gmin A♭ B♭9sus B♭
A tempo
E♭(9) B9
can't, I won't, I don't re - mem - ber you. That was an -
mp colla voce
Appassionato
E(9) A/E Emaj7 A/E
oth - er time, An - oth - er time and place. Al - though you
mf espress.
E(9) A/E E9sus E7
Allargando
bear a faint re - sem - blance, You're an - oth - er face. Yes, I was

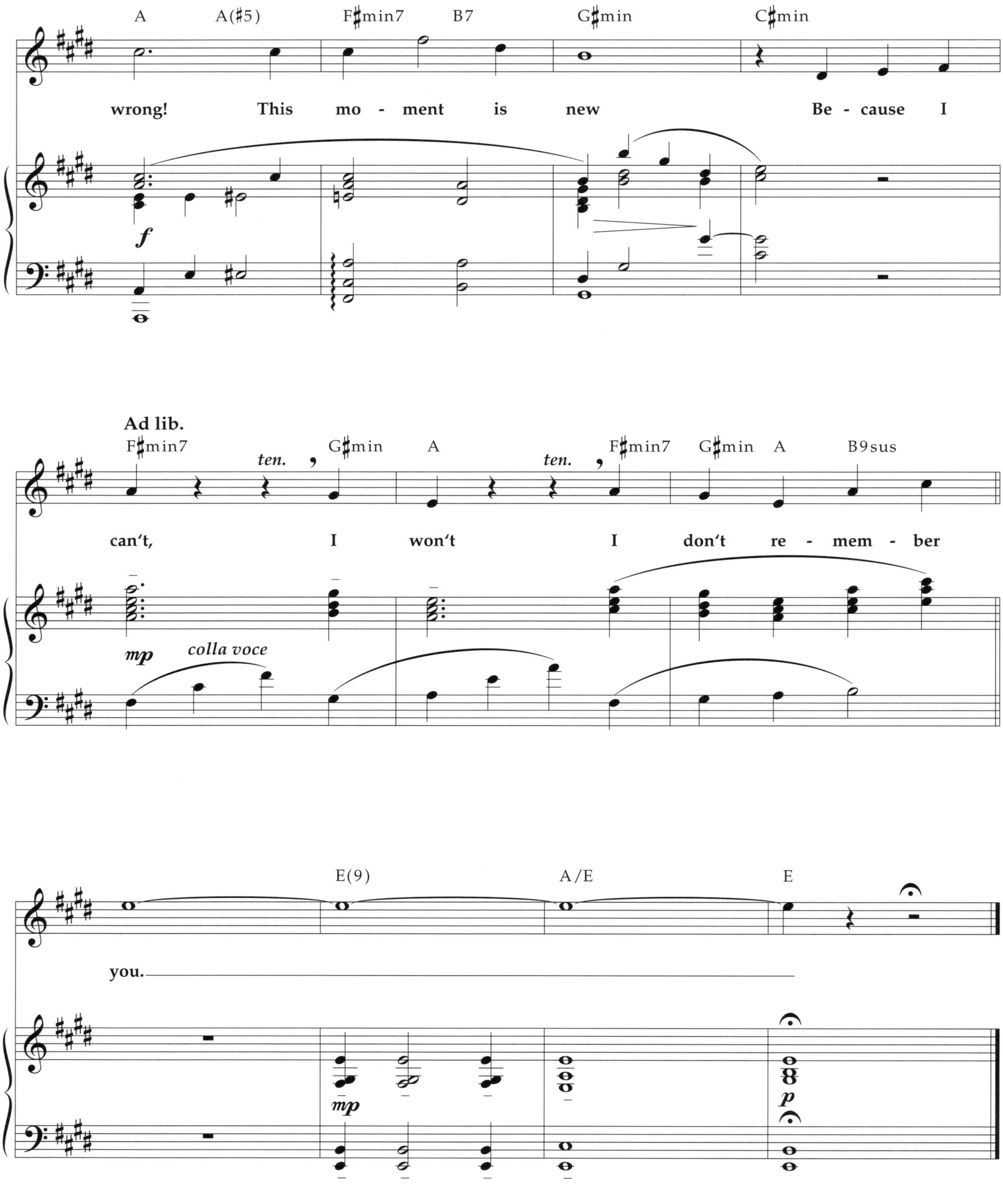
A A(♯5) F♯min7 B7 G♯min C♯min
wrong! This mo - ment is new Be - cause I
f
Ad lib.
F♯min7 ten. G♯min A ten. F♯min7 G♯min A B9sus
can't, I won't I don't re - mem - ber
mp colla voce
E(9) A/E E
you.
mp
p

# I Move On

*from the Motion Picture* **CHICAGO**

Words by
**FRED EBB**

Music by
**JOHN KANDER**

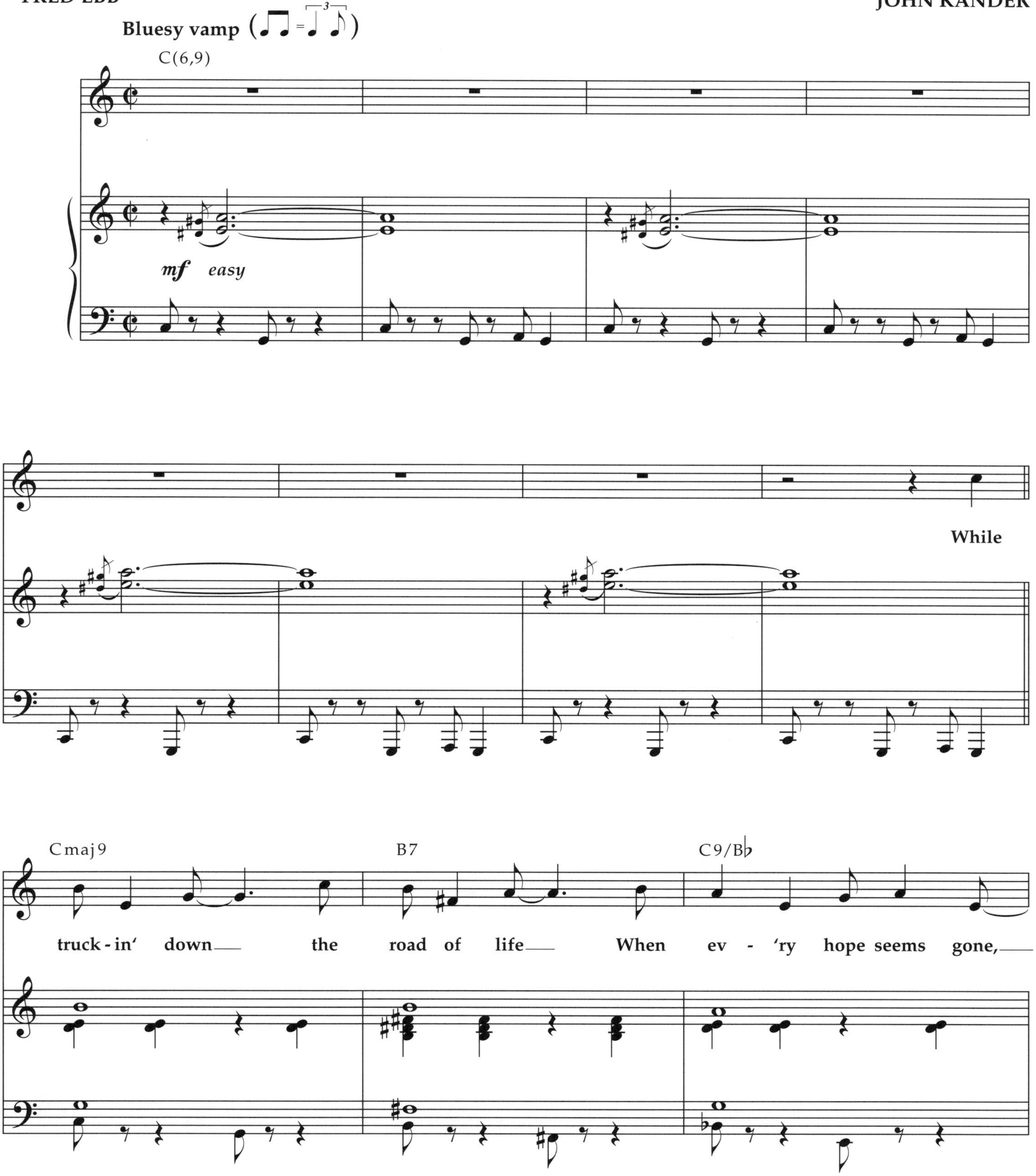

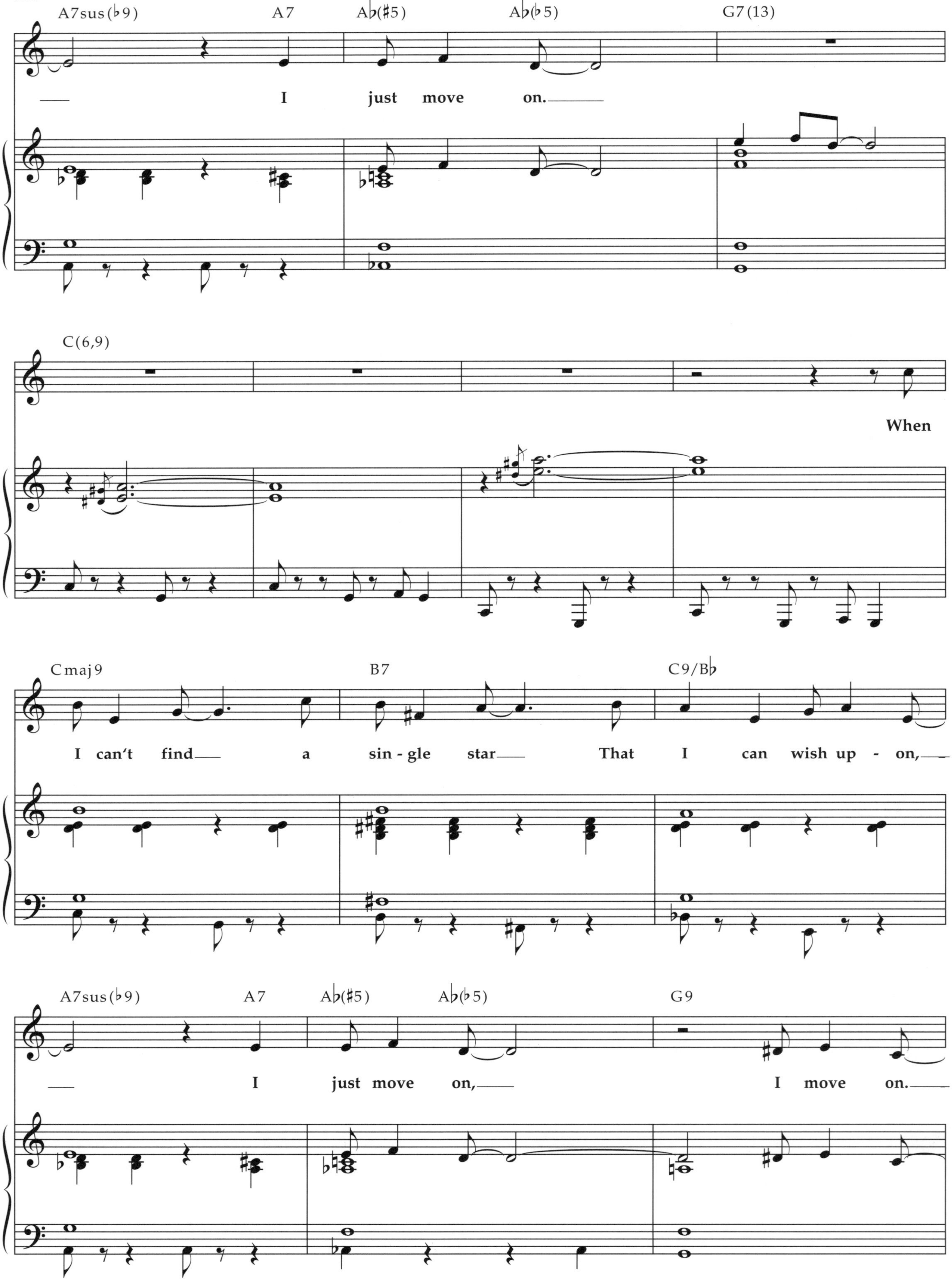
A7sus(♭9)
A7
A♭(♯5)
A♭(♭5)
G7(13)
I just move on.
C(6,9)
When
Cmaj9
B7
C9/B♭
I can't find a sin-gle star That I can wish up-on,
A7sus(♭9)
A7
A♭(♯5)
A♭(♭5)
G9
I just move on, I move on.

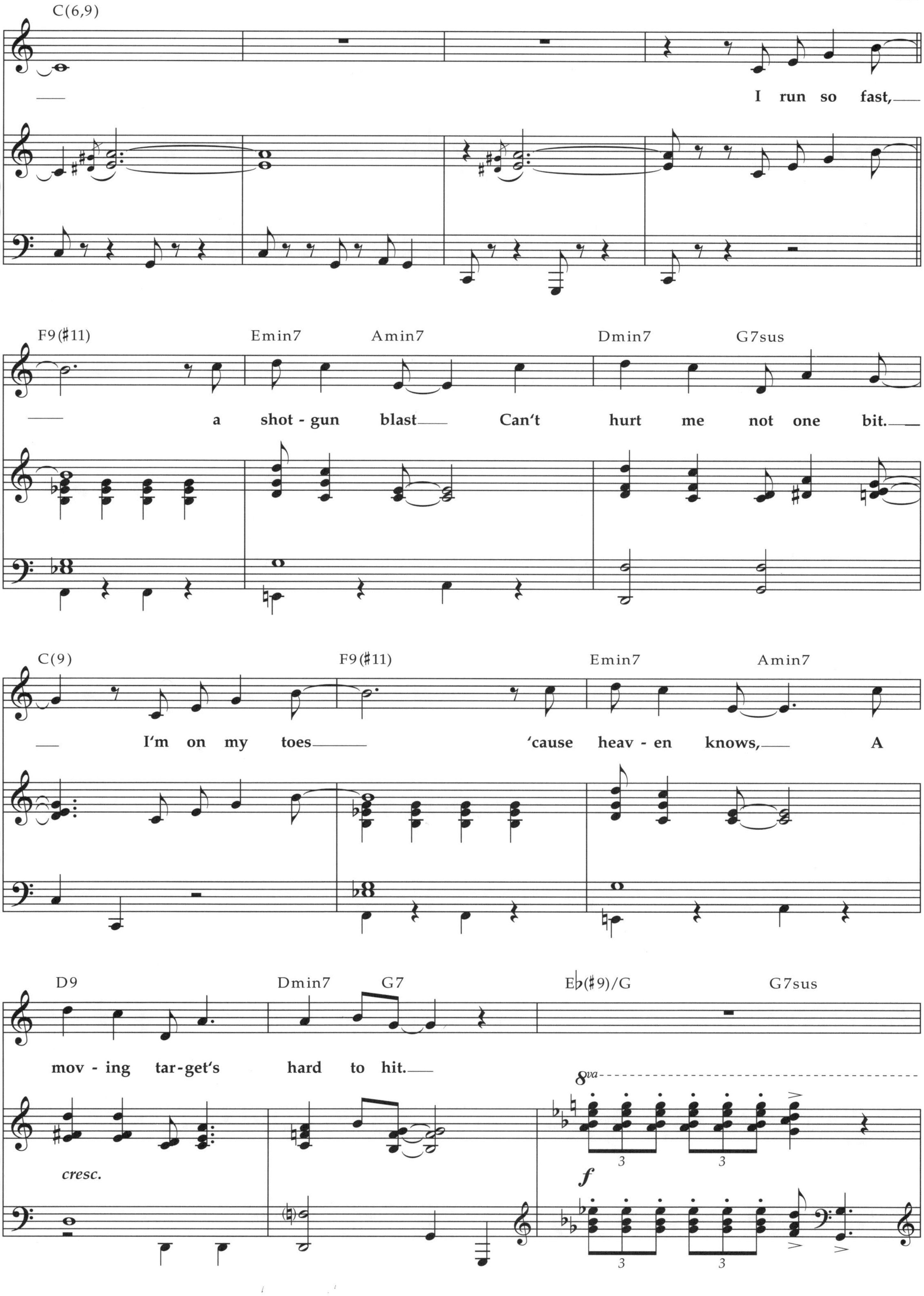
C(6,9)
I run so fast,
F9(♯11)
Emin7
Amin7
Dmin7
G7sus
a shot - gun blast Can't hurt me not one bit.
C(9)
F9(♯11)
Emin7
Amin7
I'm on my toes 'cause heav - en knows, A
D9
Dmin7
G7
E♭(♯9)/G
G7sus
mov - ing tar-get's hard to hit.
8va
cresc.
f

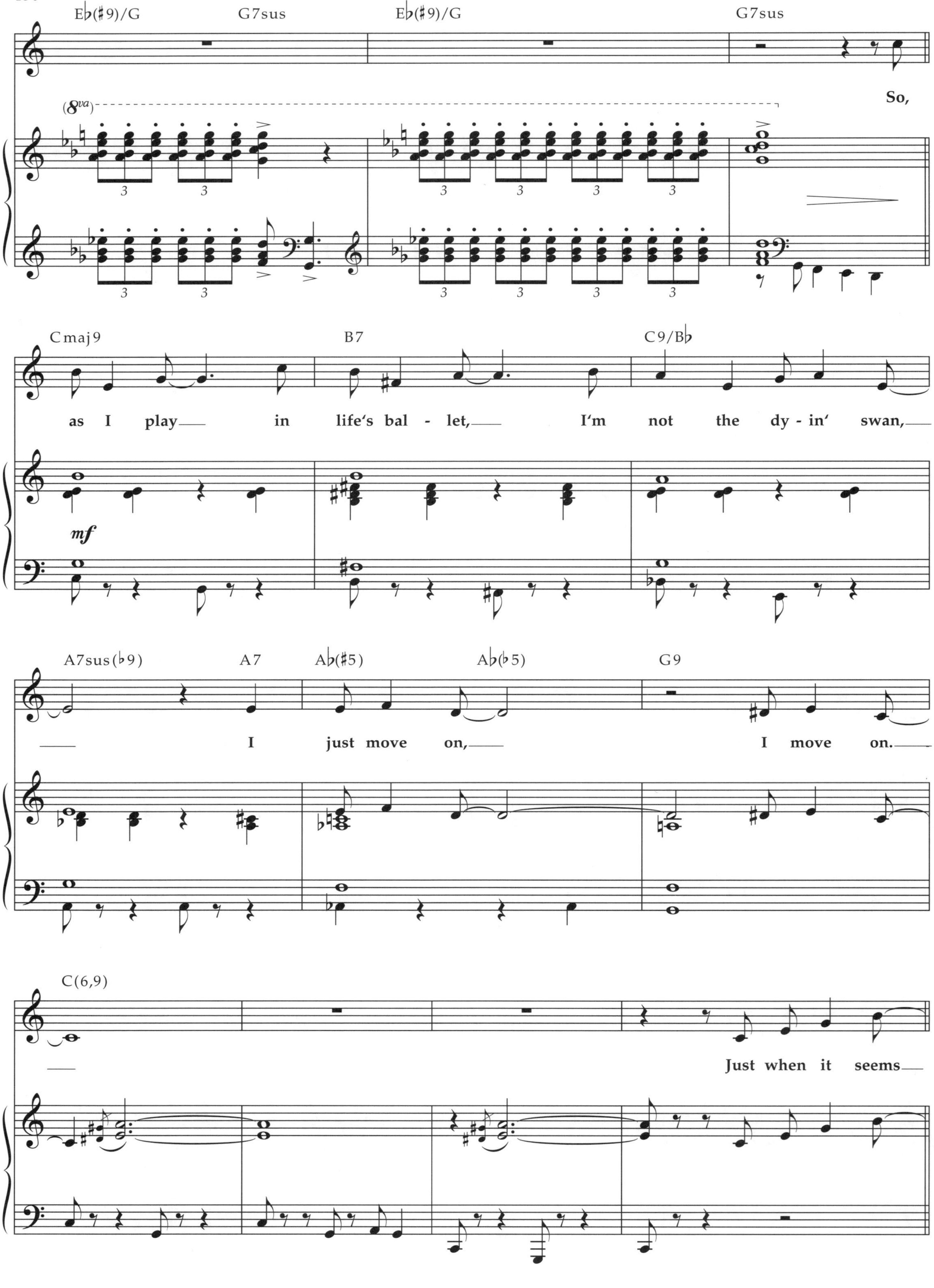
E♭(♯9)/G
G7sus
E♭(♯9)/G
G7sus
So,
(8va)
Cmaj9
B7
C9/B♭
as I play in life's bal - let, I'm not the dy - in' swan,
mf
A7sus(♭9)
A7
A♭(♯5)
A♭(♭5)
G9
I just move on, I move on.
C(6,9)
Just when it seems

F9(♯11) Emin7 Amin7 Dmin7 G7sus
I'm out of dreams And life has got me down,
C(9) F9(♯11) Emin7 Amin7
I don't de - spair, I don't go there. I
D9 Dmin7 G7 E♭(♯9)/G G7sus
hang my bon-net out of town.
8va
f
3
3
3
3

E♭(♯9)/G G7sus E♭(♯9)/G G7sus
(8va)
So,
mf
Cmaj9 B7 C9/B♭
there's no doubt I'm well cut out To run life's mar - a - thon
A7sus(♭9) A7 Dmin9(♭5) G7sus(♭9) G9sus
'Cause I move on. I

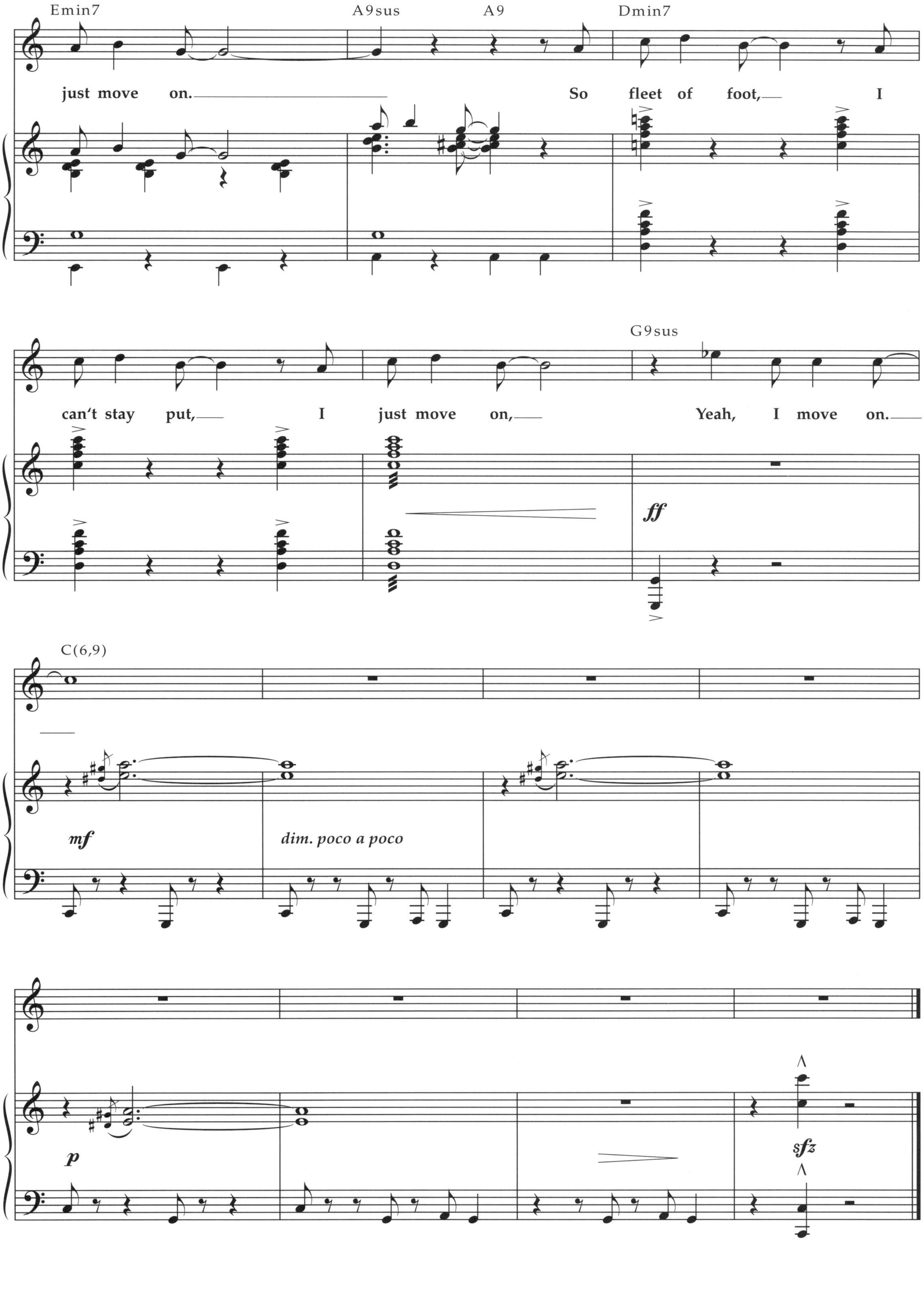
Emin7
A9sus
A9
Dmin7
just move on.
So fleet of foot,
I
can't stay put,
I just move on,
G9sus
Yeah, I move on.
ff
C(6,9)
mf
dim. poco a poco
p
sfz

# If You Could See Her

*from the Musical* ***CABARET***

Words by
**FRED EBB**

Music by
**JOHN KANDER**

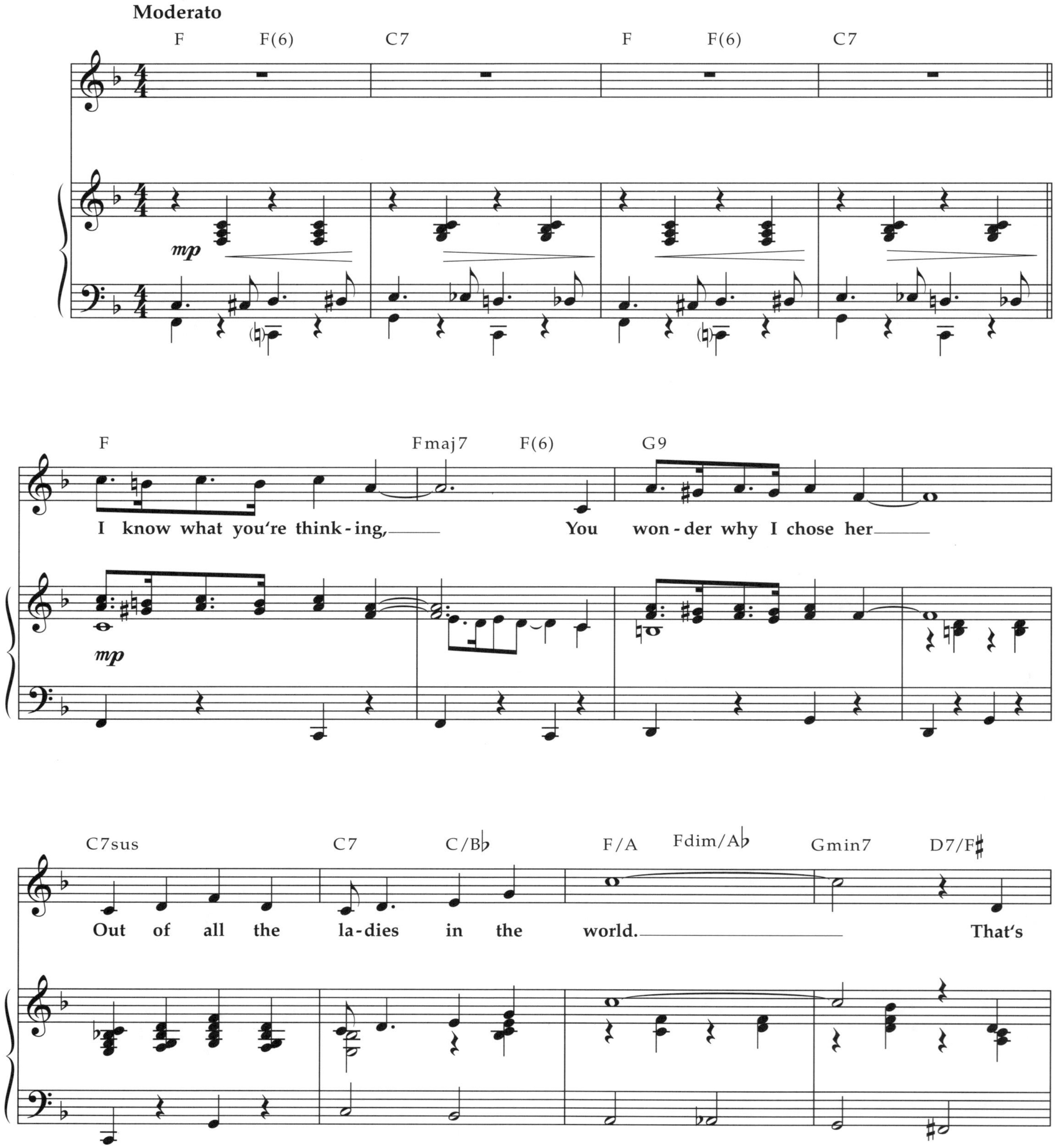
Moderato
F F(6) C7 F F(6) C7
mp
F Fmaj7 F(6) G9
I know what you're think-ing, You won-der why I chose her
mp
C7sus C7 C/B♭ F/A Fdim/A♭ Gmin7 D7/F♯
Out of all the la-dies in the world. That's

Gmin
just a first im-pres - sion,
What good's a first im-pres - sion?
ad lib.
C
C9sus
C9
If you knew her like I do,
It would change your point of
Cmin7
F7
view.
Moderato
B♭
B♭maj7
B♭(6)
If you could see her through my eyes,
How can I speak of her vir - tues?
B♭
B♭maj7
D♭dim
Cmin7
F7
Cmin7
You would - n't won - der at all.
I don't know where to be - gin.
If you could see her through
She's clev - er, she's sweet, she reads

C F7 F7(♯5) B♭ B♭/D D♭dim F7/C
my eyes, I guar - an - tee you would fall, (like I did).
mu - sic, She does - n't smoke or drink gin, (like I do).
B♭ B♭maj7 B♭(6) B♭7 B♭9
When we're in pub - lic to - geth - er, I hear so - ci - e - ty
Yet when we're walk - ing to - geth - er, They sneer if I'm hold - ing her
E♭ C9 B♭/F Dmin7(♭5) G7
moan, But if they could see her through my eyes,
hand, If they could see her through my eyes,
Cmin7 F7(13) 1. B♭ B♭(6) F7
May - be they'd leave us a - lone.
May - be they'd all un - der -

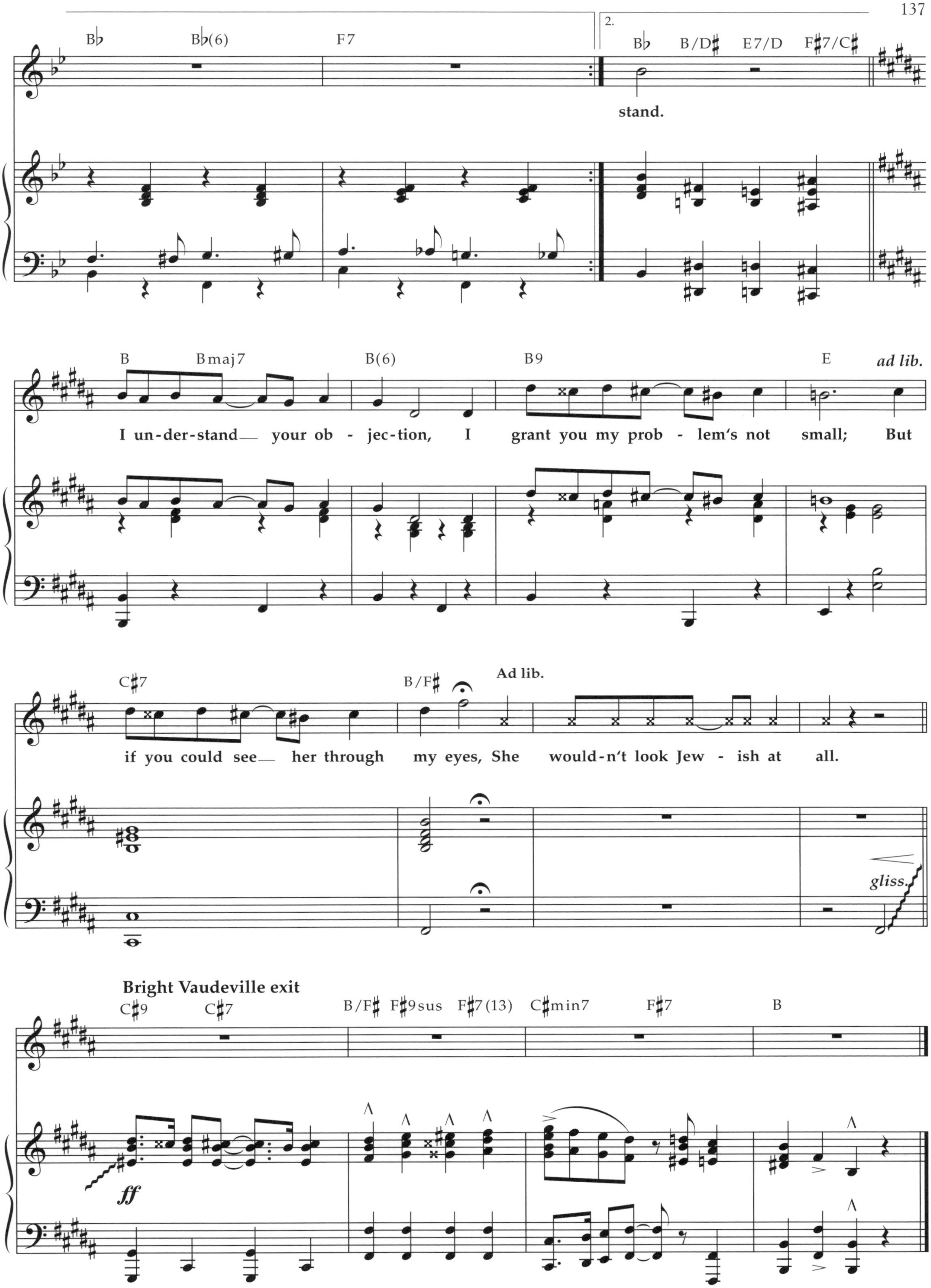
2.
B♭ B♭(6) F7 B♭ B/D♯ E7/D F♯7/C♯
stand.
B Bmaj7 B(6) B9 E
ad lib.
I un-der-stand your ob - jec-tion, I grant you my prob - lem's not small; But
C♯7 B/F♯
Ad lib.
if you could see her through my eyes, She would-n't look Jew - ish at all.
gliss.
Bright Vaudeville exit
C♯9 C♯7 B/F♯ F♯9sus F♯7(13) C♯min7 F♯7 B
ff

# Isn't This Better?

*from the Motion Picture* ***FUNNY LADY***

Words by
**FRED EBB**

Music by
**JOHN KANDER**

G♭(9)
G♭(6,9)
G♭9
Some-bod - y nice, Some-bod - y new, Some - one who lets me re - act as I
p
C♭(9)
B♭7(♭9)
E♭min7
A♭min7
B♭7
nor - mal - ly do. Is - n't this bet - ter?
poco cresc.
E♭sus
E♭(♯5)
E♭
E♭sus
B♭9sus
B♭7
E♭sus
E♭(♯5)
E♭
Pas - sion is fine, but pas - sion burns fast. Pas - sion's de - sign seems
mp
E♭sus
B♭9sus
B♭7
E♭min9
A♭7(13)
F7
nev - er to last. Bet - ter a match, bet - ter a blend.
poco accel.

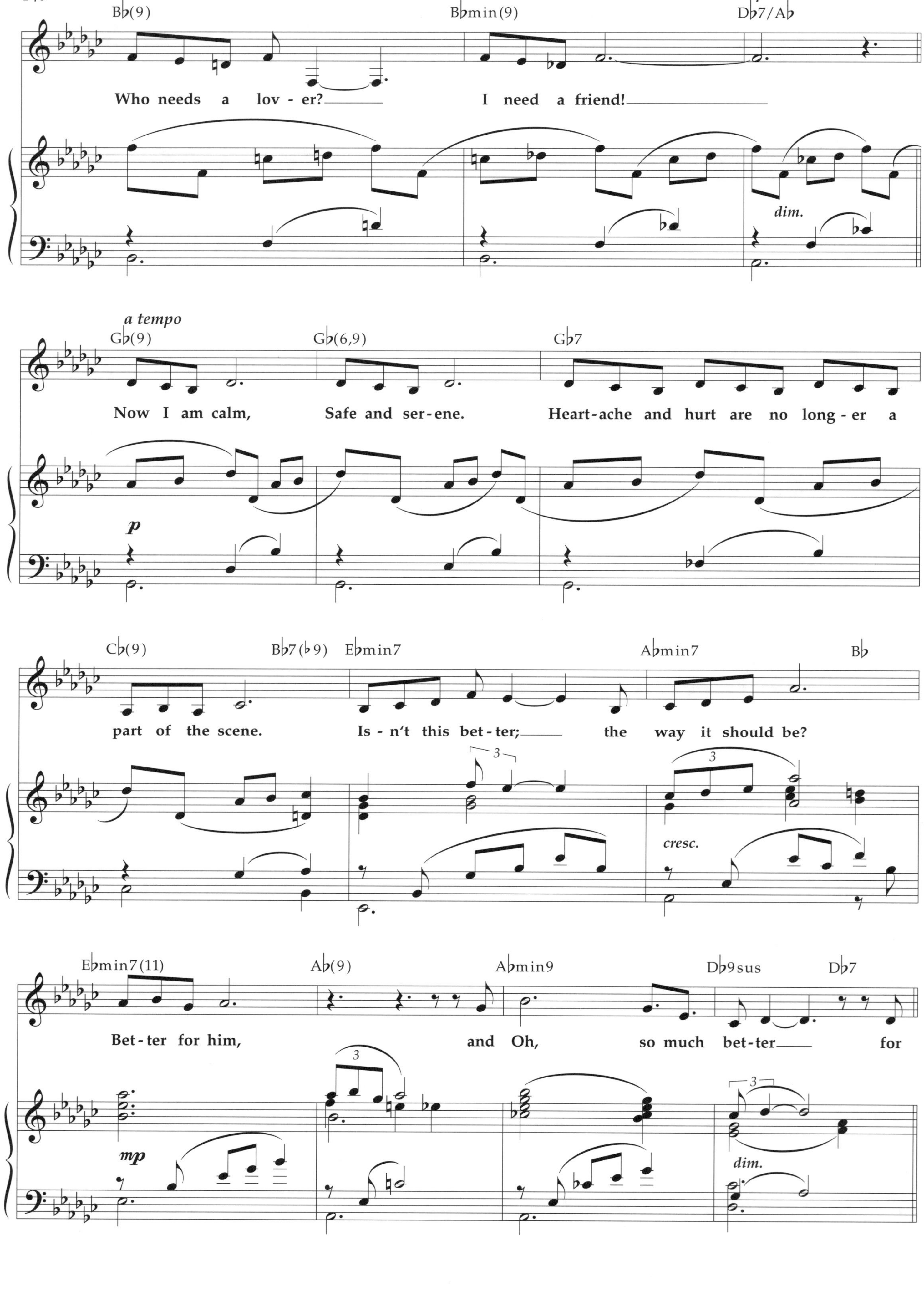
poco rit.
B♭(9)
B♭min(9)
D♭7/A♭
Who needs a lov - er?
I need a friend!
dim.
a tempo
G♭(9)
G♭(6,9)
G♭7
Now I am calm,
Safe and ser - ene.
Heart - ache and hurt are no long - er a
p
C♭(9)
B♭7(♭9)
E♭min7
A♭min7
B♭
part of the scene.
Is - n't this bet - ter;
the way it should be?
3
cresc.
E♭min7(11)
A♭(9)
A♭min9
D♭9sus
D♭7
Bet - ter for him,
and Oh,
so much
bet - ter
for
mp
dim.

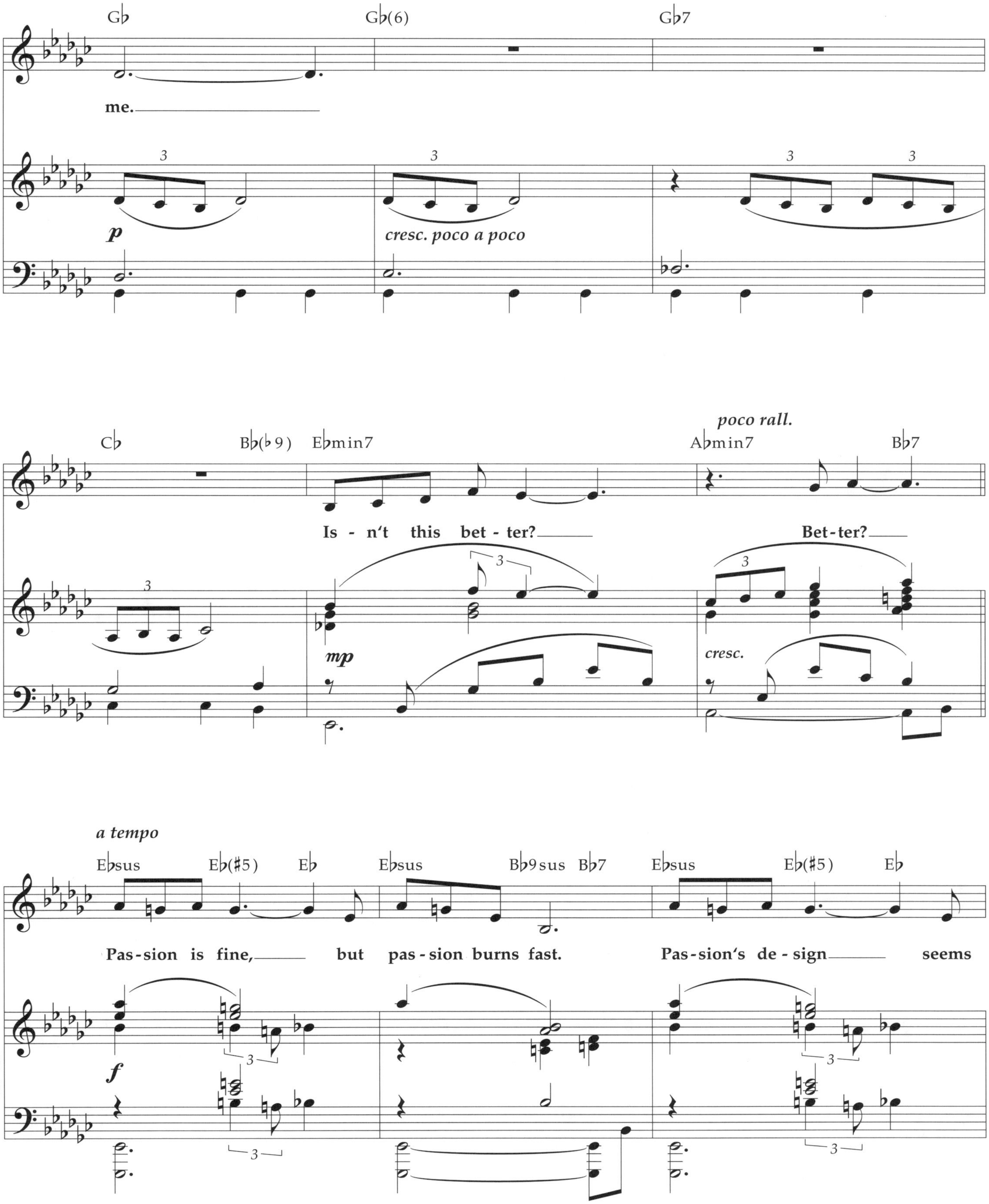
G♭
G♭(6)
G♭7
me.
p
cresc. poco a poco
C♭
B♭(♭9)
E♭min7
poco rall.
A♭min7
B♭7
Is - n't this bet - ter?
Bet - ter?
mp
cresc.
a tempo
E♭sus
E♭(♯5)
E♭
E♭sus
B♭9sus
B♭7
E♭sus
E♭(♯5)
E♭
Pas - sion is fine,
but pas - sion burns fast.
Pas - sion's de - sign
seems
f

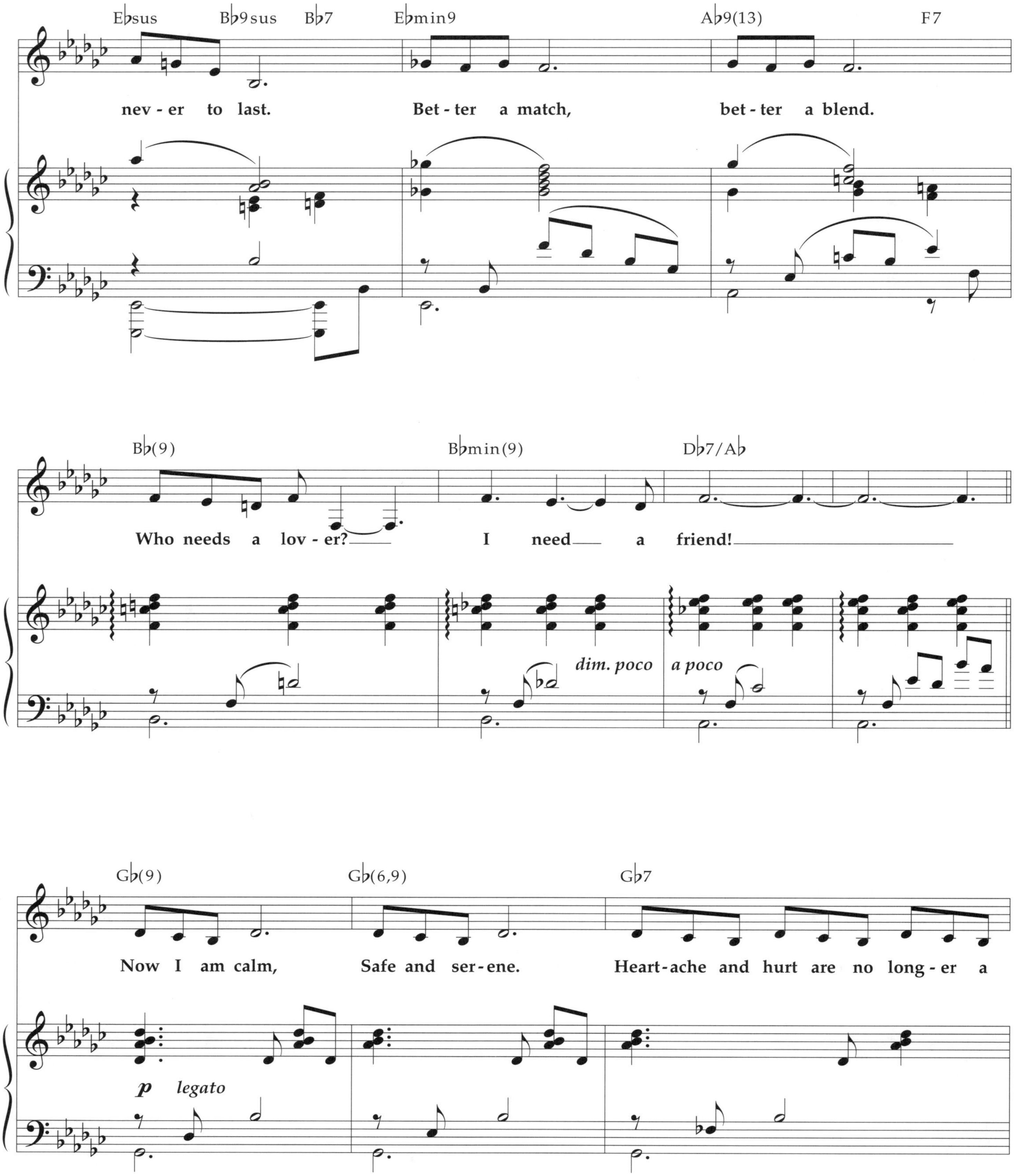
E♭sus B♭9sus B♭7 E♭min9 A♭9(13) F7
nev - er to last. Bet - ter a match, bet - ter a blend.
B♭(9) B♭min(9) D♭7/A♭
Who needs a lov - er? I need a friend!
dim. poco a poco
G♭(9) G♭(6,9) G♭7
Now I am calm, Safe and ser - ene. Heart - ache and hurt are no long - er a
p legato

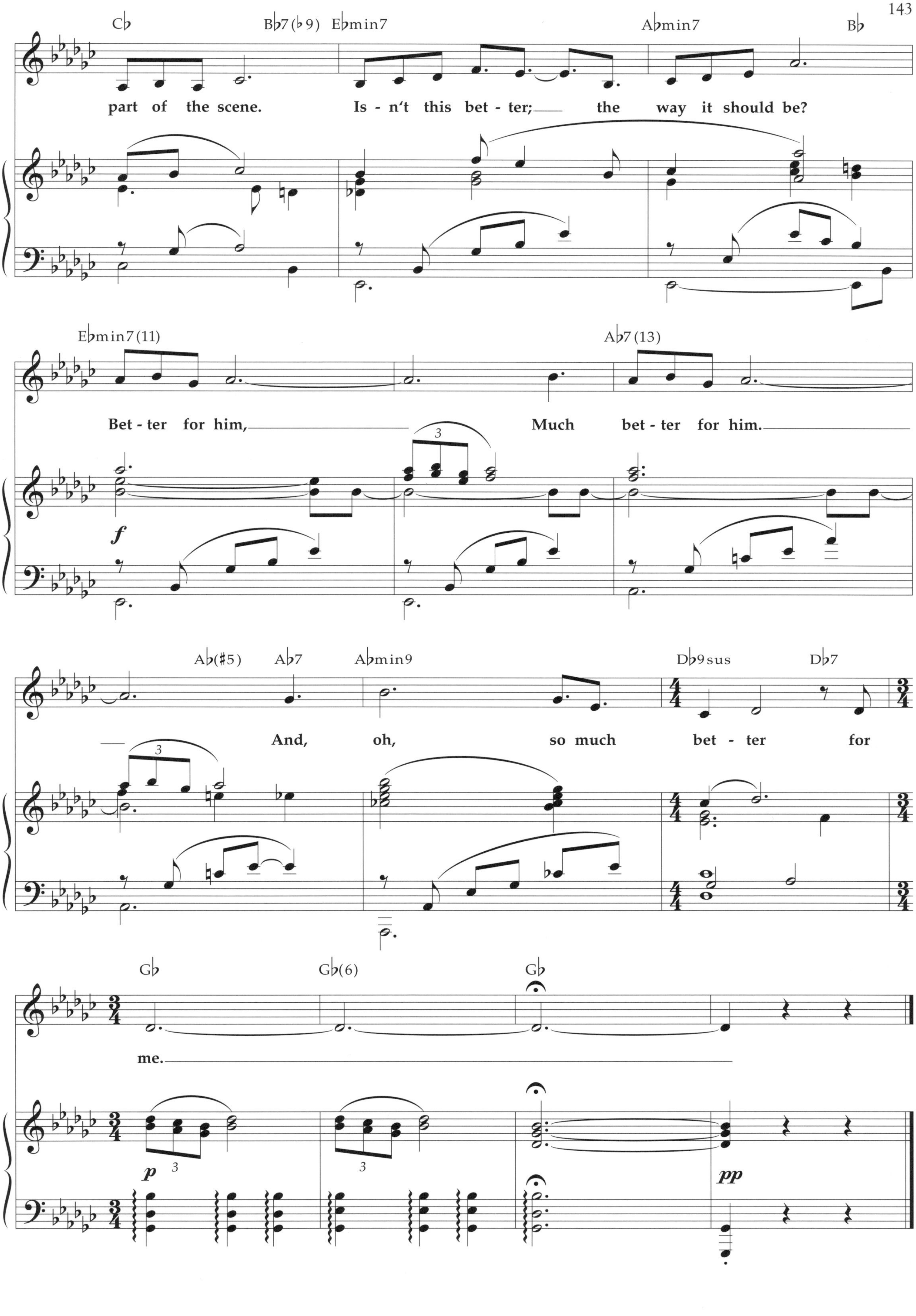

C♭
B♭7(♭9)
E♭min7
A♭min7
B♭
part of the scene. Is - n't this bet - ter; the way it should be?
E♭min7(11)
A♭7(13)
Bet - ter for him, Much bet - ter for him.
A♭(♯5)
A♭7
A♭min9
D♭9sus
D♭7
And, oh, so much bet - ter for
G♭
G♭(6)
G♭
me.

# Kiss of the Spider Woman

*from the Musical* **KISS OF THE SPIDER WOMAN**

Words by
**FRED EBB**

Music by
**JOHN KANDER**

C♯min G♯7 C♯min G♯7
bed - room, the par - lor or e - ven the street. There's
C♯min F♯ C♯min F♯
no place on earth You're like - ly to miss Her
G♯7sus G♯7
kiss.
cresc.
C♯min C♯sus C♯min C♯sus(9)
Soon - er or lat - er in sun - light or gloom When the
mp

C♯min C♯sus C♯min C♯sus(9)
red can - dles flick - er she'll walk in the room And the
C♯min F♯ C♯min F♯
cur - tain will shake And the fi - re will hiss. Here comes her
G♯7sus G♯9
kiss. And the
cresc.
rall. poco a poco
A tempo
C♯min C♯min/B D♯7/A♯ F♯min/A G♯7
moon grows dim - mer At the
f marc.

C♯min
C♯min/B
D♯7/A♯
tide's low ebb And her
F♯min(6)/A
G♯7
C♯min
C♯min/B
black beads shim - mer And you're
D♯7/A♯
F♯min(6)/A
G♯7sus
G♯7
ach - ing to move But you're caught in the web Of the
rall.
C♯min
C♯min/B
D♯7/A♯
F♯min/A
G♯7
Spi - der - wom - an With her
a tempo

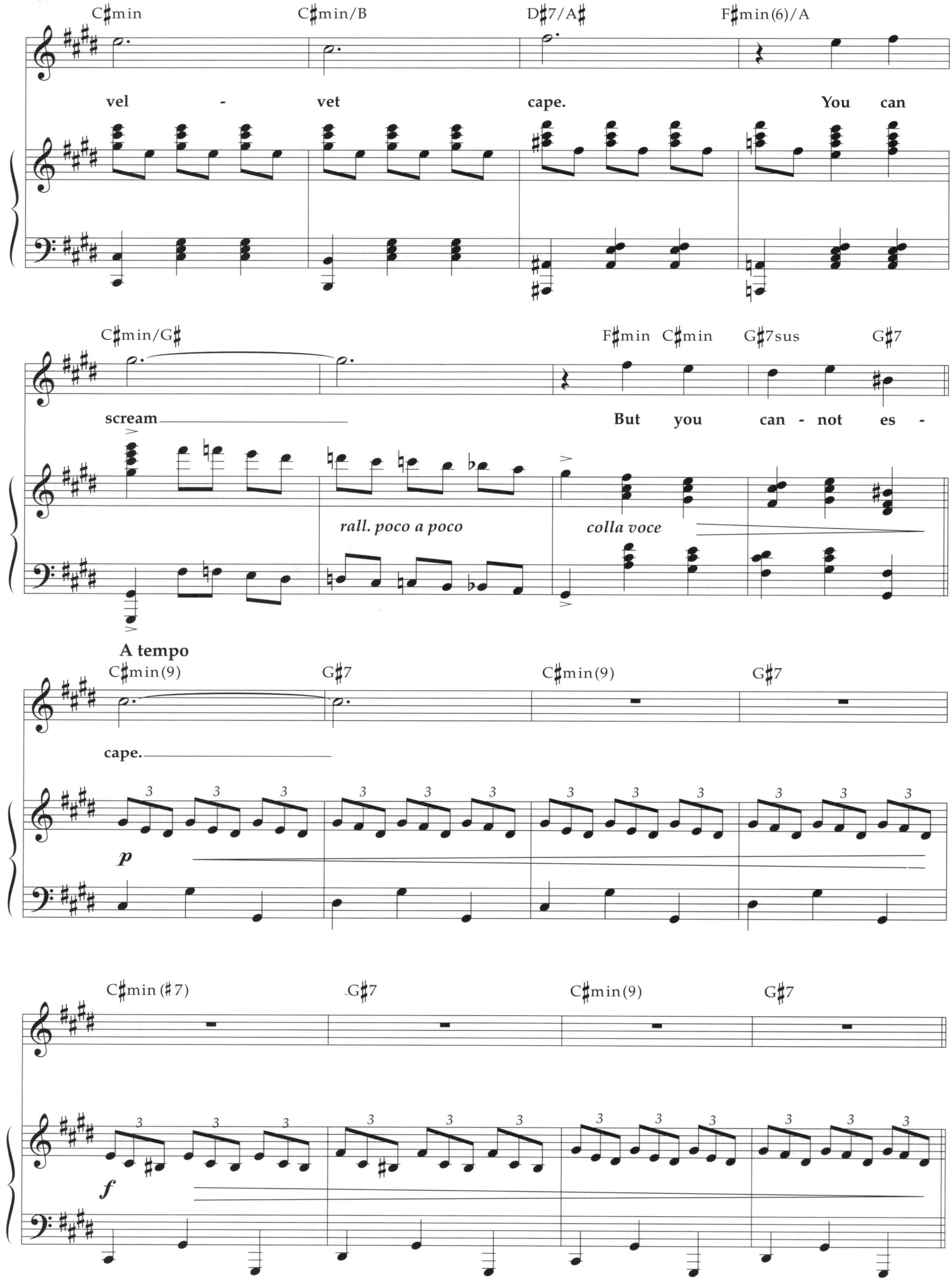
C♯min
C♯min/B
D♯7/A♯
F♯min(6)/A
vel - vet cape. You can
C♯min/G♯
F♯min C♯min G♯7sus G♯7
scream
But you can - not es -
rall. poco a poco
colla voce
A tempo
C♯min(9) G♯7 C♯min(9) G♯7
cape.
p
C♯min (♯7) G♯7 C♯min(9) G♯7
f

C♯min G♯7 C♯min G♯7
Soon - er or lat - er your love will ar - rive And he
mp stacc.
C♯min G♯7 C♯min G♯7
touch - es your heart. You're a - lert and a - live. And there's
C♯min F♯ C♯min F♯
on - ly one pin That can punc - ture such bliss: Her
G♯7sus G♯7
kiss.
poco cresc.

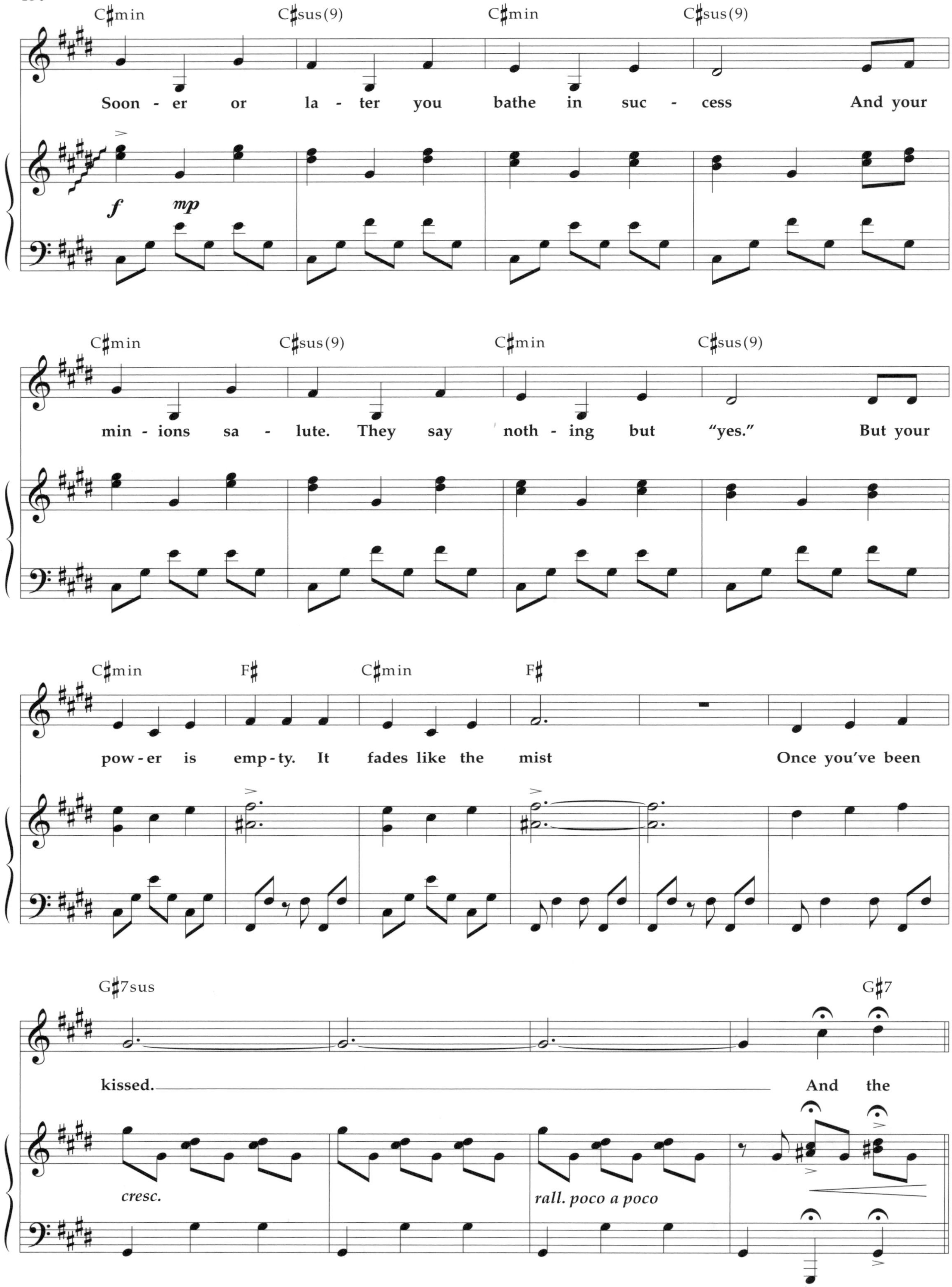
C♯min C♯sus(9) C♯min C♯sus(9)
Soon - er or la - ter you bathe in suc - cess And your
f mp
C♯min C♯sus(9) C♯min C♯sus(9)
min - ions sa - lute. They say noth - ing but "yes." But your
C♯min F♯ C♯min F♯
pow - er is emp - ty. It fades like the mist Once you've been
G♯7sus G♯7
kissed. And the
cresc.
rall. poco a poco

A tempo
C♯min
C♯min/B
D♯7/A♯
F♯min(6)/A
moon grows dim - mer___ At the
f marc.
C♯min
C♯min/B
D♯7/A♯
tide's low ebb. And your
F♯min(6)/A
G♯7
C♯min
C♯min/B
breath comes fast - er___ And you're

D♯7/A♯
F♯min(6)/A
G♯7sus
G♯7
ach - ing to move But you're caught in the web Of the
cresc. e rall.
A tempo
C♯
C♯/B
F♯(6)/A♯
F♯min(6)/A
G♯7
Spi - der - wom - an In her
ff
C♯
C♯/B
F♯/A♯
F♯min/A
vel - - vet cape. You can
rall.

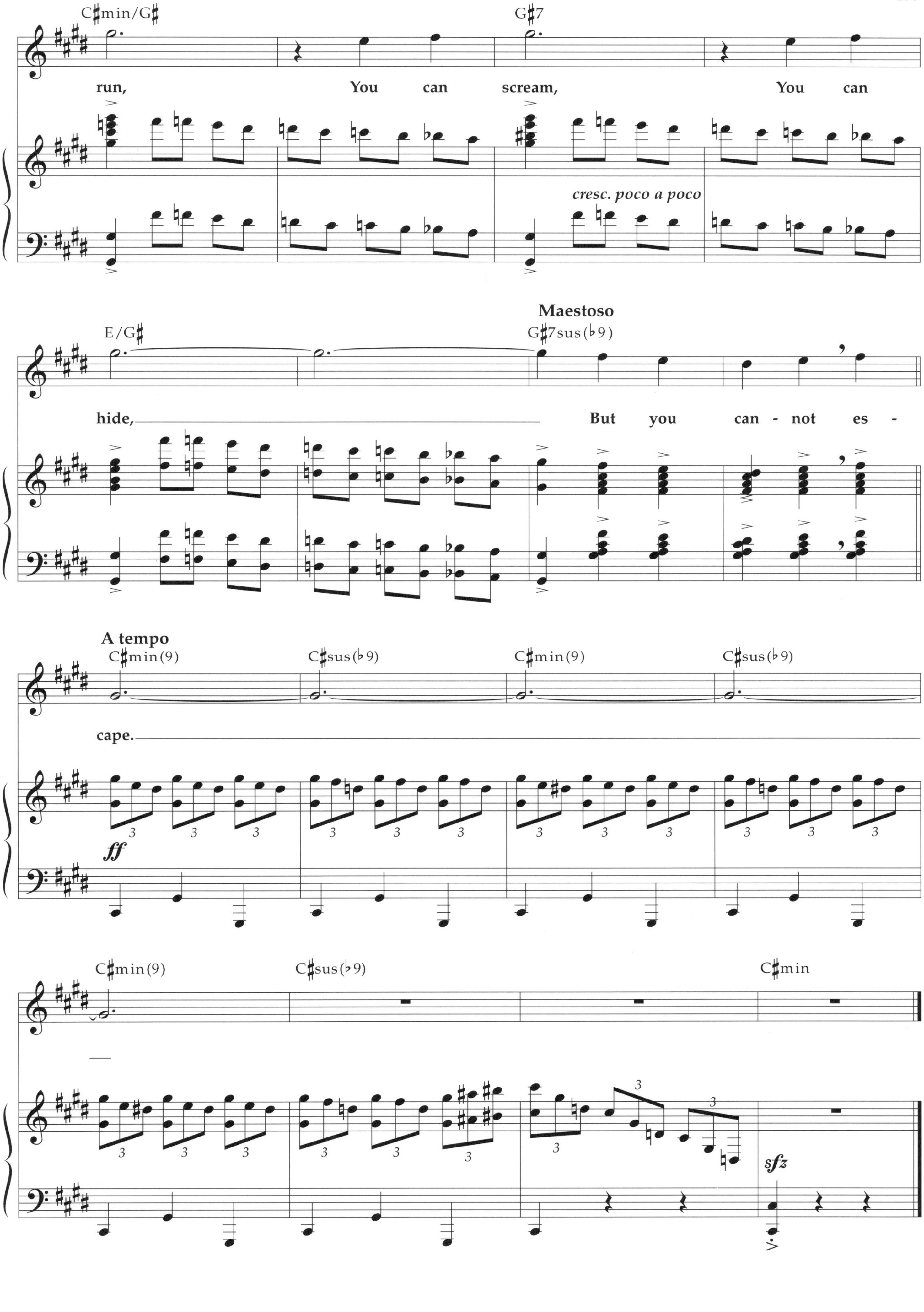
C♯min/G♯
G♯7
run, You can scream, You can
cresc. poco a poco
E/G♯
Maestoso
G♯7sus(♭9)
hide, But you can - not es -
A tempo
C♯min(9)
C♯sus(♭9)
C♯min(9)
C♯sus(♭9)
cape.
ff
C♯min(9)
C♯sus(♭9)
C♯min
sfz

# Life Is

*from the Musical* **ZORBA**

Words by
**FRED EBB**

Music by
**JOHN KANDER**

E♭(9)
Life is where you wait while you're wait-ing to leave.
Life is where you grin and
E♭9
E♭9sus
cresc.
C(9)
grieve.
mf
C
C/B
Hav-ing if you're luck-y, want-ing if you're not. Look-ing for the ru-by
mp

C/B♭
A9sus
un - der-neath the rot. Hun-gry for the pi - laf in some-one els - e's pot. But
D
B♭7
E♭(9)
that's the on - ly choice you've got!
f
E♭(9)
Life is where you stand just be -
p
3
E♭9sus
fore you are flat. Life is on - ly that. Mis - ter,

E♭9sus
Life is sim-ply that, Mis-ter, That and noth-ing more than
E♭(9)
that.
p
Life is what you feel till you can't feel at all.
mf
E♭9sus
Life is where you fly and

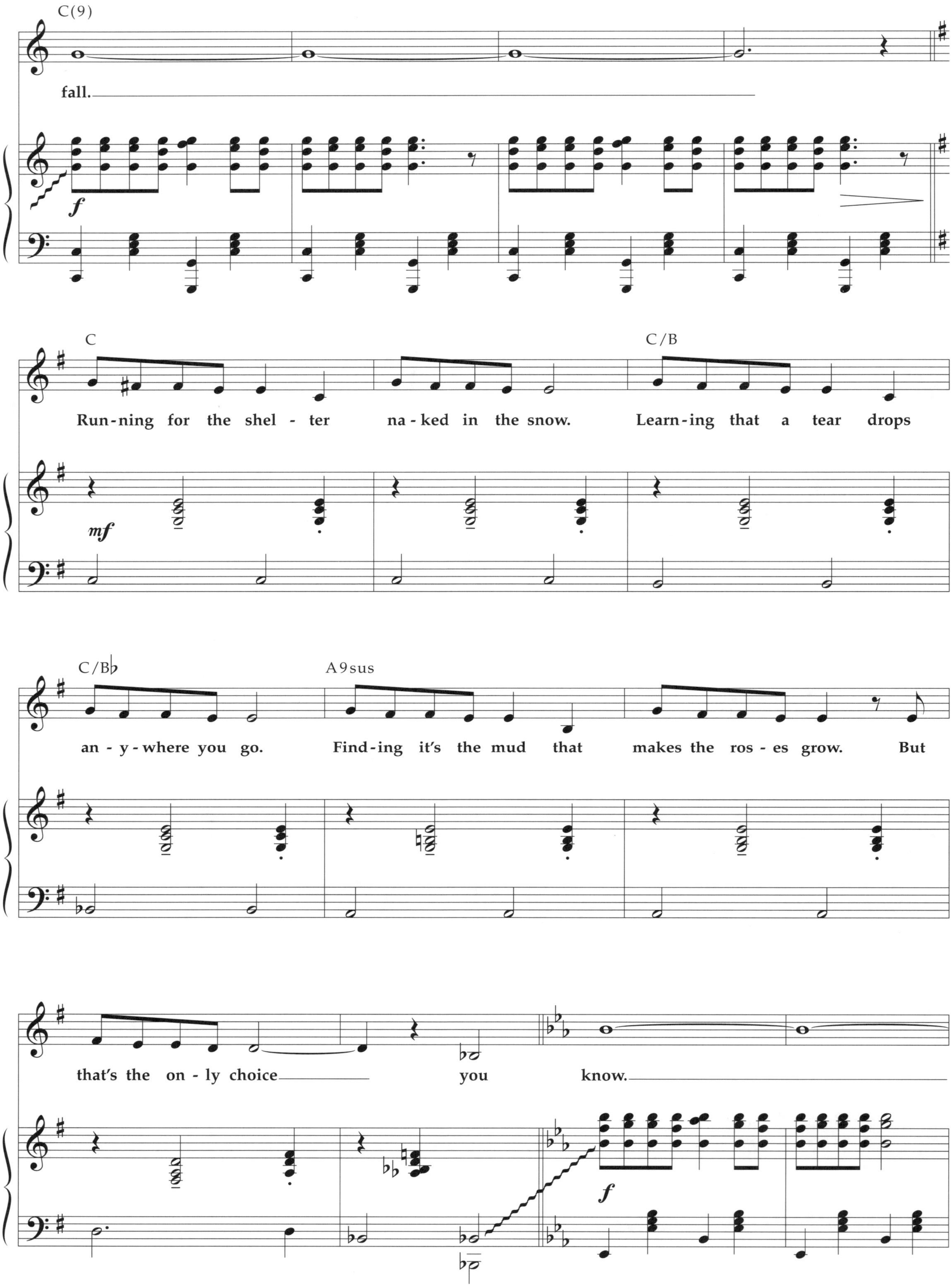
C(9)
fall.
f
C
C/B
Run-ning for the shel - ter na-ked in the snow. Learn-ing that a tear drops
mf
C/B♭
A9sus
an - y - where you go. Find-ing it's the mud that makes the ros - es grow. But
that's the on - ly choice you know.
f

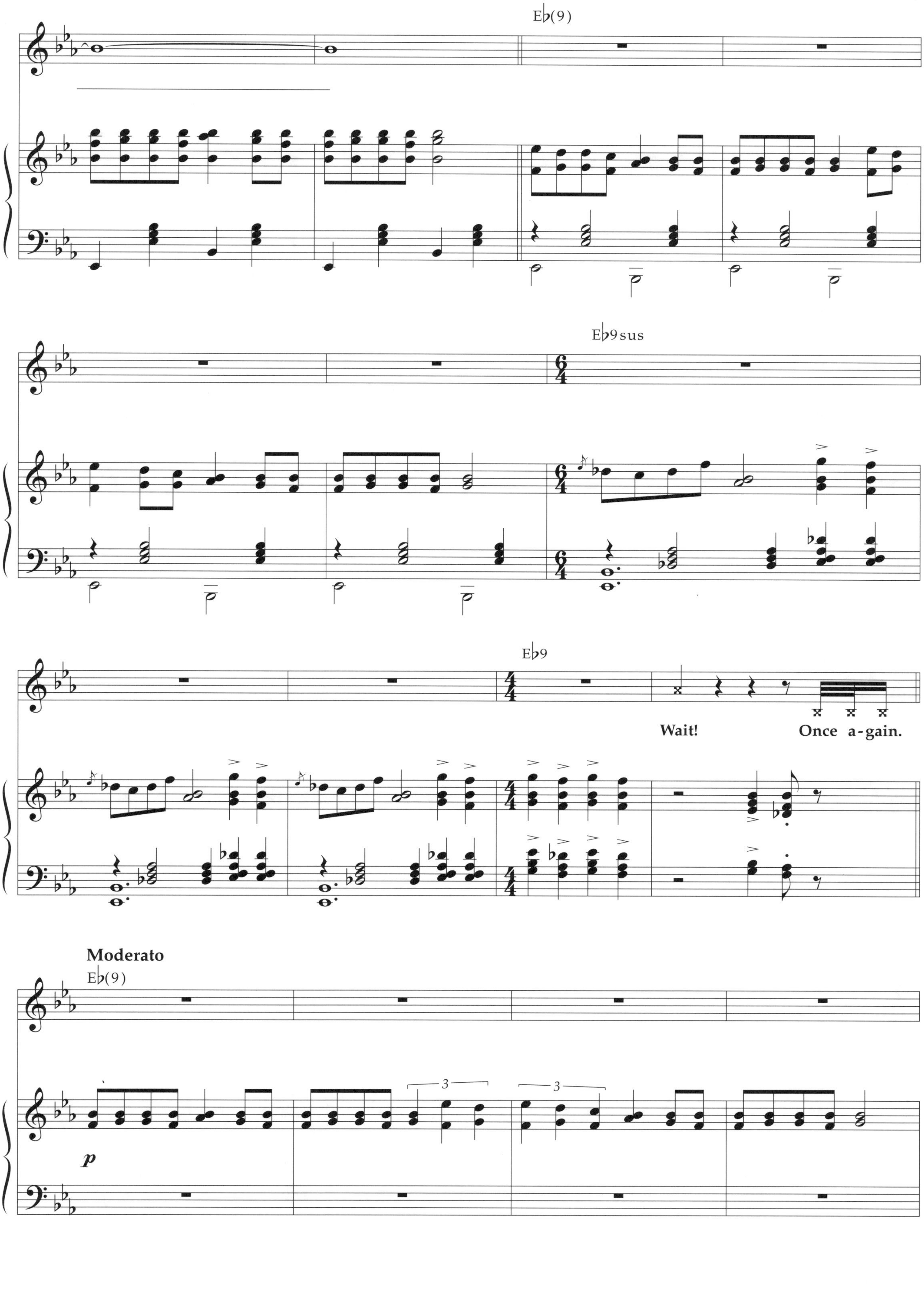
E♭(9)
E♭9sus
E♭9
Wait! Once a-gain.
Moderato
E♭(9)
p

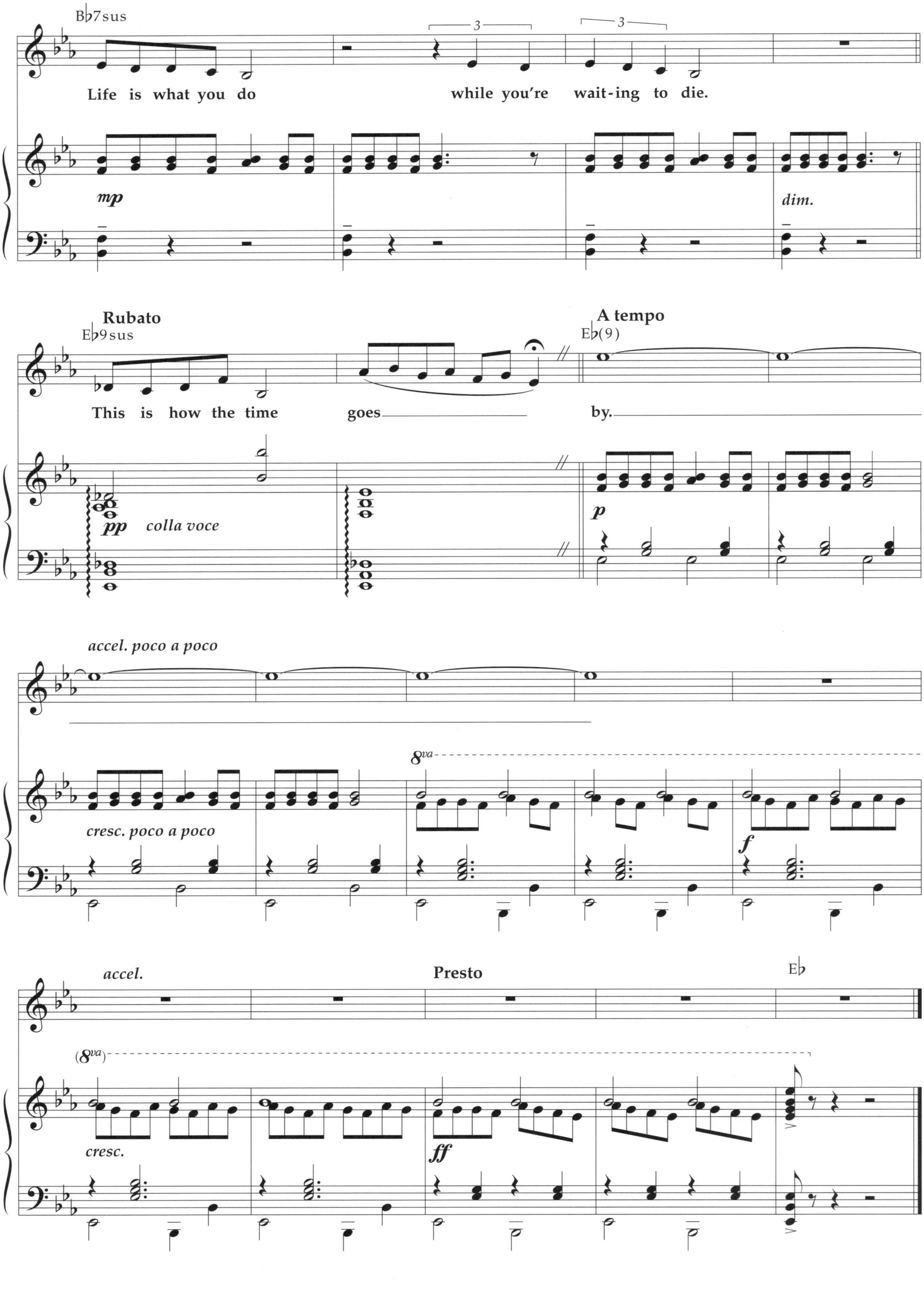

B♭7sus
3
3
Life is what you do while you're wait-ing to die.
mp
dim.
Rubato
E♭9sus
A tempo
E♭(9)
This is how the time goes by.
pp colla voce
p
accel. poco a poco
8va
cresc. poco a poco
f
accel.
Presto
E♭
(8va)
cresc.
ff

# Maybe This Time

*from the Musical* ***CABARET***

Words by
**FRED EBB**

Music by
**JOHN KANDER**

**Slowly, with a steady pulse**

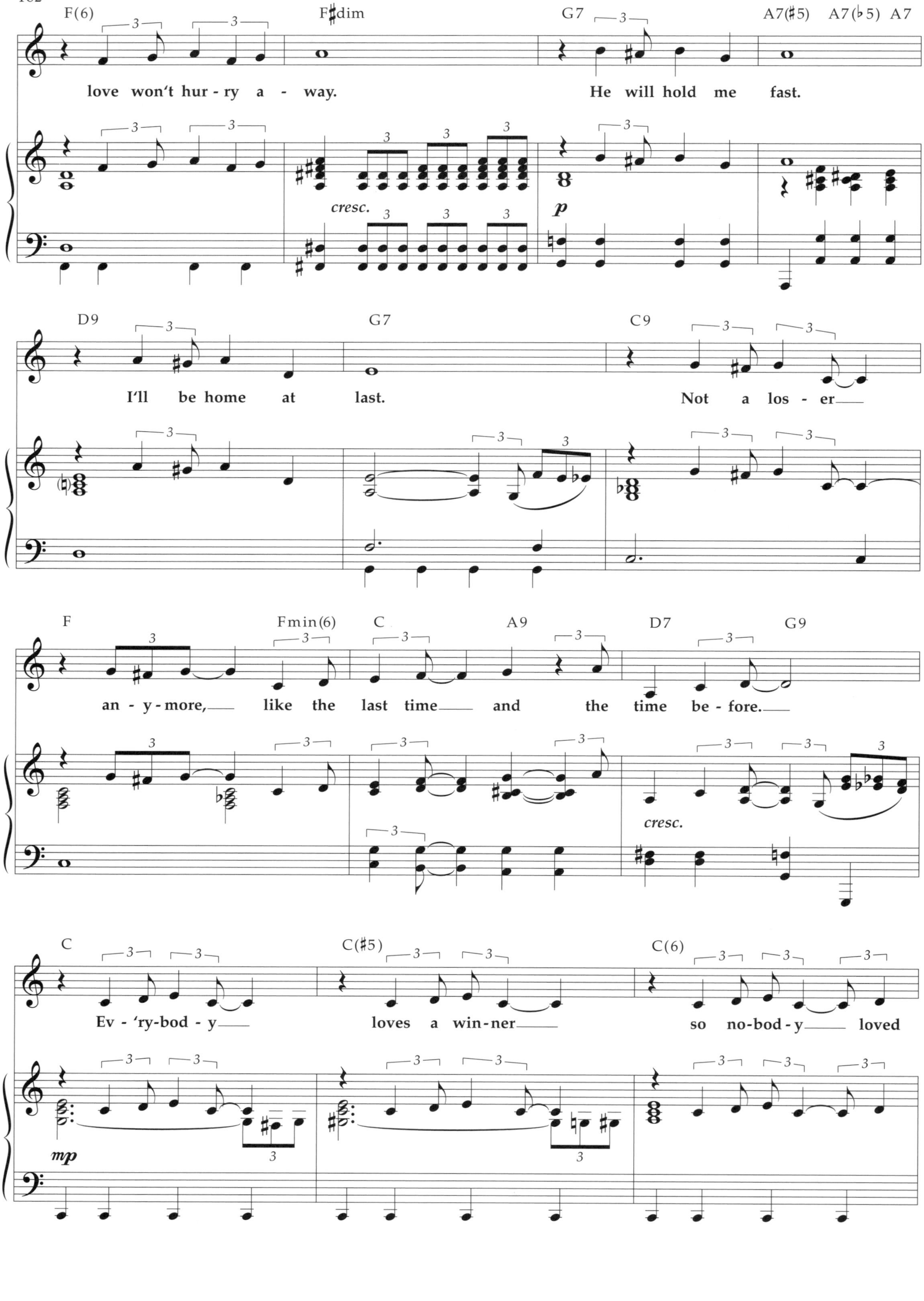
F(6)
F♯dim
G7
A7(♯5) A7(♭5) A7
love won't hur-ry a - way.
He will hold me fast.
cresc.
p
D9
G7
C9
I'll be home at last.
Not a los-er
F
Fmin(6)
C
A9
D7
G9
an - y-more, like the last time and the time be-fore.
cresc.
C
C(♯5)
C(6)
Ev - 'ry-bod - y loves a win-ner so no-bod-y loved
mp

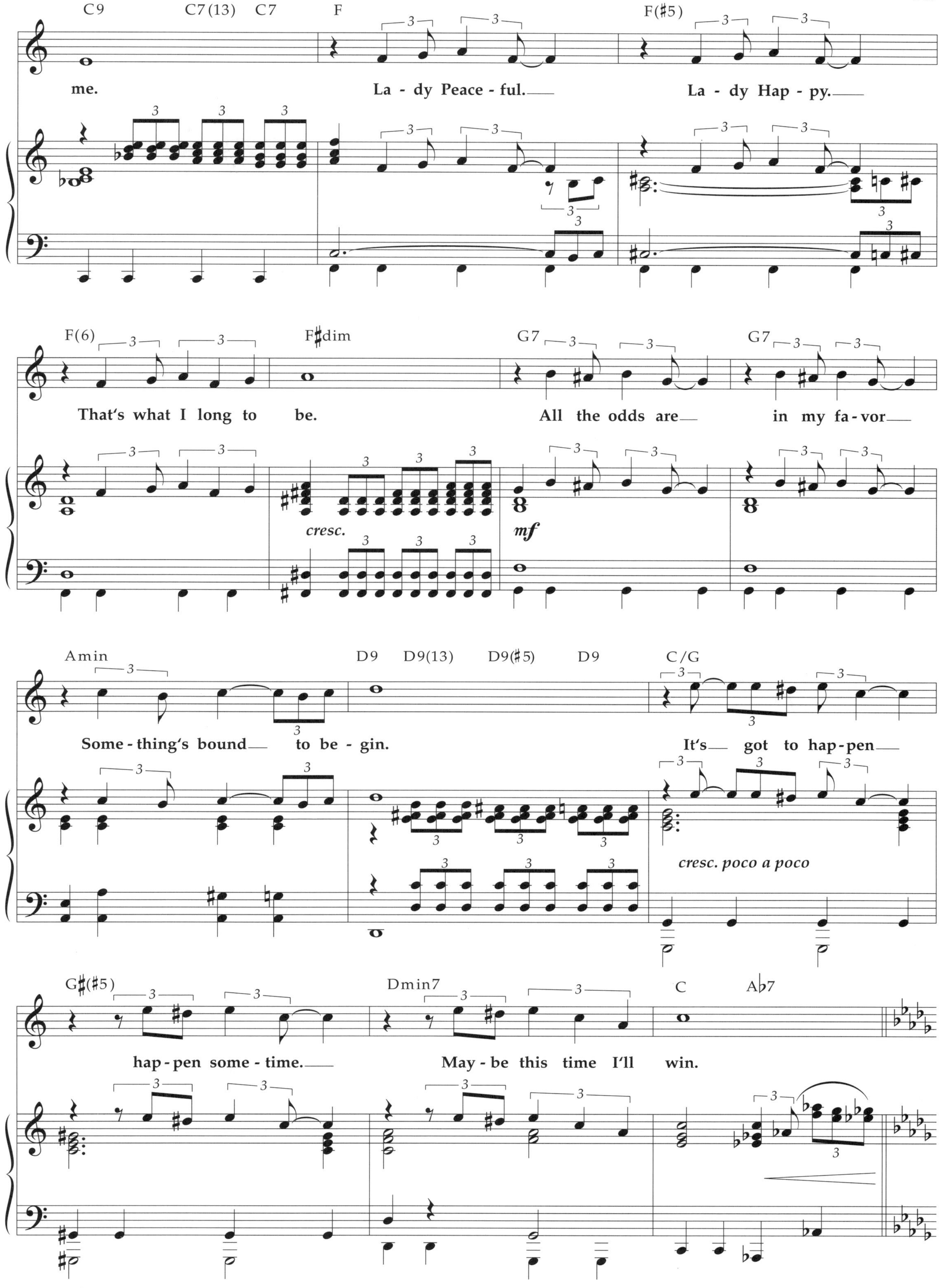

C9 C7(13) C7 F F(♯5)
me. La - dy Peace - ful. La - dy Hap - py.
F(6) F♯dim G7 G7
That's what I long to be. All the odds are in my fa - vor
cresc.
mf
Amin D9 D9(13) D9(♯5) D9 C/G
Some - thing's bound to be - gin. It's got to hap - pen
cresc. poco a poco
G♯(♯5) Dmin7 C A♭7
hap - pen some - time. May - be this time I'll win.

Steadily building
D♭
D♭(♯5)
D♭(6)
Ev - 'ry-bod - y loves a win-ner so no-bod - y loved
f
D♭9
D♭7
D♭7(♯5)
G♭
G♭(♯5)
me. La - dy Peace - ful. La - dy Hap - py.
G♭(6)
Gdim
A♭7
That's what I long to be. All the odds are

A♭7
B♭min
B♭min(♯7)
B♭min7
E♭9(13)
E♭9(♯5)
E♭9
in my fa - vor
Some - thing's bound
to be - gin.
cresc.
D♭/A♭
D♭(♯5)/A♭
B♭min/A♭
It's got to hap - pen
hap - pen some - time.
May - be this time.
ff
Rubato
E♭min9
E♭min9/A♭
Dictated
D♭
A/D♭
D♭(6)
May - be this time I'll
win.

# Love and Love Alone

*from the Musical* ***THE VISIT***

Words by
**FRED EBB**

Music by
**JOHN KANDER**

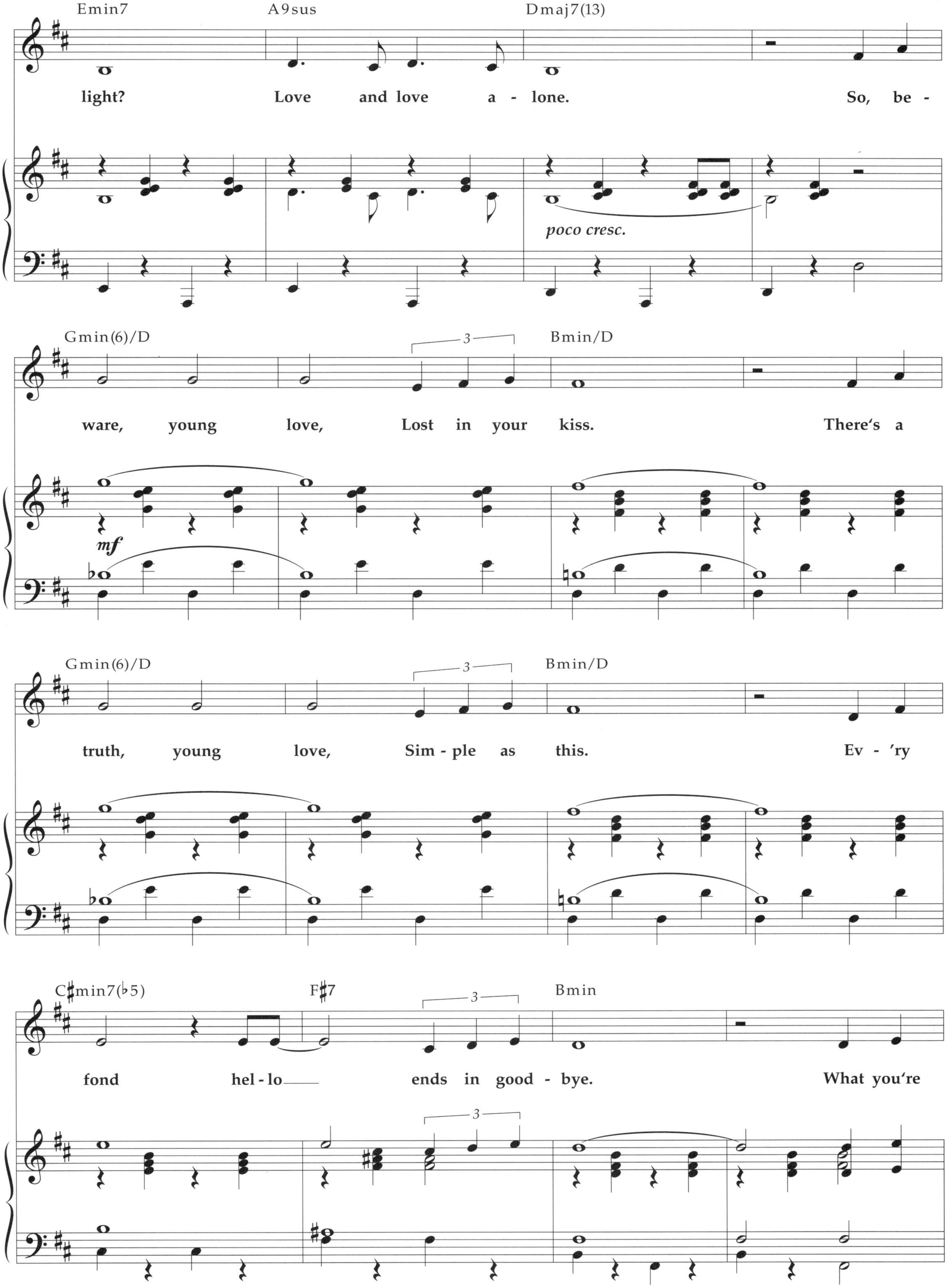

Emin7
A9sus
Dmaj7(13)
light? Love and love a - lone. So, be -
poco cresc.
Gmin(6)/D
Bmin/D
3
ware, young love, Lost in your kiss. There's a
mf
Gmin(6)/D
Bmin/D
3
truth, young love, Sim - ple as this. Ev - 'ry
C♯min7(♭5)
F♯7
Bmin
3
fond hel - lo ends in good - bye. What you're

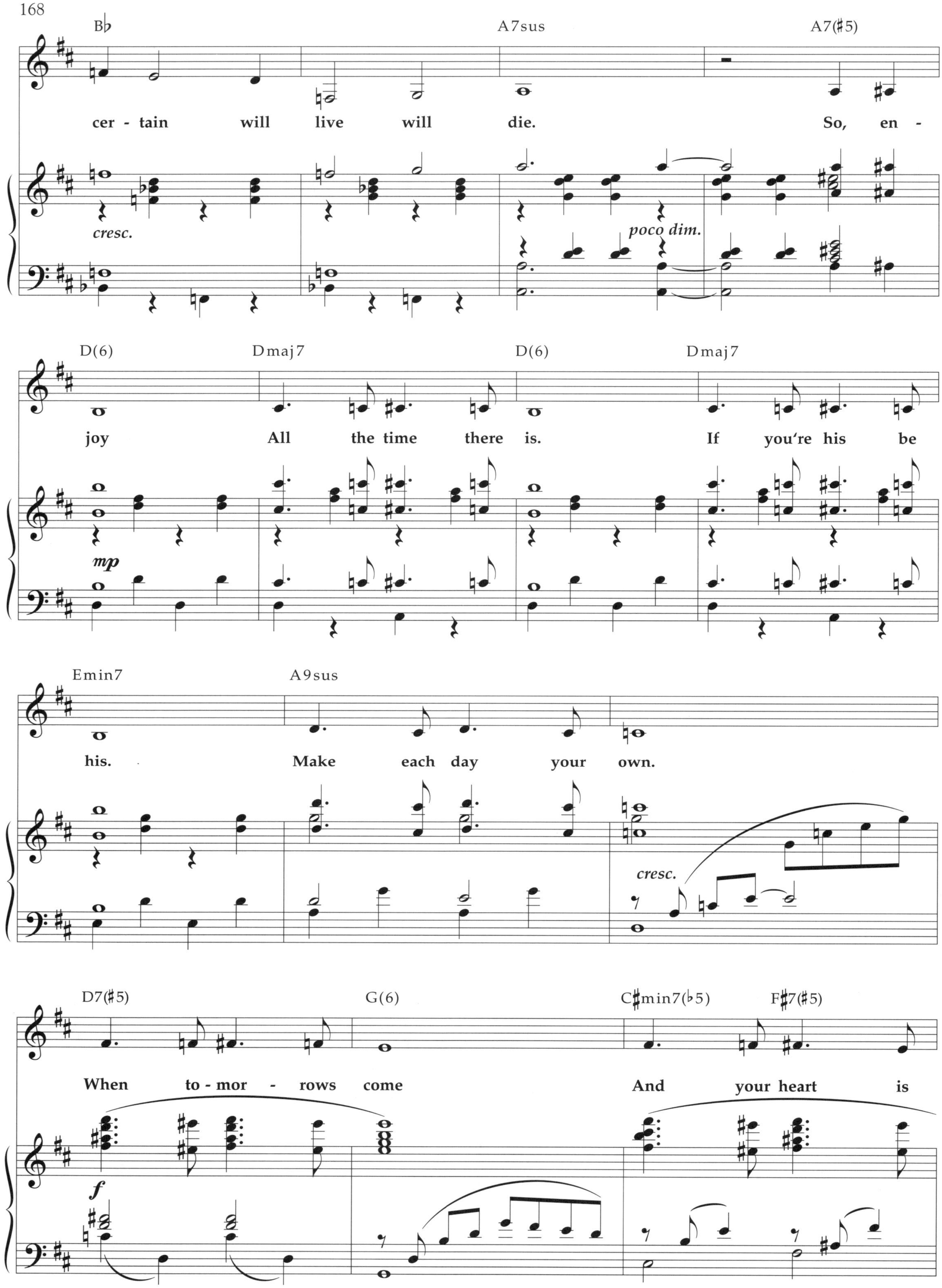
B♭
A7sus
A7(♯5)
cer - tain will live will die. So, en -
cresc.
poco dim.
D(6)
Dmaj7
D(6)
Dmaj7
joy All the time there is. If you're his be
mp
Emin7
A9sus
his. Make each day your own.
cresc.
D7(♯5)
G(6)
C♯min7(♭5)
F♯7(♯5)
When to - mor - rows come And your heart is
f

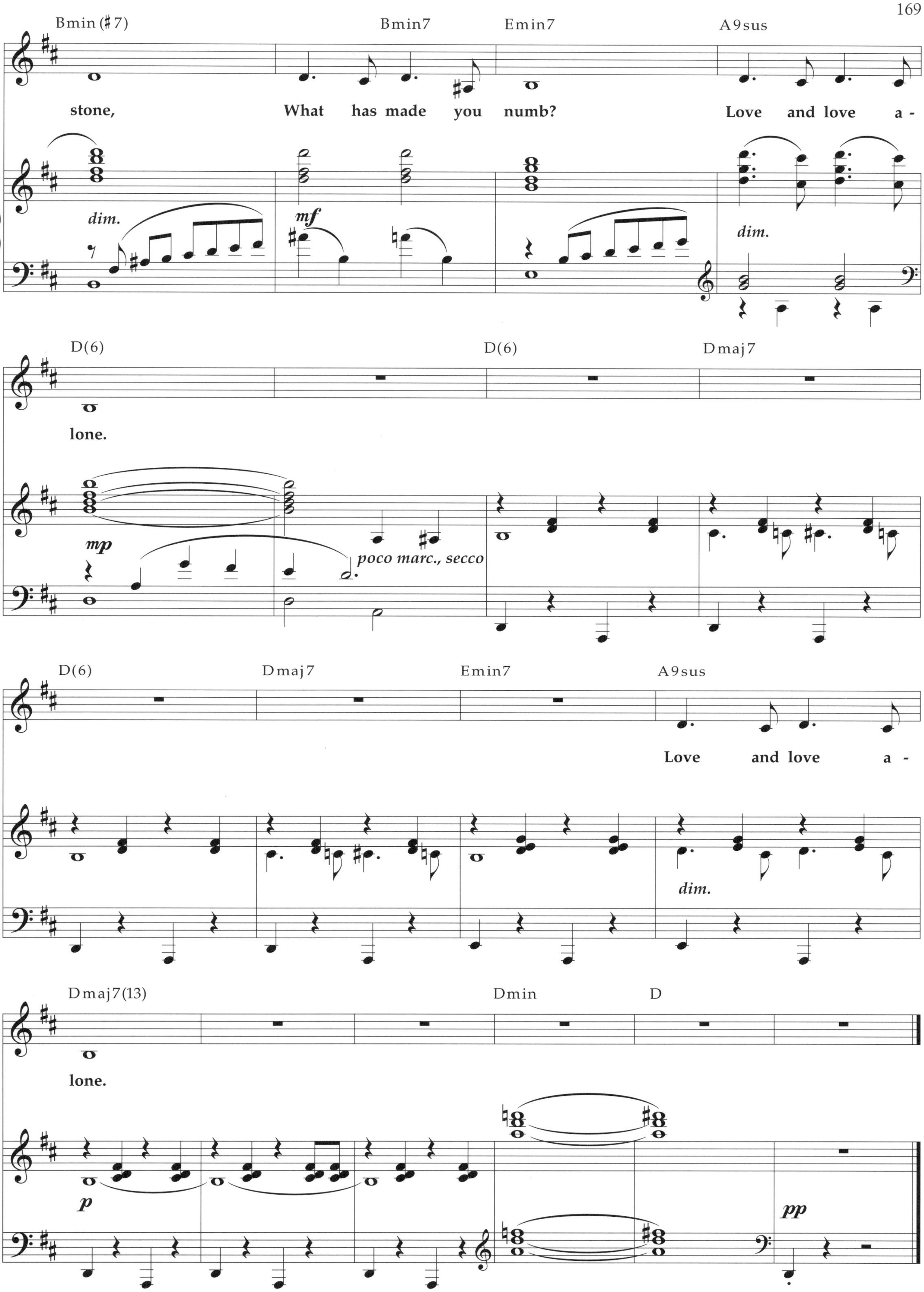
Bmin(♯7)
Bmin7
Emin7
A9sus
stone, What has made you numb? Love and love a -
dim.
mf
dim.
D(6)
D(6)
Dmaj7
lone.
mp
poco marc., secco
D(6)
Dmaj7
Emin7
A9sus
Love and love a -
dim.
Dmaj7(13)
Dmin
D
lone.
p
pp

# Mein Herr

*from the Musical* ***CABARET***

Words by
**FRED EBB**

Music by
**JOHN KANDER**

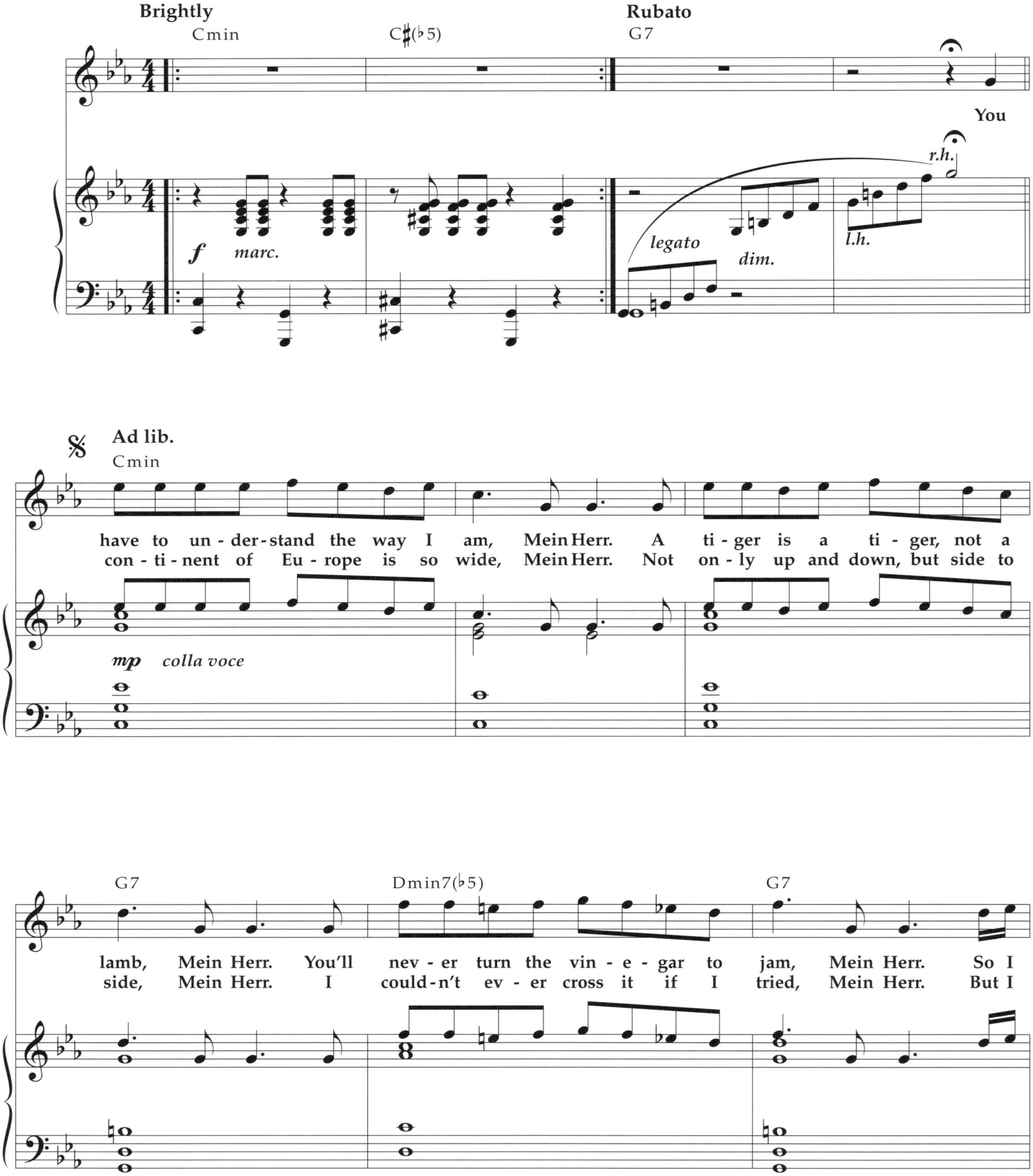
Brightly
Cmin
C♯(♭5)
Rubato
G7
You
r.h.
f marc.
legato
dim.
l.h.
Ad lib.
Cmin
have to un - der - stand the way I am, Mein Herr. A ti - ger is a ti - ger, not a
con - ti - nent of Eu - rope is so wide, Mein Herr. Not on - ly up and down, but side to
mp colla voce
G7
Dmin7(♭5)
G7
lamb, Mein Herr. You'll nev - er turn the vin - e - gar to jam, Mein Herr. So I
side, Mein Herr. I could - n't ev - er cross it if I tried, Mein Herr. But I

G7sus(♭9)
do what I do. When I'm through then I'm through and I'm
do what I can, inch by inch, step by step. mile by
through. Too - dle oo!
mile, man by man.
Bye bye mein
f
p
Slowly at first, then gradually faster
Cmin
1. & 3. lie - ber Herr, Fare - well mein lie - ber Herr. It was a
2. & 4. eye, Mein Herr, or won - der why, Mein Herr. I've al - ways
p – mp – mf marc.
G7
fine af - fair but now it's o - ver. And though I
said that I was a rov - er. You must - n't

G7
used to care, I need the o - pen air
knit your brow. You should have known by now
(accel.)
You're bet - ter off with - out me, Mein
You'd ev - 'ry cause to doubt me, Mein
To Coda
(Last time)
1.,3.
Cmin
Herr. Don't dab your
Herr. Bye bye Mein
r.h.
2.
Cmin
D.S. al Coda
Herr. The
r.h.

Coda
Still faster
Cmin
C
Herr. Bye bye mein lie - ber Herr. Auf wei - der -
lie - ber Herr. Fare - well, mein
ff
G7sus/D
sehen, Mein Herr. Es war sehr gut Mein Herr, und vor - bei.
lie - ber Herr. It was a fine af - fair, but now it's o - ver
8va
G7
Du kennst mich wohl, Mein Herr. Ach, le - be wohl, Mein Herr. Du sollst mich
And though I used to care, I need the o - pen air. You're bet - ter
1.
C
nie mehr se - hen, Mein Herr Bye, bye mein

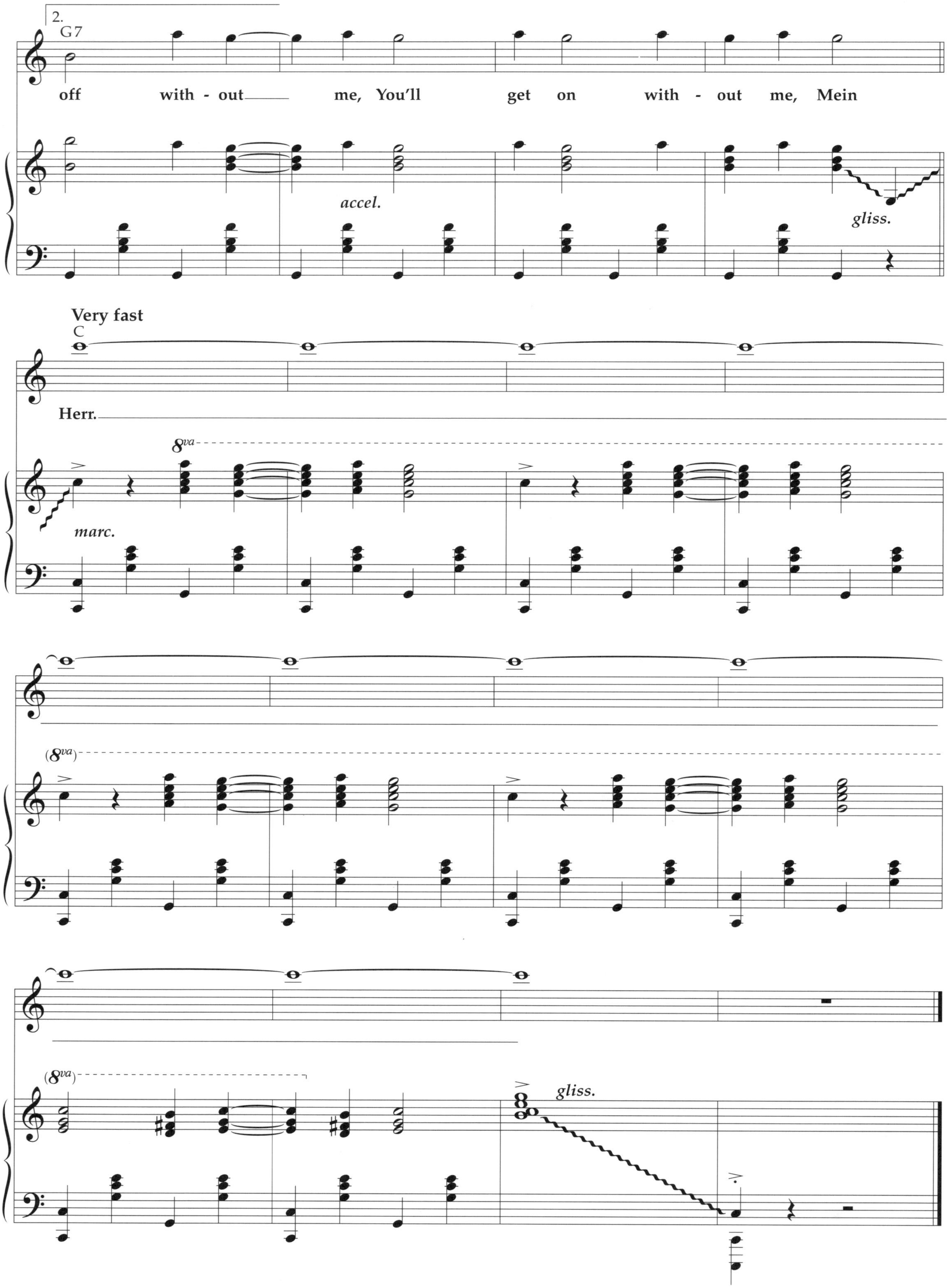
2.
G7
off with - out me, You'll get on with - out me, Mein
accel.
gliss.
Very fast
C
Herr.
8va
marc.
(8va)
(8va)
gliss.

# Money, Money

*from the Musical* **CABARET**

Words by
**FRED EBB**

Music by
**JOHN KANDER**

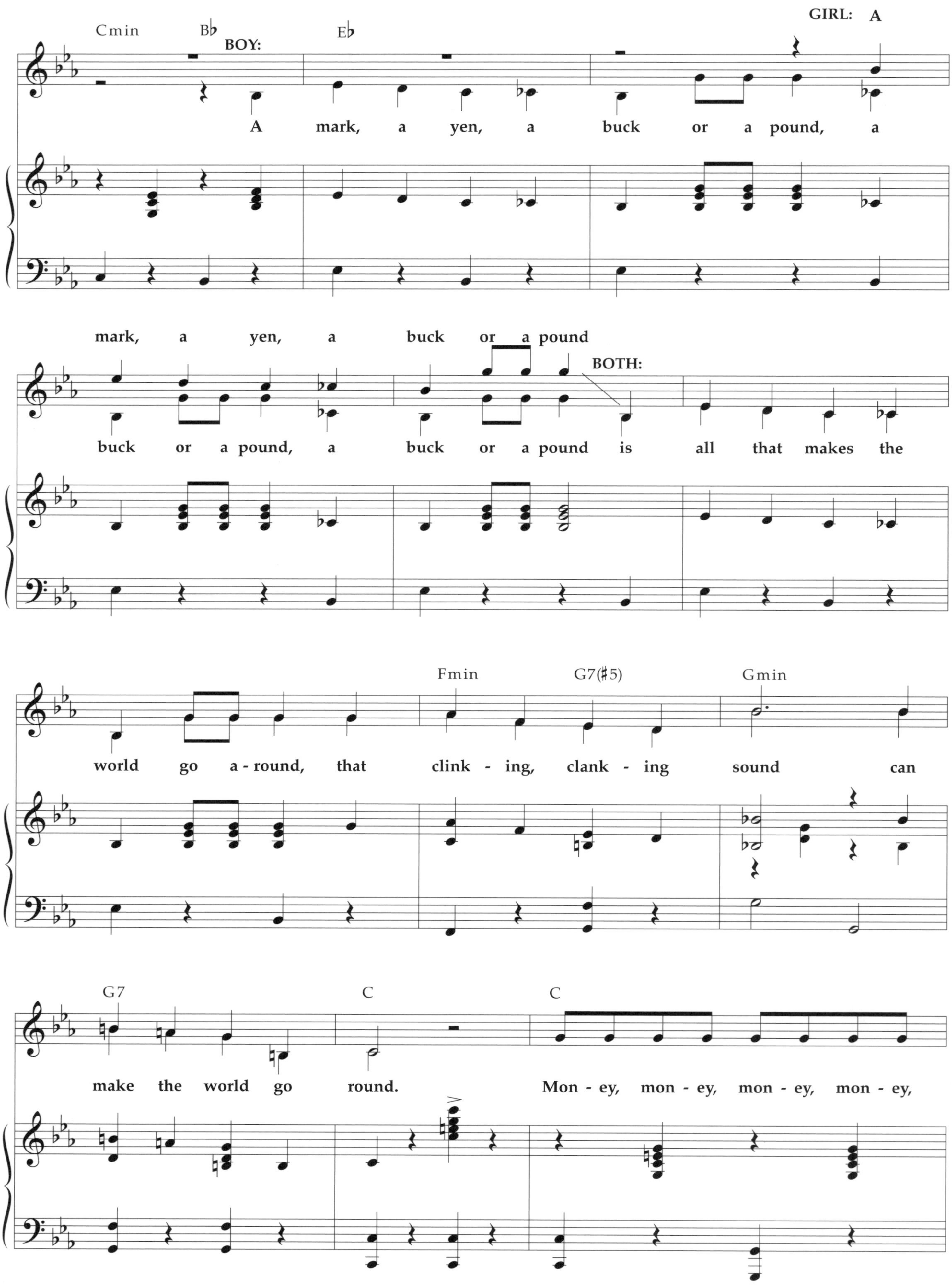
Cmin
B♭
E♭
BOY:
GIRL: A
A mark, a yen, a buck or a pound, a
mark, a yen, a buck or a pound
BOTH:
buck or a pound, a buck or a pound is all that makes the
Fmin
G7(♯5)
Gmin
world go a-round, that clink-ing, clank-ing sound can
G7
C
C
make the world go round. Mon-ey, mon-ey, mon-ey, mon-ey,

GIRL: Mon-ey, mon-ey, mon-ey, mon-ey,
Cmin
mon-ey, mon-ey, mon-ey, mon-ey, mon-ey, mon-ey, mon-ey, mon-ey.
BOY: If you hap-pen to be
G7
mon-ey, mon-ey, mon-ey, mon-ey, mon-ey, mon-ey, mon-ey, mon-ey,
Cmin
mon-ey, mon-ey, mon-ey, mon-ey,
rich, and you feel like a night's en-ter-tain-ment, you can pay for a gay es-ca-
mon-ey, mon-ey, mon-ey, mon-ey,
G7
mon-ey, mon-ey, mon-ey, mon-ey, mon-ey, mon-ey, mon-ey, mon-ey,
pade. If you hap-pen to be rich, and a-lone, and you need a com-pan-ion, you can

Cmin
mon-ey, mon-ey, mon-ey, mon-ey.
A7
Mon-ey, mon-ey, mon-ey, mon-ey,
ring ting-a-ling for the maid. If you hap-pen to be rich and you find you are
Dmin
mon-ey, mon-ey, mon-ey, mon-ey, mon-ey, mon-ey, mon-ey, mon-ey, mon.
left by your lov-er, tho you moan and you groan quite a lot, you can take it on the
A7
Dmin
C♯dim
chin, call a cab, and be-gin to re-cov-er on your four-teen car-at

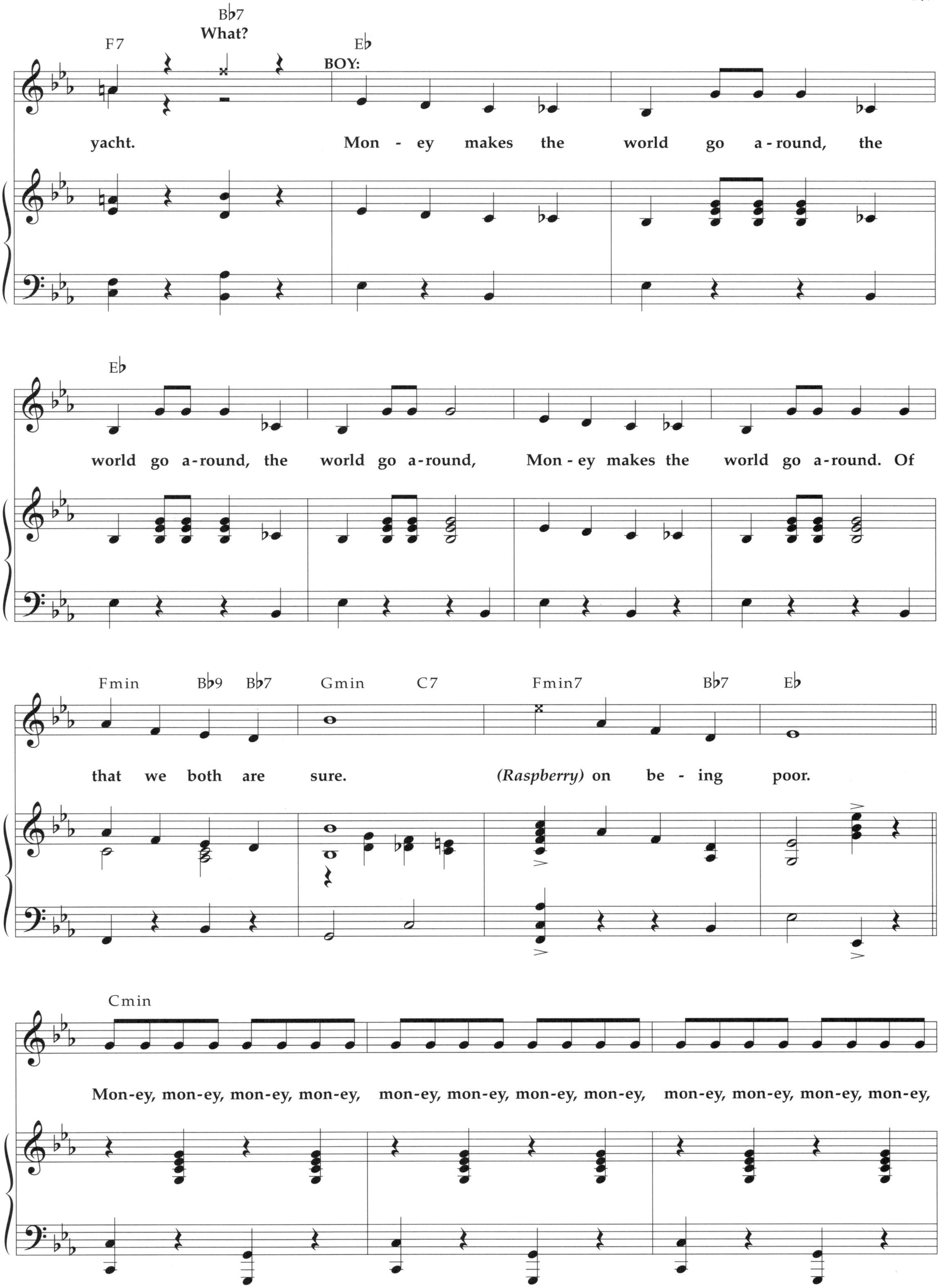

F7 B♭7 E♭
What?
BOY:
yacht. Mon - ey makes the world go a - round, the
E♭
world go a - round, the world go a - round, Mon - ey makes the world go a - round. Of
Fmin B♭9 B♭7 Gmin C7 Fmin7 B♭7 E♭
that we both are sure. (Raspberry) on be - ing poor.
Cmin
Mon-ey, mon-ey, mon-ey, mon-ey, mon-ey, mon-ey, mon-ey, mon-ey, mon-ey, mon-ey, mon-ey, mon-ey,

G7
Cmin
When you have-n't an - y coal in the stove and you
mon. When you have-n't an-y coal in the stove and you freeze in the win-ter and you
Cmin
G7
freeze in the win-ter and you curse to the wind at your fate. When you have-n't an - y
curse to the wind at your fate. When you have-n't an - y shoes on your feet and your
Cmin
shoes on your feet and your coat's thin as pa-per and you look thir - ty pounds un-der
coat's thin as pa-per and you look thir-ty pounds un-der weight. When you go to get a

A7
weight. When you go to get a word of ad-vice
Dmin
from the fat lit-tle pas-tor, he will
word of ad-vice from the fat lit-tle pas-tor, he will tell you to love ev-er-
tell you to love ev - er -
A7
more. But when hun - ger comes to
more. But when hun - ger comes to rap, rat - a - tat, rat - a -
rap, at the win - dow, see how
Dmin
A7
BOTH:
tat, at the win - dow, see how love flies out the

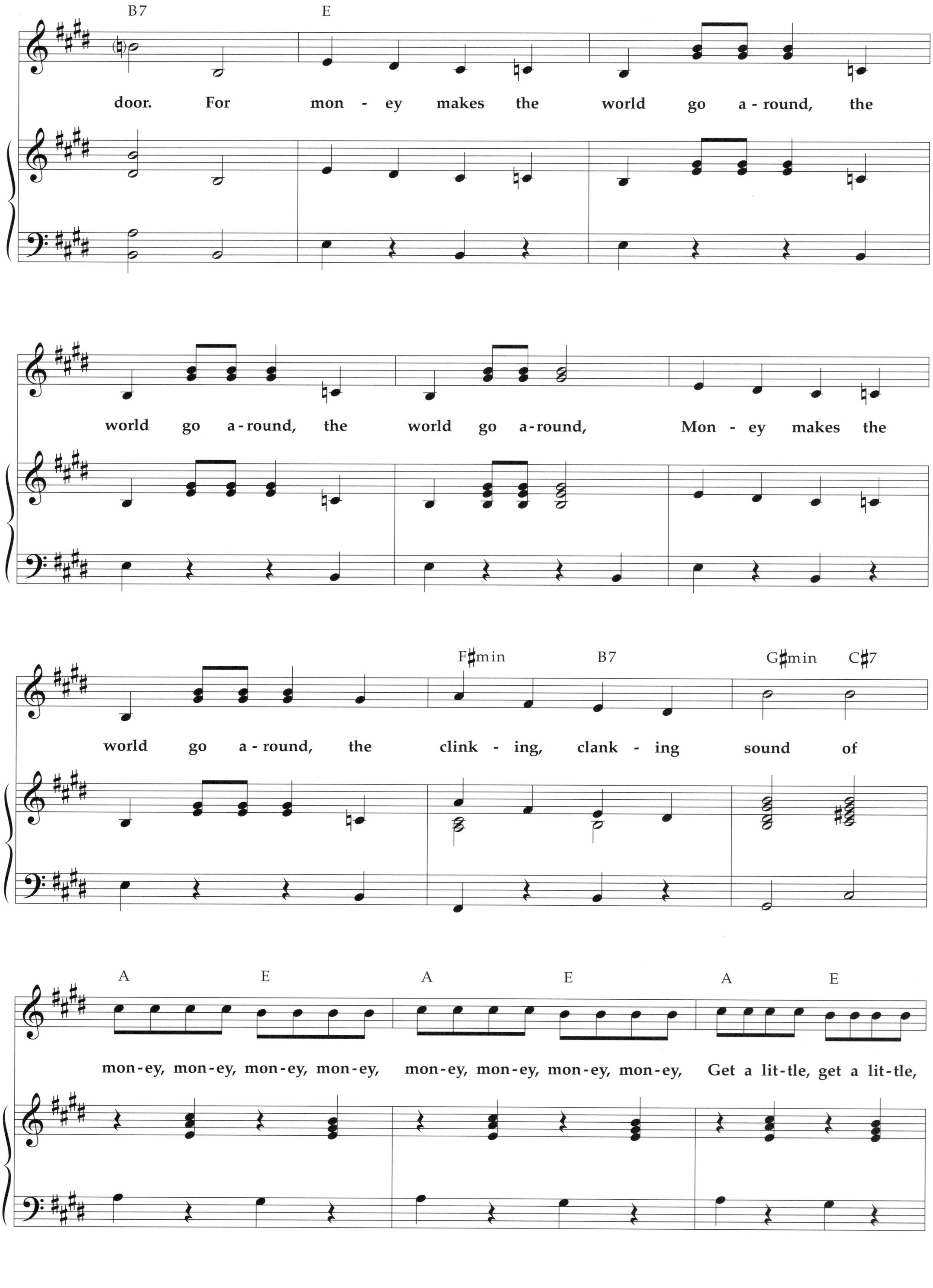
B7 E
door. For mon - ey makes the world go a - round, the
world go a - round, the world go a - round, Mon - ey makes the
F♯min B7 G♯min C♯7
world go a - round, the clink - ing, clank - ing sound of
A E A E A E
mon-ey, mon-ey, mon-ey, mon-ey, mon-ey, mon-ey, mon-ey, mon-ey, Get a lit-tle, get a lit-tle,

A E A E A E
mon - ey, mon - ey, mon - ey, mon - ey, mark, a yen, a buck or a pound, that
A E A E A E
clink - ing, clank - ing clunk - ing sound is all that makes the
A E A B7 E
world go round, It makes the world go round.

# Mister Cellophane

*from the Musical* ***CHICAGO***

Words by
**FRED EBB**

Music by
**JOHN KANDER**

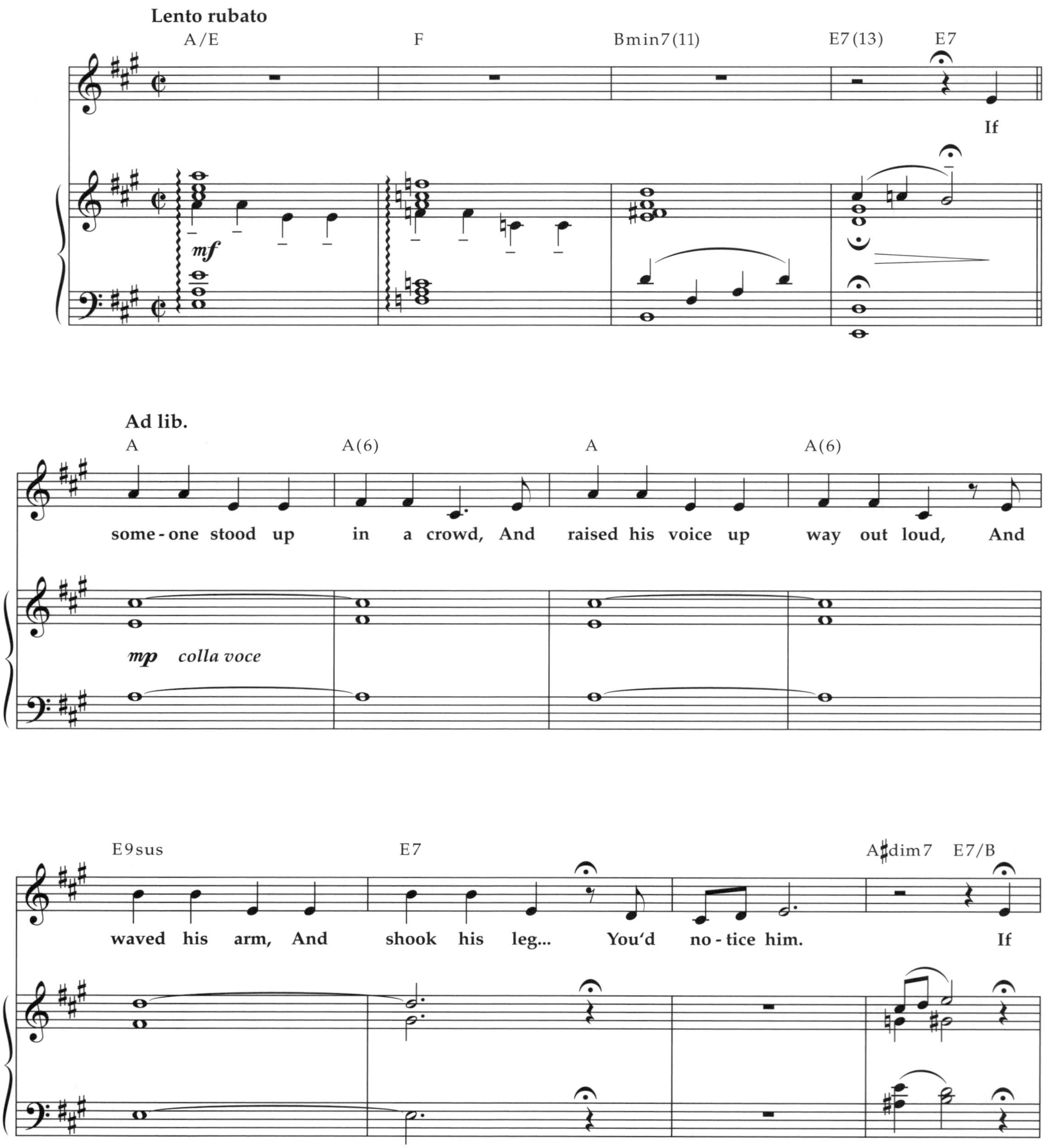

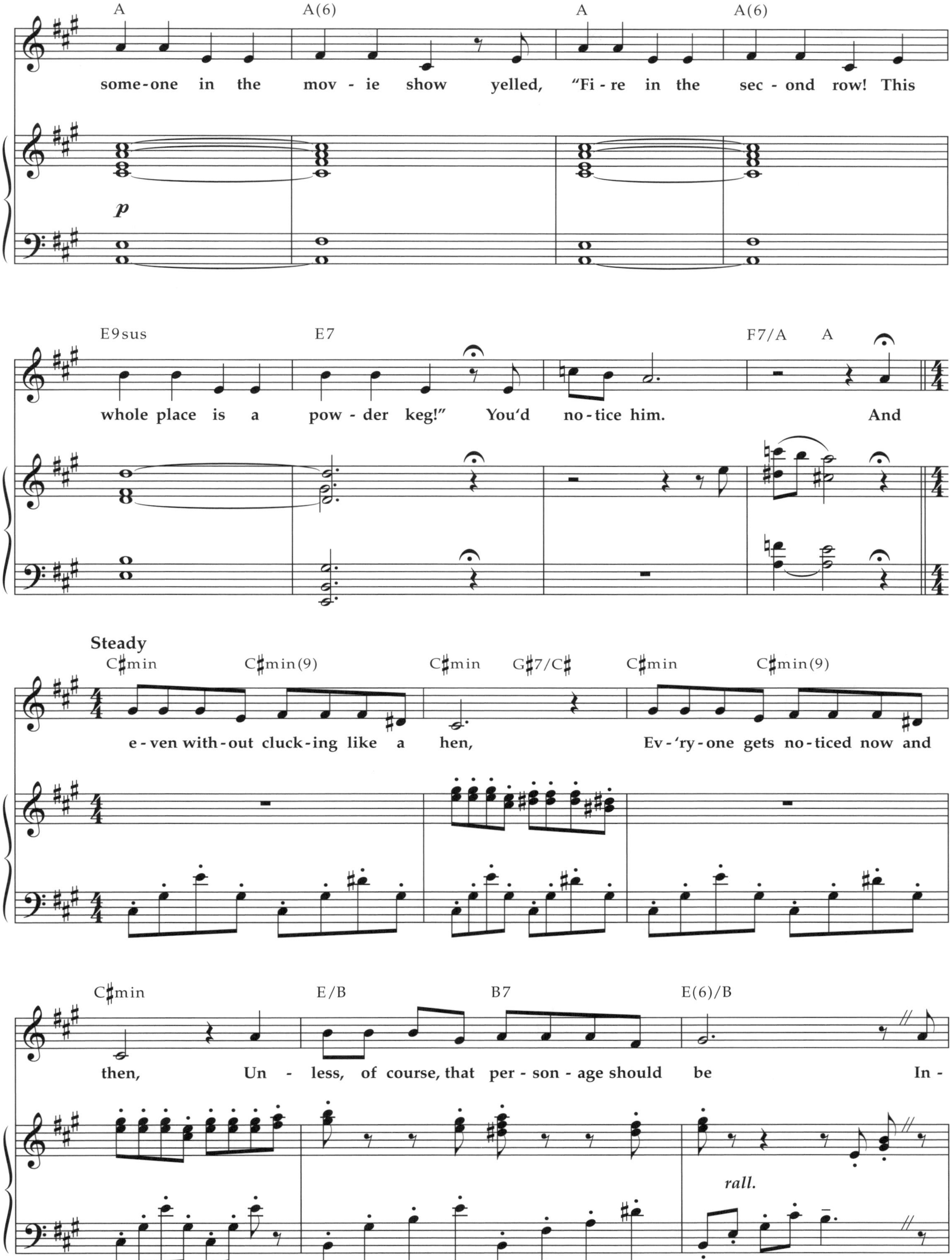
A
A(6)
A
A(6)
some-one in the mov - ie show yelled, "Fi - re in the sec - ond row! This
p
E9sus
E7
F7/A
A
whole place is a pow - der keg!" You'd no - tice him. And
Steady
C♯min
C♯min(9)
C♯min
G♯7/C♯
C♯min
C♯min(9)
e - ven with - out cluck - ing like a hen, Ev - 'ry - one gets no - ticed now and
C♯min
E/B
B7
E(6)/B
then, Un - less, of course, that per - son - age should be In -
rall.

B7/F#
E9sus
E7
vis - i - ble, in - con - se - quen - tial me.
Slow Rag (in 4)
E9
A(6)
Cel - lo - phane, Mis - ter Cel - lo - phane. Should have been my name, Mis - ter
mf
E9
Cel - lo - phane, 'Cause you can look right through me,
F7
E7
A
Walk right by me And nev - er know I'm there. I tell ya,

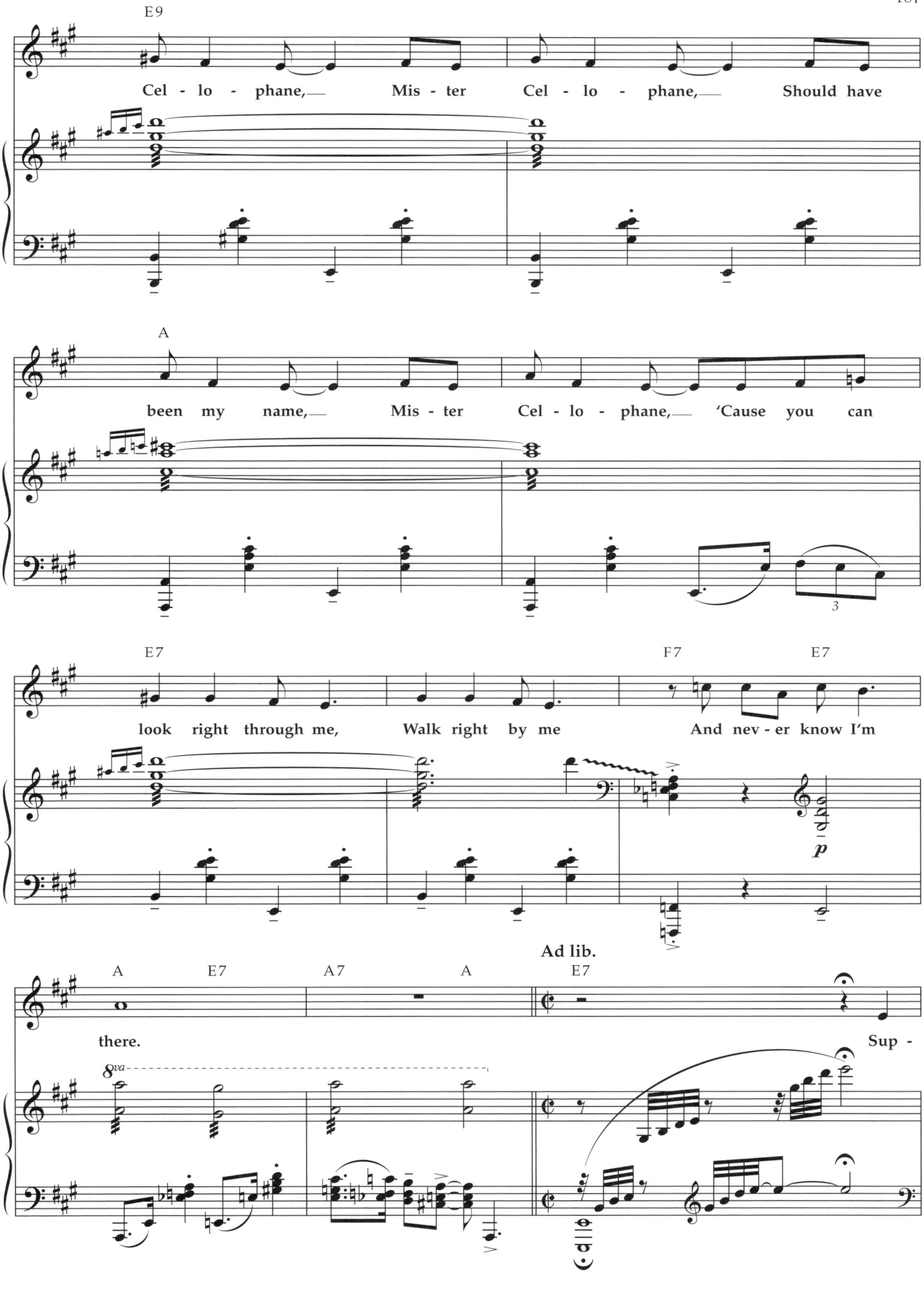
E9
Cel - lo - phane, Mis - ter Cel - lo - phane, Should have
A
been my name, Mis - ter Cel - lo - phane, 'Cause you can
3
E7 F7 E7
look right through me, Walk right by me And nev - er know I'm
p
Ad lib.
A E7 A7 A E7
there. Sup -
8va

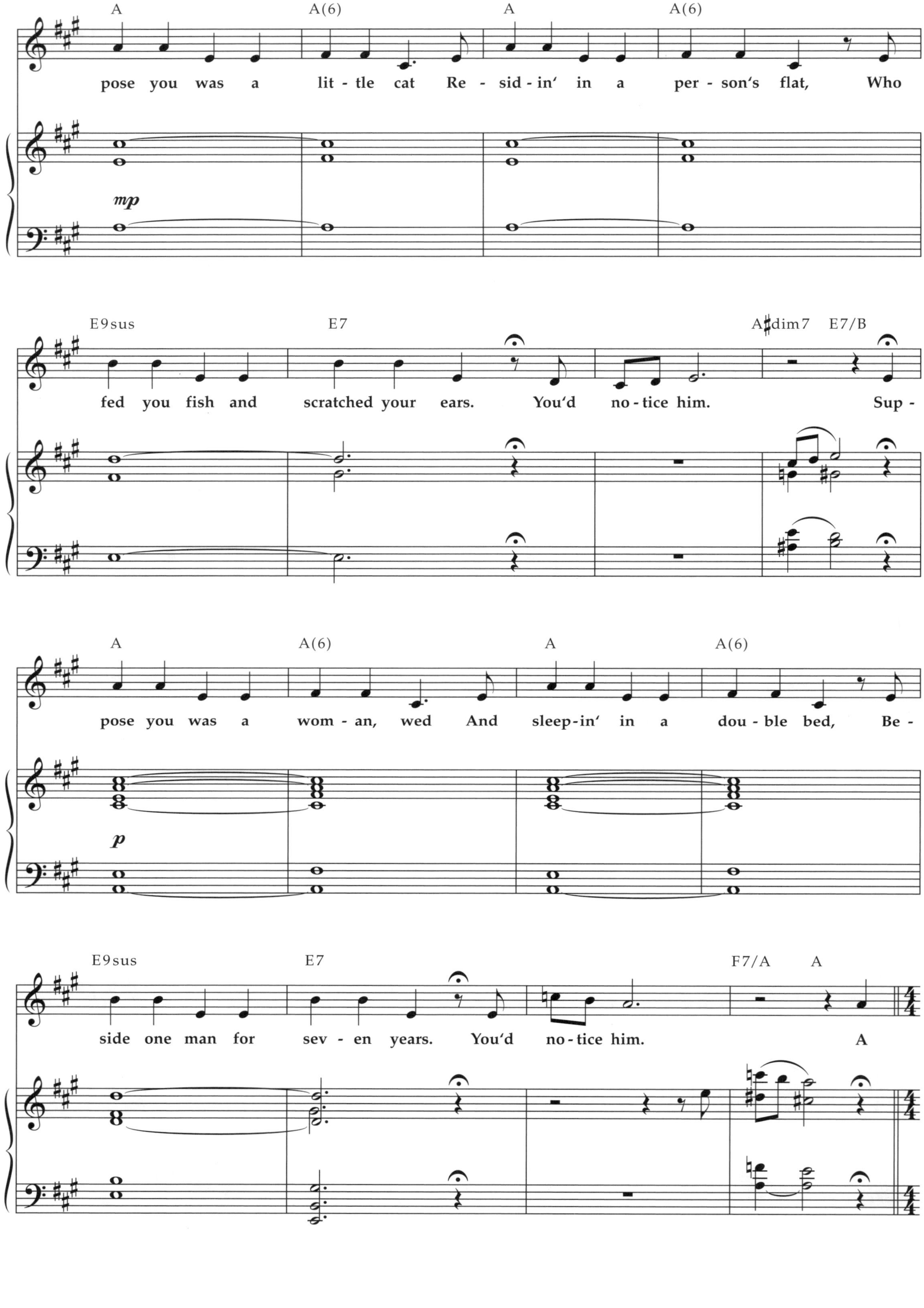
A A(6) A A(6)
pose you was a lit - tle cat Re - sid - in' in a per - son's flat, Who
mp
E9sus E7 A♯dim7 E7/B
fed you fish and scratched your ears. You'd no - tice him. Sup -
A A(6) A A(6)
pose you was a wom - an, wed And sleep - in' in a dou - ble bed, Be -
p
E9sus E7 F7/A A
side one man for sev - en years. You'd no - tice him.
A

Steady
C♯min
C♯min(9)
G♯7/C♯
hu - man be - ing's made of more than air. With
all that bulk, you're bound to see him there. Un - less that hu-man be-ing next to
E/B
B7
B7/E
you Is un - im - pres - sive, un - dis - tin - guished
rit.
E7
F♯dim/E
you know who.

Slow, smoothly
F7
B♭(6)
Should have been my name, Mis - ter
8va
mp cresc. poco a poco
mf
F7
Cel - lo - phane, 'Cause you can look right through me, Walk right by me
(8va)
f
G♭7
F7
B♭
And nev - er know I'm there. I tell ya
(8va)
F♯7
Cel - lo - phane, Mis - ter Cel - lo - phane, Should have
ff

B(6)
been my name, Mis - ter Cel - lo - phane, 'Cause you can
F♯7
G7
F♯7
look right through me, Walk right by me And nev - er know I'm
G♯min
C♯7
B/F♯
F♯7sus
F♯7
there. Nev - er e - ven know I'm
sfz
Molto rubato
Bmin
G7
B(6)
there.
p
dim.
pp

# My Coloring Book

Words by
**FRED EBB**

Music by
**JOHN KANDER**

E♭
most un - u - su - al col - or - ing book, The kind you nev - er
a tempo
D♭9
B7
B♭9
see, Cray-ons read - y? Ver - y well, be - gin to col - or
8va
rall.
Gentle Waltz
E♭
B♭9sus
E♭maj7
me.
poco rall.
cresc.
A tempo
E♭
B♭9sus
E♭(9)
B♭7sus
These are the eyes that watched him as he walked a -
p sempre legato

E♭maj7
E♭7
Fmin7
B♭7
way.
Col - or them
E♭
B♭9sus
E♭maj7
B♭9sus
grey.
cresc. e poco rall.
E♭maj7
B♭9sus
E♭(9)
B♭7sus
This is the heart that thought he would al - ways be
a tempo
mp
E♭maj7
E♭7
Fmin7
B♭7sus
true.
Col - or it

E♭
B♭9sus
E♭7
E♭9sus
E♭
blue. These are the
poco rit.
With a little motion
A♭
A♭(♯5)
A♭(6)
A♭(♯5)
arms that held him and touched him, Then lost him some -
A♭
A♭maj7
A♭(6)
A♭
how. Col - or them
mf
colla voce
poco rall.
Poco rubato
Gmin7
C9(13)
emp - ty now.
dim.

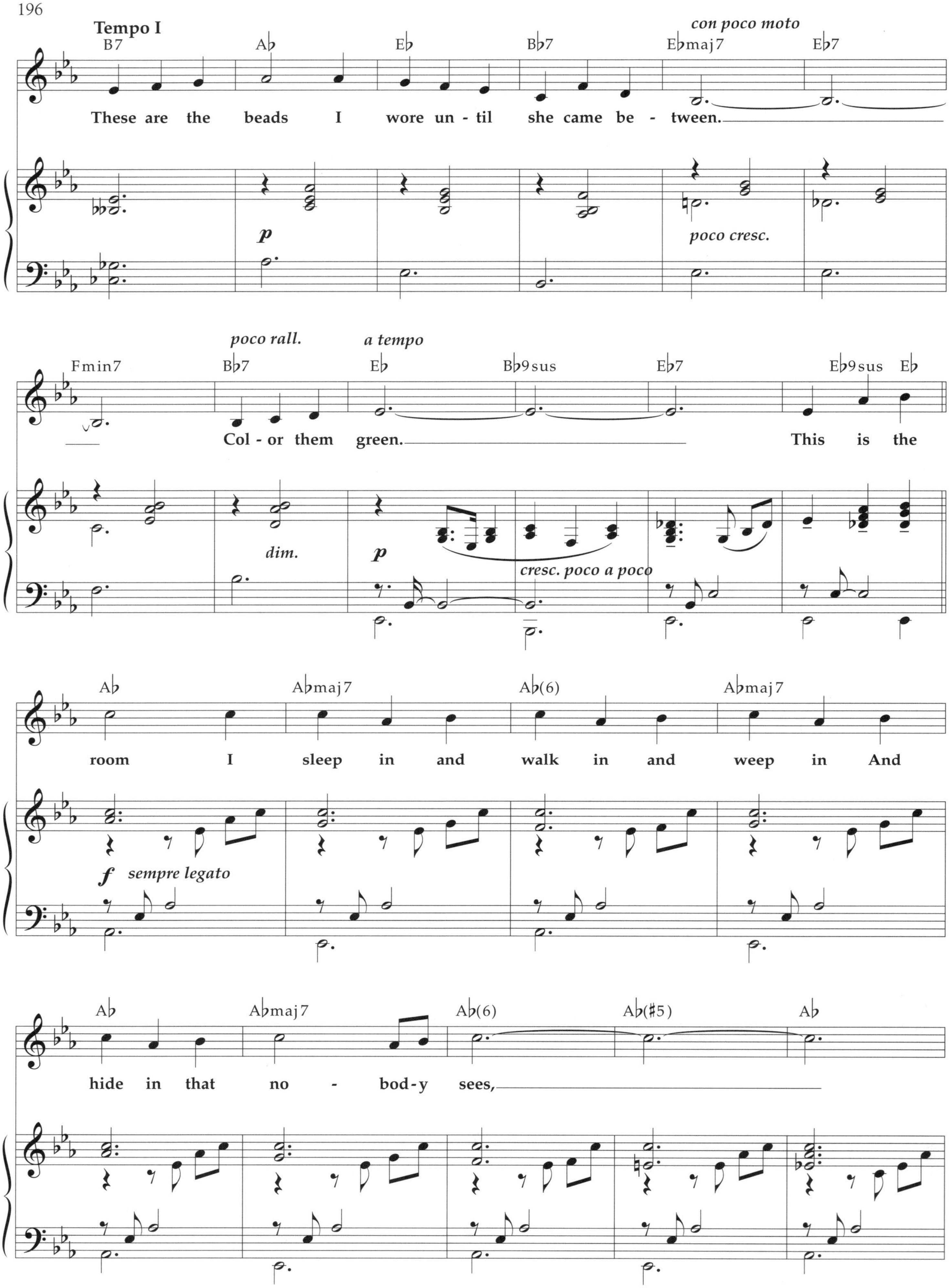
Tempo I
con poco moto
B7 A♭ E♭ B♭7 E♭maj7 E♭7
These are the beads I wore un - til she came be - tween.
p
poco cresc.
poco rall.
a tempo
Fmin7 B♭7 E♭ B♭9sus E♭7 E♭9sus E♭
Col - or them green. This is the
dim.
p
cresc. poco a poco
A♭ A♭maj7 A♭(6) A♭maj7
room I sleep in and walk in and weep in And
f sempre legato
A♭ A♭maj7 A♭(6) A♭(♯5) A♭
hide in that no - bod - y sees,

Poco rubato
A♭
Gmin7
C9(13)
Col - or it lone - ly, please.
mp
8va
Rubato
B7
A♭maj7
E♭maj9
B♭9sus
This is the man, The one I de - pend - ed up -
E♭
E♭maj7
Fmin7
B♭7
on.
Col - or him
Slowly
E♭
B♭9sus
E♭maj7
B♭9sus
E♭(9)
gone.
p
pp

# Theme from "New York, New York"

*from the Motion Picture* **NEW YORK, NEW YORK**

Words by
**FRED EBB**

Music by
**JOHN KANDER**

F
Gmin7 C7
Gmin7 C7 C9sus C7
shoes Are long-ing to stray, And step a -
F
Fmaj7
F7
round the heart of it New York, New York. I wan-na
B♭maj7
B♭min(6)
Fmaj9
F(6) Gmin7 Fmaj7
wake up in the cit - y that does - n't sleep To find I'm
Amin7
D9
Gmin7
C7
king of the hill, Top of the heap. My lit - tle town
cresc.
mf

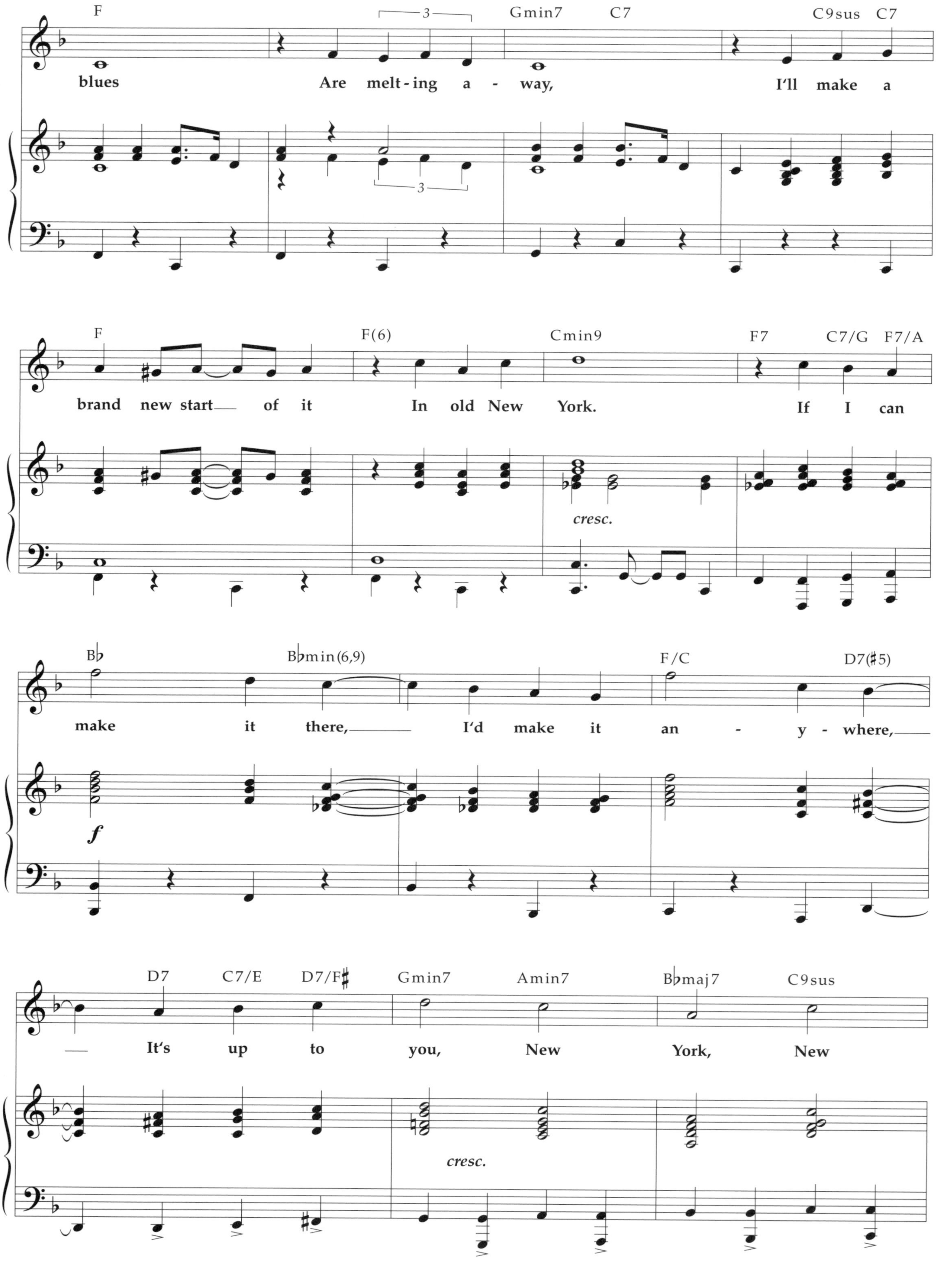
F
Gmin7 C7
C9sus C7
blues Are melt-ing a - way, I'll make a
F
F(6)
Cmin9
F7 C7/G F7/A
brand new start of it In old New York. If I can
cresc.
B♭
B♭min(6,9)
F/C
D7(♯5)
make it there, I'd make it an - y - where,
f
D7 C7/E D7/F♯
Gmin7 Amin7
B♭maj7 C9sus
It's up to you, New York, New
cresc.

F
Gmin7
C9sus
York.
ff
dim.
F
F(6)
F7
C7/G
F7/A
New York, New York. I wan - na
mp
cresc.
B♭maj7
B♭min
Fmaj9
wake up in the cit - y that does - n't sleep
mf
3

F(6)
Amin7
D9
To find I'm king of the hill, Head of the list,
rall. poco a poco
Bbmin7
Db7
Cream of the crop At the top of the heap. My lit - tle town
cresc.
f
colla voce
Pesante
Gb
Abmin7 Db7
Ebdim Fmin7(b5)
blues Are melt-ing a - way, I'll make a

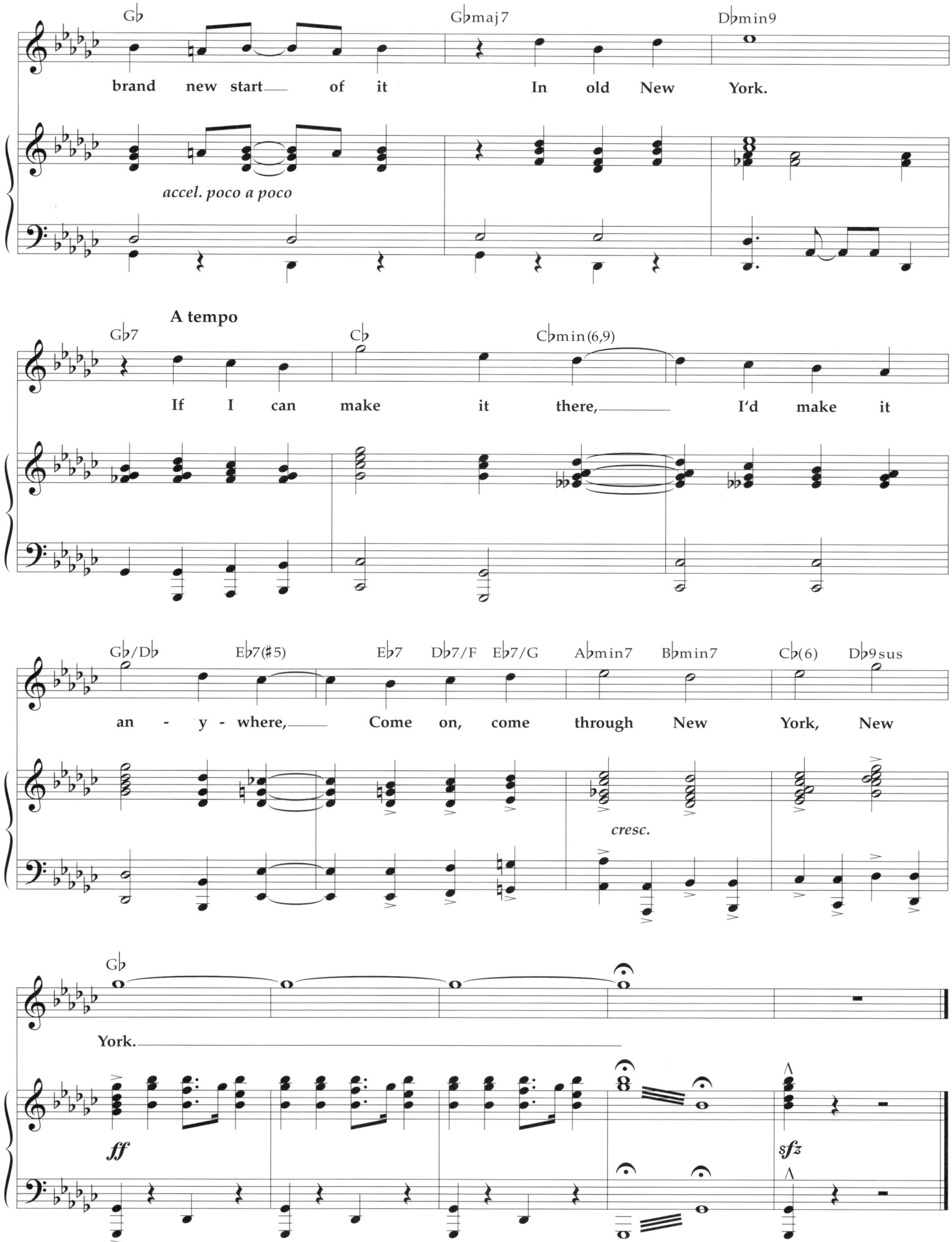
G♭
G♭maj7
D♭min9
brand new start of it In old New York.
accel. poco a poco
A tempo
G♭7
C♭
C♭min(6,9)
If I can make it there, I'd make it
G♭/D♭
E♭7(♯5)
E♭7
D♭7/F
E♭7/G
A♭min7
B♭min7
C♭(6)
D♭9sus
an - y - where, Come on, come through New York, New
cresc.
G♭
York.
ff
sfz

# Only Love

*from the Musical* ***ZORBA***

Words by
**FRED EBB**

Music by
**JOHN KANDER**

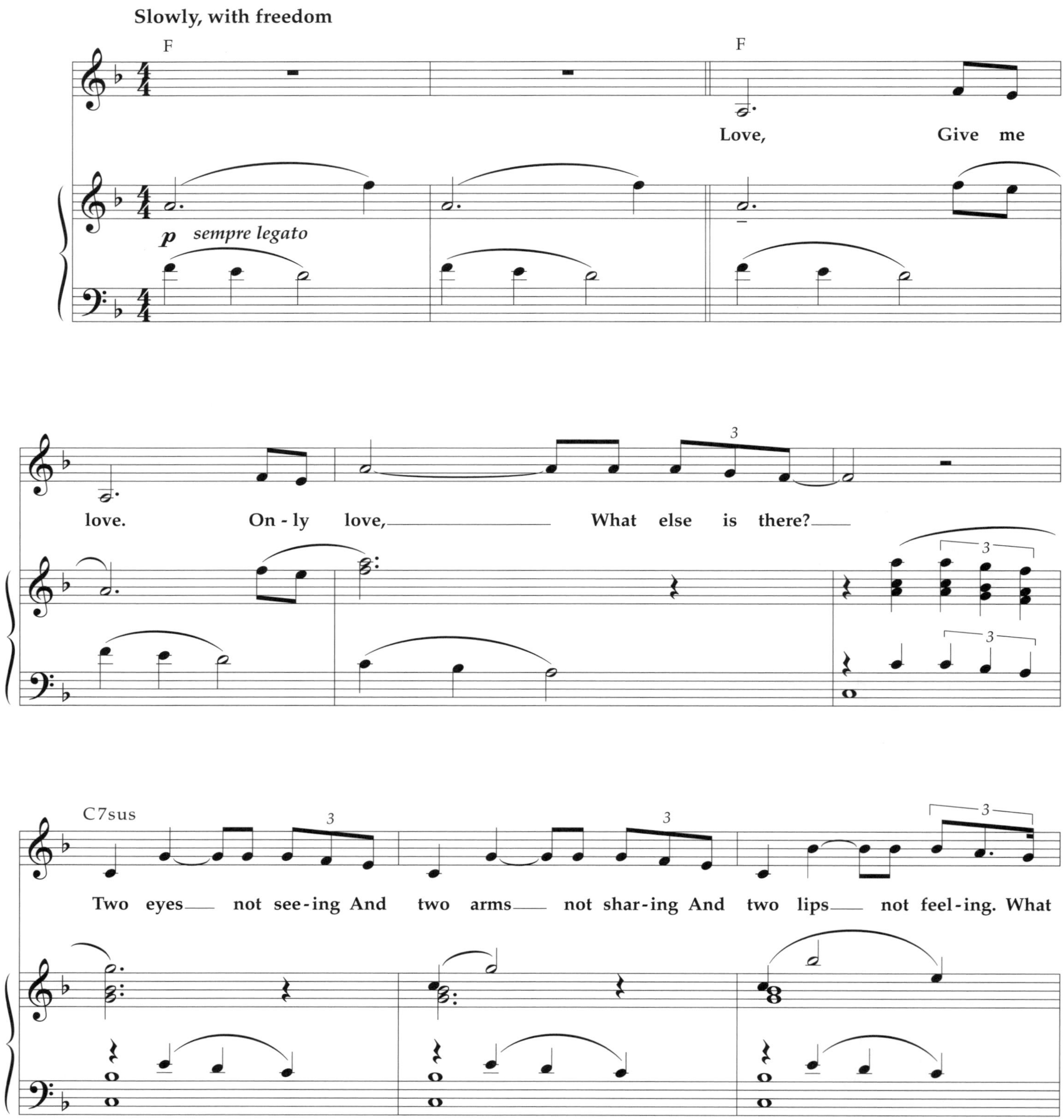

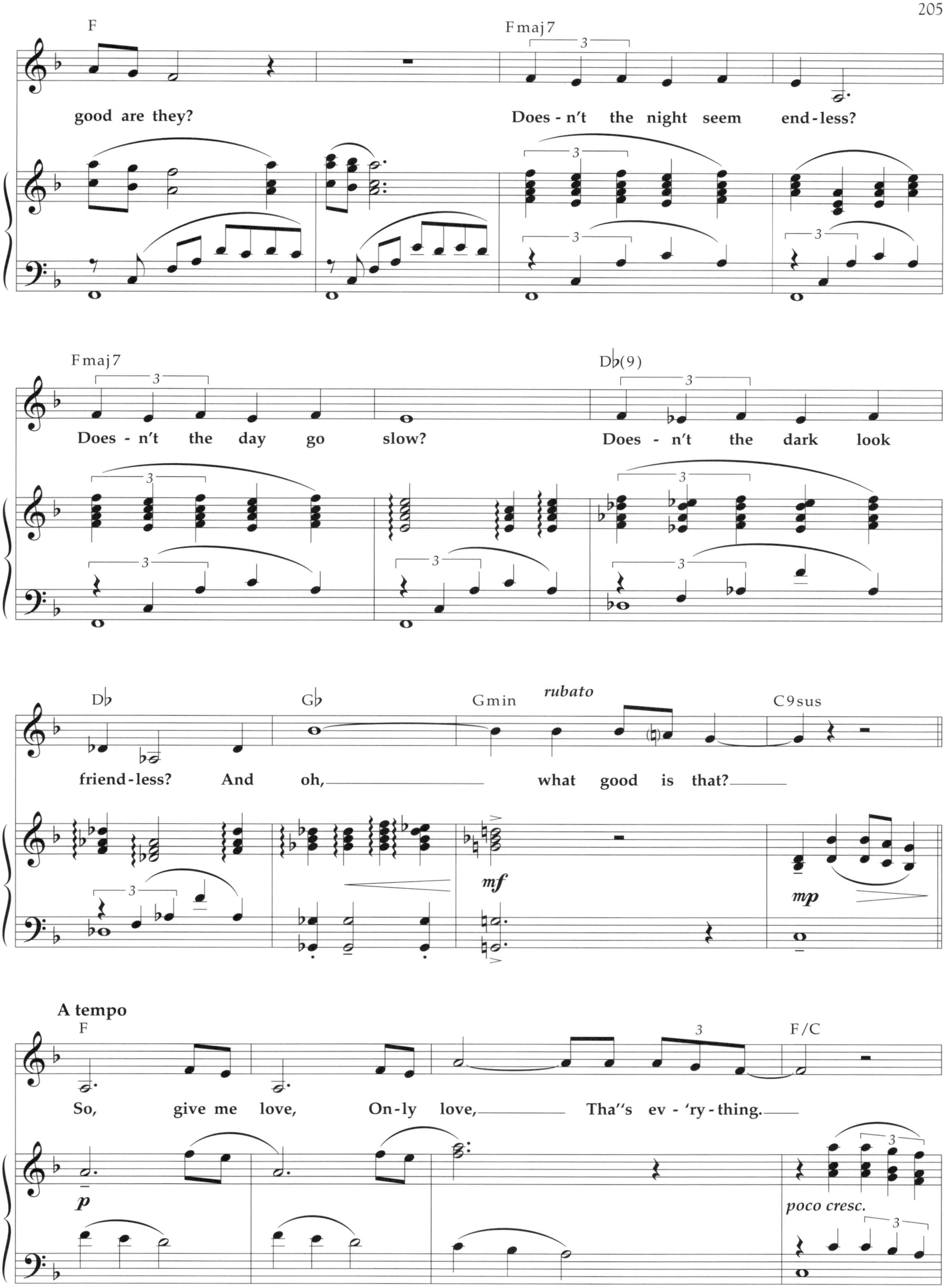
F
Fmaj7
good are they?
Does - n't the night seem end - less?
Fmaj7
Db(9)
Does - n't the day go slow?
Does - n't the dark look
Db
Gb
Gmin
rubato
C9sus
friend - less? And oh,
what good is that?
mf
mp
A tempo
F
F/C
So, give me love, On - ly love,
Tha''s ev - 'ry - thing.
p
poco cresc.

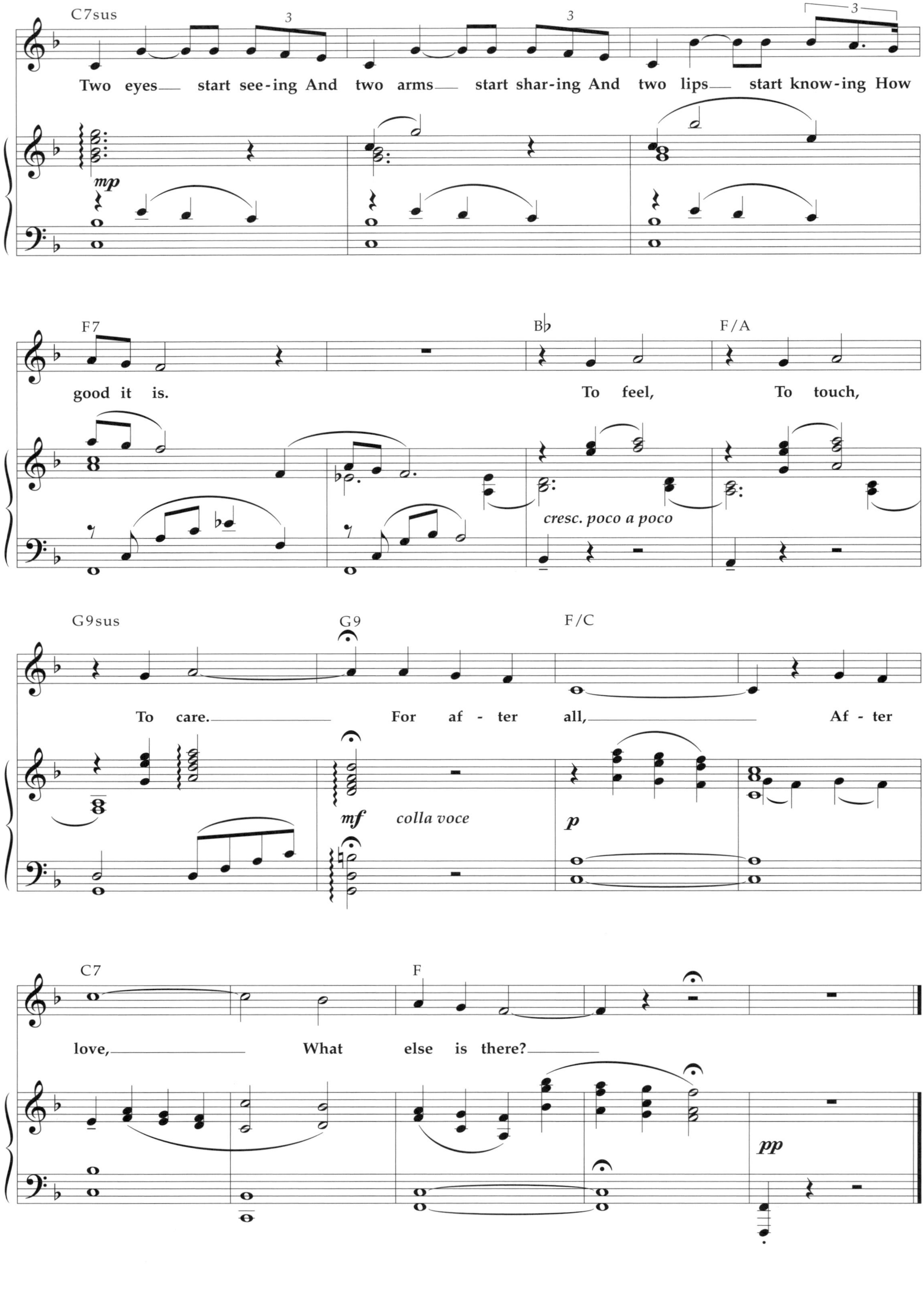
C7sus
Two eyes start see-ing And two arms start shar-ing And two lips start know-ing How
mp
F7
good it is.
B♭
F/A
To feel, To touch,
cresc. poco a poco
G9sus
G9
F/C
To care. For af - ter all, Af - ter
mf
colla voce
p
C7
F
love, What else is there?
pp

# Sara Lee

*featured in the Revue* **AND THE WORLD GOES 'ROUND**

Words by
**FRED EBB**

Music by
**JOHN KANDER**

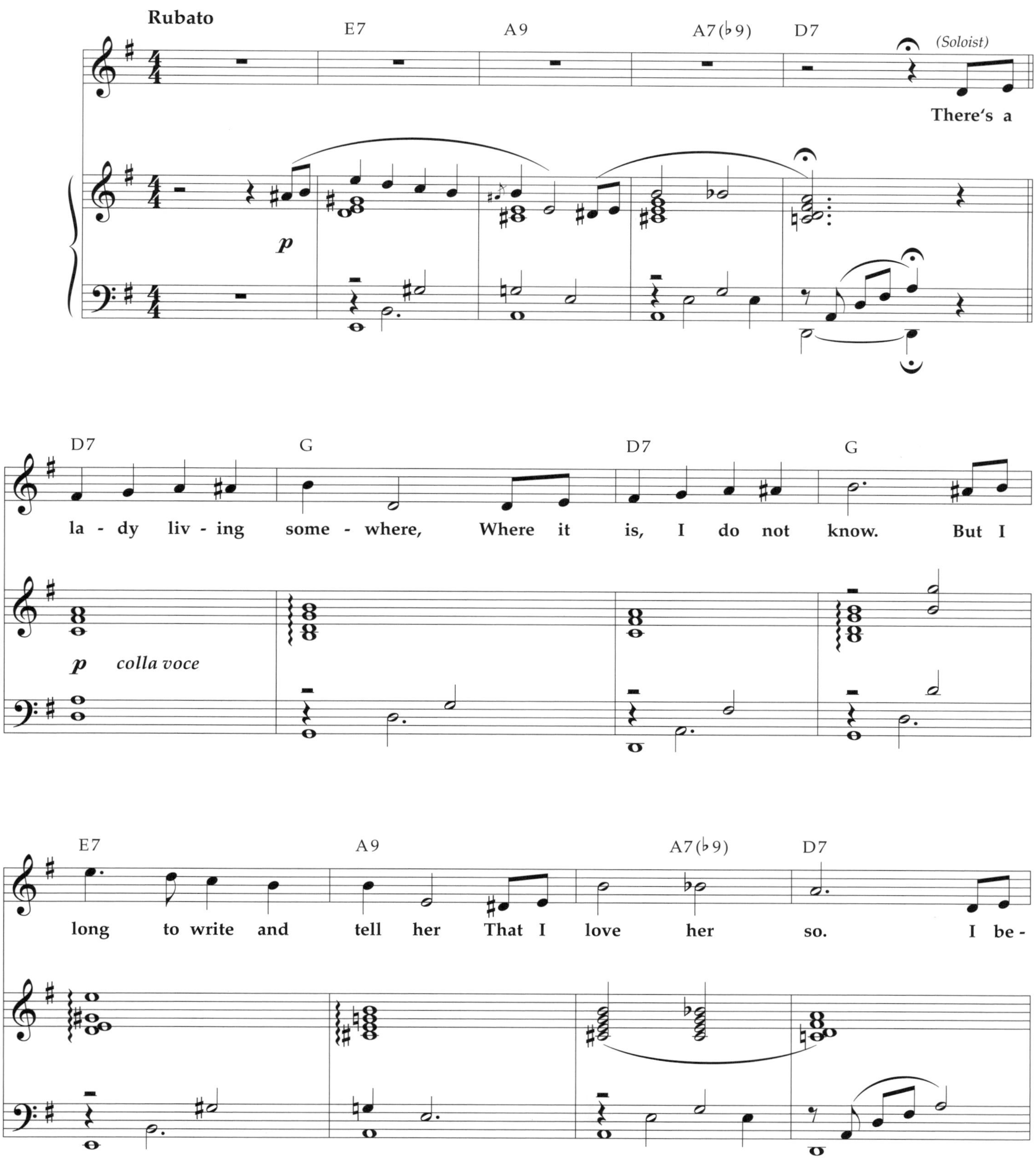

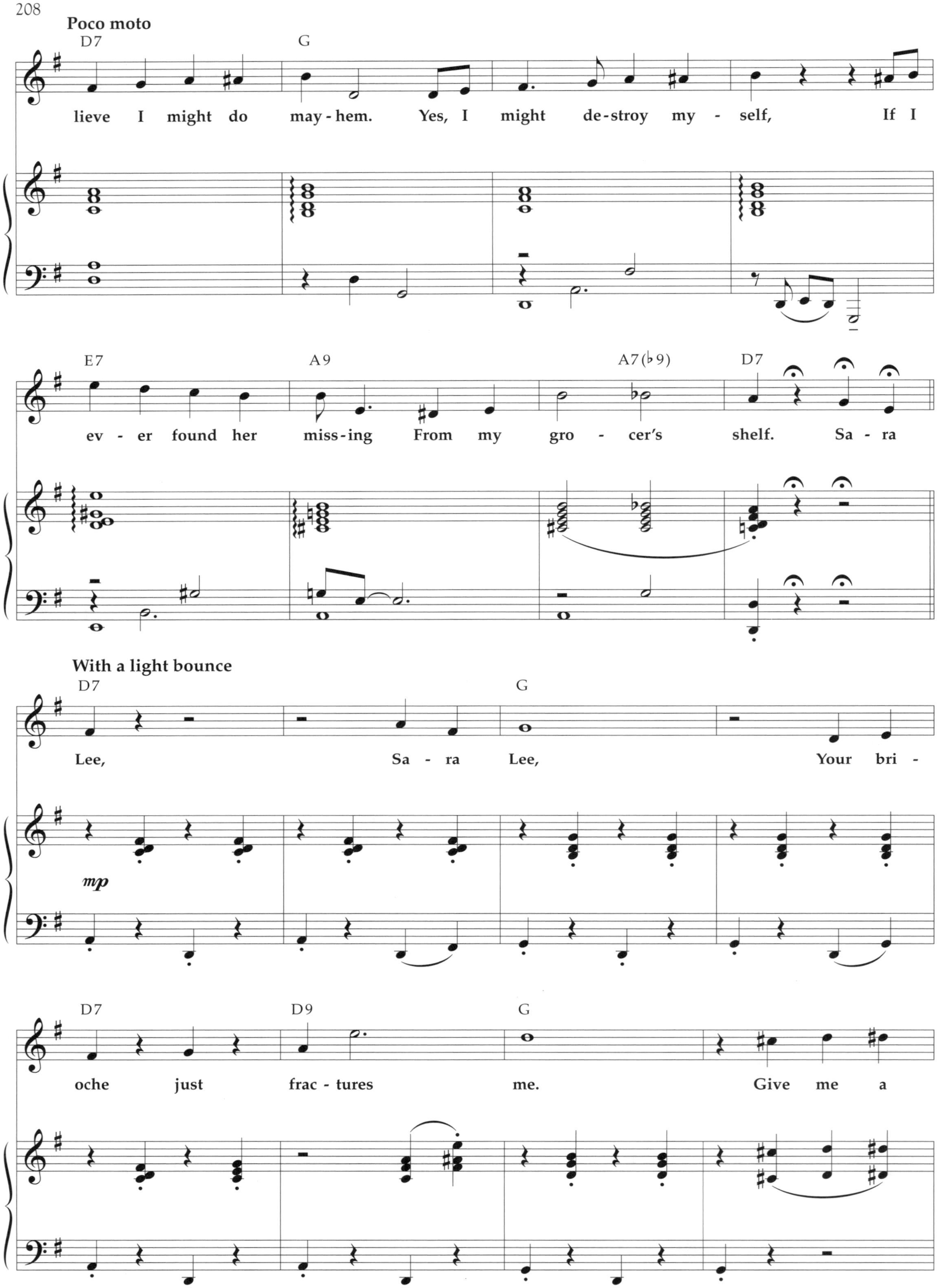
Poco moto
D7 G
lieve I might do may - hem. Yes, I might de - stroy my - self, If I
E7 A9 A7(♭9) D7
ev - er found her miss - ing From my gro - cer's shelf. Sa - ra
With a light bounce
D7 G
Lee, Sa - ra Lee, Your bri -
mp
D7 D9 G
oche just frac - tures me. Give me a

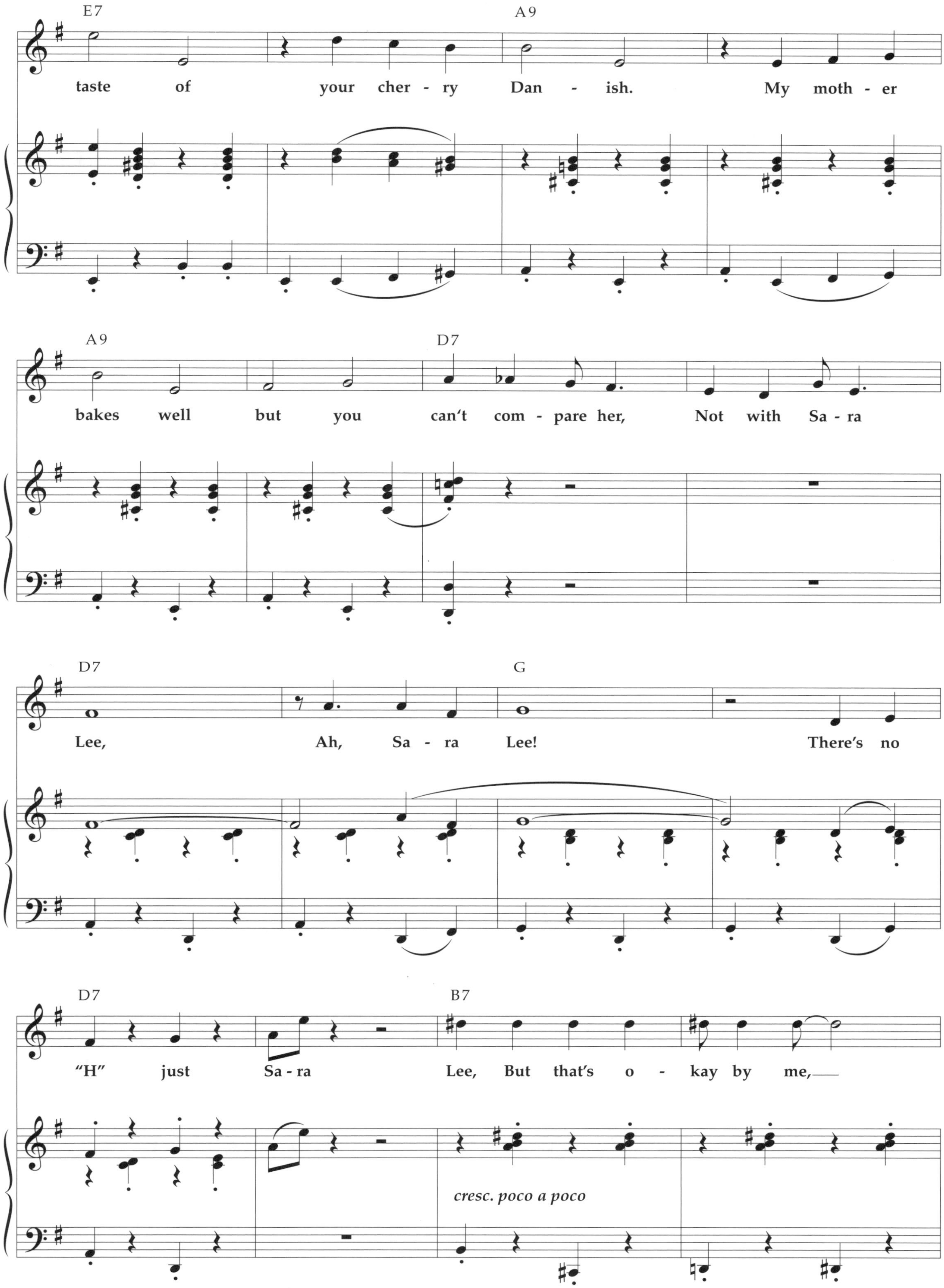
E7 A9
taste of your cher - ry Dan - ish. My moth - er
A9 D7
bakes well but you can't com - pare her, Not with Sa - ra
D7 G
Lee, Ah, Sa - ra Lee! There's no
D7 B7
"H" just Sa - ra Lee, But that's o - kay by me,
cresc. poco a poco

E7
A9
A9
'Cause I'm liv-in' in Par-a-dise When I'm nib-bl-in' Ap-ple Spice. From the
G(6)
Bmin7(♭5)
E7
A9
D7
kitch-ens of the one I love, Won-der-ful Sa-ra
mf
G(6)
D7
(Soloist)
And it thrills me right to my soul,
(Backup singers)
Lee. Sa-ra Lee, Sa-ra
mp

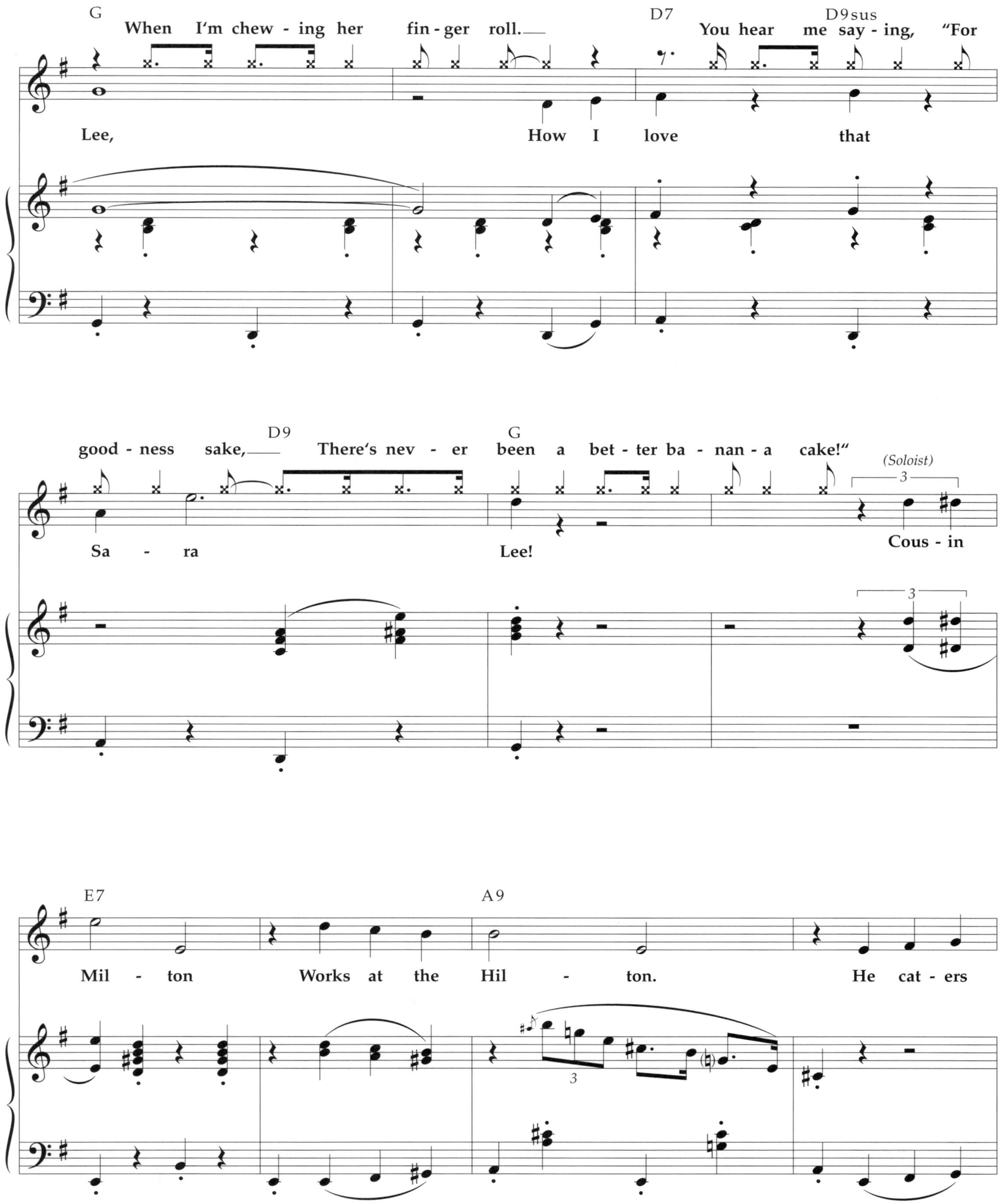
G
When I'm chew - ing her fin - ger roll.
D7
D9sus
You hear me say - ing, "For
Lee,
How I love that
good - ness sake,
D9
There's nev - er been a bet - ter ba - nan - a cake!"
G
(Soloist)
3
Sa - ra Lee!
Cous - in
E7
A9
Mil - ton Works at the Hil - ton.
He cat - ers
3

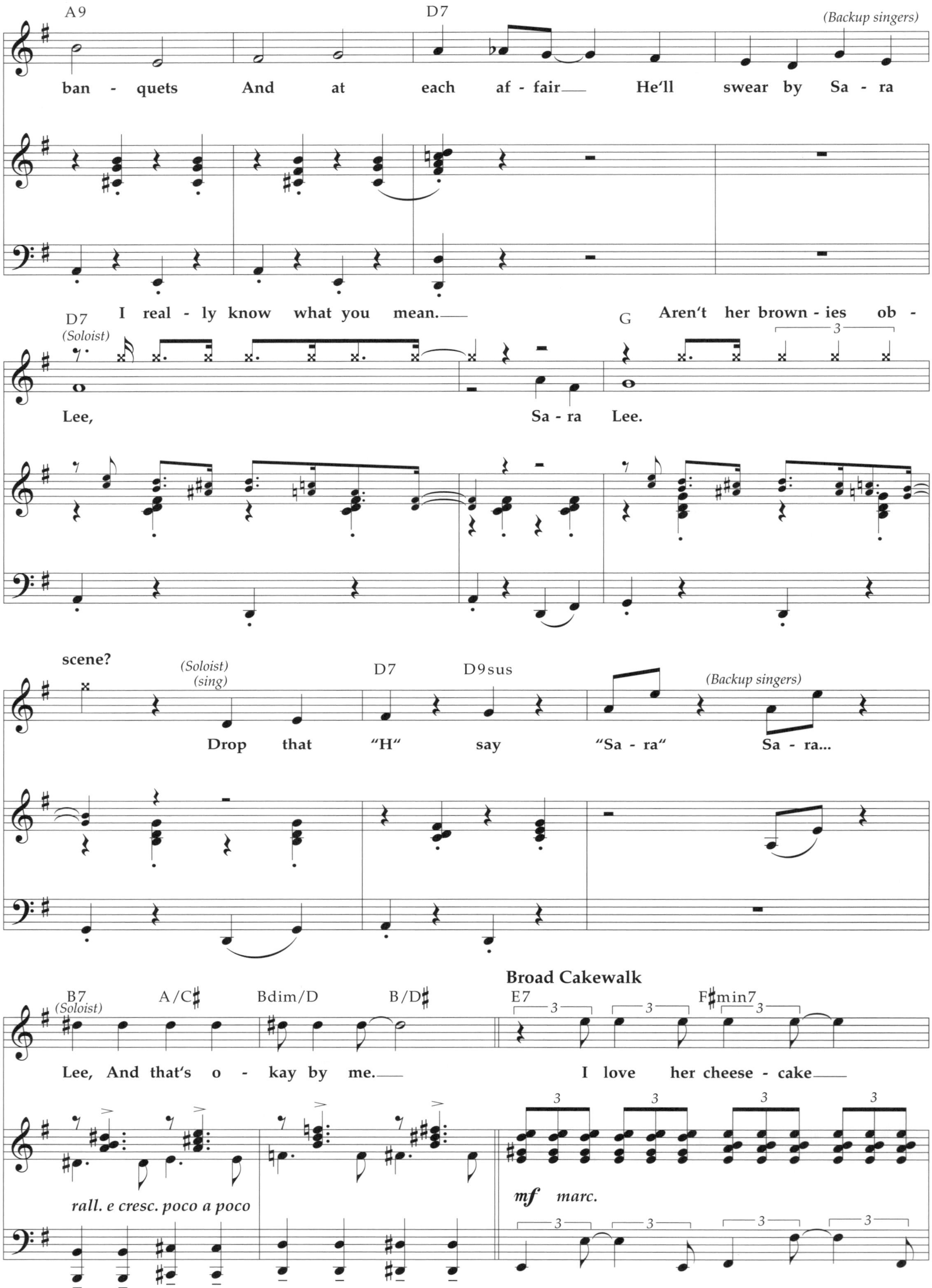

A9
D7
(Backup singers)
ban - quets And at each af - fair He'll swear by Sa - ra
D7
(Soloist)
I real - ly know what you mean.
G
Aren't her brown - ies ob -
3
Lee, Sa - ra Lee.
scene?
(Soloist)
(sing)
D7
D9sus
(Backup singers)
Drop that "H" say "Sa - ra" Sa - ra...
Broad Cakewalk
B7
(Soloist)
A/C♯
Bdim/D
B/D♯
E7
F♯min7
Lee, And that's o - kay by me. I love her cheese - cake
rall. e cresc. poco a poco
mf marc.

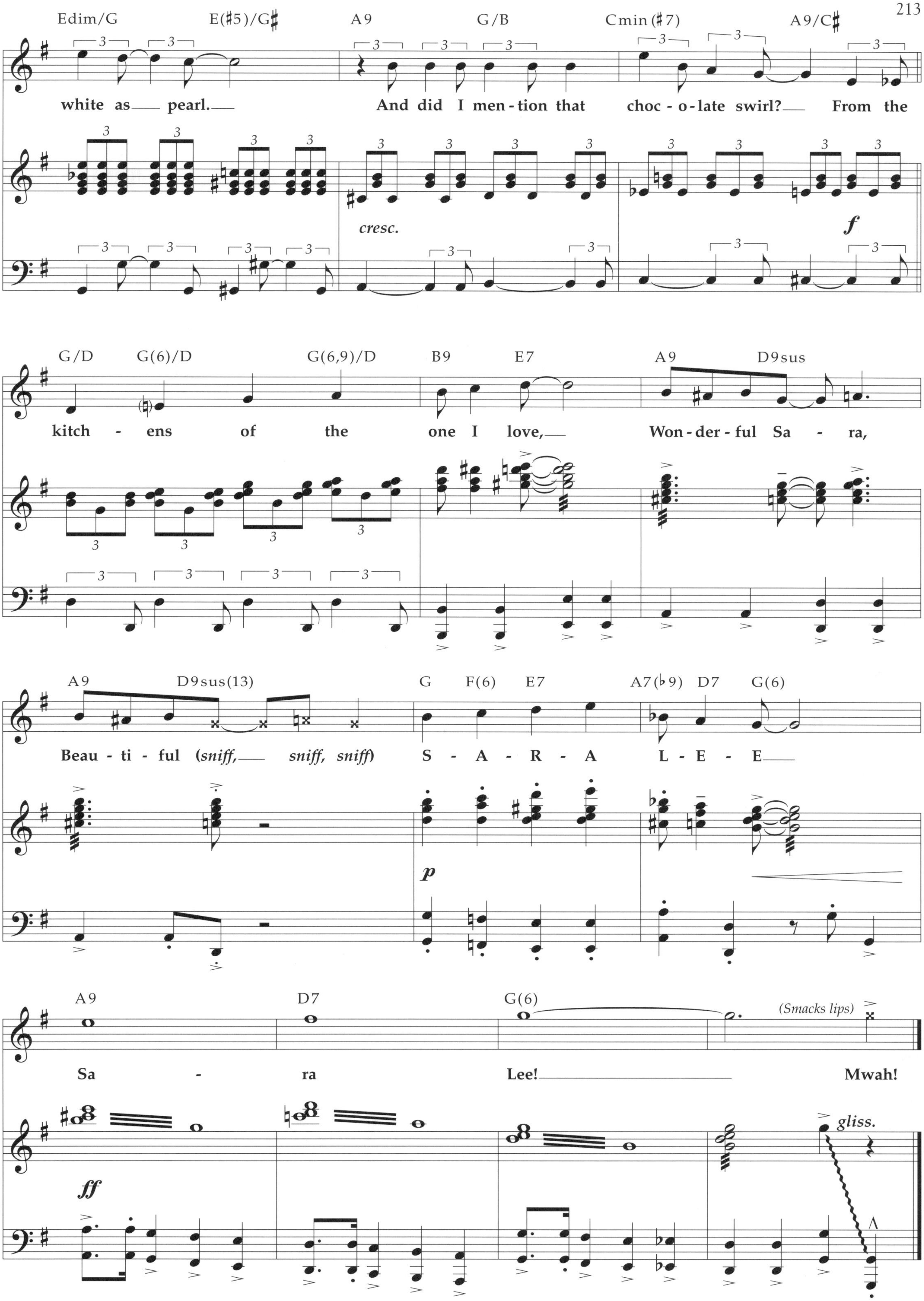
Edim/G E(♯5)/G♯ A9 G/B Cmin(♯7) A9/C♯
white as pearl. And did I men-tion that choc-o-late swirl? From the
cresc.
f
G/D G(6)/D G(6,9)/D B9 E7 A9 D9sus
kitch - ens of the one I love, Won-der-ful Sa - ra,
A9 D9sus(13) G F(6) E7 A7(♭9) D7 G(6)
Beau-ti-ful (sniff, sniff, sniff) S - A - R - A L - E - E
p
A9 D7 G(6)
(Smacks lips)
Sa - ra Lee! Mwah!
ff
gliss.

# A Quiet Thing

*from the Musical* ***FLORA, THE RED MENACE***

Words by
**FRED EBB**

Music by
**JOHN KANDER**

Poco rubato
B♭min7 E♭9sus Cmin D♭ E♭
ring. It's a qui - et thing.
colla voce
A little faster
A♭maj7 Fmin7 B♭min7
When you hold the world In your trem - bling
mp
E♭7(13) Cmin7 Fmin7
hand, You'd think you'd hear a cho - ir
B♭min7 E♭9sus Cmin C Cmin C
sing. It's a qui - et thing.
cresc. e poco accel.

Con moto
C
Cmaj7
Dmin
C
Cmaj7
C(6)
There are no ex - plod - ing fi - re - works. Where's the roar - ing of the
mf
Dmin7
G9
E/B
B9sus
crowds? May - be it's the strange new at - mo - sphere
Eb9sus
Eb7
Way up here a - mong the clouds. But
Tempo I
Ab
Fmin7
Bbmin7
Eb7(13)
I don't hear the drums, I don't hear the band, The
mp

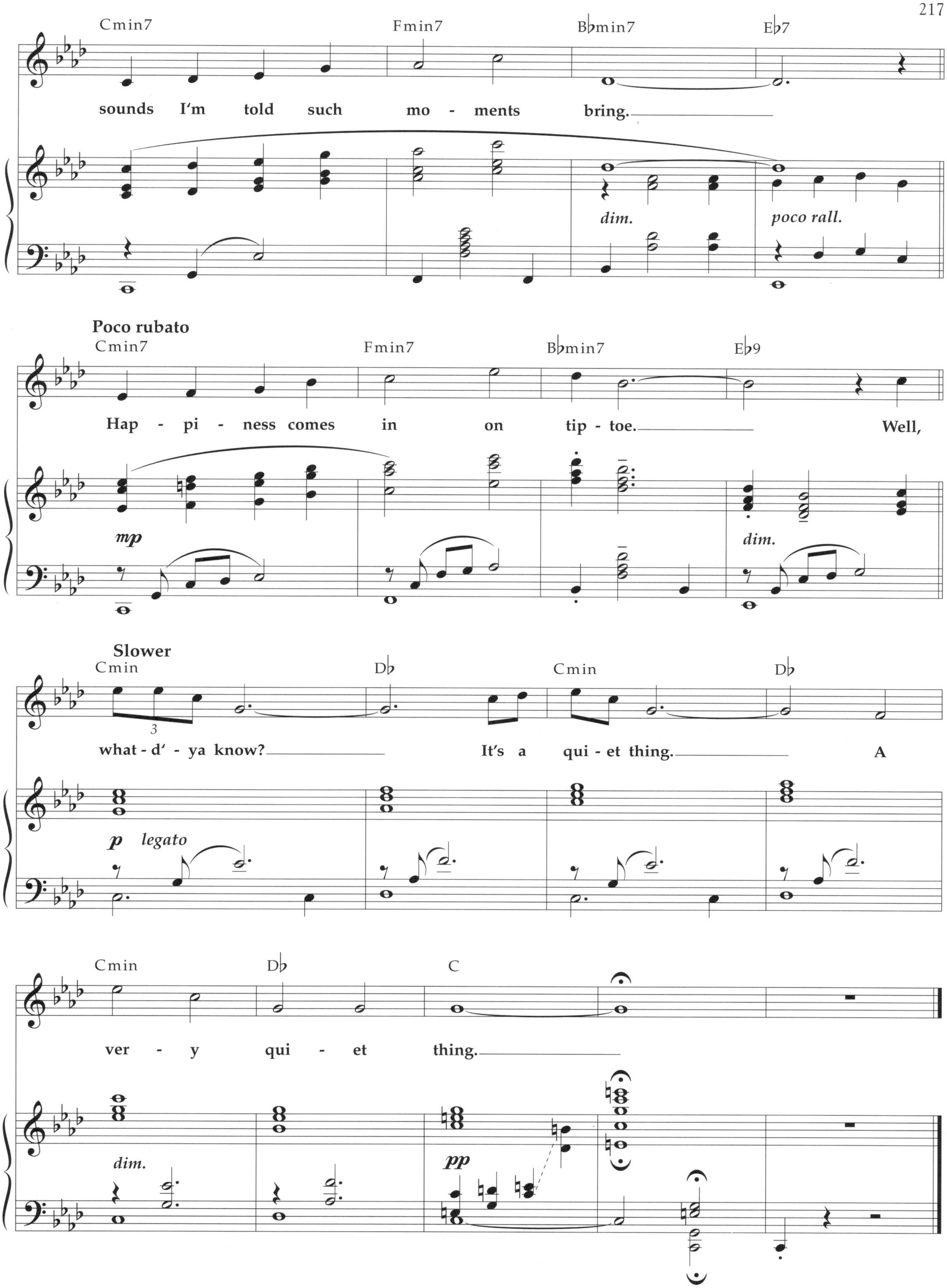
Cmin7
Fmin7
B♭min7
E♭7
sounds I'm told such mo - ments bring.
dim.
poco rall.
Poco rubato
Cmin7
Fmin7
B♭min7
E♭9
Hap - pi - ness comes in on tip - toe. Well,
mp
dim.
Slower
Cmin
D♭
Cmin
D♭
what - d' - ya know? It's a qui - et thing. A
p legato
Cmin
D♭
C
ver - y qui - et thing.
dim.
pp

# Second Chance

*from the Musical* **STEEL PIER**

Words by
**FRED EBB**

Music by
**JOHN KANDER**

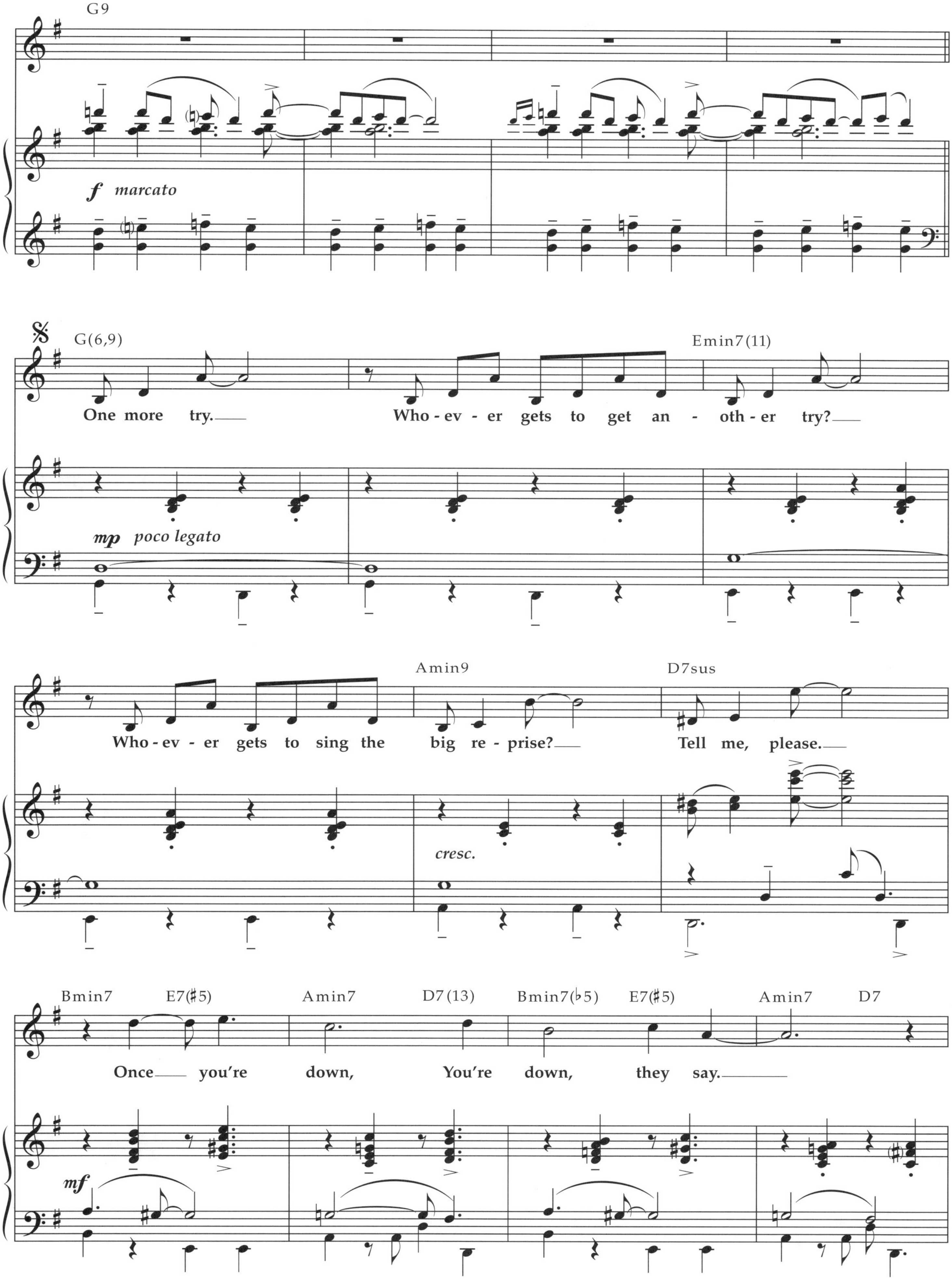
G9
f marcato
G(6,9)
One more try.
Who-ev-er gets to get an-oth-er try?
Emin7(11)
mp poco legato
Who-ev-er gets to sing the big re-prise?
Amin9
D7sus
Tell me, please.
cresc.
Bmin7
E7(♯5)
Amin7
D7(13)
Bmin7(♭5)
E7(♯5)
Amin7
D7
Once you're down, You're down, they say.
mf

Bmin7 E7(♯5) Amin7 D7(13) Bmin7(♭5) E7(♯5) Amin7 D7
Once you're out, You're out to stay.
Emin Emin(♯7) Emin7
No one tells you You can get right up
A7(13) Amin7 D7(♭9) E♭(6,9) D7(13)
And you can start all o - ver With a
cresc.
f
dim.
G(6,9) Emin7(11)
sec - ond chance. When - ev - er life has gone from bad to worse,

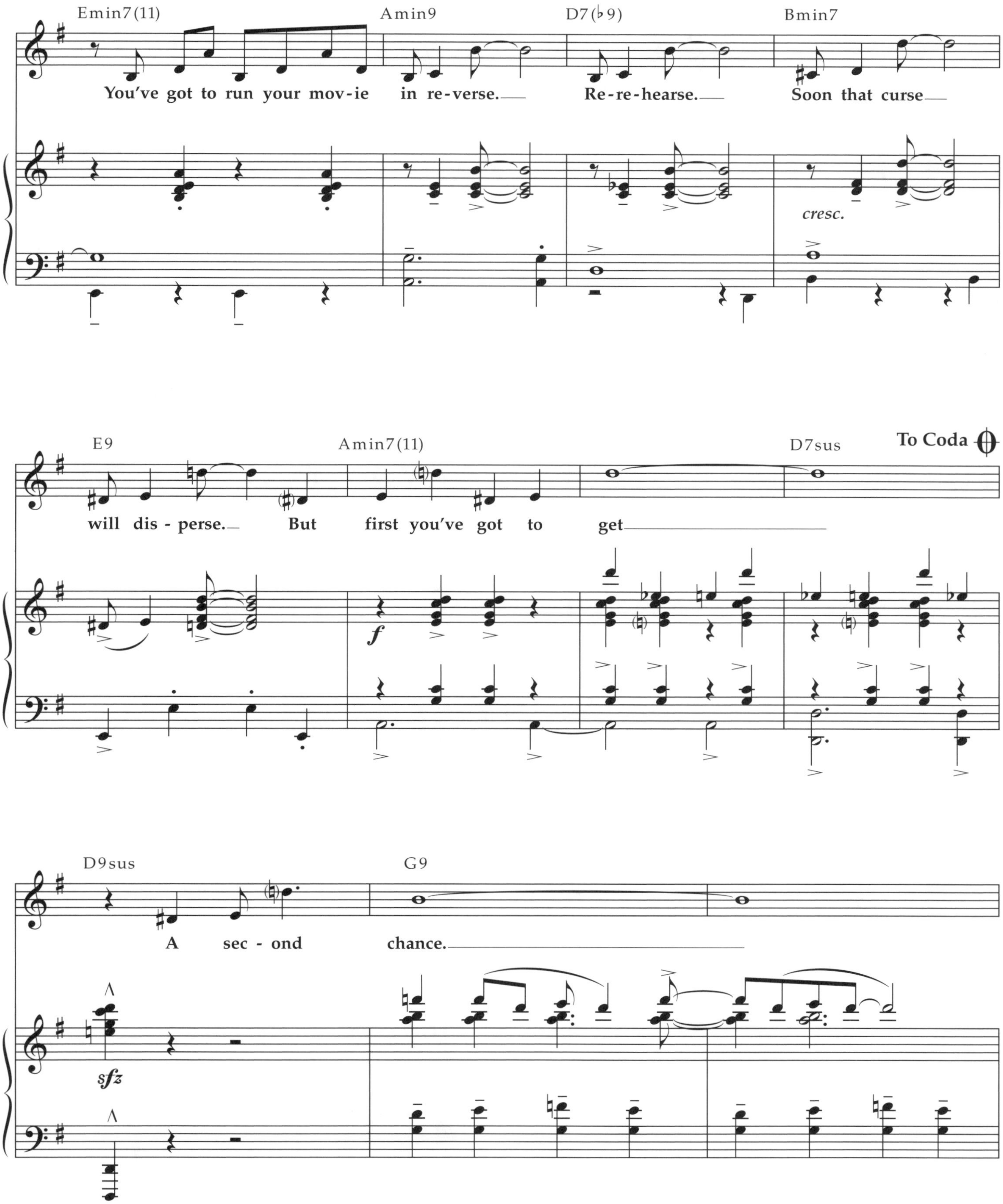
Emin7(11)
Amin9
D7(♭9)
Bmin7
You've got to run your mov-ie in re-verse. Re-re-hearse. Soon that curse
cresc.
E9
Amin7(11)
D7sus
To Coda
will dis - perse. But first you've got to get
f
D9sus
G9
A sec - ond chance.
sfz

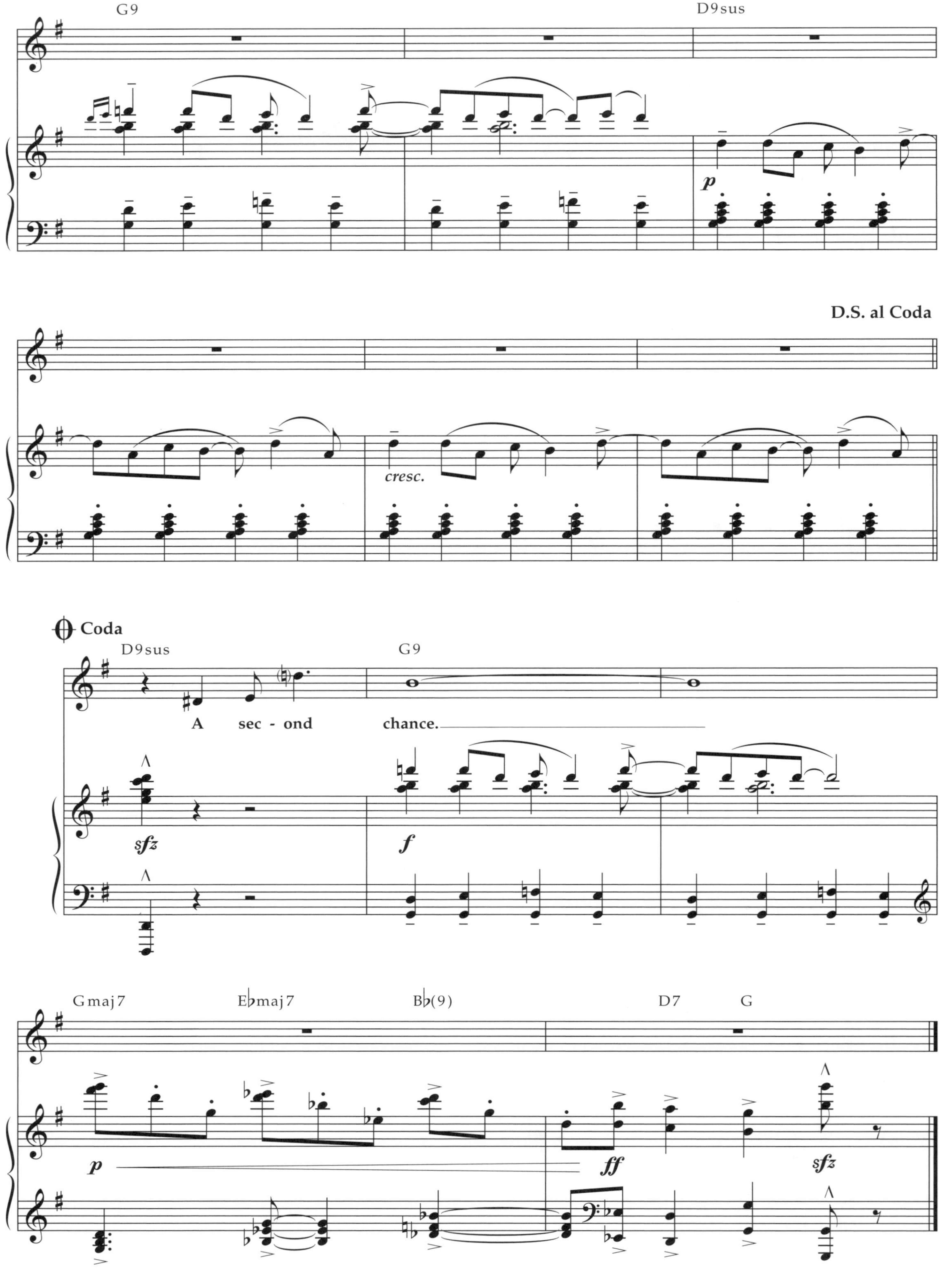
G9
D9sus
p
D.S. al Coda
cresc.
Coda
D9sus
G9
A sec - ond chance.
sfz
f
Gmaj7
E♭maj7
B♭(9)
D7
G
p
ff
sfz

# Sing Happy

*from the Musical* ***FLORA, THE RED MENACE***

Words by
**FRED EBB**

Music by
**JOHN KANDER**

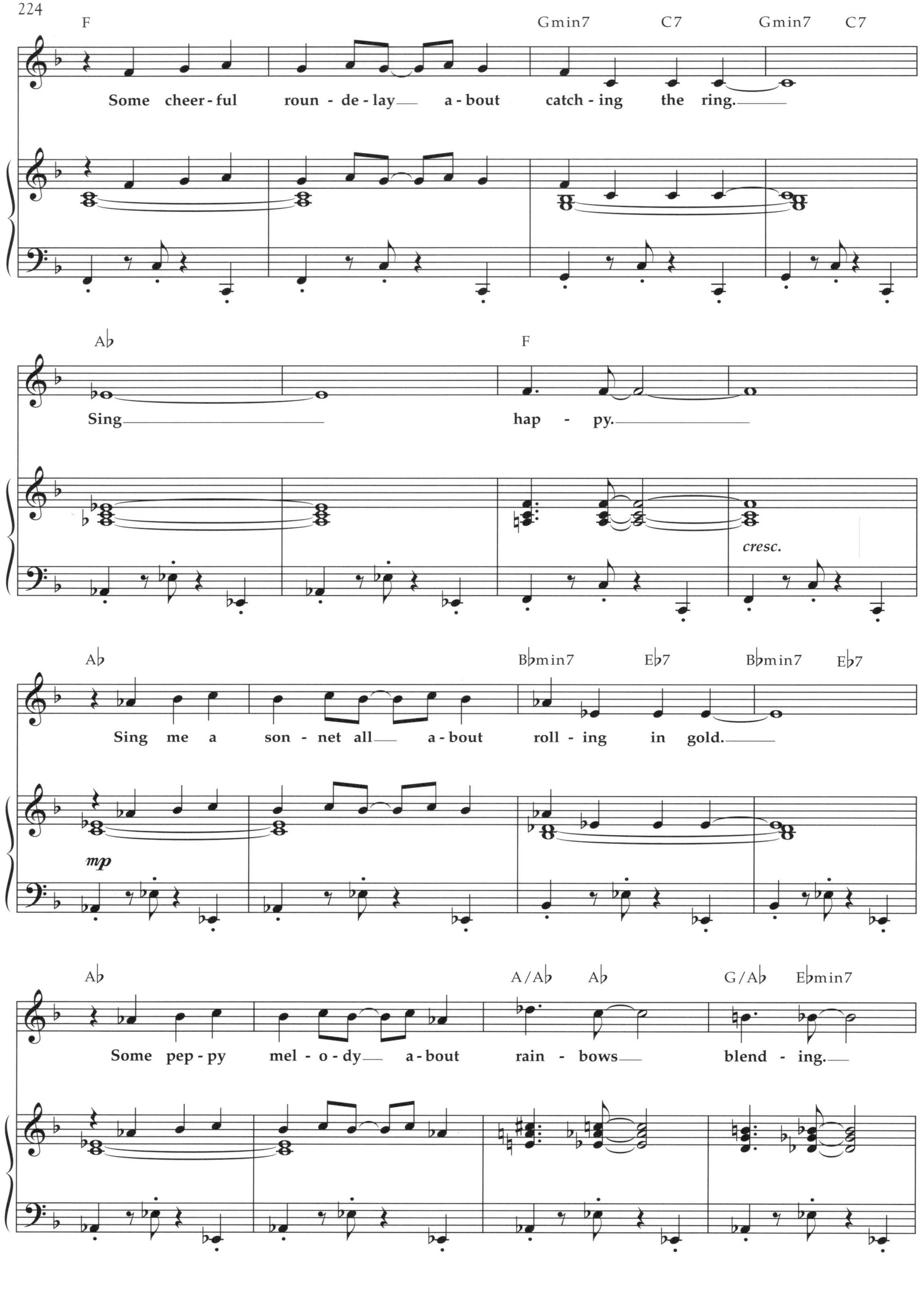
F
Gmin7
C7
Gmin7
C7
Some cheer-ful roun-de-lay a-bout catch-ing the ring.
A♭
F
Sing hap-py.
cresc.
A♭
B♭min7
E♭7
B♭min7
E♭7
Sing me a son-net all a-bout roll-ing in gold.
mp
A♭
A/A♭
A♭
G/A♭
E♭min7
Some pep-py mel-o-dy a-bout rain-bows blend-ing.

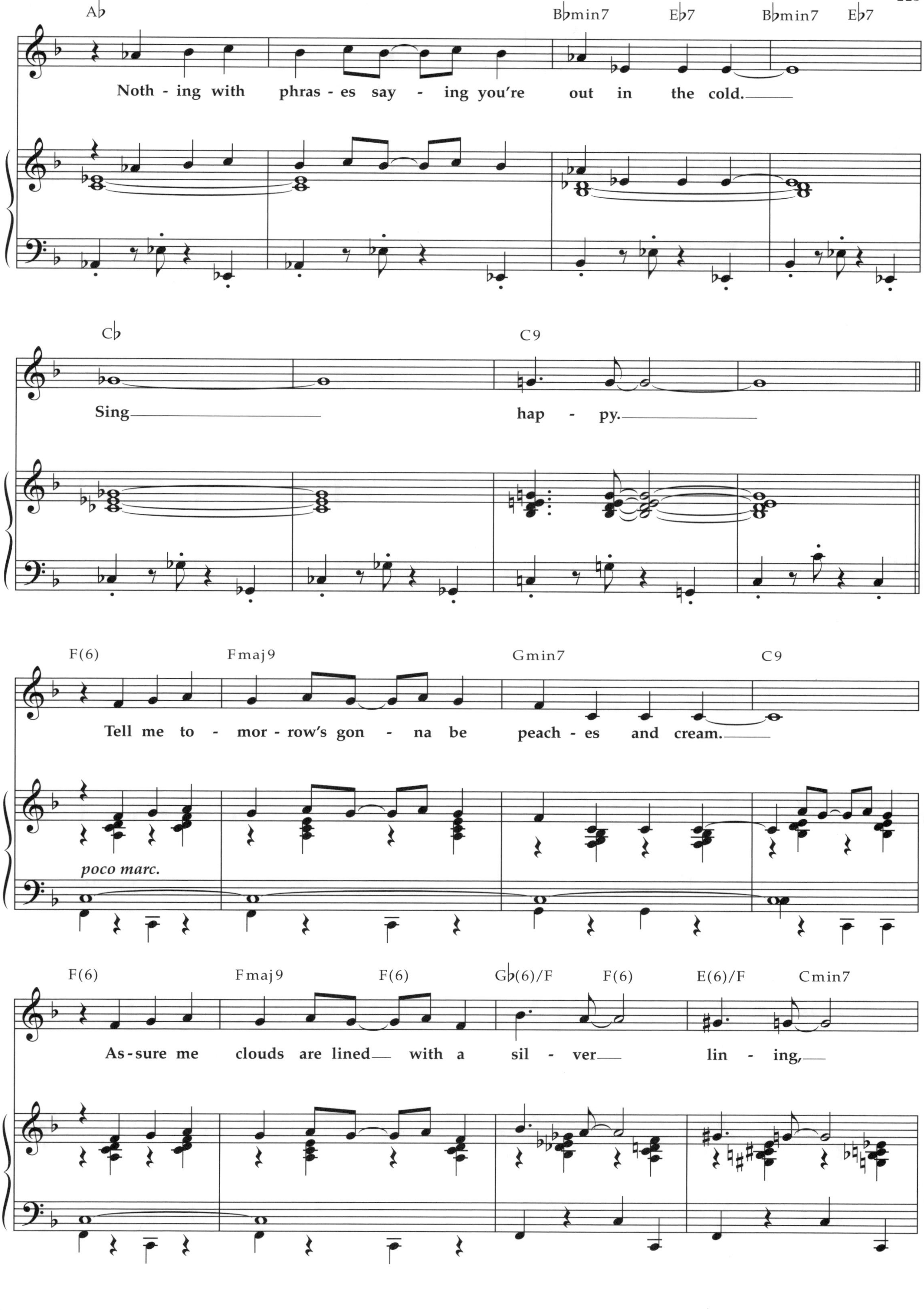
A♭
B♭min7 E♭7 B♭min7 E♭7
Noth - ing with phras - es say - ing you're out in the cold.
C♭
C9
Sing hap - py.
F(6) Fmaj9 Gmin7 C9
Tell me to - mor - row's gon - na be peach - es and cream.
poco marc.
F(6) Fmaj9 F(6) G♭(6)/F F(6) E(6)/F Cmin7
As-sure me clouds are lined with a sil - ver lin - ing,

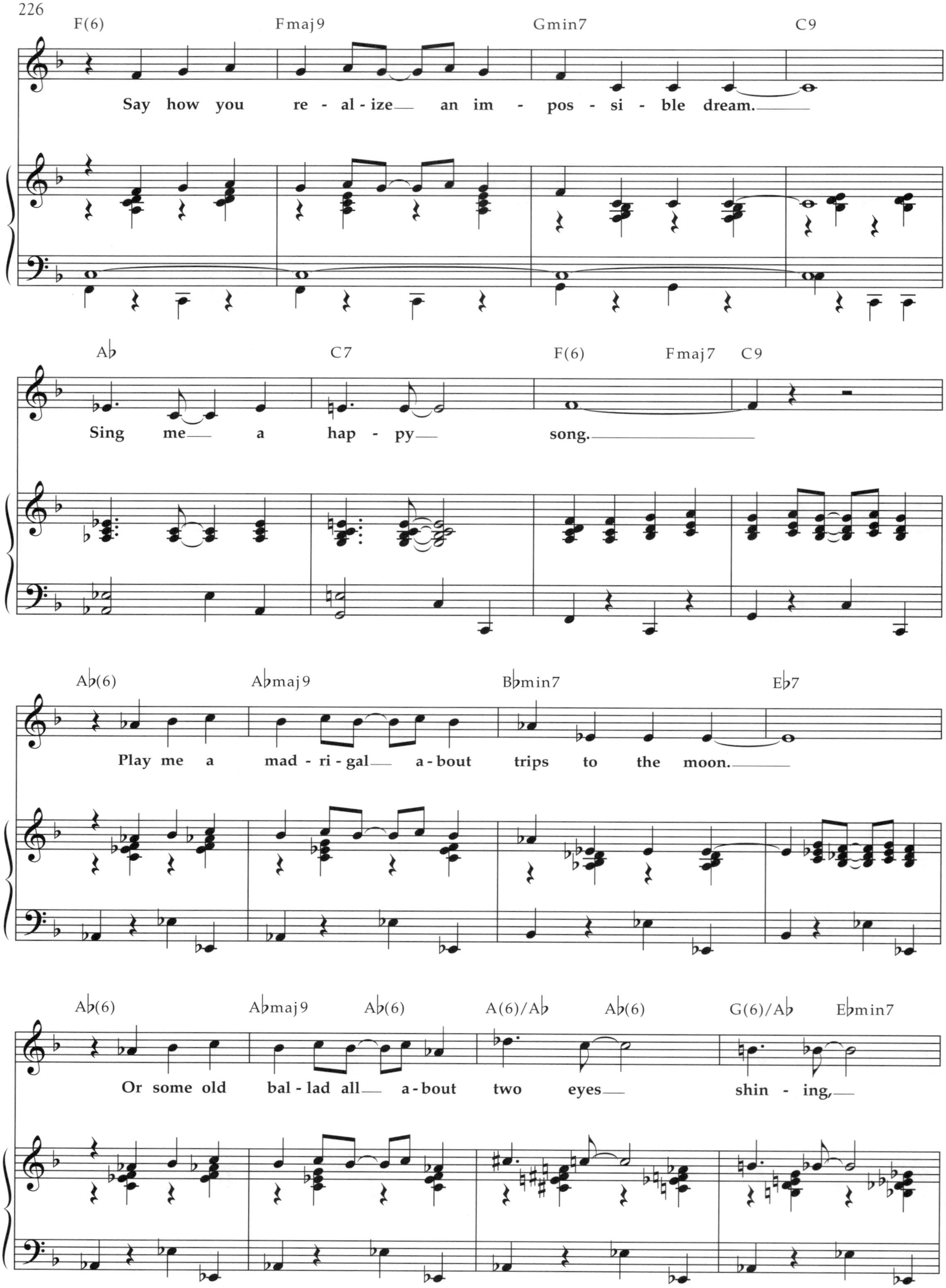
F(6) Fmaj9 Gmin7 C9
Say how you re - al - ize an im - pos - si - ble dream.
A♭ C7 F(6) Fmaj7 C9
Sing me a hap - py song.
A♭(6) A♭maj9 B♭min7 E♭7
Play me a mad - ri - gal a - bout trips to the moon.
A♭(6) A♭maj9 A♭(6) A(6)/A♭ A♭(6) G(6)/A♭ E♭min7
Or some old bal - lad all a - bout two eyes shin - ing,

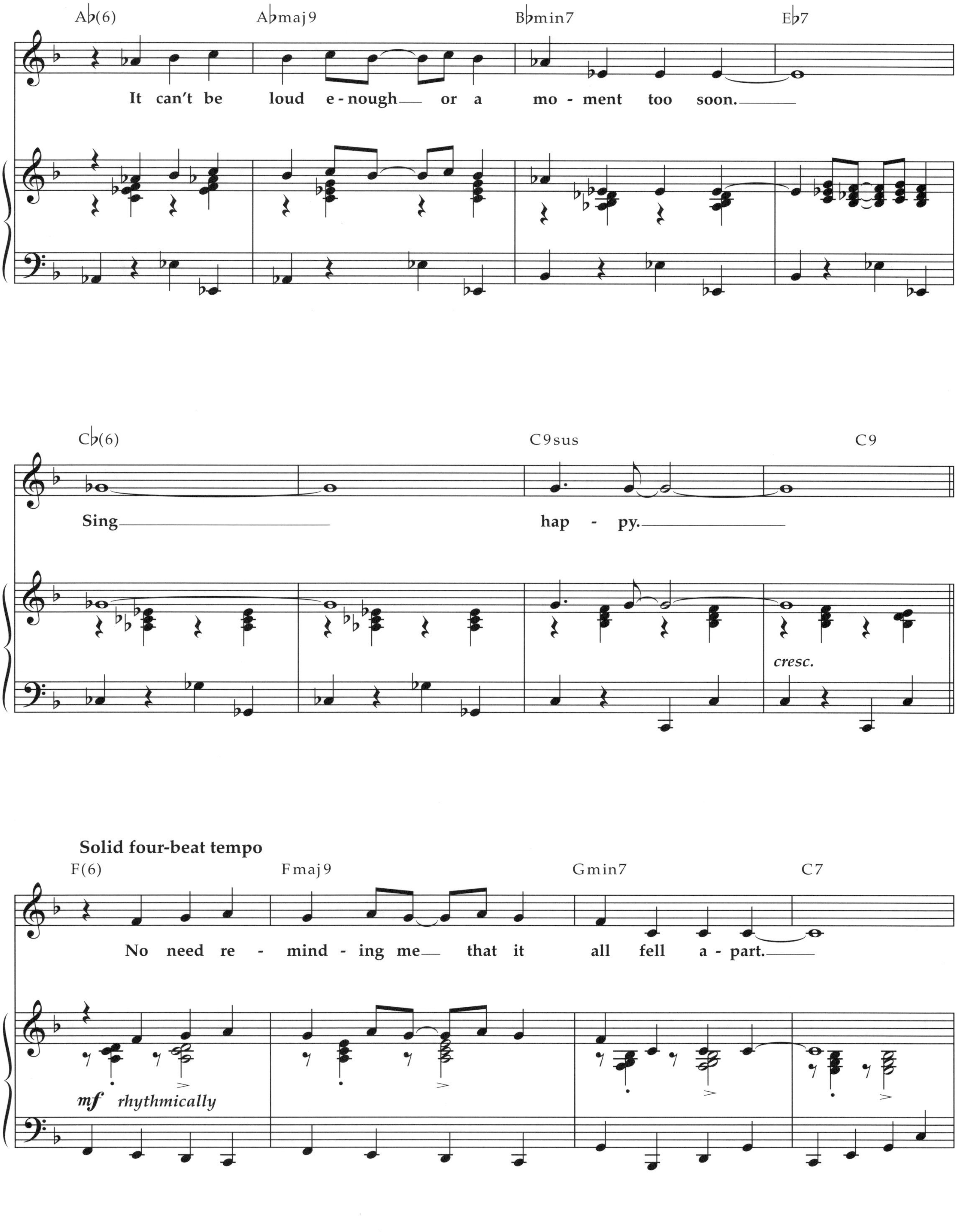
A♭(6)
A♭maj9
B♭min7
E♭7
It can't be loud e-nough or a mo-ment too soon.
C♭(6)
C9sus
C9
Sing hap - py.
cresc.
Solid four-beat tempo
F(6)
Fmaj9
Gmin7
C7
No need re - mind - ing me that it all fell a - part.
mf rhythmically

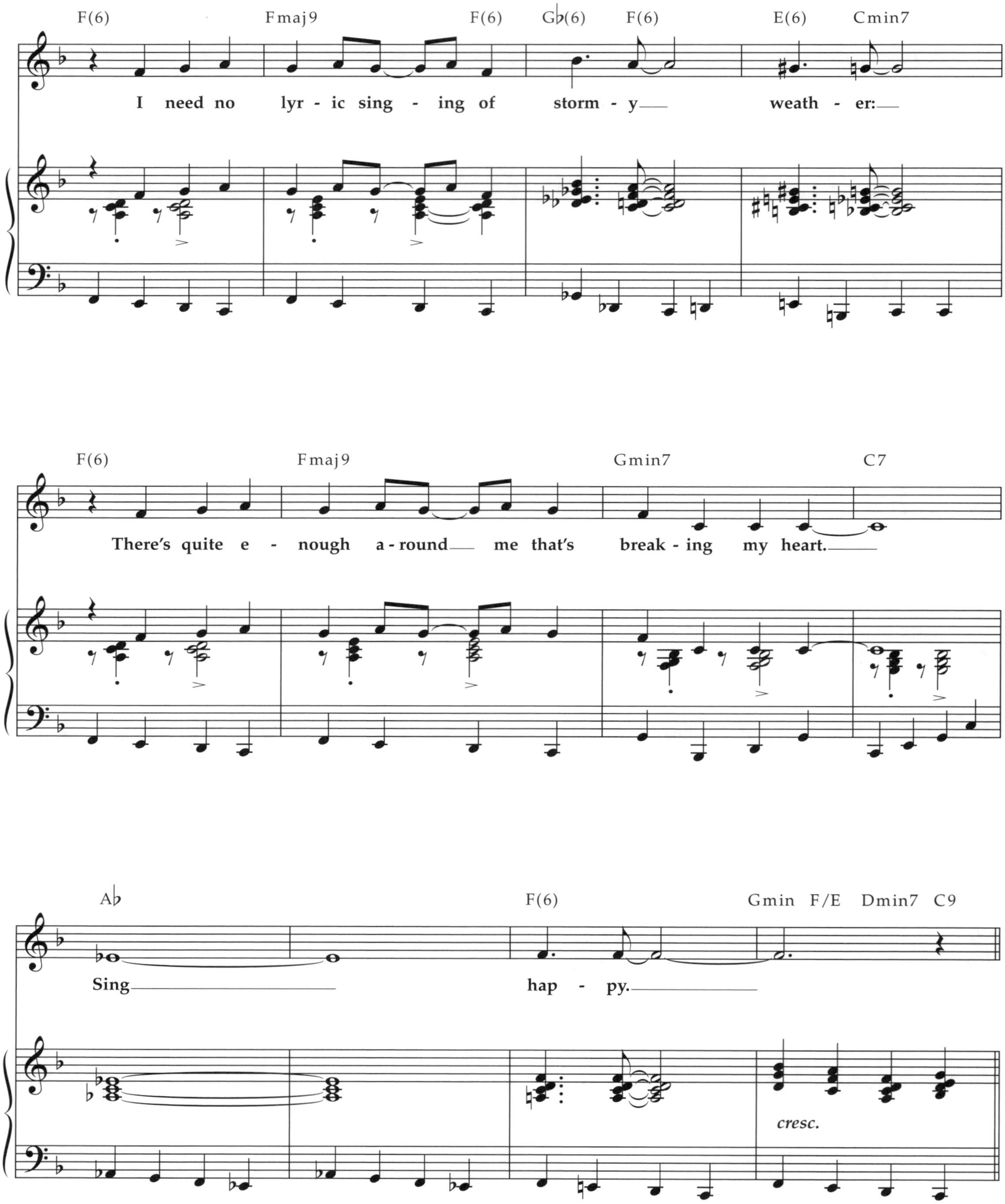
F(6) Fmaj9 F(6) G♭(6) F(6) E(6) Cmin7
I need no lyr - ic sing - ing of storm - y weath - er:
F(6) Fmaj9 Gmin7 C7
There's quite e - nough a - round me that's break - ing my heart.
A♭ F(6) Gmin F/E Dmin7 C9
Sing hap - py.
cresc.

A♭ A♭(6,9) A♭maj9 A♭(6) B♭min7 E♭7 B♭min7 E♭7
Give me a hal - le - lu - jah and get up and shout,
f
A♭ A♭(6,9) A♭maj9 A♭(6) A(6)/A♭ A♭(6) G(6)/A♭ A♭9sus
Tell me the sun is shin - ing a - round the cor - ner.
A♭ A♭(6,9) A♭maj9 A♭(6) B♭min7 E♭7 B♭min7 E♭7
Who - ev - er's in - ter - est - ed in help - ing me out,

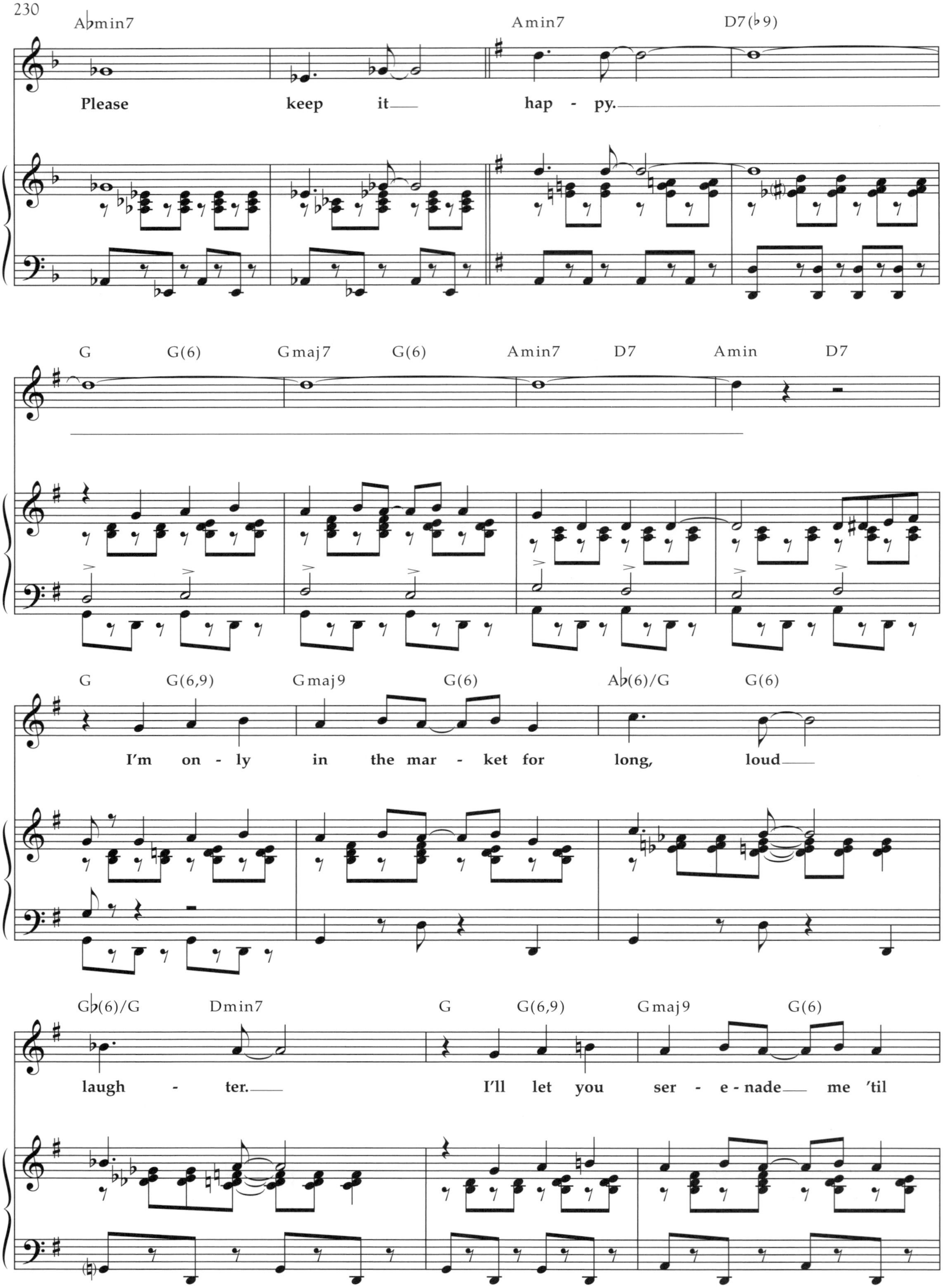
A♭min7 Amin7 D7(♭9)
Please keep it happy.
G G(6) Gmaj7 G(6) Amin7 D7 Amin D7
G G(6,9) Gmaj9 G(6) A♭(6)/G G(6)
I'm on - ly in the mar - ket for long, loud
G♭(6)/G Dmin7 G G(6,9) Gmaj9 G(6)
laugh - ter. I'll let you ser - e - nade me 'til

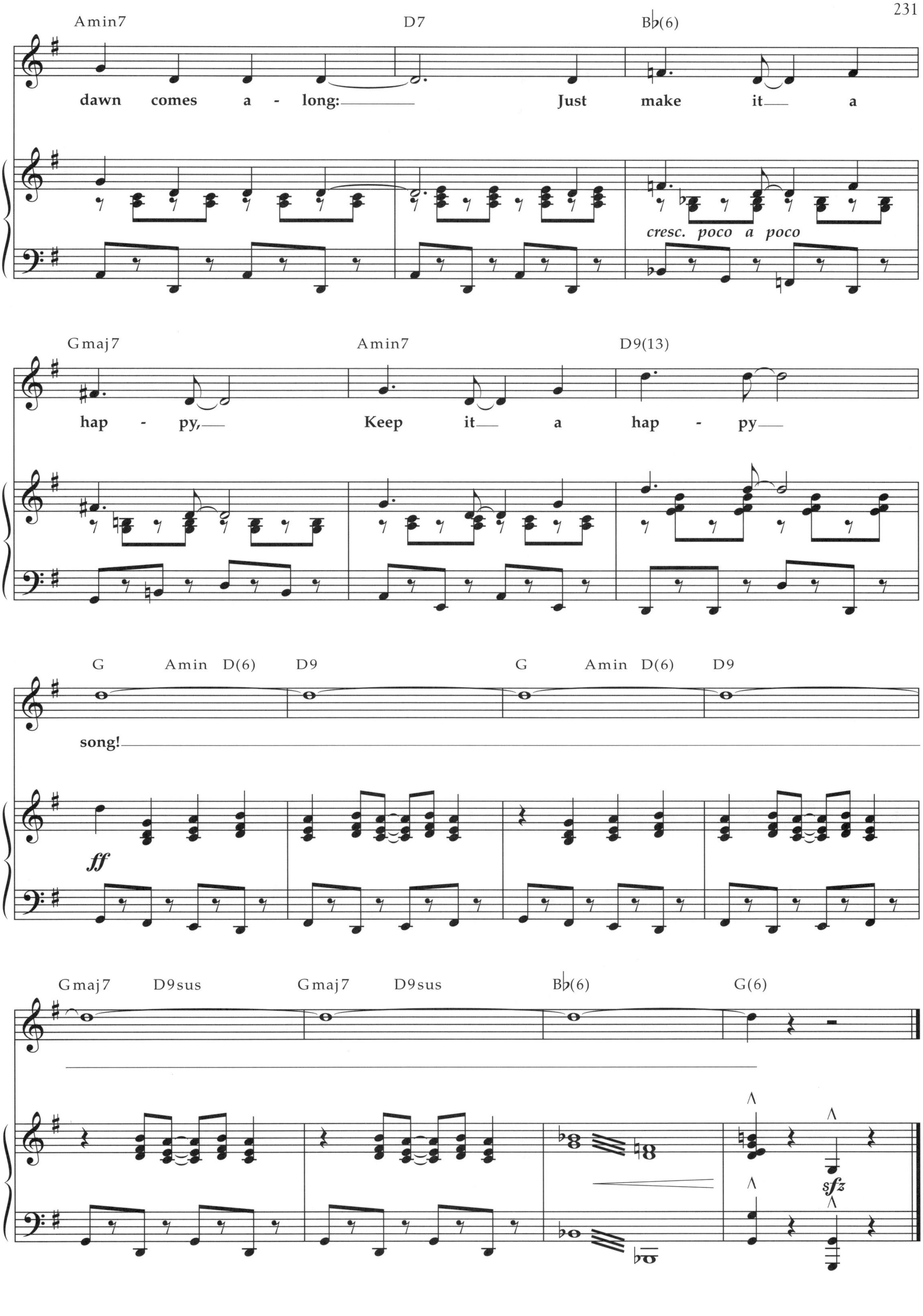
Amin7
D7
B♭(6)
dawn comes a - long:
Just make it a
cresc. poco a poco
Gmaj7
Amin7
D9(13)
hap - py,
Keep it a hap - py
G
Amin
D(6)
D9
song!
ff
Gmaj7
D9sus
G(6)
sfz

# She's a Woman

*from the Musical* ***KISS OF THE SPIDER WOMAN***

Words by
**FRED EBB**

Music by
**JOHN KANDER**

poco rall.
G9sus
Cmaj7
G9sus
G
luck-y
She's a wom-an
She wears
Flowing motion
Cmaj7
G9sus
Cmaj7
G9sus
dia-monds bright as stars
She has lov-ers o-pen doors to fan-cy cars
She's
Dmin7
G9sus
poco rall.
Emin7
E9
poco accel.
luck-y
So luck-y
She's a wom-an
A
cresc.
Più mosso
A
D/A
D(6)/A
A
D/A
per-fume by Lan-vin to dab a-cross her wrist
A se-cret rib-boned di-a-ry of

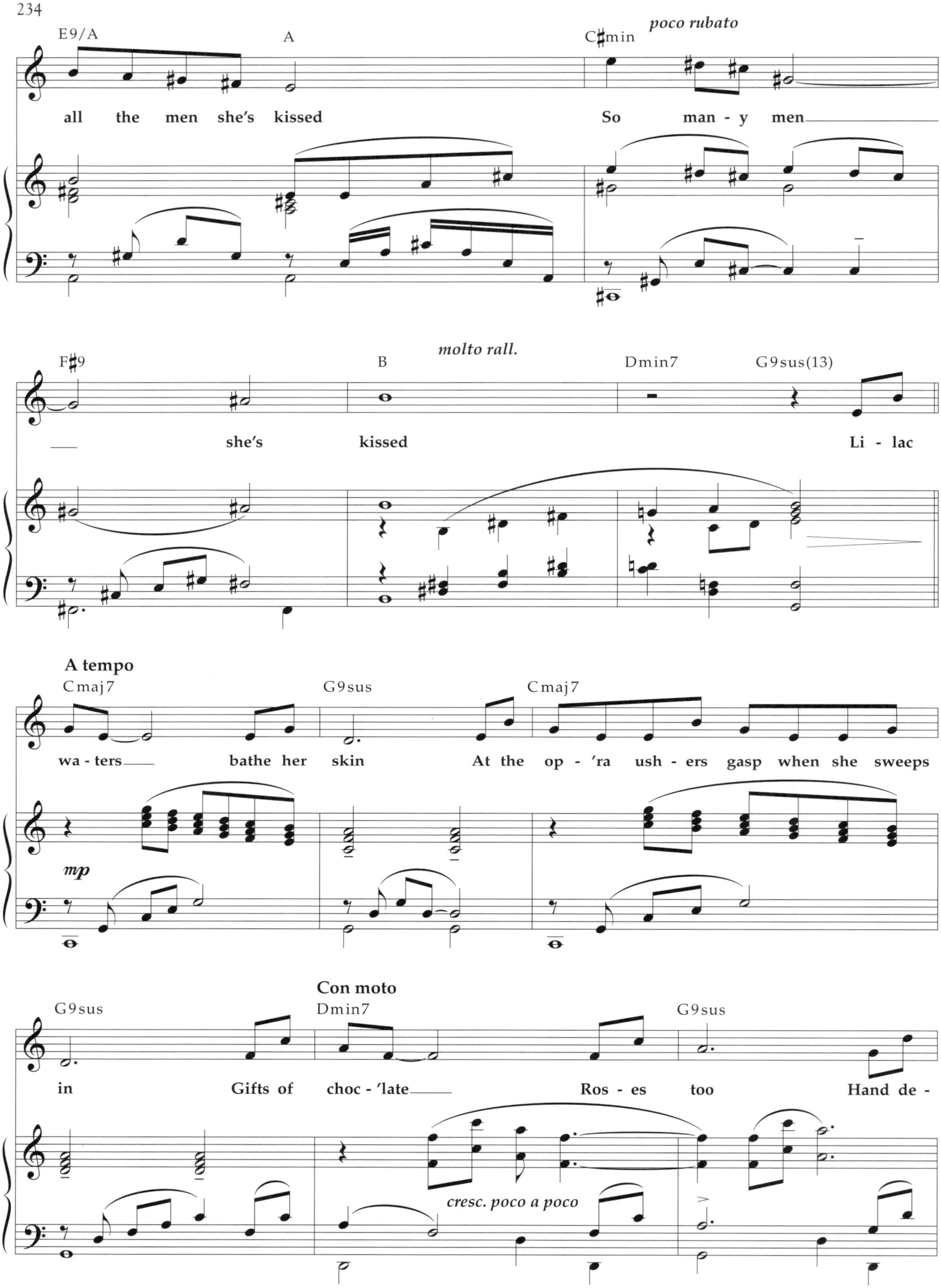
E9/A
A
C♯min
poco rubato
all the men she's kissed
So man - y men
F♯9
B
molto rall.
Dmin7
G9sus(13)
she's kissed
Li - lac
A tempo
Cmaj7
G9sus
Cmaj7
wa - ters bathe her skin
At the op - 'ra ush - ers gasp when she sweeps
mp
Con moto
G9sus
Dmin7
G9sus
in
Gifts of choc - 'late
Ros - es too
Hand de -
cresc. poco a poco

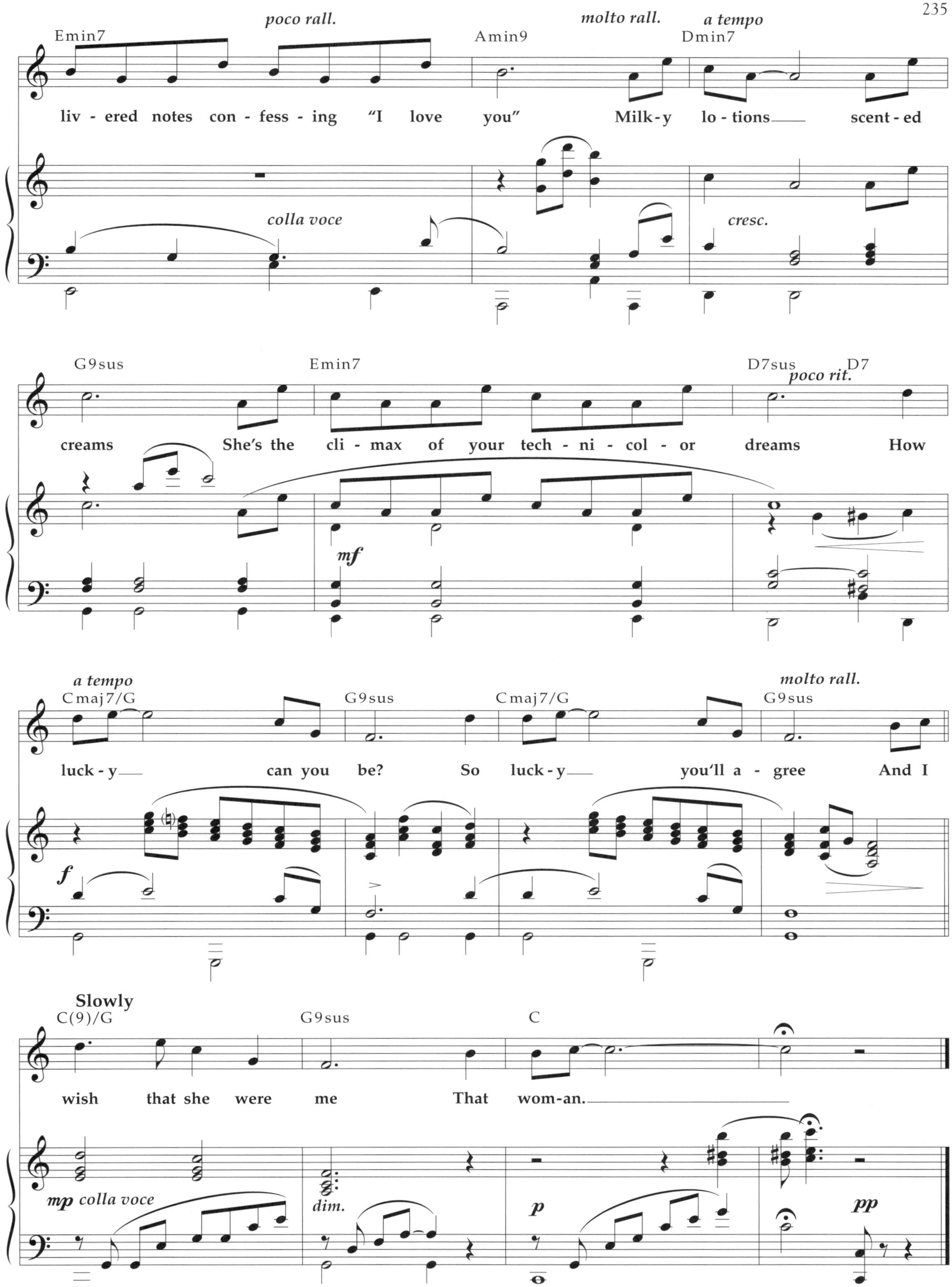
poco rall.
molto rall.
a tempo
Emin7
Amin9
Dmin7
liv - ered notes con - fess - ing "I love you" Milk - y lo - tions scent - ed
colla voce
cresc.
G9sus
Emin7
D7sus
D7
poco rit.
creams She's the cli - max of your tech - ni - col - or dreams How
mf
a tempo
molto rall.
Cmaj7/G
G9sus
Cmaj7/G
G9sus
luck - y can you be? So luck - y you'll a - gree And I
f
Slowly
C(9)/G
G9sus
C
wish that she were me That wom - an.
mp colla voce
dim.
p
pp

# The Skin of Our Teeth

*from the Musical* ***SKIN OF OUR TEETH***

Words by
**FRED EBB**

Music by
**JOHN KANDER**

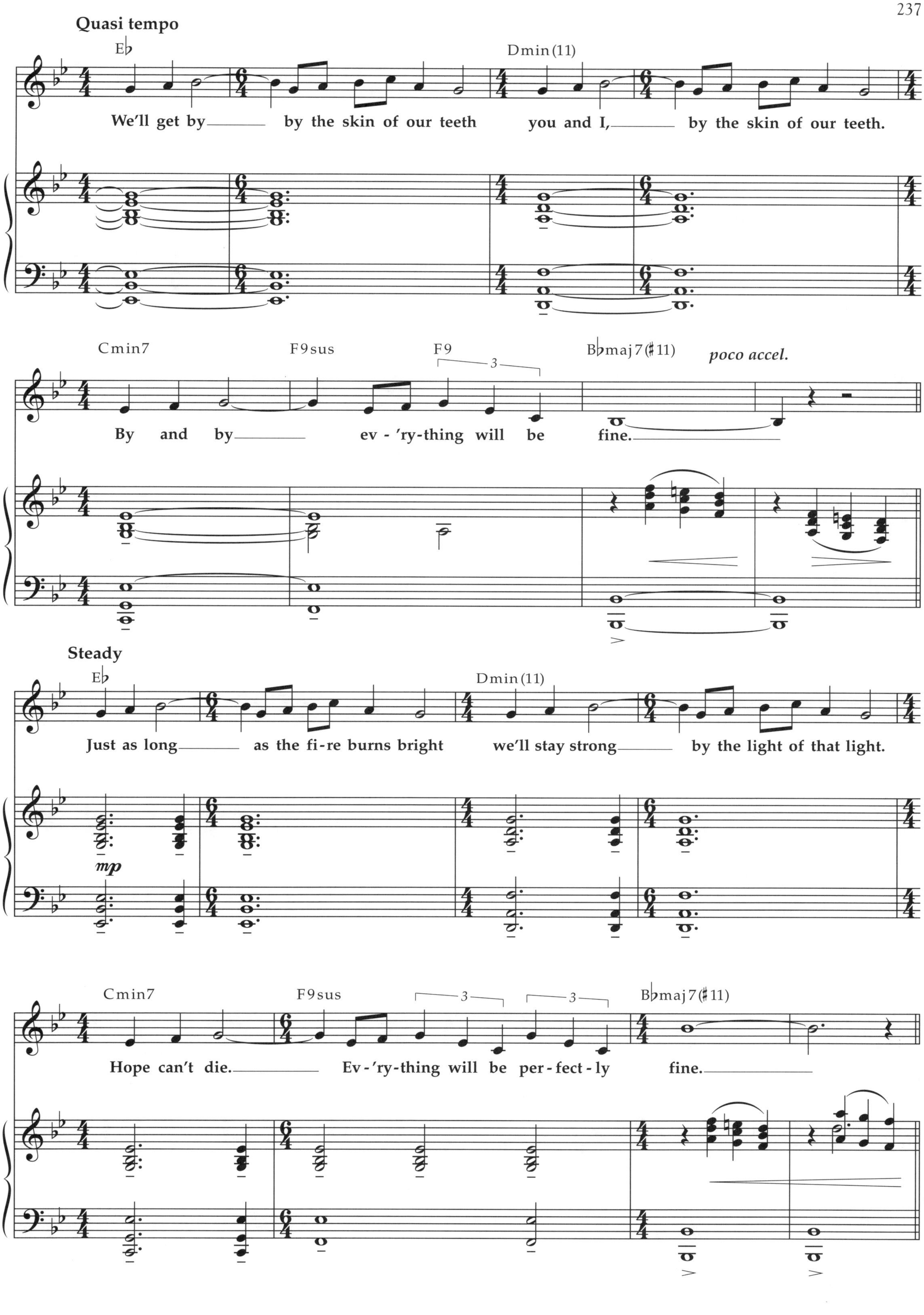
Quasi tempo
E♭
Dmin(11)
We'll get by by the skin of our teeth you and I, by the skin of our teeth.
Cmin7
F9sus
F9
3
B♭maj7(♯11)
poco accel.
By and by ev-'ry-thing will be fine.
Steady
E♭
Dmin(11)
Just as long as the fi-re burns bright we'll stay strong by the light of that light.
mp
Cmin7
F9sus
3
3
B♭maj7(♯11)
Hope can't die. Ev-'ry-thing will be per-fect-ly fine.

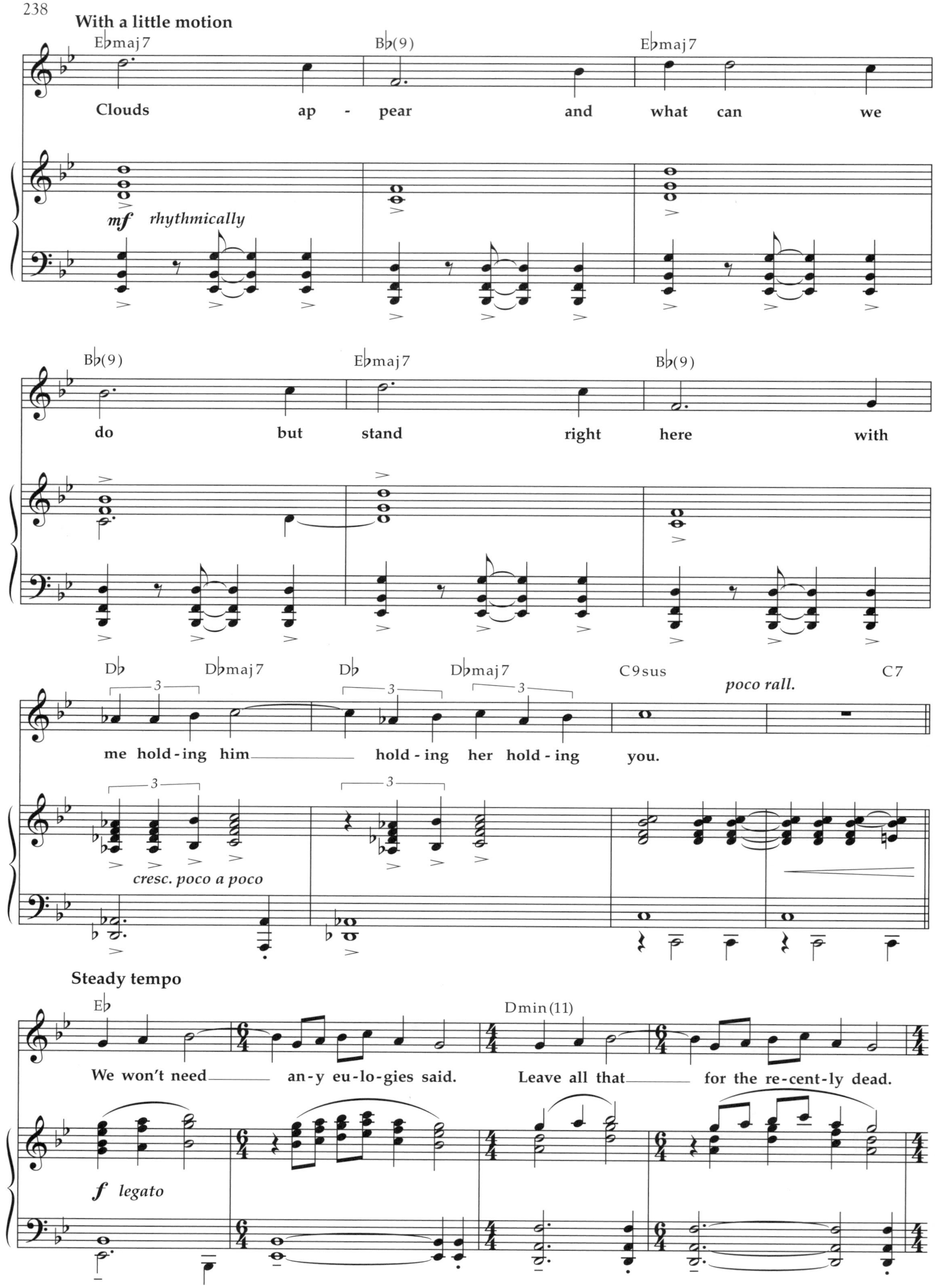
With a little motion
E♭maj7
B♭(9)
E♭maj7
Clouds ap - pear and what can we
mf rhythmically
B♭(9)
E♭maj7
B♭(9)
do but stand right here with
D♭
D♭maj7
D♭
D♭maj7
C9sus
poco rall.
C7
me hold-ing him hold-ing her hold-ing you.
3
cresc. poco a poco
Steady tempo
E♭
Dmin(11)
We won't need any eu-lo-gies said. Leave all that for the re-cent-ly dead.
f legato

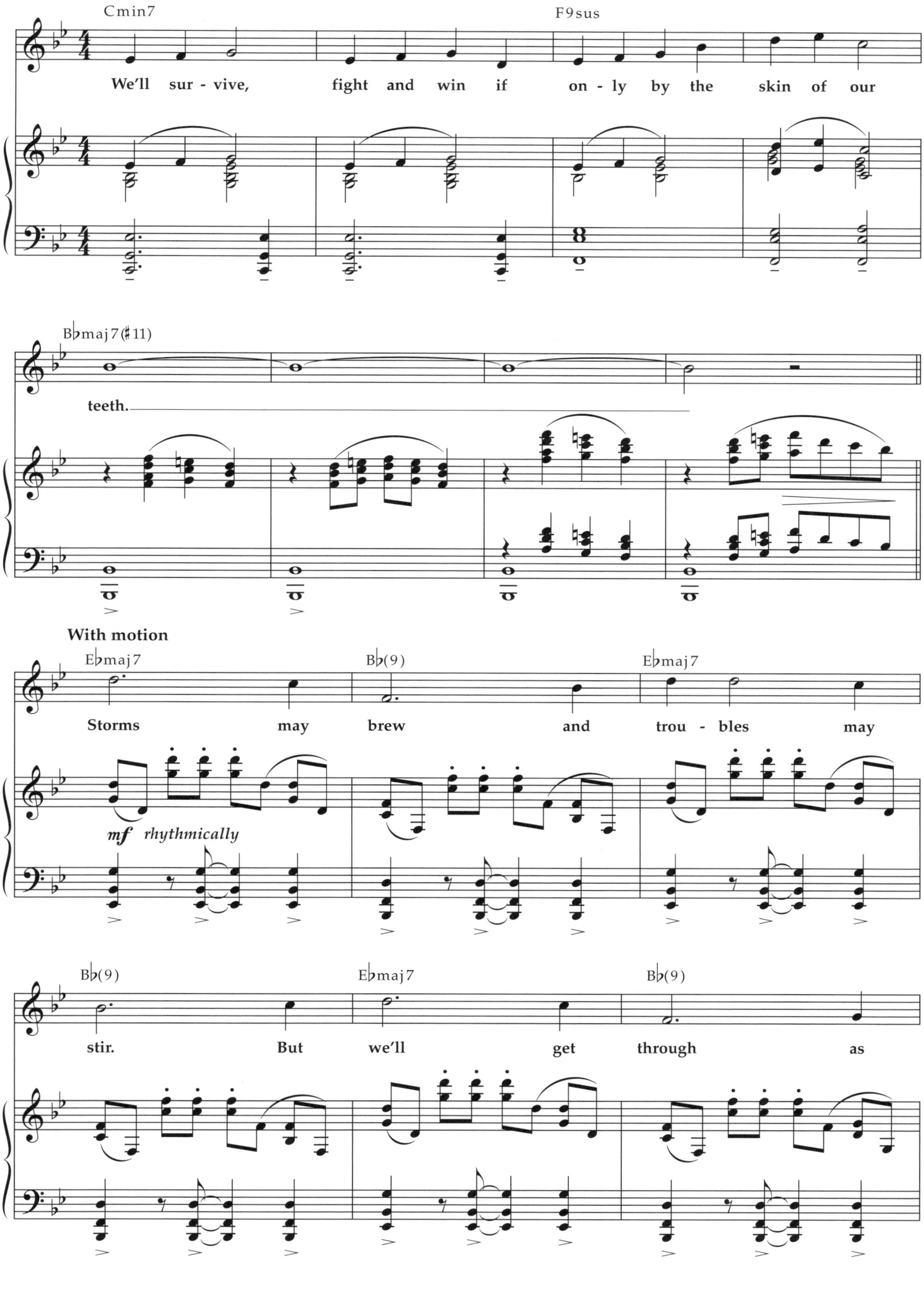
Cmin7
F9sus
We'll sur - vive, fight and win if on - ly by the skin of our
B♭maj7(♯11)
teeth.
With motion
E♭maj7
B♭(9)
E♭maj7
Storms may brew and trou - bles may
mf rhythmically
B♭(9)
E♭maj7
B♭(9)
stir. But we'll get through as

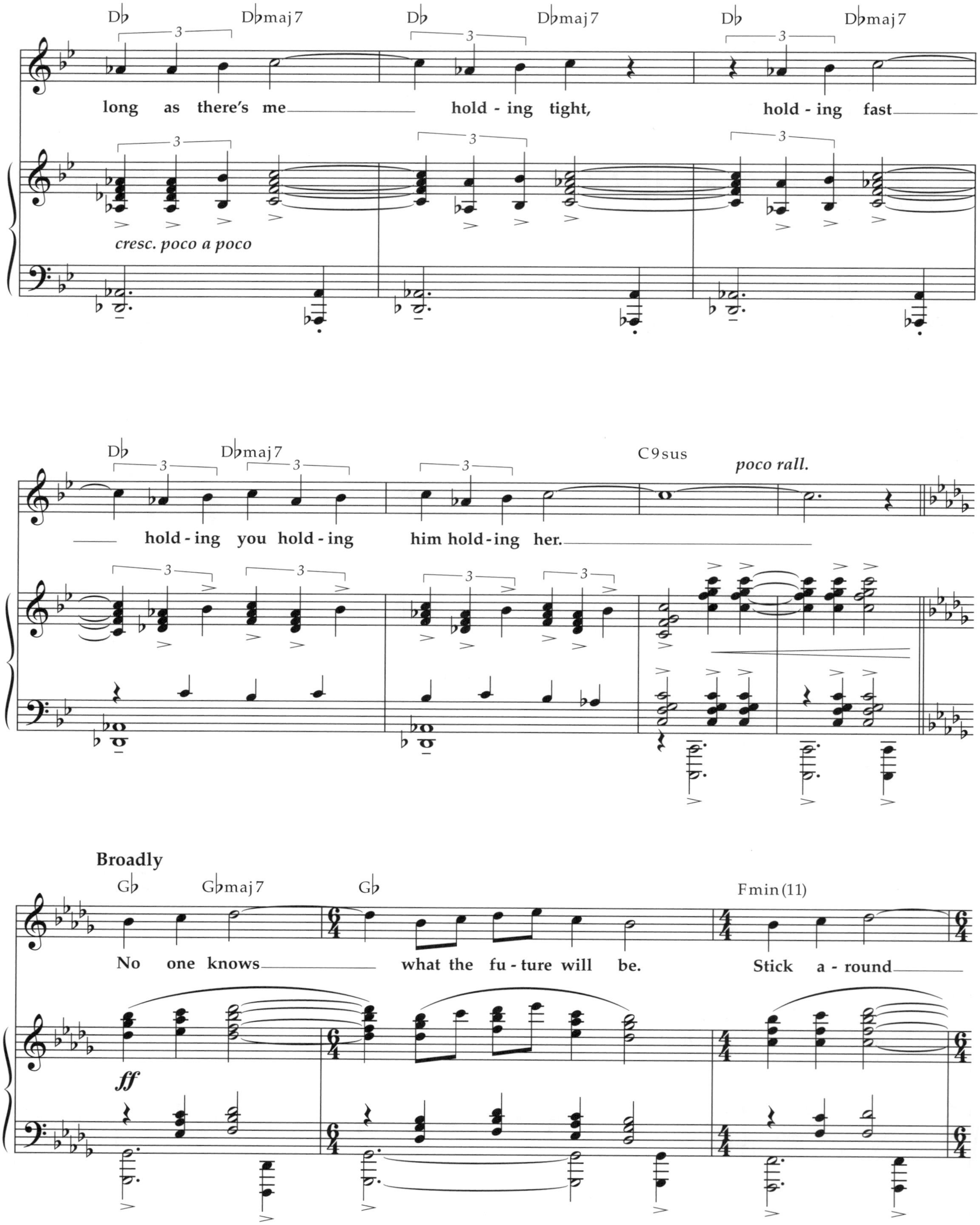
D♭ D♭maj7 D♭ D♭maj7 D♭ D♭maj7
long as there's me hold - ing tight, hold - ing fast
cresc. poco a poco
D♭ D♭maj7 C9sus
poco rall.
hold - ing you hold - ing him hold - ing her.
Broadly
G♭ G♭maj7 G♭ Fmin(11)
No one knows what the fu - ture will be. Stick a - round
ff

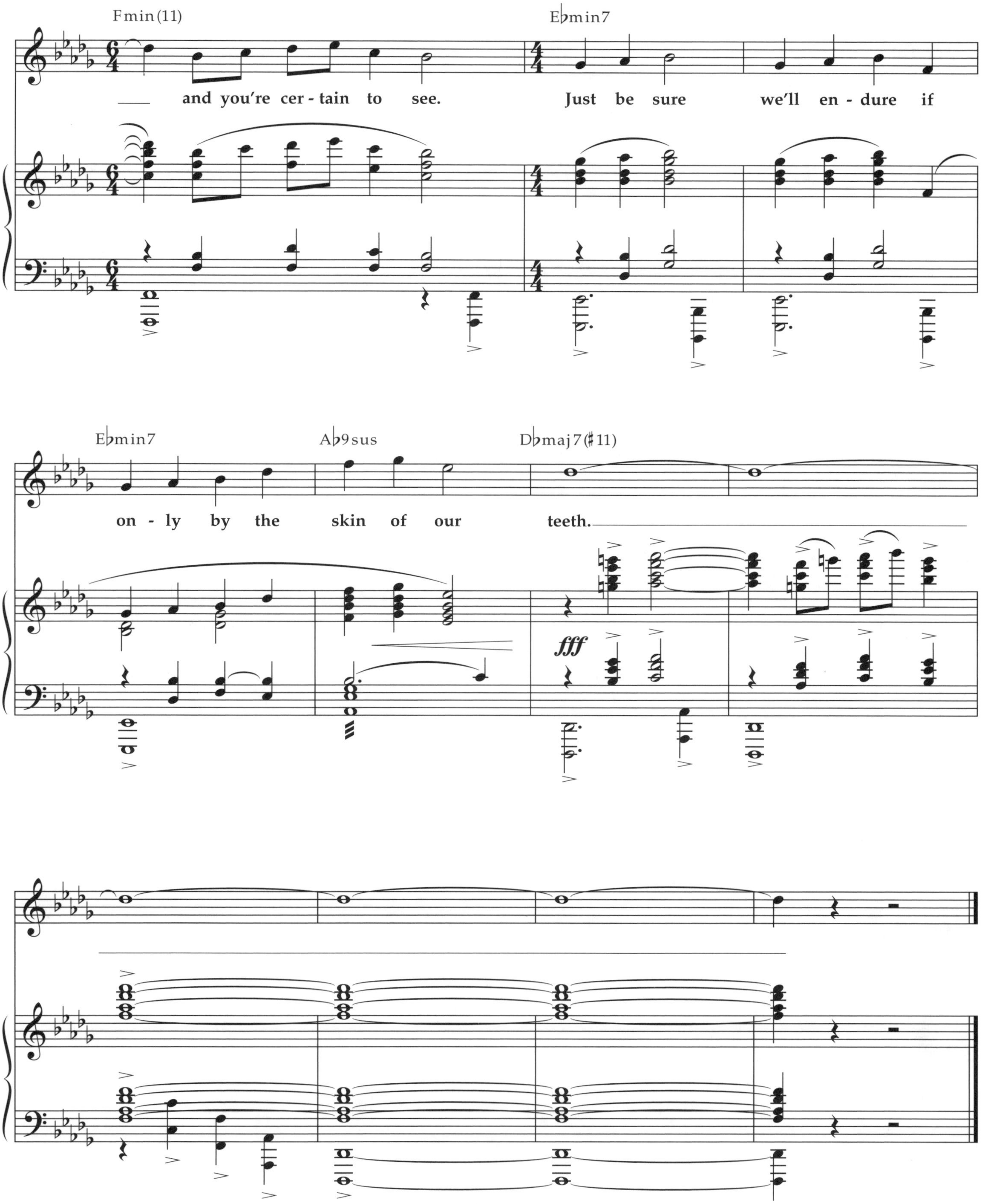
Fmin(11)
Ebmin7
and you're cer - tain to see. Just be sure we'll en - dure if
Ebmin7
Ab9sus
Dbmaj7(#11)
on - ly by the skin of our teeth.
fff

# So What?

*from the Musical* **CABARET**

Words by
**FRED EBB**

Music by
**JOHN KANDER**

**FRAULEIN SCHNEIDER:**
**You say fifty marks,**
**I say one hundred marks, a -**

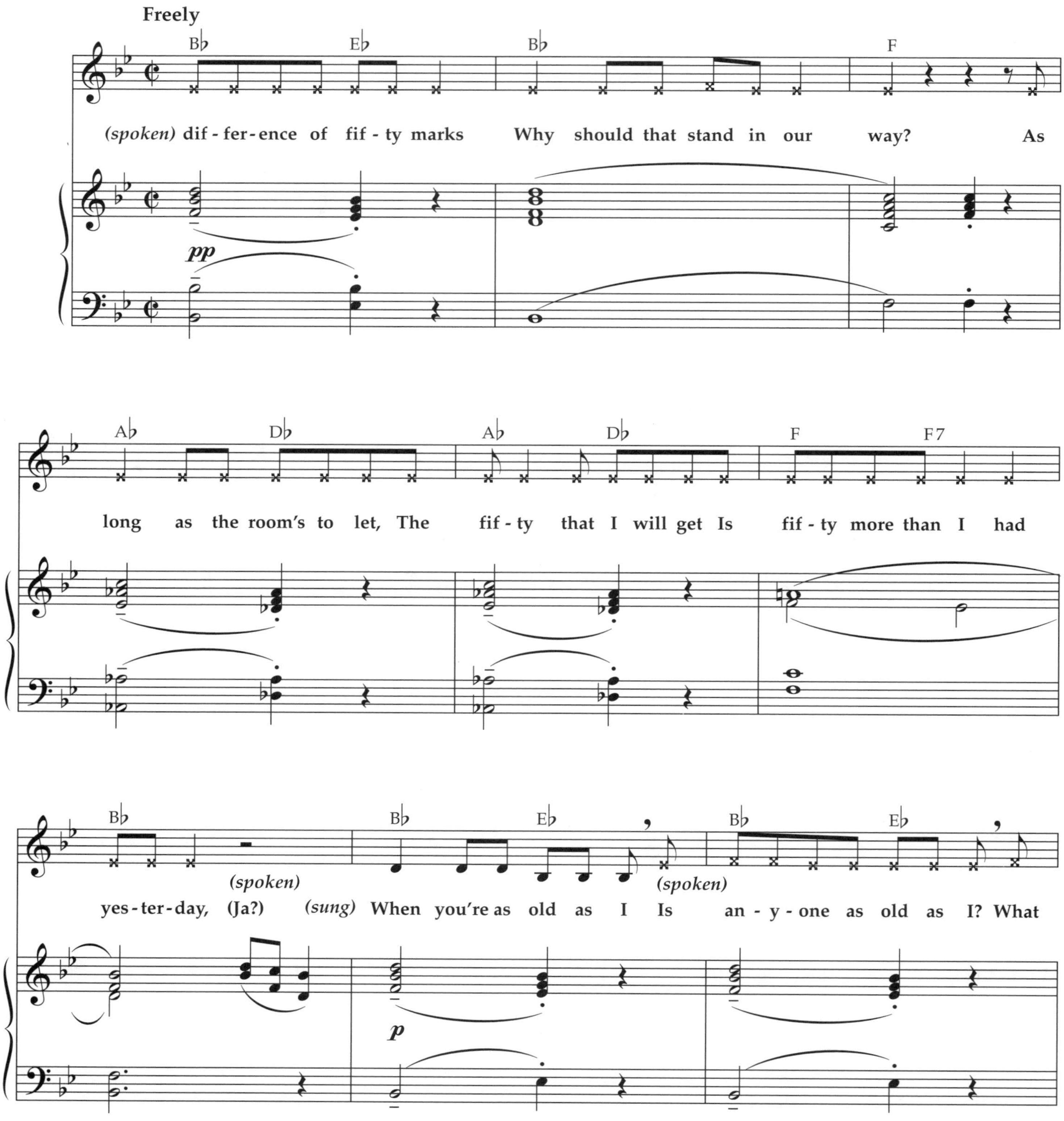

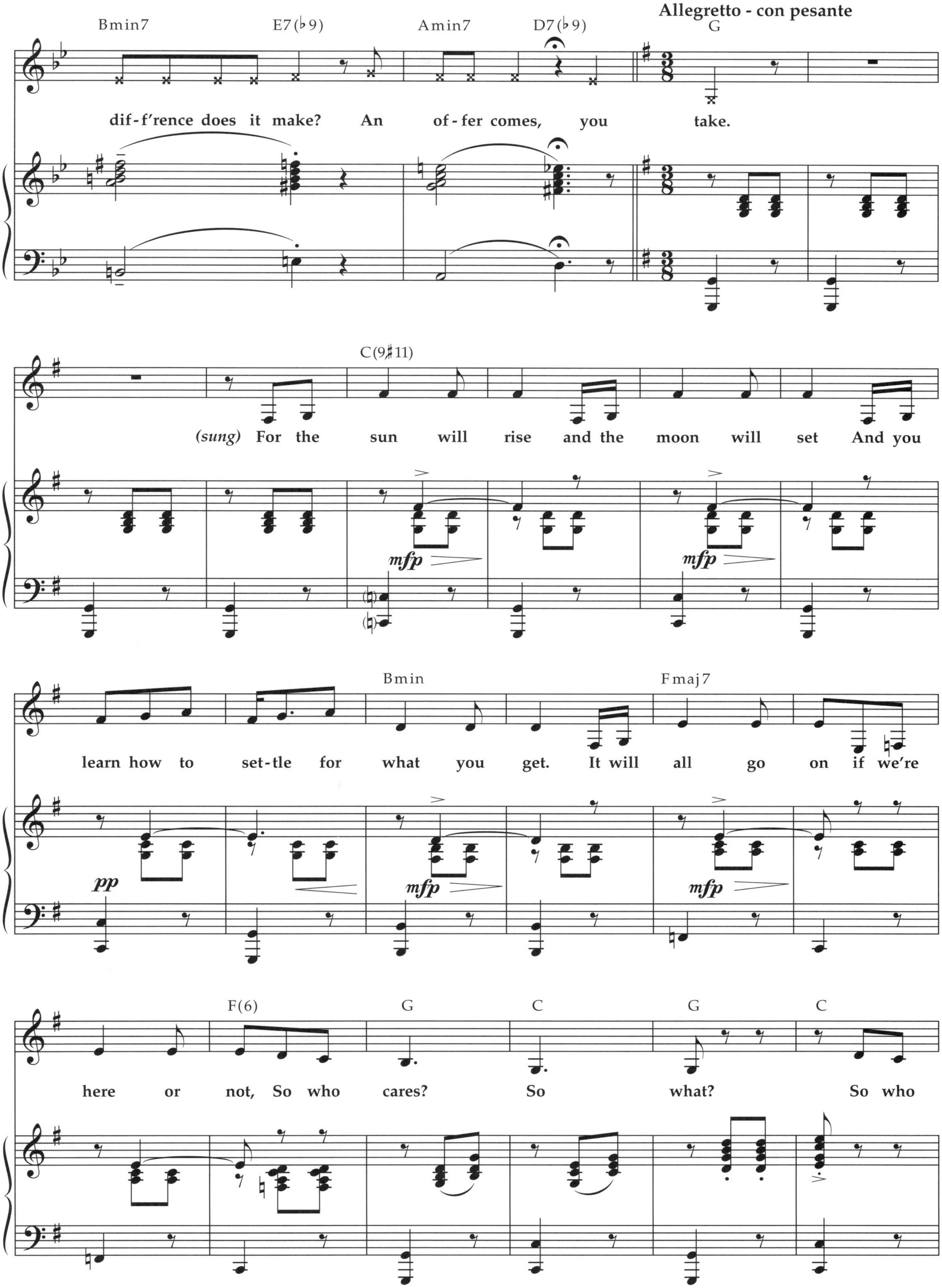
Allegretto - con pesante
Bmin7 E7(♭9) Amin7 D7(♭9) G
dif - f'rence does it make? An of - fer comes, you take.
C(9♯11)
(sung) For the sun will rise and the moon will set And you
mfp
mfp
Bmin Fmaj7
learn how to set - tle for what you get. It will all go on if we're
pp
mfp
mfp
F(6) G C G C
here or not, So who cares? So what? So who

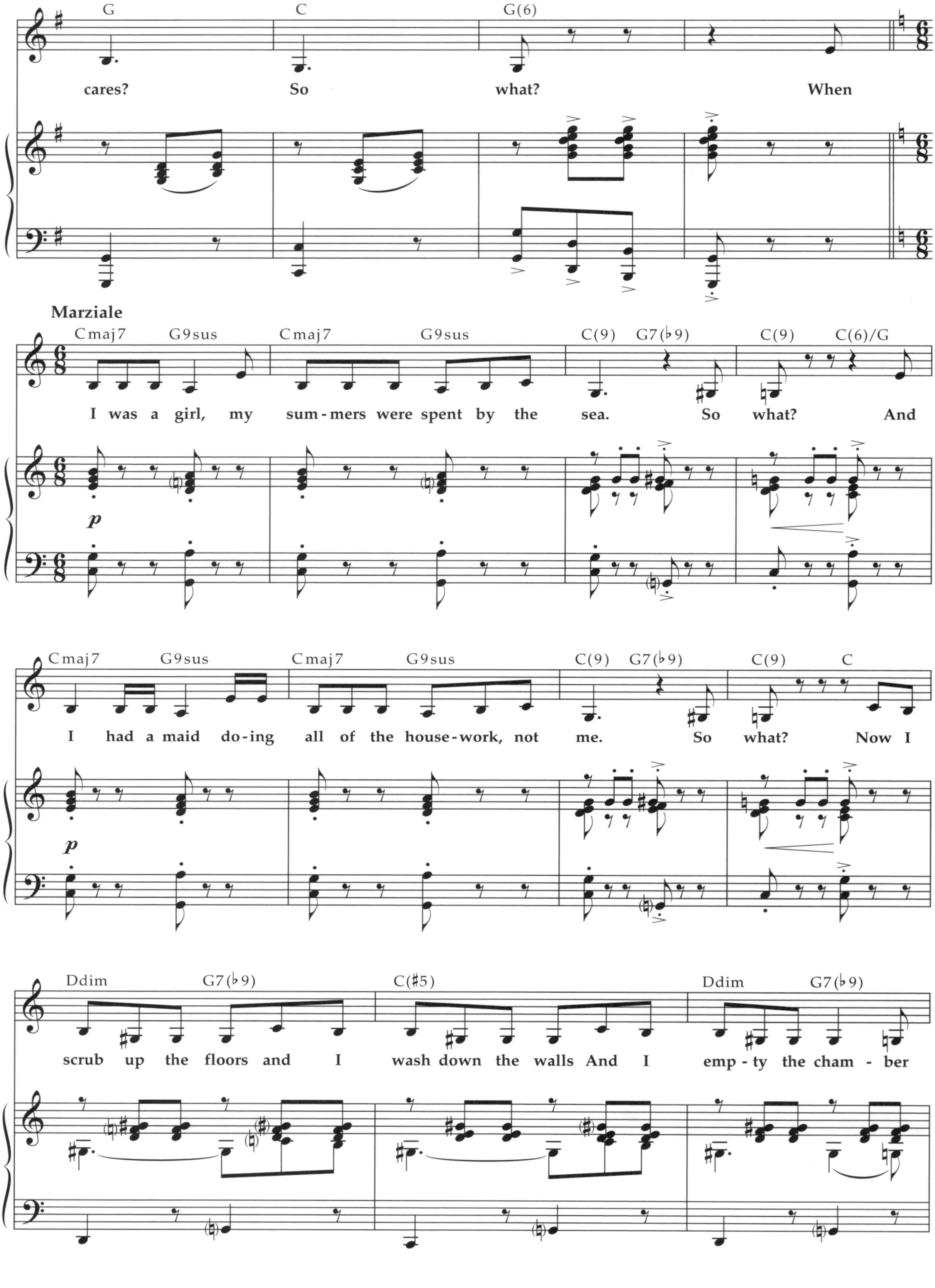
G C G(6)
cares? So what? When
Marziale
Cmaj7 G9sus Cmaj7 G9sus C(9) G7(♭9) C(9) C(6)/G
I was a girl, my sum-mers were spent by the sea. So what? And
p
Cmaj7 G9sus Cmaj7 G9sus C(9) G7(♭9) C(9) C
I had a maid do-ing all of the house-work, not me. So what? Now I
p
Ddim G7(♭9) C(♯5) Ddim G7(♭9)
scrub up the floors and I wash down the walls And I emp-ty the cham-ber

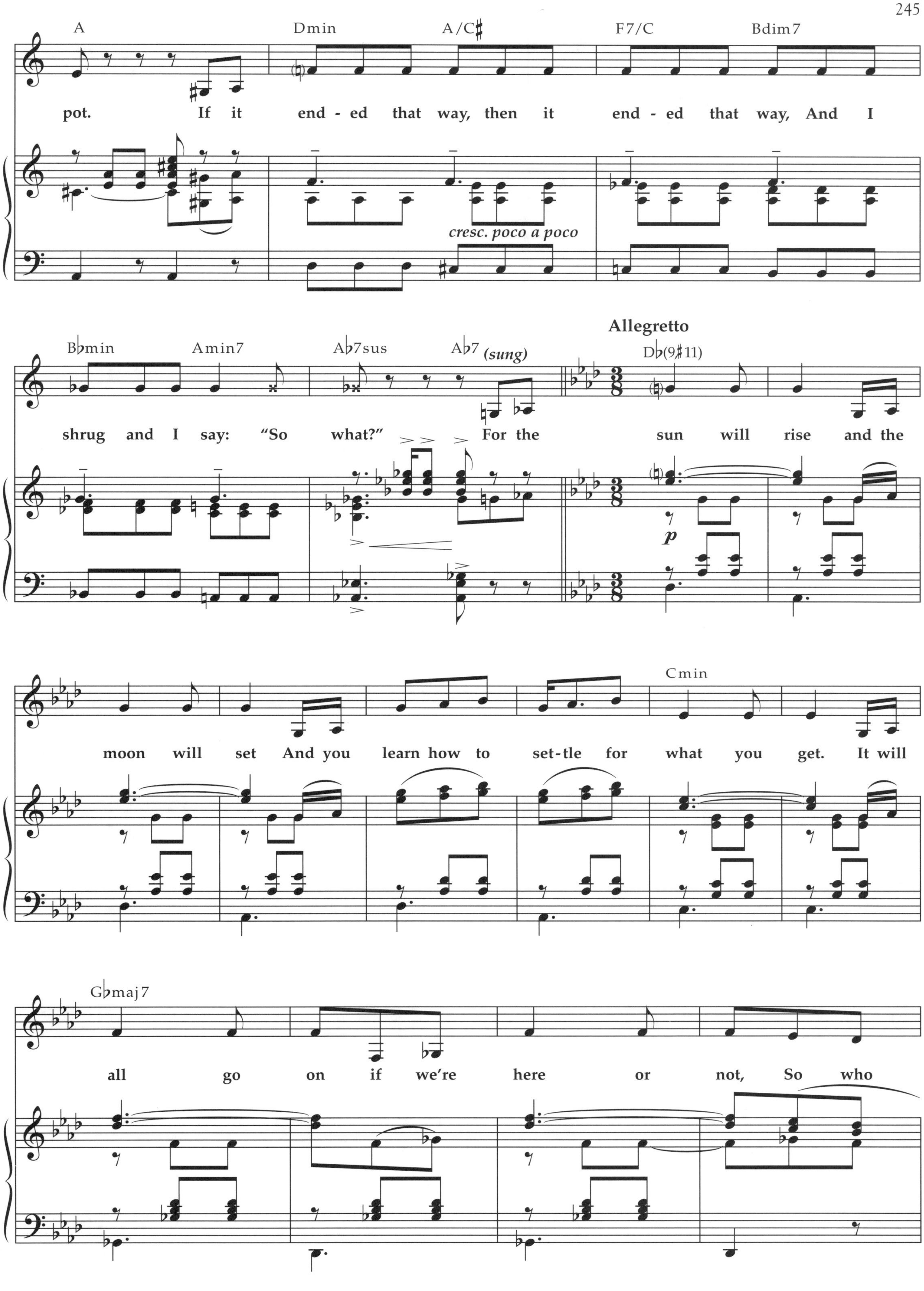
A
Dmin
A/C♯
F7/C
Bdim7
pot. If it end - ed that way, then it end - ed that way, And I
cresc. poco a poco
B♭min
Amin7
A♭7sus
A♭7
(sung)
Allegretto
D♭(9♯11)
shrug and I say: "So what?" For the sun will rise and the
p
moon will set And you learn how to set-tle for what you get. It will
Cmin
G♭maj7
all go on if we're here or not, So who

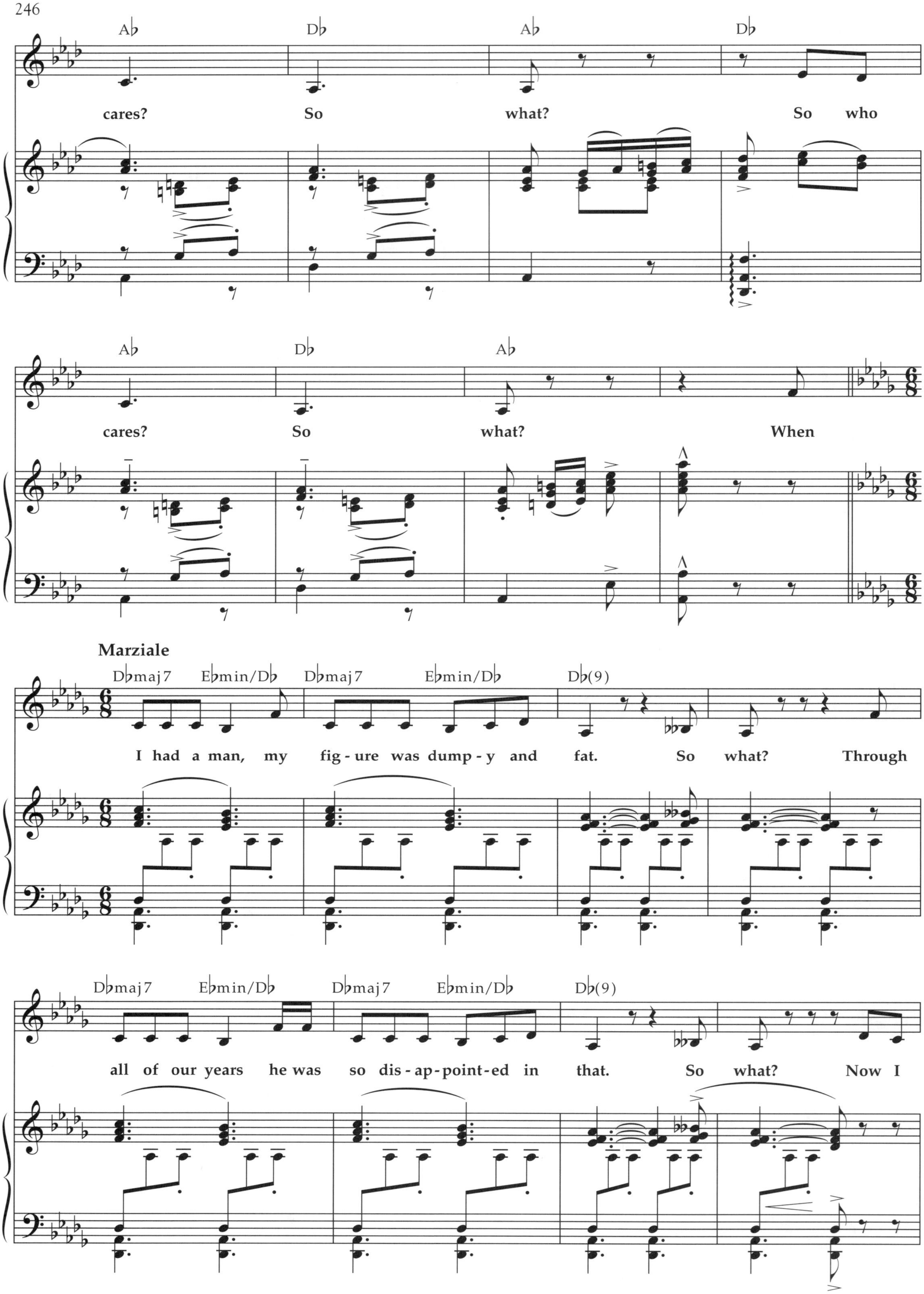
A♭ D♭ A♭ D♭
cares? So what? So who
A♭ D♭ A♭
cares? So what? When
Marziale
D♭maj7 E♭min/D♭ D♭maj7 E♭min/D♭ D♭(9)
I had a man, my fig - ure was dump - y and fat. So what? Through
D♭maj7 E♭min/D♭ D♭maj7 E♭min/D♭ D♭(9)
all of our years he was so dis - ap - point - ed in that. So what? Now I

E♭dim A♭7(♭9) E♭dim A♭7(♭9) E♭dim A♭7(♭9)
have what he missed and my fig - ure is trim, But he lies in a church - yard
p
B♭min(9) E♭min B♭/D
plot. If it was - n't to be that he
mf
G♭7/D♭ Cdim7 Gmaj7/B E♭7/B♭ Amin9
ev - er would see the un - cor - set - ed me, So what? For the
mf p
Allegretto
D(9♯11)
sun will rise and the moon will set And you

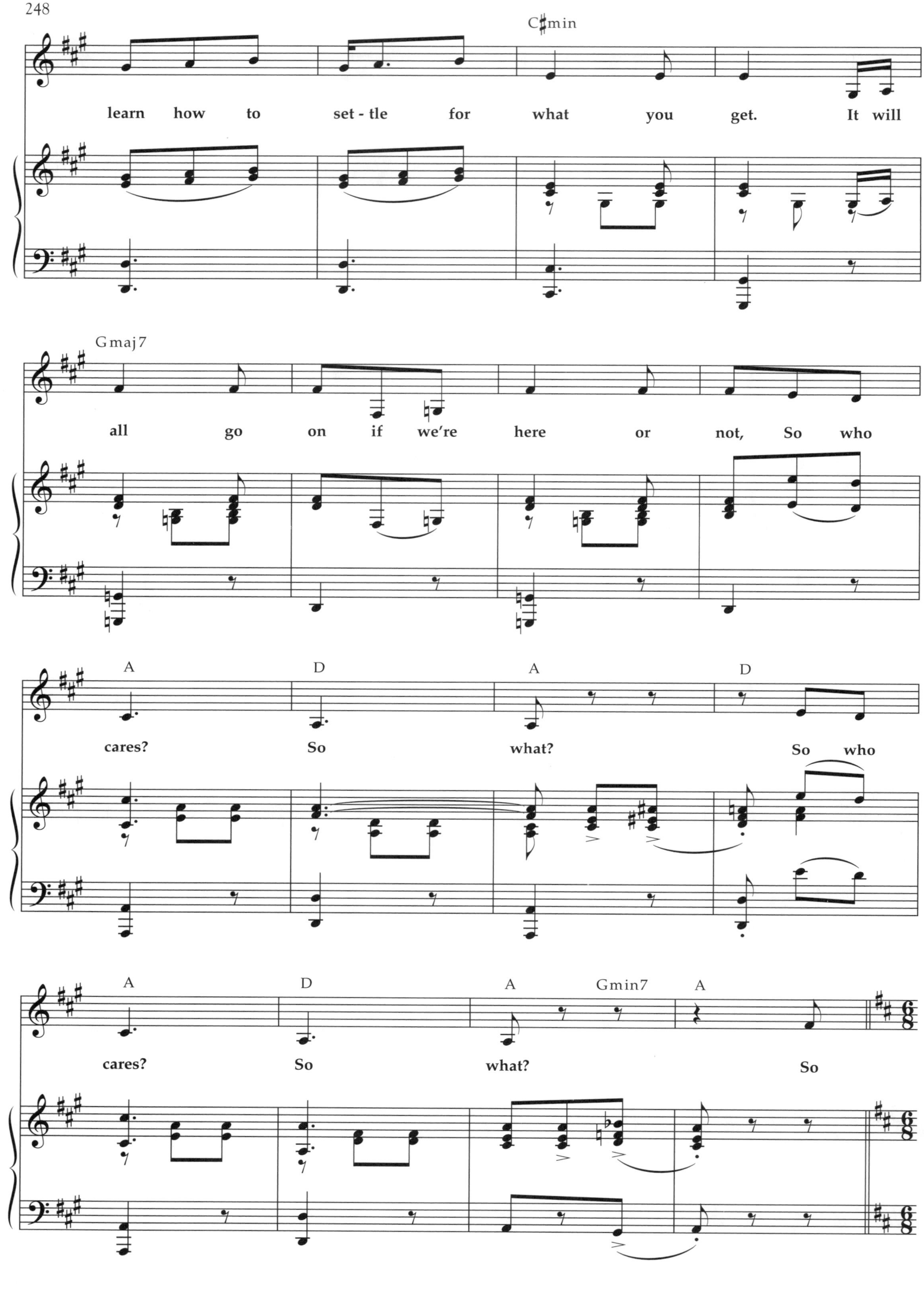
C♯min
learn how to set - tle for what you get. It will
Gmaj7
all go on if we're here or not, So who
A D A D
cares? So what? So who
A D A Gmin7 A
cares? So what? So

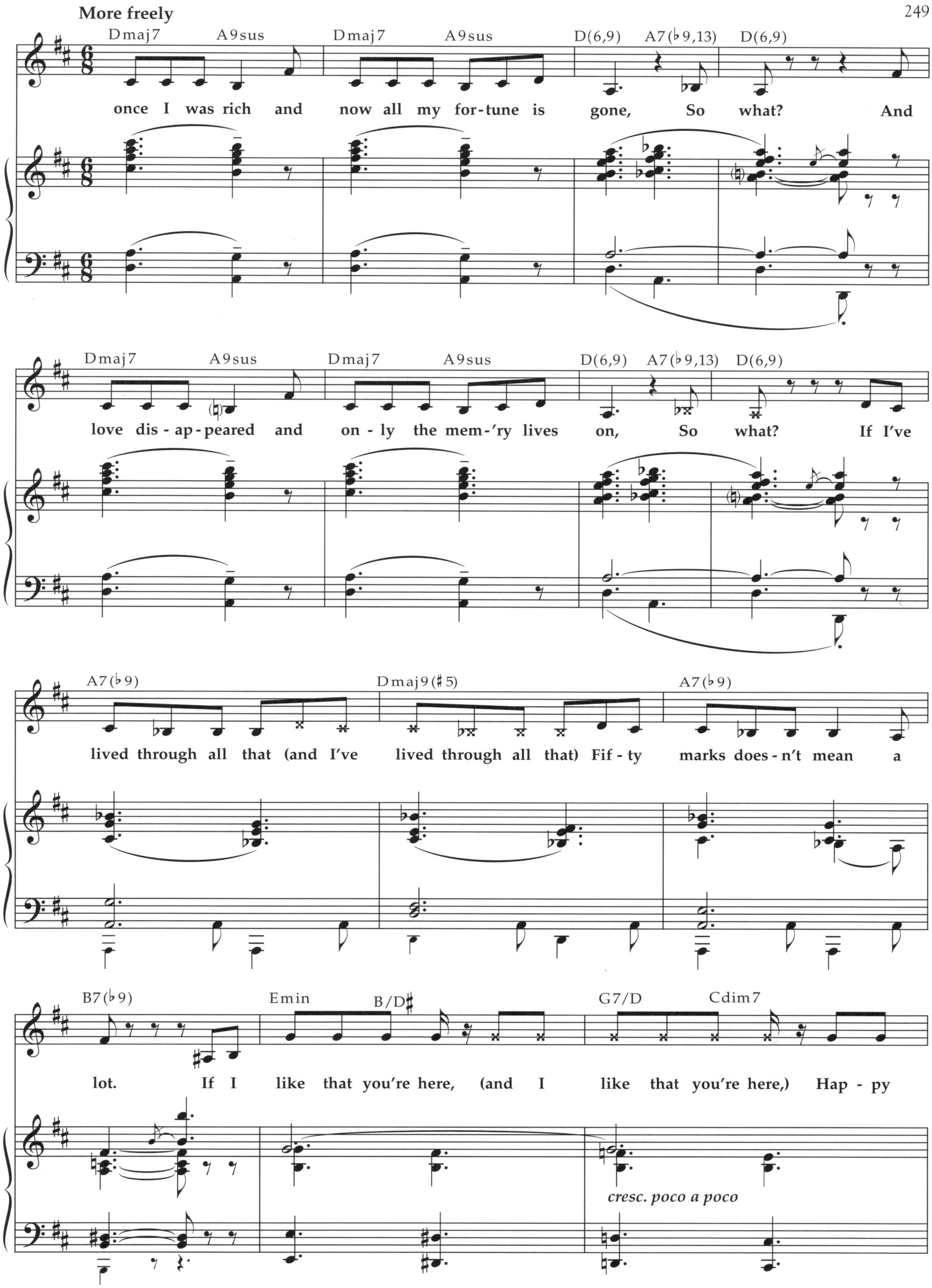
More freely
Dmaj7 A9sus Dmaj7 A9sus D(6,9) A7(♭9,13) D(6,9)
once I was rich and now all my for-tune is gone, So what? And
Dmaj7 A9sus Dmaj7 A9sus D(6,9) A7(♭9,13) D(6,9)
love dis-ap-peared and on-ly the mem-'ry lives on, So what? If I've
A7(♭9) Dmaj9(♯5) A7(♭9)
lived through all that (and I've lived through all that) Fif-ty marks does-n't mean a
B7(♭9) Emin B/D♯ G7/D Cdim7
lot. If I like that you're here, (and I like that you're here,) Hap-py
cresc. poco a poco

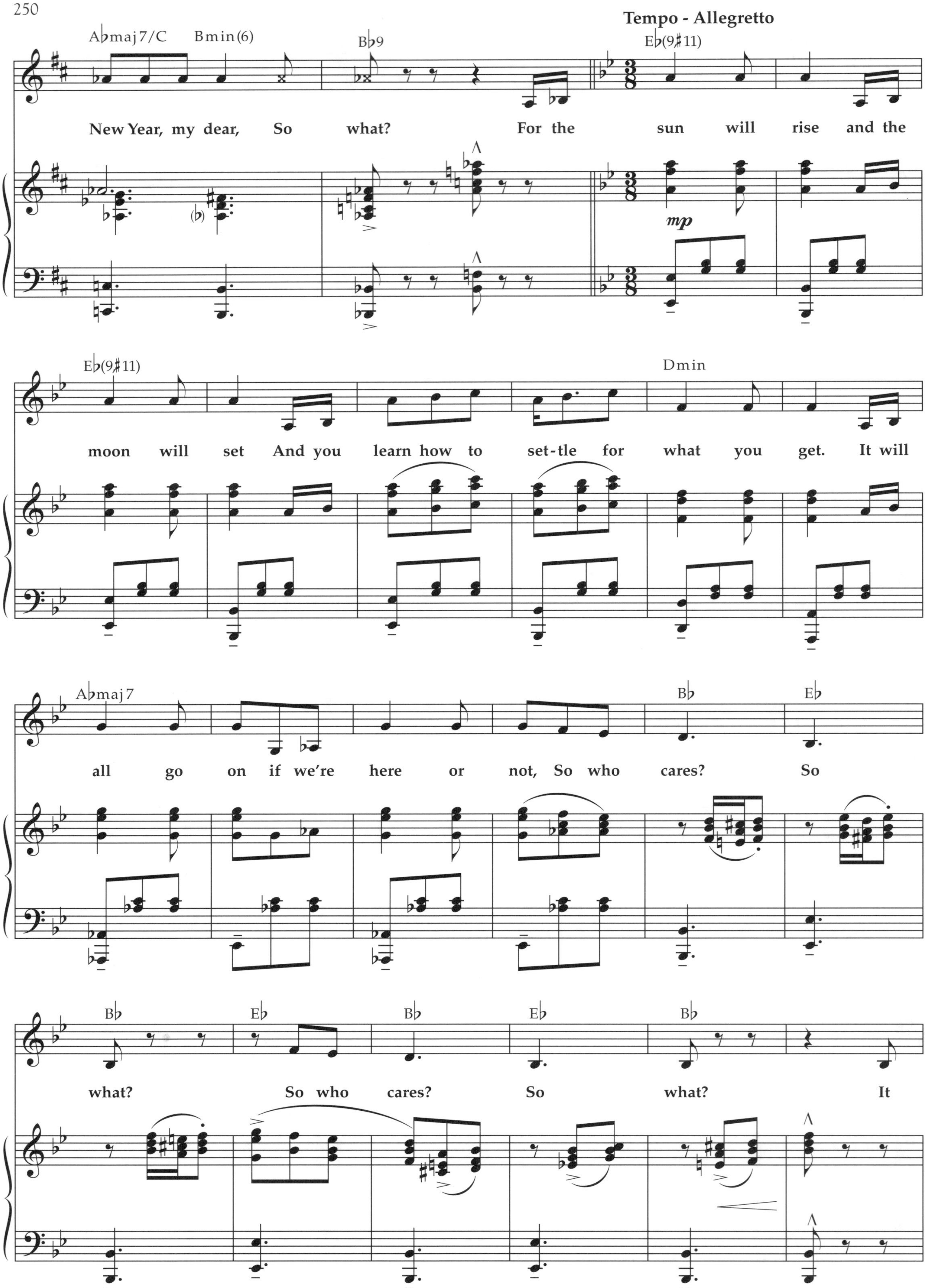
Tempo - Allegretto
A♭maj7/C Bmin(6) B♭9 E♭(9♯11)
New Year, my dear, So what? For the sun will rise and the
mp
E♭(9♯11) Dmin
moon will set And you learn how to set-tle for what you get. It will
A♭maj7 B♭ E♭
all go on if we're here or not, So who cares? So
B♭ E♭ B♭ E♭ B♭
what? So who cares? So what? It

E♭(9♯11)
all
goes
E♭(9♯11)
on.
So who
B♭
cares?
Who cares?
Who
f
cares?
So what?!
B♭maj9
ff

# Sometimes a Day Goes By

*from the Musical* ***WOMAN OF THE YEAR***

Words by
**FRED EBB**

Music by
**JOHN KANDER**

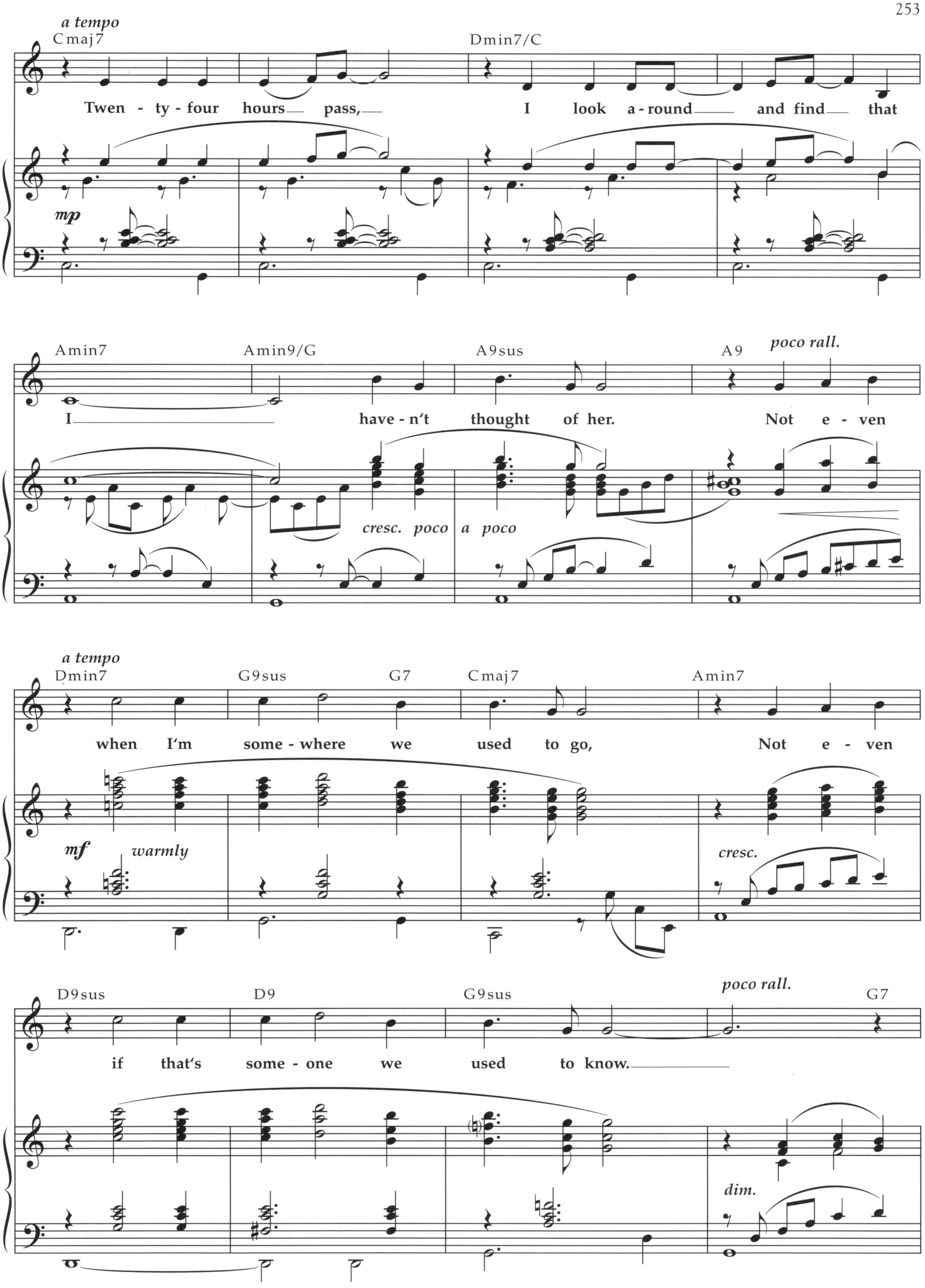
a tempo
Cmaj7
Dmin7/C
Twen - ty - four hours pass, I look a - round and find that
mp
Amin7
Amin9/G
A9sus
A9
poco rall.
I have - n't thought of her. Not e - ven
cresc. poco a poco
a tempo
Dmin7
G9sus
G7
Cmaj7
Amin7
when I'm some - where we used to go, Not e - ven
mf
warmly
cresc.
D9sus
D9
G9sus
poco rall.
G7
if that's some - one we used to know.
dim.

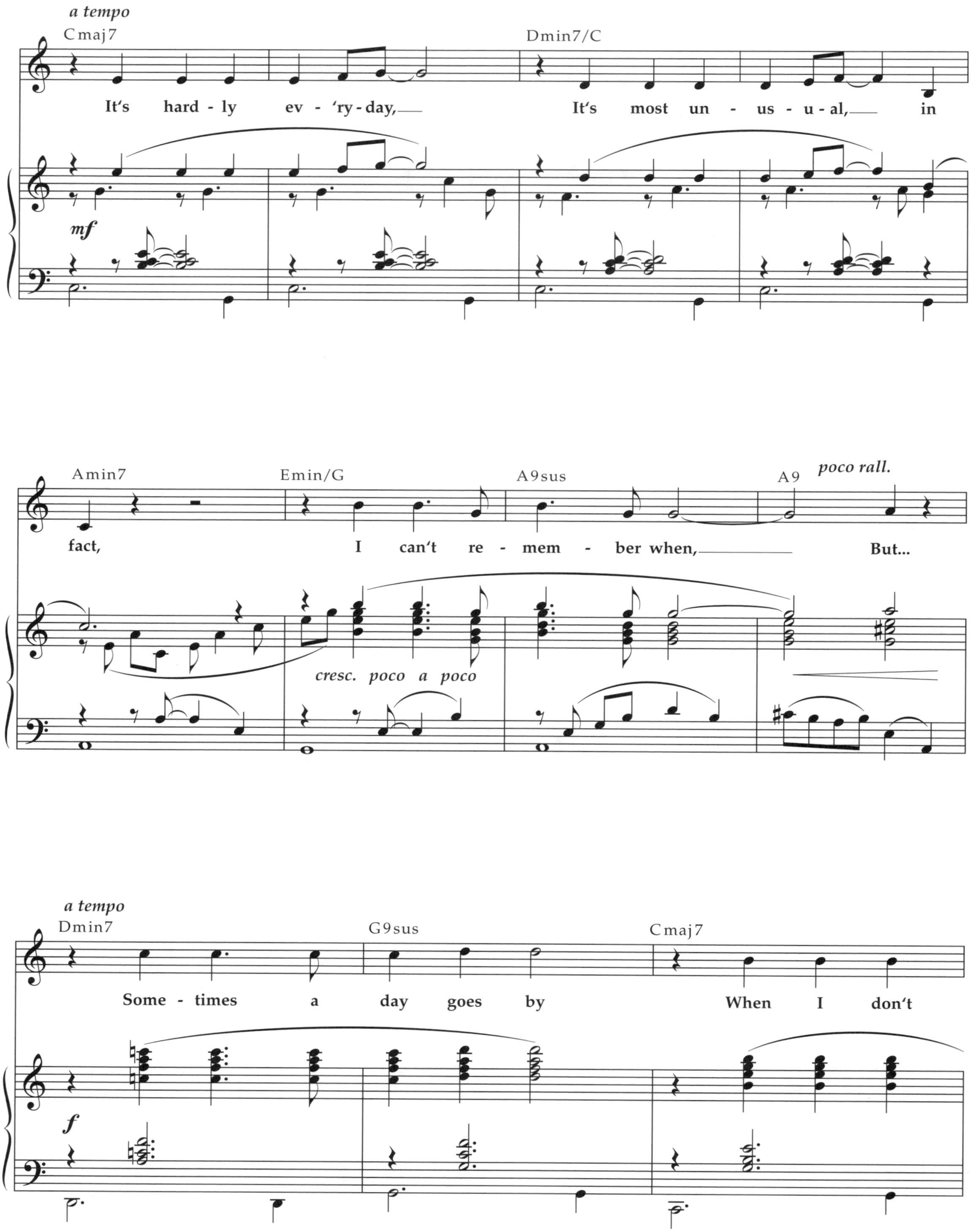
a tempo
Cmaj7
Dmin7/C
It's hard - ly ev - 'ry - day, It's most un - us - u - al, in
mf
Amin7
Emin/G
A9sus
A9
poco rall.
fact, I can't re - mem - ber when, But...
cresc. poco a poco
a tempo
Dmin7
G9sus
Cmaj7
Some - times a day goes by When I don't
f

Amin7
Dmin7
G9sus
G9
think of her Till morn - ing comes, And
Emin7
poco rall.
A7
poco rubato
Dmin7
G9sus
then there she is a -
dim.
mf
a tempo
Cmaj7(13)
rall. poco a poco
C
gain.
mp
dim.
p

# A Tough Act to Follow

*from the Musical* ***CURTAINS***

Words by
**FRED EBB**

Music by
**JOHN KANDER**

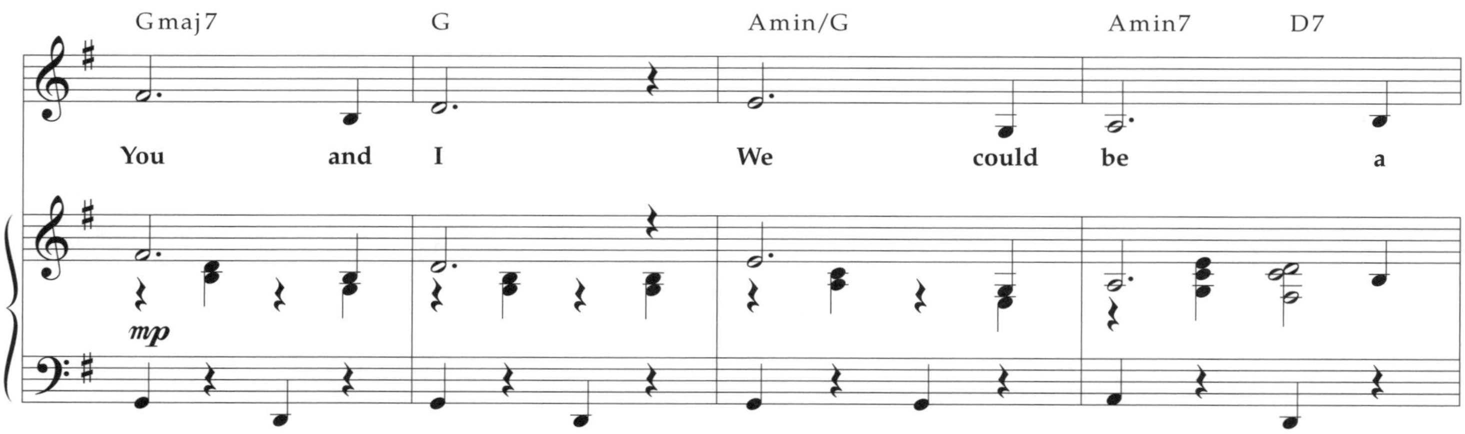


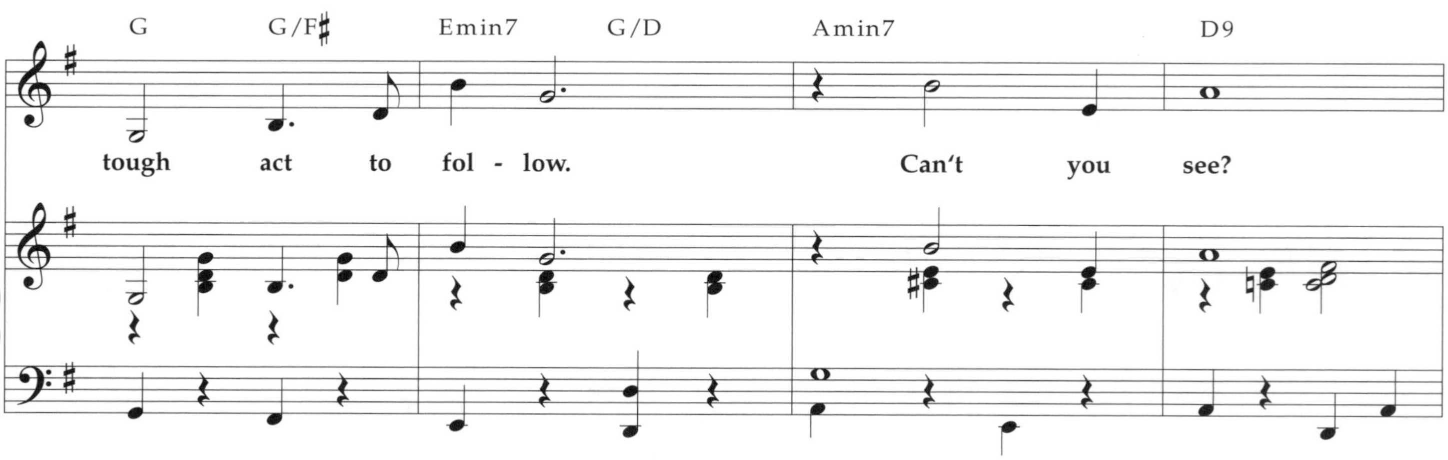

Bmin7 D♭dim7 D7/A E/G♯
Spe - cial peo - ple do - ing spe - cial things.
Amin/G D/F♯ Bdim7 E7 Amin D7
Run - ning rings a - round an - y pair. An - y - where.
poco cresc.
Gmaj7 G Amin/G Amin7 D7
You and I. We could stay a
mf
G G/F♯ Emin7 A9 F♯min7(♭5) B
tough act to fol - low in ev - 'ry way If you

Emin
G7/D
C
Cmin
hold my hand and let the mu - sic start let the
cresc. poco a poco
G7
C/G
Cmin/G
G7
cur - tains part let the spot - light
Cmaj7
Cmin (♯7)
Cmin(6)
G/D
D7sus
D7
glow. We'd be a tough act to fol - low I
dim.
p
With motion
A♭maj7
B♭min7
E♭7
know.
mf warmly

A♭
A♭/G
Fmin7
B♭9sus
B♭min7
E♭9
gliss.
ff
Cmin
Cmin7
Bdim7
B♭min7
F/A
A♭min7
mf
cresc. poco a poco
G9sus
G9
G9sus
F9(13)
rall.

A little broader
B♭maj7
Cmin7
F7
You and I. We could stay a
f legato
B♭
B♭/A
Gmin7
C9(13)
Adim7
D7
tough act to fol - low in ev - 'ry way If you
Gmin7
B♭7/F
B♭7
E♭maj7
hold my hand and let the mu - sic
ff
E♭min
B♭/D
B♭9
E♭/G
G♭dim
rit.
start let the cur - tains part let the

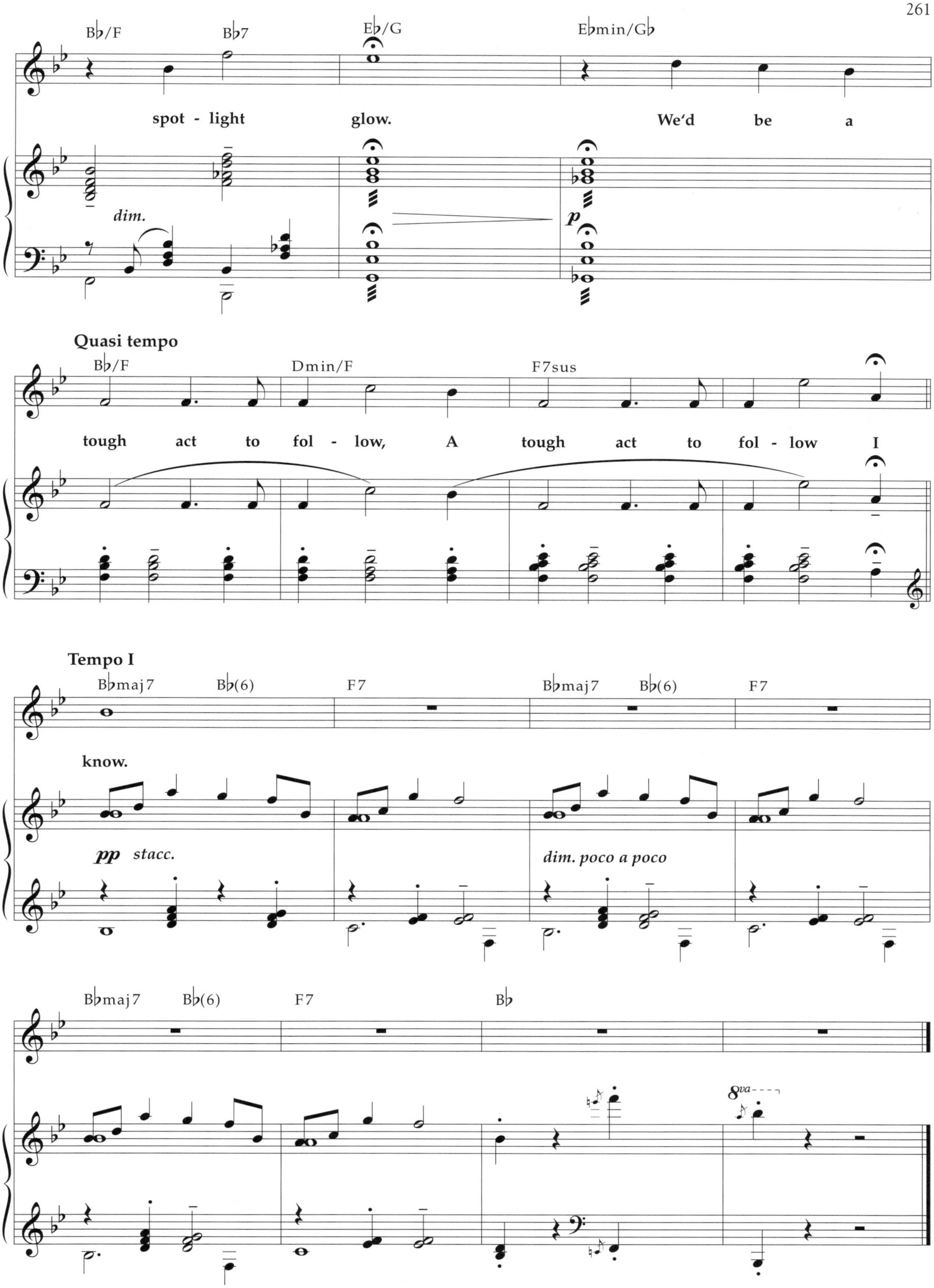
B♭/F
B♭7
E♭/G
E♭min/G♭
spot - light glow. We'd be a
dim.
p
Quasi tempo
B♭/F
Dmin/F
F7sus
tough act to fol - low, A tough act to fol - low I
Tempo I
B♭maj7
B♭(6)
F7
know.
pp stacc.
dim. poco a poco
B♭
8va

# We Can Make It

*from the Musical* **THE RINK**

Words by
**FRED EBB**

Music by
**JOHN KANDER**

**Moderately slow**

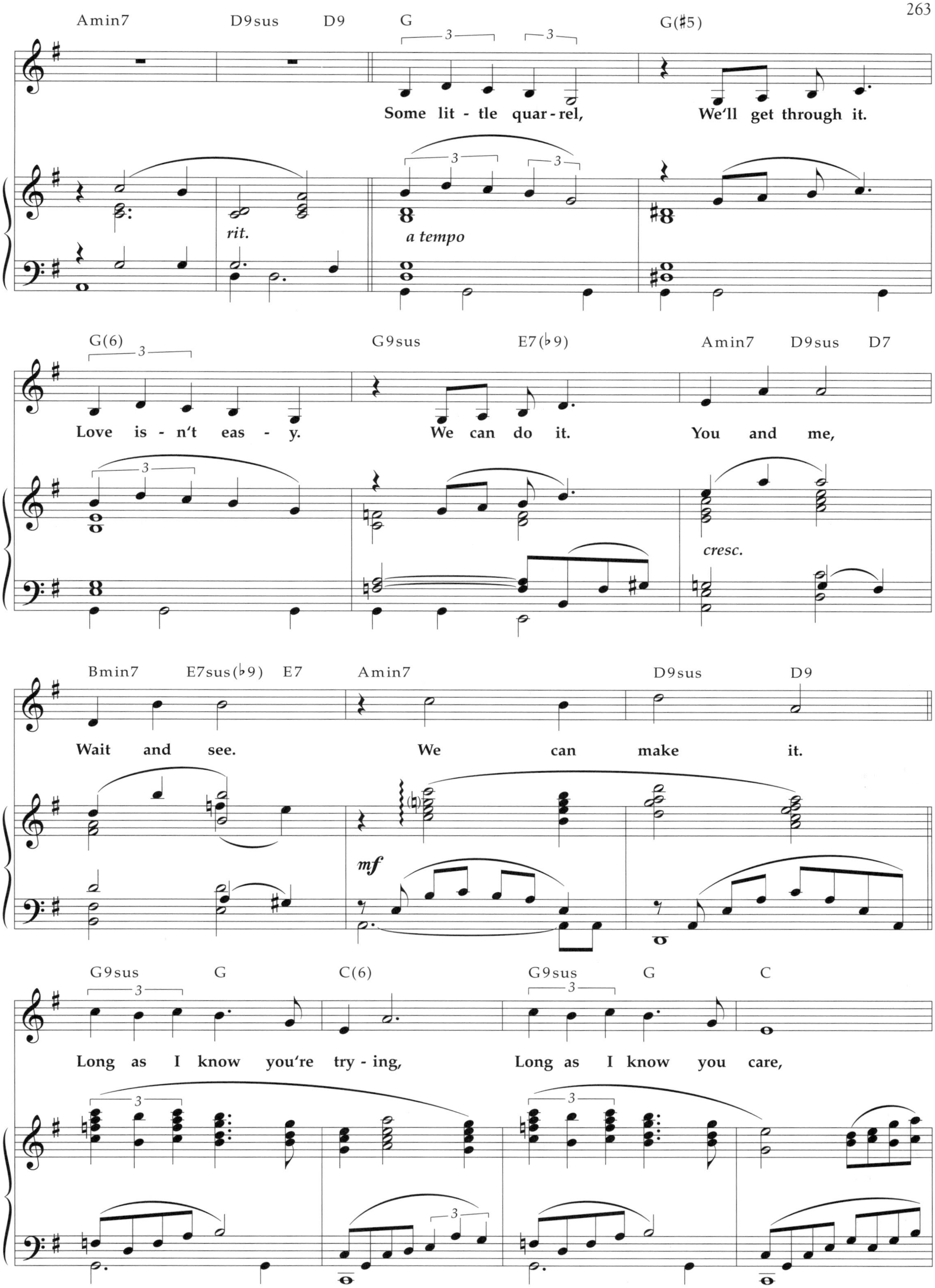
Amin7 D9sus D9 G G(♯5)
Some lit - tle quar - rel, We'll get through it.
rit.
a tempo
G(6) G9sus E7(♭9) Amin7 D9sus D7
Love is - n't eas - y. We can do it. You and me,
cresc.
Bmin7 E7sus(♭9) E7 Amin7 D9sus D9
Wait and see. We can make it.
mf
G9sus G C(6) G9sus G C
Long as I know you're try - ing, Long as I know you care,

Cmin(♯7) Cmin(6) Bmin7 B♭min7 Amin7 molto rall. D9sus D7(♭9)
Long as we pull to - geth - er We can do an - y - thing, an - y - time, an - y -
cresc.
Con moto
G G(♯5) G(6) poco rit. G9sus E7(♭9)
where.
f
dim.
A tempo
Amin7 D9sus D9 Bmin7 E7sus(♭9) E7 Amin7 D9sus D9
I have you. You have me. We can make it.
mf

G9sus G C(6) F♯min7 B7 Emin7 A9sus A7
Right to the end of al - ways, Down to the fin - ish line.
poco rit.
Con moto
D9sus G G(♯5)
We can make it fine.
cresc.
f
G(6) G9sus E7(♭9) Amin7 D9sus D9

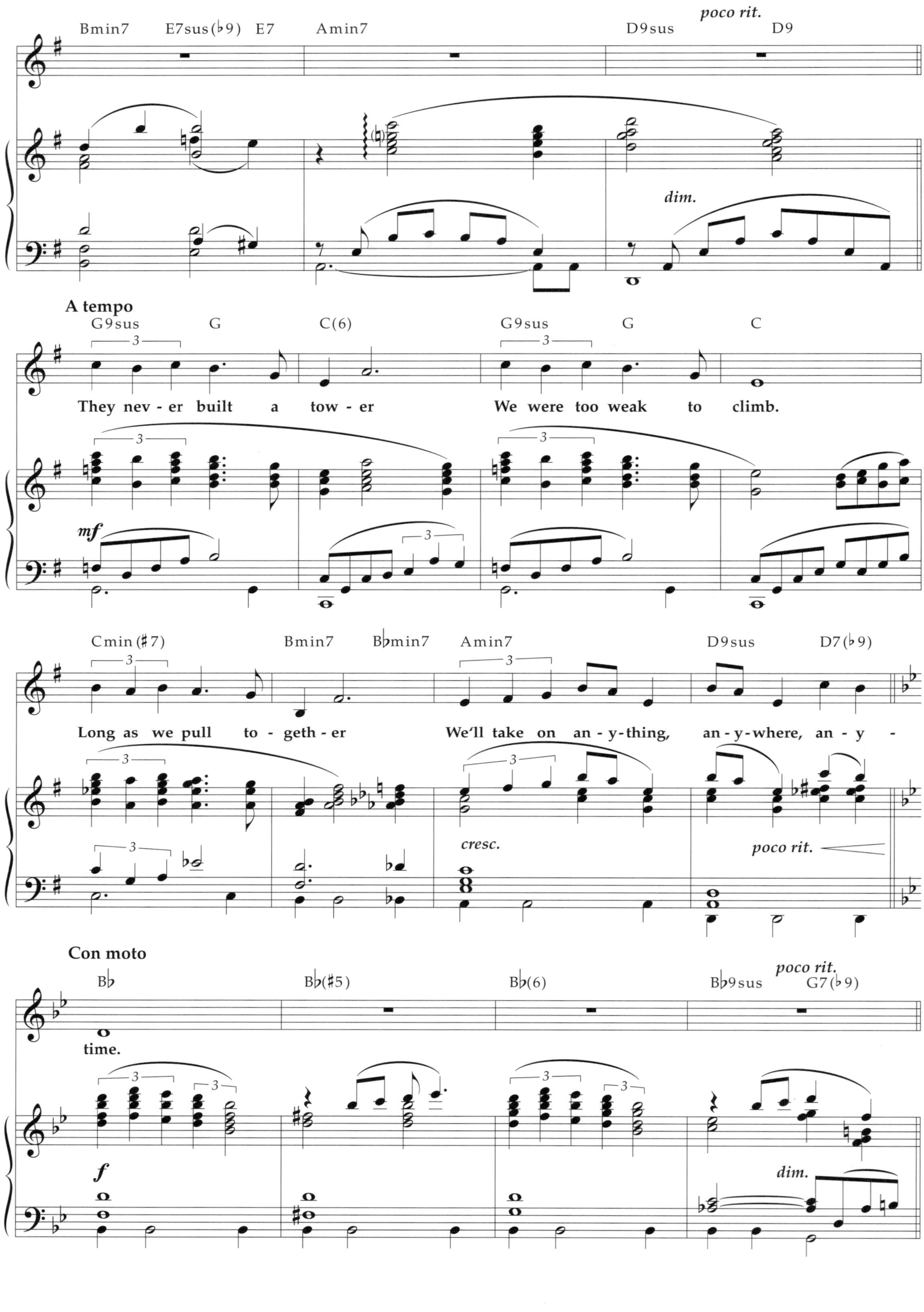
poco rit.
Bmin7 E7sus(♭9) E7 Amin7 D9sus D9
dim.
A tempo
G9sus G C(6) G9sus G C
They nev - er built a tow - er We were too weak to climb.
mf
Cmin(♯7) Bmin7 B♭min7 Amin7 D9sus D7(♭9)
Long as we pull to - geth - er We'll take on an - y - thing, an - y - where, an - y -
cresc.
poco rit.
Con moto
poco rit.
B♭ B♭(♯5) B♭(6) B♭9sus G7(♭9)
time.
f
dim.

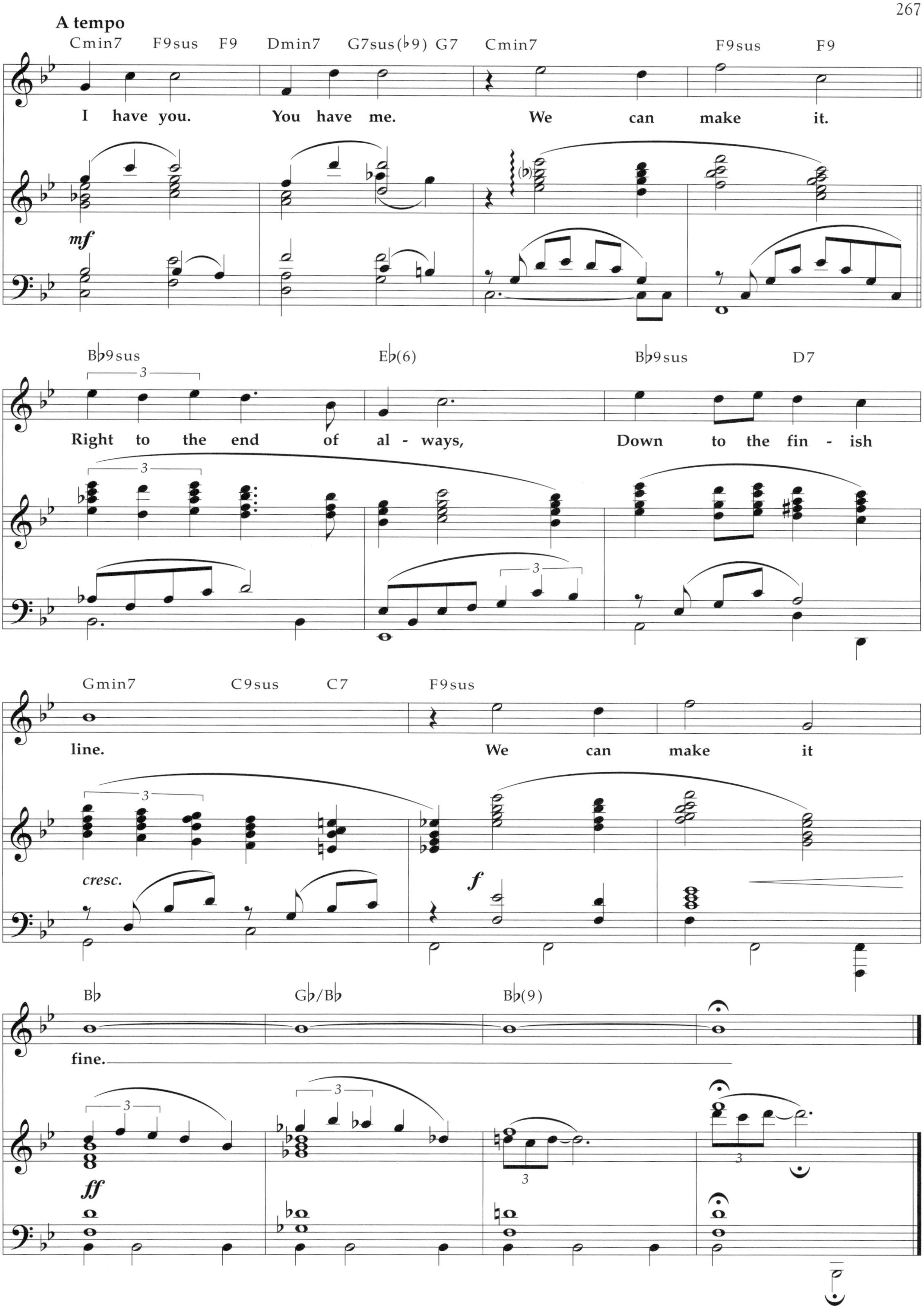
A tempo
Cmin7 F9sus F9 Dmin7 G7sus(♭9) G7 Cmin7 F9sus F9
I have you. You have me. We can make it.
mf
B♭9sus E♭(6) B♭9sus D7
Right to the end of al - ways, Down to the fin - ish
3
Gmin7 C9sus C7 F9sus
line. We can make it
cresc.
f
B♭ G♭/B♭ B♭(9)
fine.
ff
3

# When You're Good to Mama

*from the Musical* ***CHICAGO***

Words by
**FRED EBB**

Music by
**JOHN KANDER**

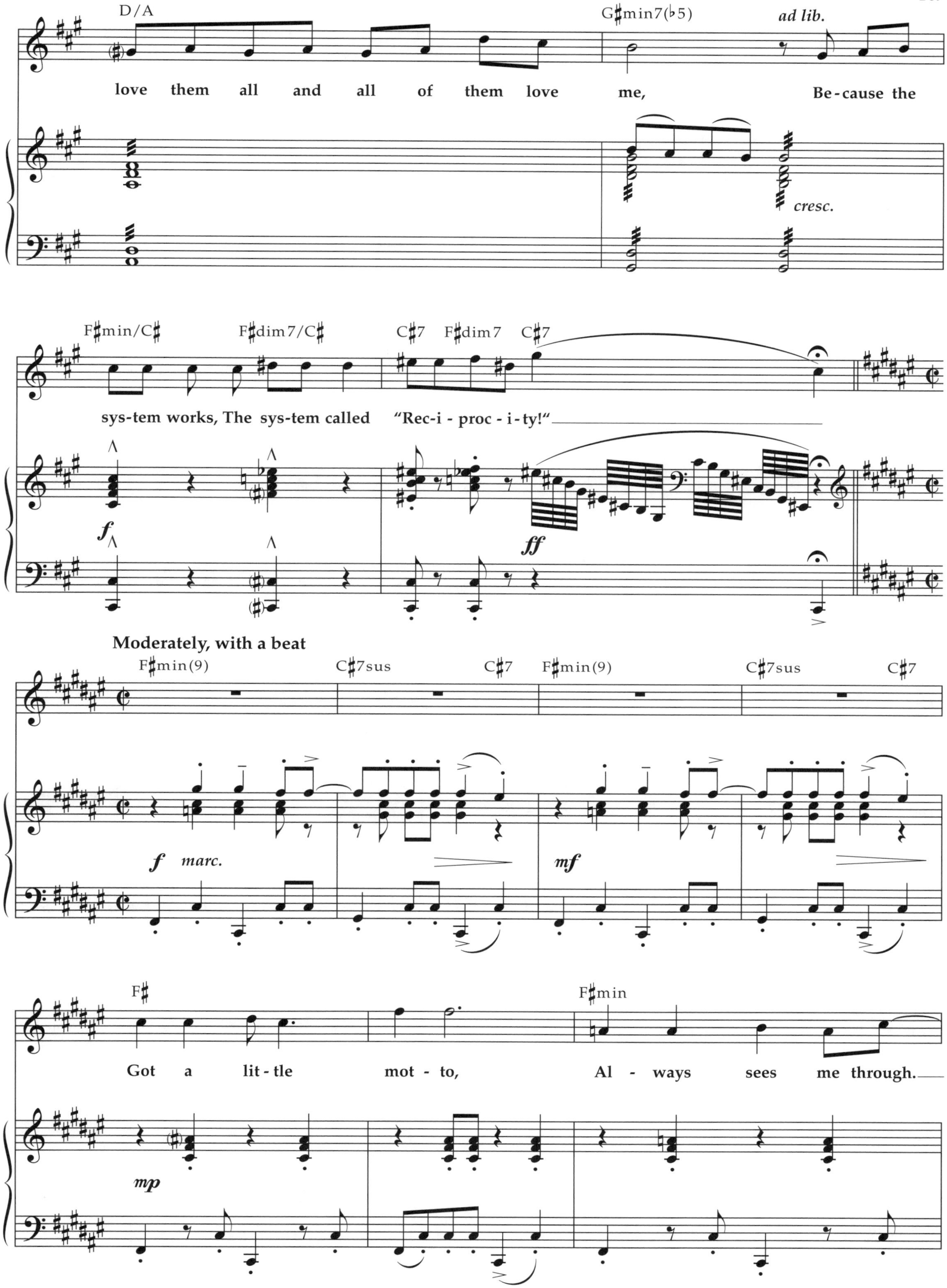
D/A
G♯min7(♭5)
ad lib.
love them all and all of them love me, Be-cause the
cresc.
F♯min/C♯
F♯dim7/C♯
C♯7 F♯dim7 C♯7
sys-tem works, The sys-tem called "Rec-i-proc-i-ty!"
f
ff
Moderately, with a beat
F♯min(9)
C♯7sus
C♯7
F♯min(9)
C♯7sus
C♯7
f marc.
mf
F♯
F♯min
Got a lit-tle mot-to, Al-ways sees me through.
mp

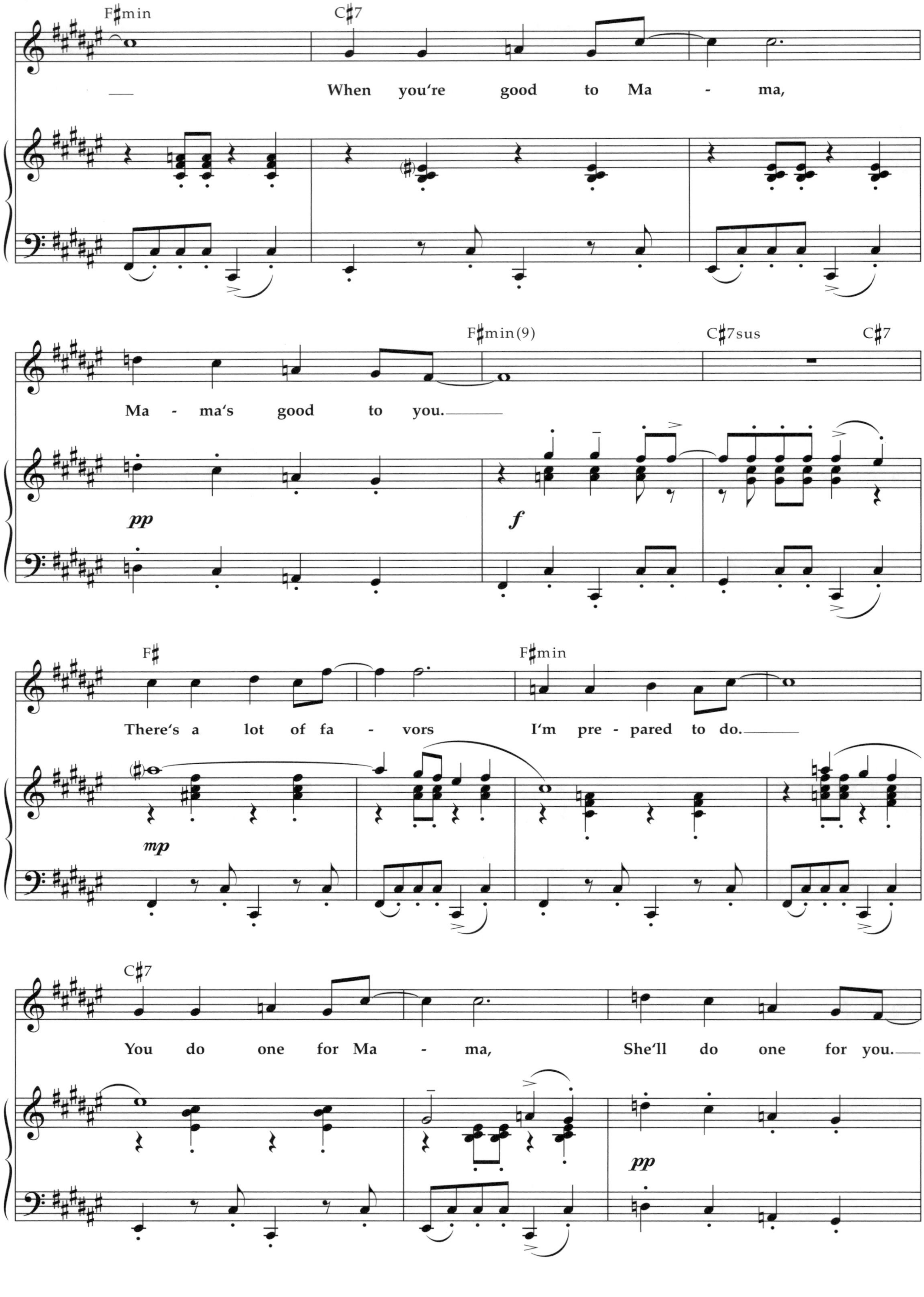
F♯min
C♯7
When you're good to Ma - ma,
F♯min(9)
C♯7sus
C♯7
Ma - ma's good to you.
pp
f
F♯
F♯min
There's a lot of fa - vors I'm pre - pared to do.
mp
C♯7
You do one for Ma - ma, She'll do one for you.
pp

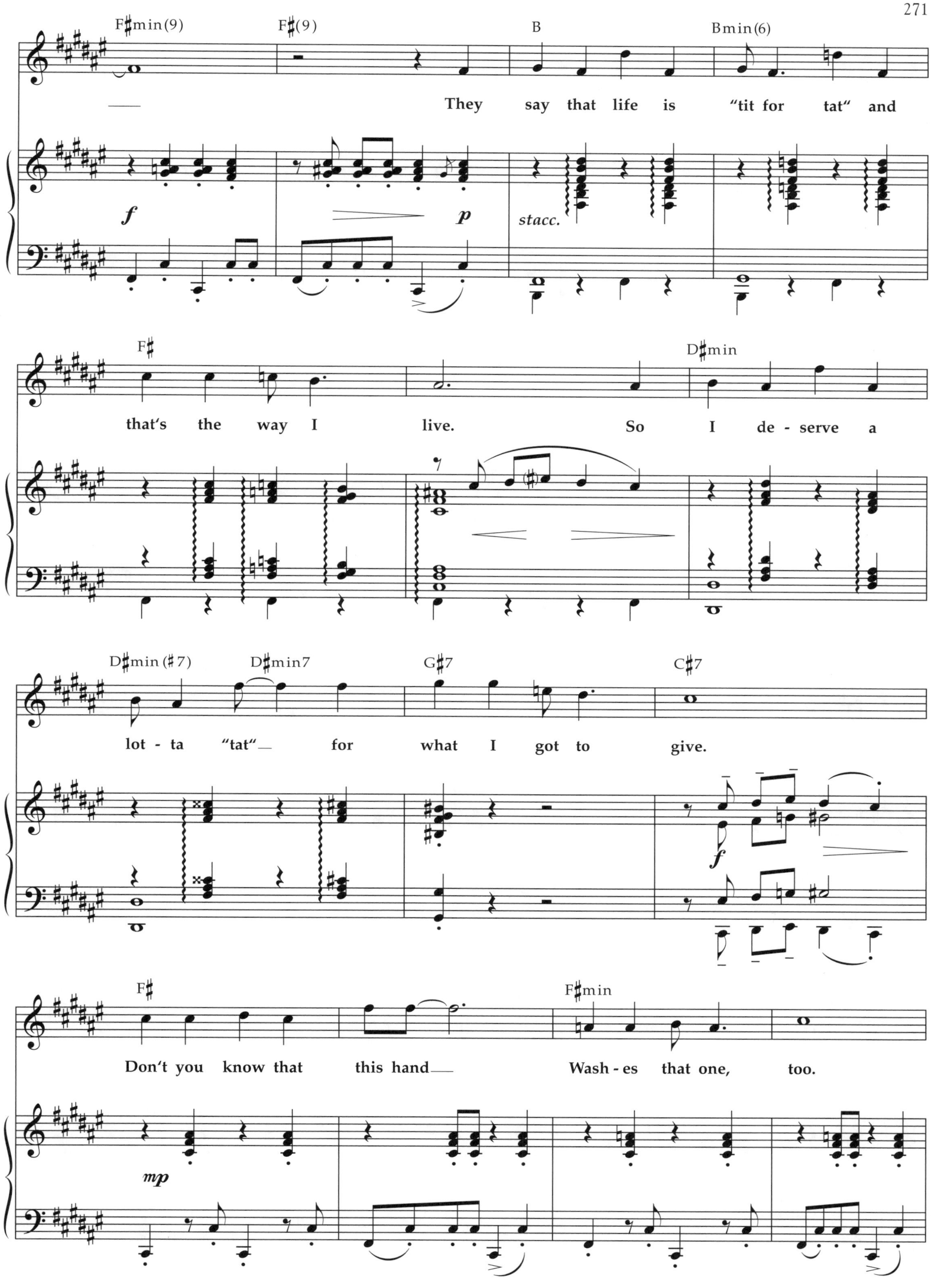
F♯min(9)
F♯(9)
B
Bmin(6)
They say that life is "tit for tat" and
f
p
stacc.
F♯
D♯min
that's the way I live. So I de - serve a
D♯min (♯7)
D♯min7
G♯7
C♯7
lot - ta "tat" for what I got to give.
f
F♯
F♯min
Don't you know that this hand Wash - es that one, too.
mp

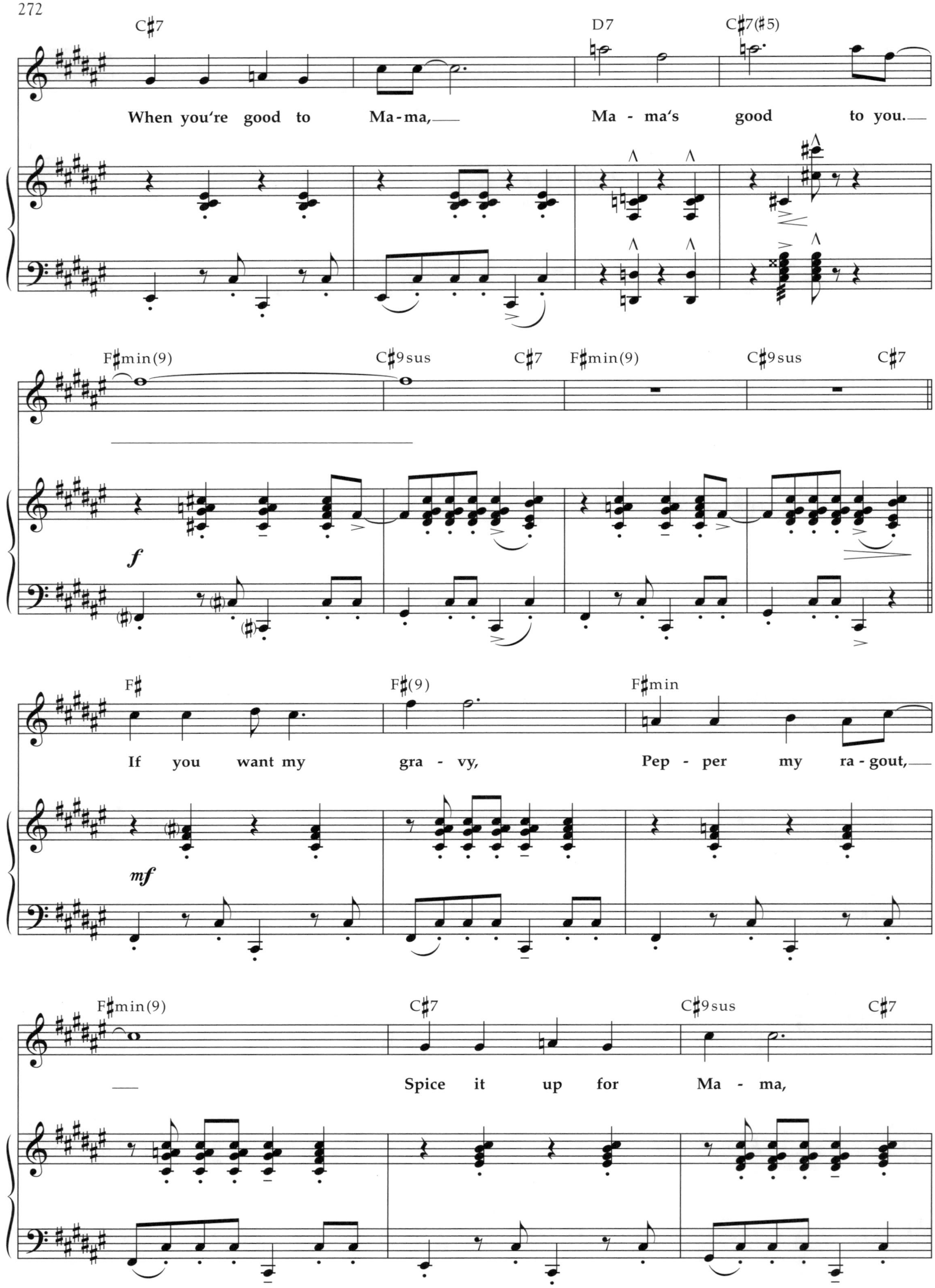
C♯7
D7
C♯7(♯5)
When you're good to Ma-ma, Ma - ma's good to you.
F♯min(9)
C♯9sus
C♯7
F♯min(9)
C♯9sus
C♯7
f
F♯
F♯(9)
F♯min
If you want my gra - vy, Pep - per my ra - gout,
mf
F♯min(9)
C♯7
C♯9sus
C♯7
Spice it up for Ma - ma,

C♯7
F♯min(9)
C♯9sus
C♯
She'll get hot for you.
f
F♯
When they pass the bas - ket
F♯min
Folks con - tri - bute to,
mf
C♯7
You put in for Ma - ma,

C♯7
F♯(9)
She'll put out for you. The
f
B
Bmin(6)
F♯
folks a - top the lad - der are the ones the world a - dores. So
mf stacc.
D♯min
D♯min (♯7)
D♯min7
G♯7
C♯7
boost me up my lad - der, kid, and I'll boost you up yours.
f

F♯
F♯(9)
F♯min
Let's all stroke to - geth - er Like the Prince - ton
mf
F♯min(9)
C♯7
crew. When you're strok - in' Ma - ma, —
D7
C♯7
F♯7
Ma - ma's strok - in' you. — So

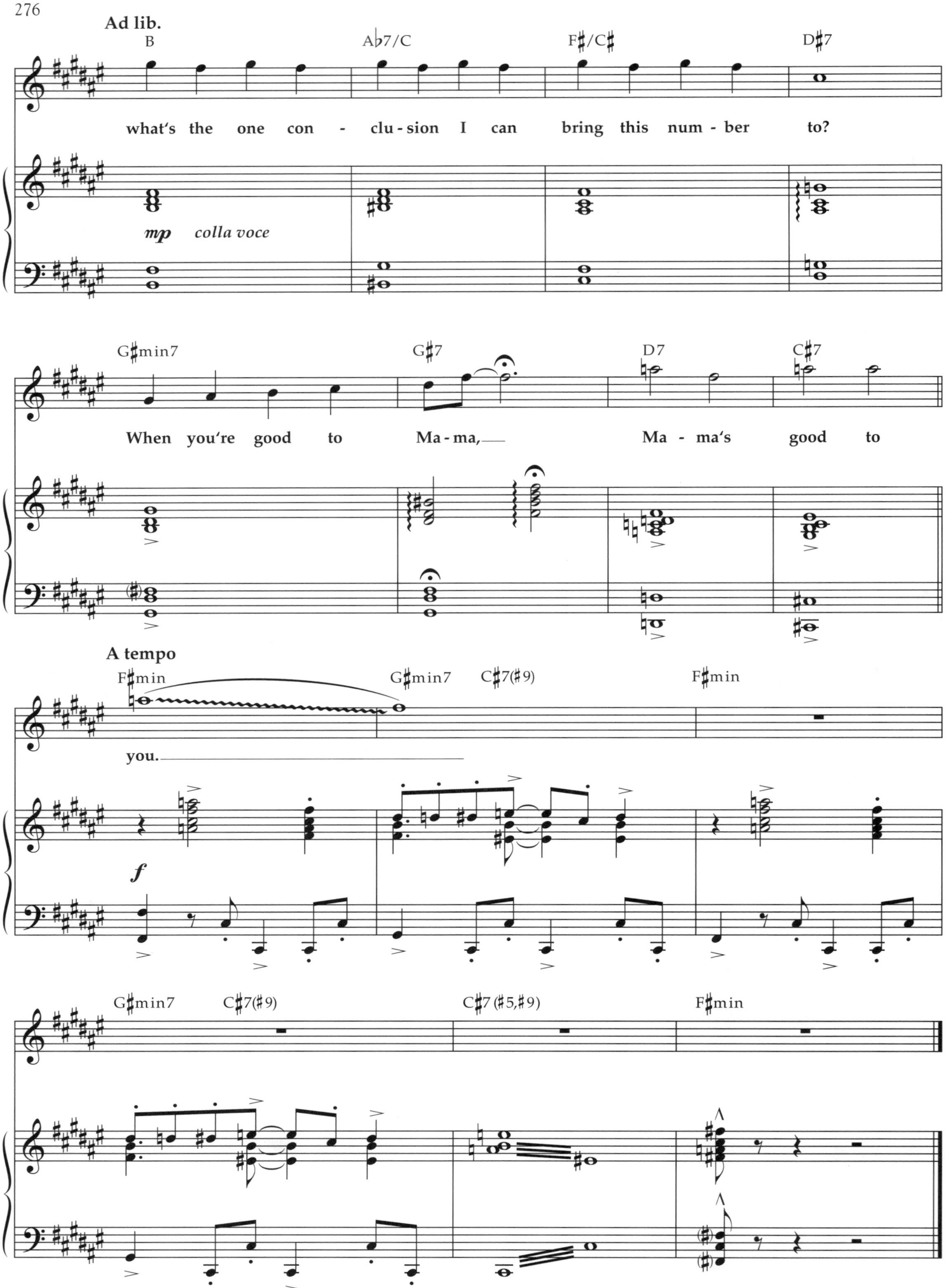
Ad lib.
B
A♭7/C
F♯/C♯
D♯7
what's the one con - clu - sion I can bring this num - ber to?
mp colla voce
G♯min7
G♯7
D7
C♯7
When you're good to Ma - ma,
Ma - ma's good to
A tempo
F♯min
G♯min7
C♯7(♯9)
F♯min
you.
f
G♯min7
C♯7(♯9)
C♯7 (♯5,♯9)
F♯min

# Willkommen

*from the Musical* ***CABARET***

Words by
**FRED EBB**

Music by
**JOHN KANDER**

**With spirit**

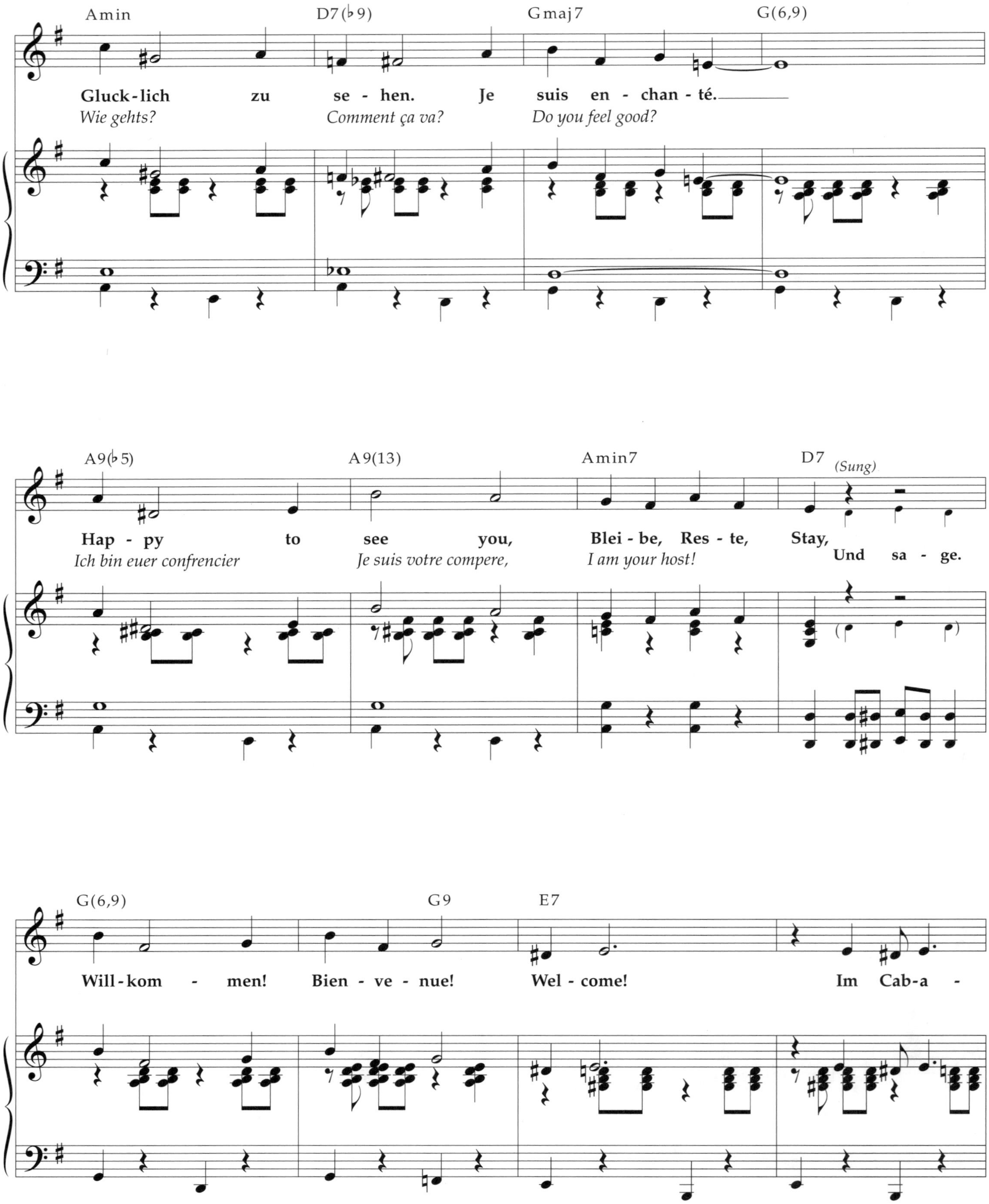
Amin
D7(♭9)
Gmaj7
G(6,9)
Gluck-lich zu se - hen. Je suis en - chan - té.
Wie gehts?
Comment ça va?
Do you feel good?
A9(♭5)
A9(13)
Amin7
D7
(Sung)
Hap - py to see you, Blei - be, Res - te, Stay,
Ich bin euer confrencier
Je suis votre compere,
I am your host!
Und sa - ge.
G(6,9)
G9
E7
Will-kom - men! Bien - ve - nue! Wel - come! Im Cab-a -

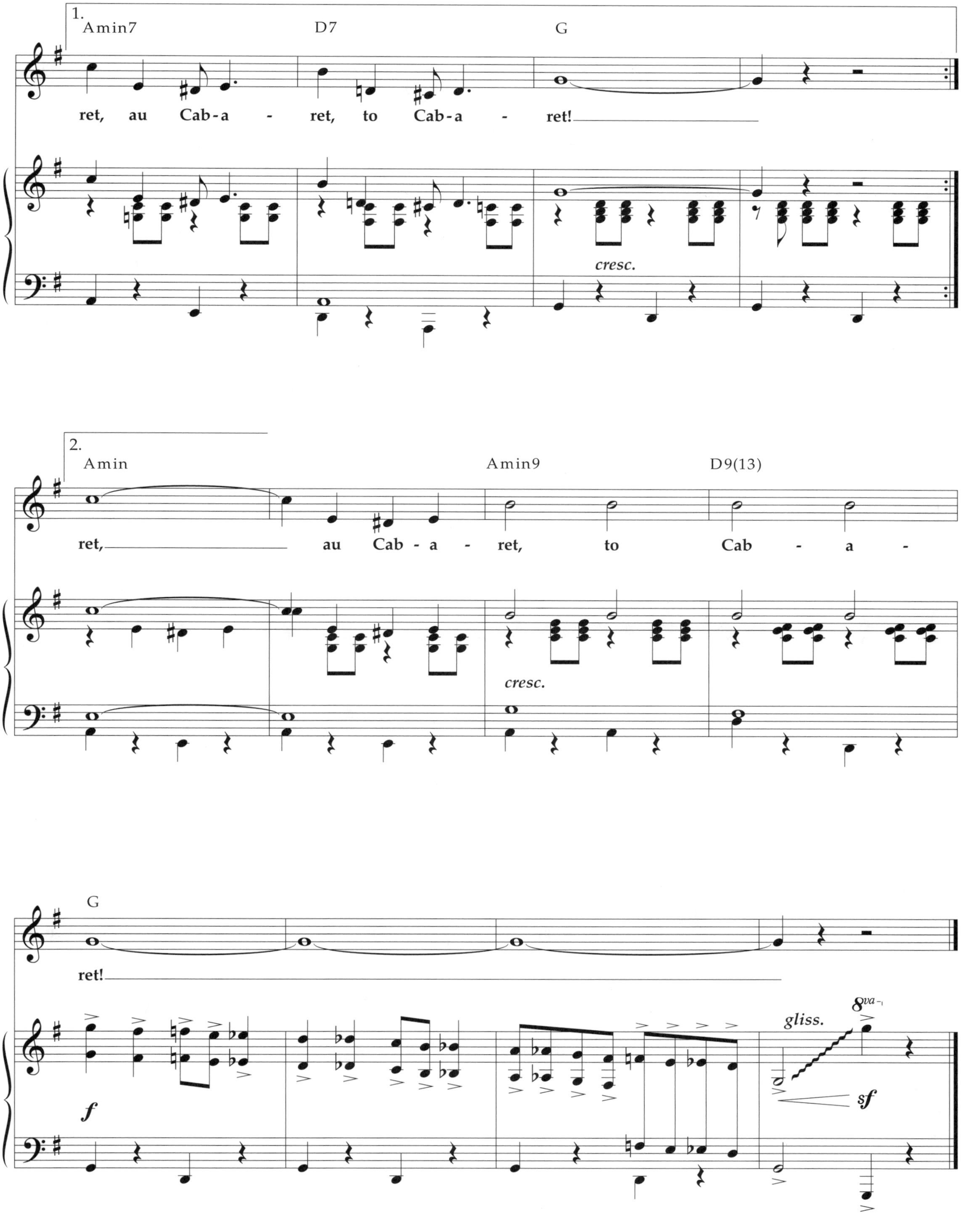
1.
Amin7
D7
G
ret, au Cab-a - ret, to Cab-a - ret!
cresc.
2.
Amin
Amin9
D9(13)
ret, au Cab - a - ret, to Cab - a -
cresc.
G
ret!
f
gliss.
8va
sf

# Yes

*from the Musical* ***70, GIRLS, 70***

Words by
**FRED EBB**

Music by
**JOHN KANDER**

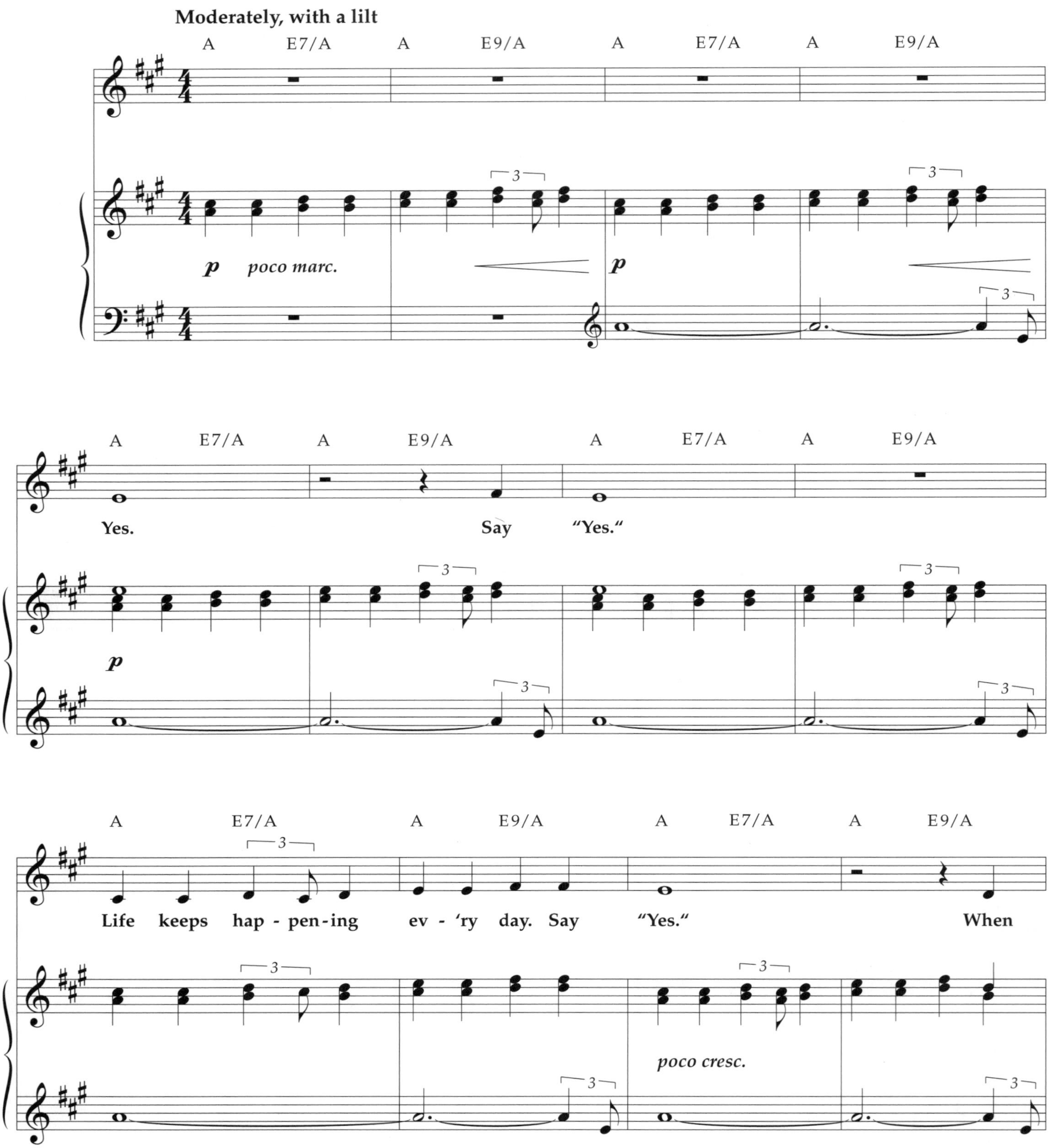

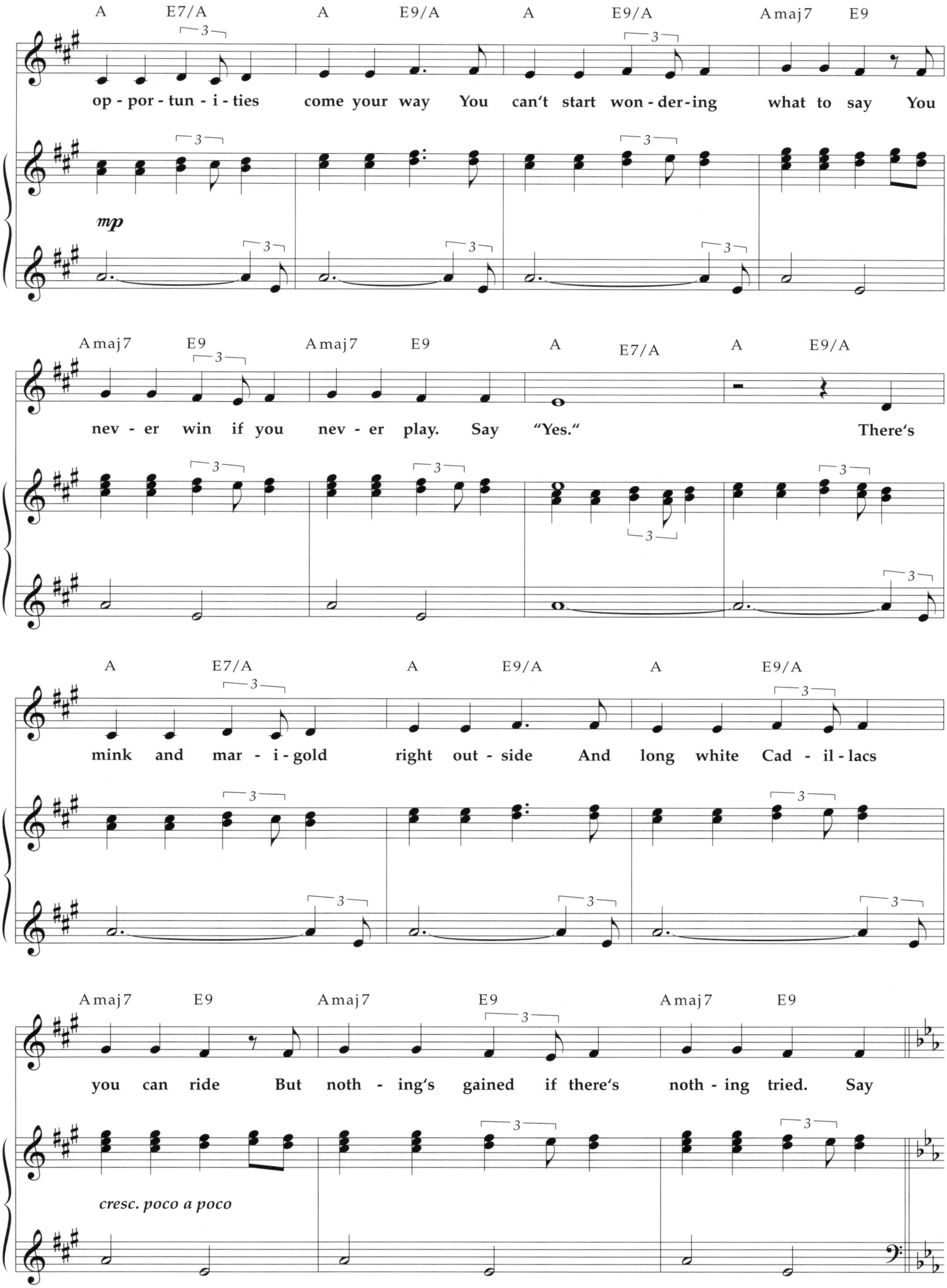
A E7/A A E9/A A E9/A Amaj7 E9
op - por - tun - i - ties come your way You can't start won - der - ing what to say You
mp
Amaj7 E9 Amaj7 E9 A E7/A A E9/A
nev - er win if you nev - er play. Say "Yes." There's
A E7/A A E9/A A E9/A
mink and mar - i - gold right out - side And long white Cad - il - lacs
Amaj7 E9 Amaj7 E9 Amaj7 E9
you can ride But noth - ing's gained if there's noth - ing tried. Say
cresc. poco a poco

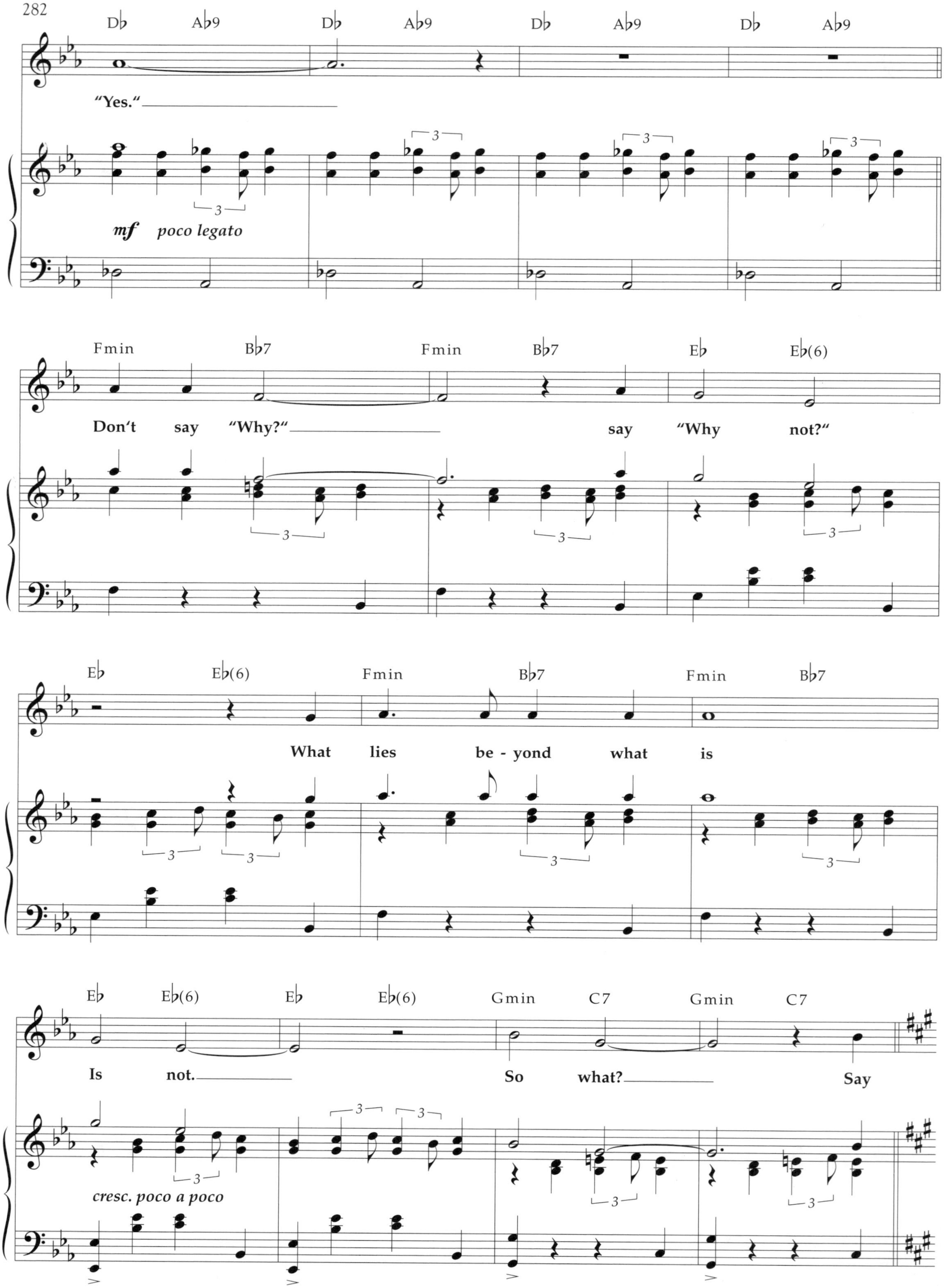
D♭ A♭9 D♭ A♭9 D♭ A♭9 D♭ A♭9
"Yes."
mf poco legato
Fmin B♭7 Fmin B♭7 E♭ E♭(6)
Don't say "Why?" say "Why not?"
E♭ E♭(6) Fmin B♭7 Fmin B♭7
What lies be - yond what is
E♭ E♭(6) E♭ E♭(6) Gmin C7 Gmin C7
Is not. So what? Say
cresc. poco a poco

D A7/D D A7/D D A9/D D A9/D
"Yes."
f
F♯min B7 F♯min B7 E E(6)/B E E(6)/B
Yes, I can. Yes, I will. Yes, I'll take a sip. Yes, I'll touch.
mf
F♯min B7 F♯min B7 G G(6)/D G G(6)/D
Yes, of course. Yes, how nice. Yes, I'd hap-pi-ly thank you ver-y much.
cresc.
E9sus E(6)/B E9sus E(6)/B E9sus E(6)/B E9sus E(6)/B
Yes. Oh, yes. There's
f

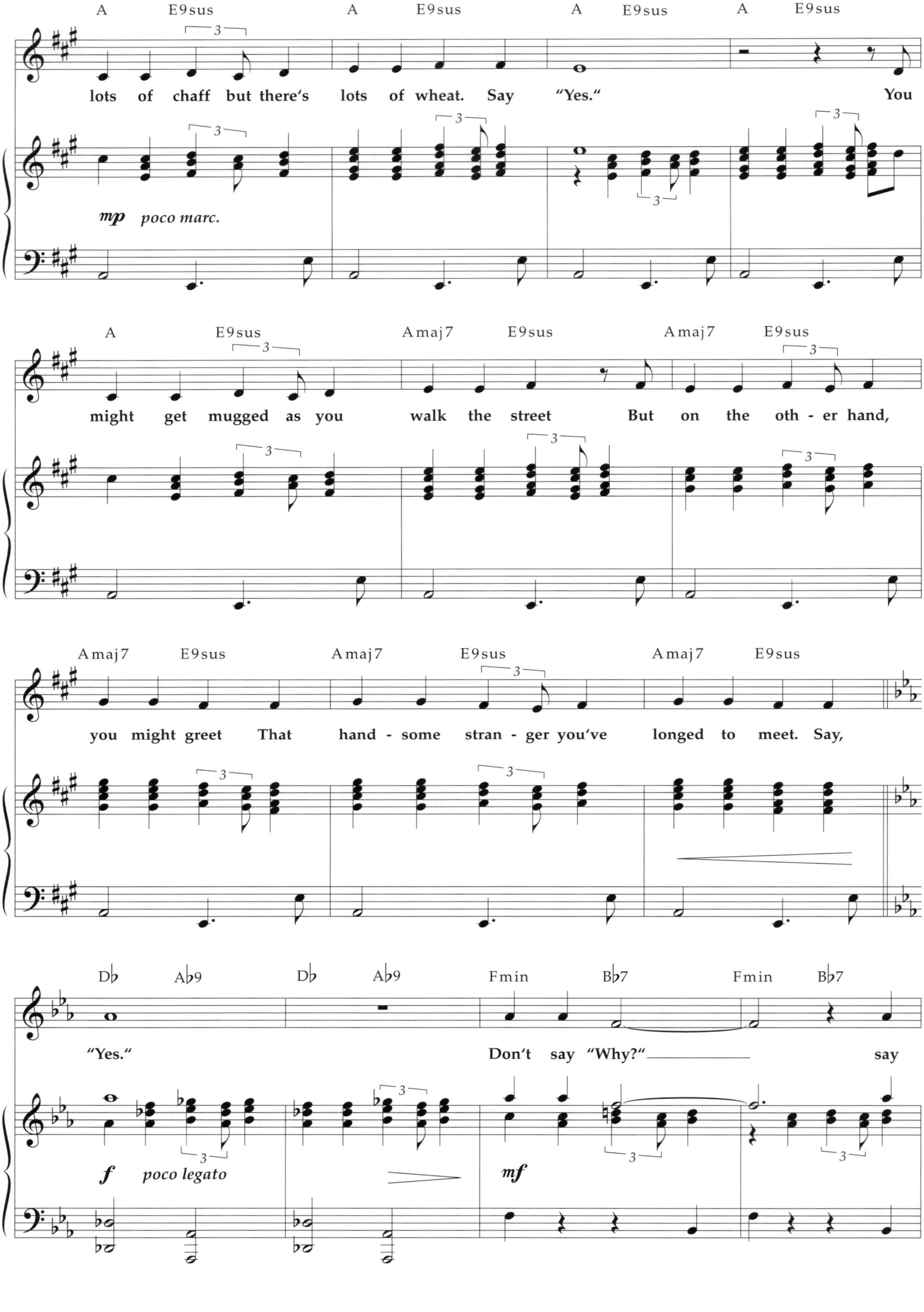
A E9sus A E9sus A E9sus A E9sus
lots of chaff but there's lots of wheat. Say "Yes." You
mp poco marc.
A E9sus Amaj7 E9sus Amaj7 E9sus
might get mugged as you walk the street But on the oth - er hand,
Amaj7 E9sus Amaj7 E9sus Amaj7 E9sus
you might greet That hand - some stran - ger you've longed to meet. Say,
D♭ A♭9 D♭ A♭9 Fmin B♭7 Fmin B♭7
"Yes." Don't say "Why?" say
f poco legato
mf

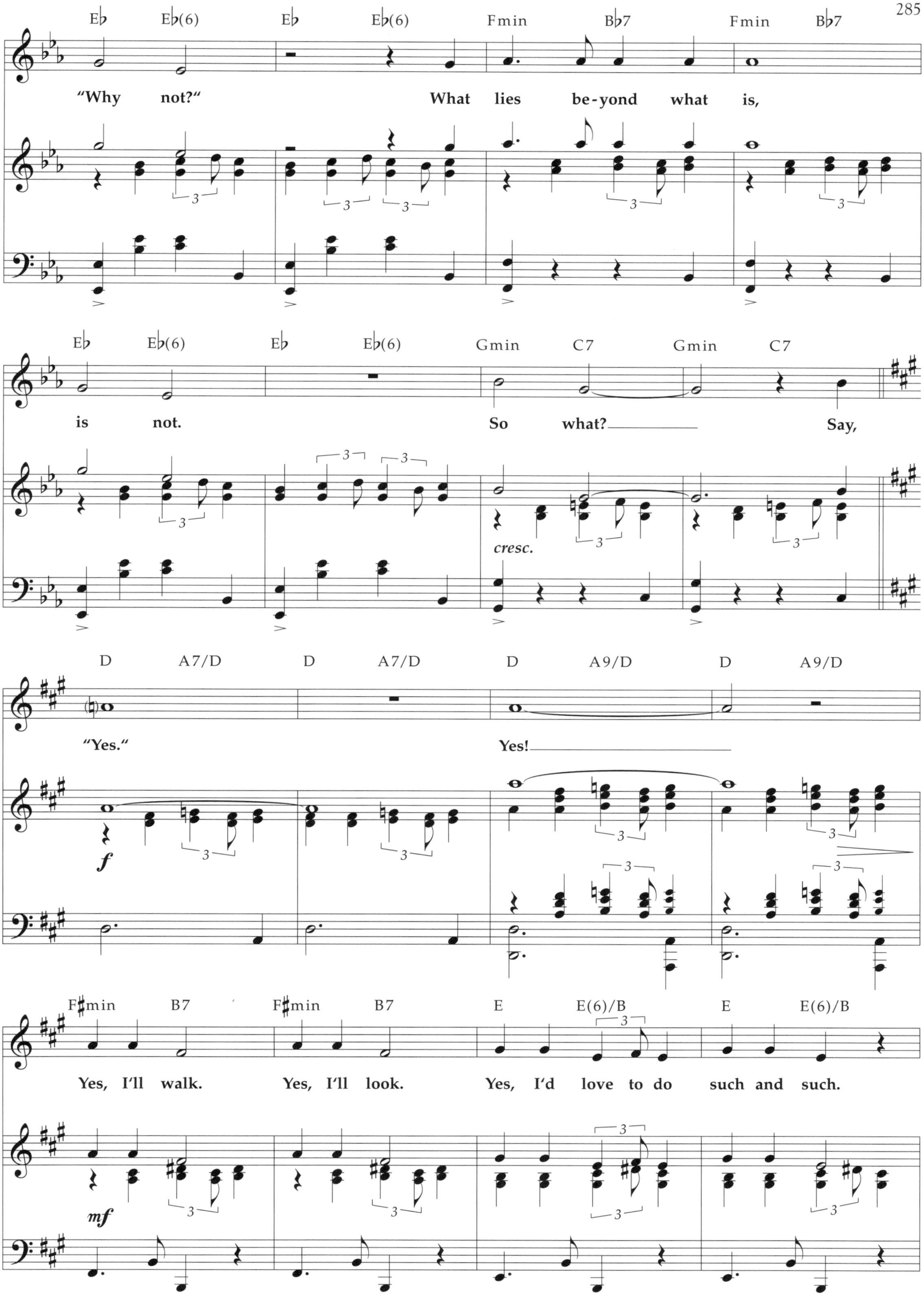

E♭ E♭(6) E♭ E♭(6) Fmin B♭7 Fmin B♭7
"Why not?" What lies be-yond what is,
E♭ E♭(6) E♭ E♭(6) Gmin C7 Gmin C7
is not. So what? Say,
cresc.
D A7/D D A7/D D A9/D D A9/D
"Yes." Yes!
f
F♯min B7 F♯min B7 E E(6)/B E E(6)/B
Yes, I'll walk. Yes, I'll look. Yes, I'd love to do such and such.
mf

F♯min B7 F♯min B7 G G(6)
Yes, I'll try. Yes, I'll dare. Yes, I'll fly.
G G(6) G G(6) G G(6)
Yes, I'll share. Yes, I'd hap - pi - ly thank you ver - y much.
E9
Yes! Oh, yes! Oh,
cresc. poco a poco

F9
B♭
F9sus
yes! You can't look back on a
f
poco marc.
B♭
F9sus
B♭
F9sus
B♭
F9sus
chance that's lost. Say, "Yes." Yes! The
B♭
F9sus
B♭
F9sus
B♭
F9sus
dice mean noth - ing un - less they're tossed. The throw is u - sual - ly

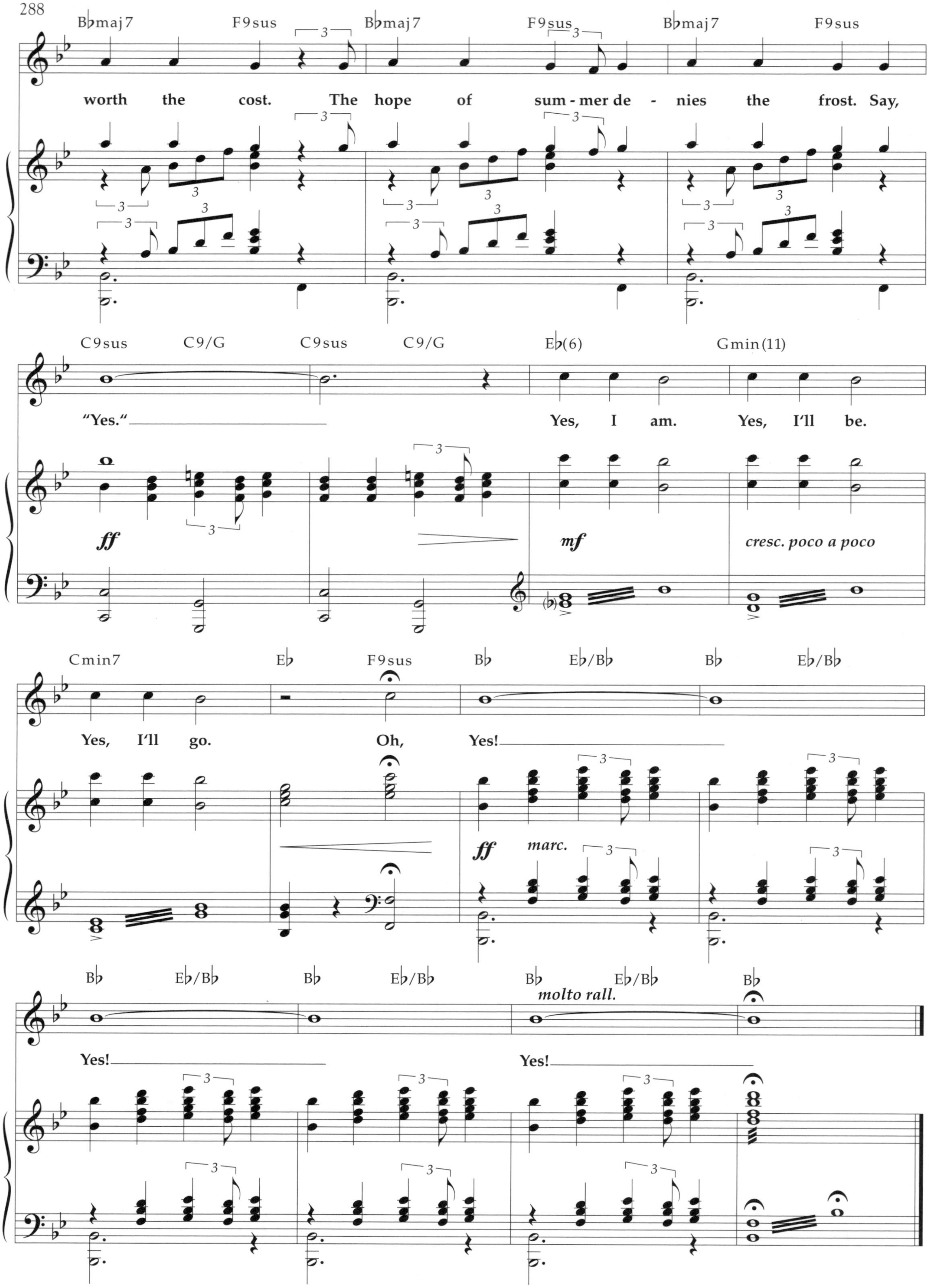
B♭maj7 F9sus B♭maj7 F9sus B♭maj7 F9sus
worth the cost. The hope of sum - mer de - nies the frost. Say,
C9sus C9/G C9sus C9/G E♭(6) Gmin(11)
"Yes." Yes, I am. Yes, I'll be.
ff
mf
cresc. poco a poco
Cmin7 E♭ F9sus B♭ E♭/B♭ B♭ E♭/B♭
Yes, I'll go. Oh, Yes!
ff
marc.
B♭ E♭/B♭ B♭ E♭/B♭ B♭ E♭/B♭ B♭
molto rall.
Yes! Yes!